Who
Will Pay?

Coping with Aging Societies,
Climate Change, and Other
Long-Term Fiscal Challenges

Peter S. Heller

Foreword by Jeffrey D. Sachs

International Monetary Fund

© 2003 International Monetary Fund

Production: IMF Multimedia Services Division
Cover design: Dale Glasgow
Figures: Theodore Peters
Composition: Julio R. Prego

Cataloging-in-Publication Data

Heller, Peter S.
    Who will pay? : coping with aging societies, climate change, and other long-term fiscal challenges / Peter S. Heller with a foreword by Jeffrey D. Sachs — [Washington, D.C.] : International Monetary Fund, [2003].
        p.   cm.

    Includes bibliographical references and index

    1. Fiscal policy.   2. Aging—Economic aspects.   3. Climatic changes—Economic aspects.   I. International Monetary Fund.
HJ192.5.H35 2003

ISBN 1-58906-223-X

Price: $28.00

Please send orders to:
International Monetary Fund, Publication Services
700 19th Street, N.W., Washington, D.C. 20431, U.S.A.
Tel.: (202) 623-7430   Telefax: (202) 623-7201
E-mail: publications@imf.org
Internet: http://www.imf.org

recycled paper

Here's what the experts are saying about:

Who Will Pay?
Coping with Aging Societies, Climate Change, and Other Long-Term Fiscal Challenges

By Peter S. Heller

"Peter Heller has made a critical contribution with this book. Political leaders in this day are perilously short-sighted. This book helps us all see into a troublesome future, but with a perspective that can help policymakers avoid the worst that might lie ahead."

—John J. Hamre
President and CEO, Center for Strategic and International Studies

"For too long, politicians, civil servants, and international organizations have had an obsessively myopic focus on this year's budget spending, revenues, and deficits. Peter Heller brings a breath of fresh air to this claustrophobic debate, arguing that we need to look ahead to the looming budgetary challenges posed by aging populations, global warming, AIDS, and other crises with severe fiscal implications. He sounds the alarm that failing to anticipate the long-run challenges will leave both present and future generations at risk of punitive tax hikes and/or arbitrary losses of benefits and essential public services as catastrophic spending crowds out everything else. Sound the call in Washington and around the world: *listen to Heller!*"

—William Easterly
Professor of Economics, New York University and
Senior Fellow, Center for Global Development

"Peter Heller's volume offers a sweeping survey of what may well prove to be the key issue of fiscal design over the coming decades— how to secure a sustainable fiscal policy, given the massive outside uncertainties which confront it. Yet we must try. Proceeding in that spirit, Heller examines the potential impact of structural changes— demographic, environmental, and political—each doubly uncertain when the interdependence of their impacts is considered. Drawing on a rich literature, old approaches are found insufficient and new techniques are offered. This is a splendid contribution to a most timely theme."

—Richard A. Musgrave
H.H. Burbank Professor of Political Economy, Emeritus, Harvard University

"Peter Heller's book on the long-run fiscal challenges facing industrial and Third World nations is right on target: timely, comprehensive, and important. While there are many books which address the crises facing the public pension programs of the industrial nations, this book addresses the fiscal crisis in a much more comprehensive way, and there is none other like it. This book is distinguished from others by its careful attention to a broader array of problems including not only population aging, but rising expenditures on health and climate change as well. It carefully considers the uncertainty surrounding these long-run challenges and how long run plans should be formulated in the context of such uncertainty. It considers the international dimension of these issues, and pays careful attention to the institutional context of policy formation."

—Ronald Lee
Professor of Demography and Economics, University of California–Berkeley

"This book is an analytic tour de force—it brings together state-of-the-art thinking from many disparate fields to show the importance of a long-term fiscal policy viewpoint. It persuasively challenges both experts and policymakers to do a far better job of addressing the future."

—Stanford G. Ross,
Former U.S. Commissioner of Social Security

"In this well-written and thought-provoking book, Peter Heller looks at the main challenges for government finances in the long term such as population aging, climate change, deadly diseases, and growing security problems. He provides an overview of the state-of-the-art thinking on these challenges, what analysts and governments currently do to understand and prepare for them, and why policymakers rather prefer to delay appropriate action. Moreover and most importantly, the book provides a road map for change via better analysis, more transparency, and reformed budget processes that are conducive to long-term planning.

The book is, therefore, a must-read for all those who are interested in learning about long-term policy challenges and their fiscal implications, in filling our knowledge gaps about them and in inducing societies to demand policymakers to undertake sufficient preparatory action."

—Ludger Schuknecht
Principal Economist, European Central Bank

"Stimulating, provocative, and well-researched reading for those interested in international finance, business, and sustainable development.
In our era of pre-occupation with quarterly balance sheets, Peter Heller
challenges our short-sightedness with penetrating and convincing
analyses of long-term demographic, environmental, and economic
changes that will inevitably impact upon fiscal policy. His prescription
of a multi-pronged approach to fiscal risk management to meet these
powerful forces contains much wisdom, backed by solid research."

—Lincoln C. Chen
John F. Kennedy School of Government, Harvard University
(formerly Executive Vice President, The Rockefeller Foundation)

"The potential for profound developments over coming decades driven by demographic change, technological advance, and globalisation
will provide challenges for policy and have potentially significant fisal
implications.... It would be a grave mistake to defer addressing the
emerging risks. Countries that fail to begin adjusting early may find
they pay a significant penalty, requiring excessive adjustment in a
short period or experiencing a loss of financial market confidence. The
ramifications for policy of these developments, and of continuing
closer global economic integration, also highlights the importance of
effective, credible, and authoritative IMF surveillance. [This] book
makes a timely and valuable contribution in highlighting the need to
begin building the capacity to respond to these demographic and
other structural developments."

—Peter Costello
Treasurer of the Commonwealth of Australia

Contents

Foreword   ix

Acknowledgments   xiii

List of Abbreviations   xiv

1   Introduction and Overview   1

2   Why Consider Long-Term Issues
in Thinking About Fiscal Policy?   10

3   How Governments (and Academics)
Address Long-Term Issues in Fiscal Policy Planning   58

4   Some Conceptual Issues in Addressing
Long-Term Fiscal Developments   120

5   The Way Forward: Embedding Long-Term Issues
in the Fiscal Policy Framework   151

6   Summary and Conclusions   221

Appendix Tables   231

References   273

Index   291

About the Author   315

List of Tables

3.1   Fiscal Sustainability in OECD Countries:
      Primary Fiscal Balance Approach   71

5.1   General Government Net Financial Liabilities
      in OECD Countries   184

5.2   Tax Ratios in OECD Countries   187

5.3   Composition of General Government Expenditure
      in OECD Countries   191

List of Figures

2.1   Projected Shares of Elderly in Total Population by
      World Region   12

2.2   Projected Government Pension and Health Spending,
      Selected OECD Countries   14

2.3   Projected Climate Change Indicators   22

2.4   Global Costs of Extreme Weather Events   24

2.5a Measures of Global Interconnectivity   27

2.5b Value of Business Conducted by eCommerce by
      World Region   27

2.6   Projected Population of World's Largest Megacities   30

2.7   Shares of World Population in 2025 in Countries with
      Physical or Economic Water Scarcity   31

List of Boxes

2.1   Conclusions of Recent Studies on the Fiscal Impact
      of Aging Industrial Country Populations   16

2.2   Speculating on Technological Change in Medicine
      in the Next Half Century   33

2.3   What Constitutes a Fiscal Commitment?   43

2.4   The Implications of Uncertainty about the Discount Rate   51

3.1   Forecasting, Budgeting, and Addressing the Long Run:
      The Perspectives of Henry Aaron, Rudolph Penner,
      and Allen Schick   95

3.2   IMF Views on Good Practices for Realistic
      Fiscal Sustainability Assessments   98

5.1   Some Useful Indicators for Clarifying
      Long-Term Fiscal Issues   164

5.2   Is There Scope for Higher Tax Burdens?   188

Foreword

Peter Heller emphasizes one overriding theme in this important new book: *think ahead* in managing public sector budgets. One might suppose such a message to be superfluous. After all, do we really need reminding that our actions today affect our choices tomorrow, whether in our personal decisions or in our collective decisions regarding a national budget? Yet Heller is thoroughly persuasive in demonstrating that current fiscal practices around the world fall far short of the necessary intertemporal logic and rigor. He goes far to explain why that is so, and why thinking ahead in fiscal affairs is much harder than it looks. Even more important, he shows how governments can improve their fiscal policymaking by adopting new tools for intertemporal analysis and budget implementation. The lessons are so powerful, indeed, that they would do much to transform the practices of Heller's own institution, the International Monetary Fund, in its role of helping countries escape the trap of extreme poverty.

The intertemporal constraints on fiscal policy can be summarized by a government's long-term budget constraint. In one version of this measure, the discounted present value of government spending on goods and services starting today and continuing until the distant future cannot exceed the discounted value of government revenue less the current stock of net government debt to the public. If the government commits to a new program involving increased spending today and in the future, it must pay for that by making offsetting cuts in other areas of spending today or in the future, or by increasing the net present value of its revenue, perhaps through tax rate increases. If these choices are not planned sensibly, a government may well someday find itself resorting in desperation to inflationary financing, which is a tax on holders of the national money, collected without explicit public approval as the government "borrows" from the central bank. Or the government might be pushed into abrupt cuts in future programs or even to a default on its debt servicing, with all of the painful consequences likely to ensue from the collapse of the government's financial credit and credibility. Similarly, if a government accumulates debt in the short term by running budget deficits, it will eventually have to service that debt by increased revenue in the future or by off-setting cuts in the discounted value of its spending. Debt financing may postpone hard choices, but it does not eliminate them.

Heller stresses the complexities that arise naturally from these long-term considerations. Government spending is typically set in programmatic terms, not in fixed dollar amounts determined in advance over several years. The annual flows attached to long-term programs are then appropriated in annual budgets. A government may be committed to providing a certain amount of health coverage without knowing precisely the future demands for health services as the population ages or as health care risks and costs change. A government may be committed to providing a given level of retirement security yet lack a clear sense of the changing age distribution of the workforce and the timing of retirement decisions. Or a government may be committed to a program of income support, for example the purchase of farm outputs at a predetermined price, without knowing how fluctuations in the weather, world market prices, and myriad other factors will affect crop yields and the supply of outputs to government purchase programs. In short, outlays associated with long-term government programs are likely to be highly uncertain. The time path of revenue associated with a given tax system is at least as complex.

The complexities multiply when we set the short-term electoral cycle alongside the long-term fiscal constraints and uncertainties. Politicians notoriously support short-run tax cuts or spending increases for the electoral boost that they offer, without giving their constituents much insight into the longer-term implications. Hard choices are pushed off until after the election, at which point a new election is on the horizon. And it is hard enough for the general public to get a rough sense of the budget at any given moment in time, much less to be able to factor in the consequences of today's budgetary decisions for the distant future.

Heller's book is particularly powerful in reminding us of some of the key drivers of longer-term change in the world economy today—from population dynamics, to climate change, to geopolitical shocks such as global terrorism—and how systematic thinking about those forces can intelligently be incorporated into budgetary debate, planning, and implementation. He reviews in detail how various governments around the world have begun to grapple with the forecasting uncertainties and the politics of intertemporal budgetary planning. And he asks the right questions. How can the public become informed of the relevant long-term trade-offs, so that these can be considered in a democratic manner? What are the best summary statistics with which to convey that information? How useful are novel tools such as generational accounts, which measure the long-term income transfers between generations? And what kinds of institutional constraints (budget rules, reporting rules, or other procedures) are best at limiting the manipulation of long-term budgets for the sake of short-term electoral considerations?

Three issues jump to mind that cry out for Heller's approach. The first is the increasingly erratic performance of U.S. fiscal policy. In just three years—as a result of massive tax cuts, unexpected shortfalls in tax revenue, the bursting of a financial bubble, and the aftermath of September 11—the U.S. budget has gone from projections of unending and massive surpluses to projections of massive deficits for years to come. The overall swings are mind-boggling. In January 2001, just as President George W. Bush was coming into office, the U.S. Congressional Budget Office projected a cumulative "on-budget" surplus (that is, excluding Social Security) of $3,122 billion over 2002–11. By March 2003 the 10-year forecast had shifted to a cumulative on-budget *deficit* of $1,678 billion. Thus in just two years we have seen an astounding, indeed unprecedented, swing of nearly $5 trillion! The projected deficits might indeed be much larger under some plausible assumptions about future policies. One feels, strongly, that the U.S. public has not been fully informed about the implications of the federal government's budget choices in recent years. How are the cumulative deficits to be handled in the future? Will cuts in popular programs be necessary? Will taxes have to be raised again? The issues have hardly yet been joined in public debate, and the multiyear tax cuts have been peddled as short-run stimulus measures.

A second and pervasive fiscal phenomenon is the strain on retirement and health financing as a result of population aging. Most countries rely on pay-as-you-go financing for some or all of their public pension and health systems. As populations age, the ratio of beneficiaries of social support to contributors will rise markedly, putting huge strains on the public financing of these programs. Indeed, the strains are already in evidence. One recent study of the United States, discussed by Heller, suggests that the net difference between government commitments and revenue (net of public debt) is on the order of $44 trillion, suggesting that massive spending cuts or tax increases will be required in the future. The bulk of the shortfall revolves around the costs of pensions and, especially, health care. Although Heller is right to underscore the uncertainties of such calculations, there is no doubt that a first-order fiscal adjustment lies ahead, yet the broad public is mostly unaware of this. The situation in many of the countries of Europe, with generous yet partly or wholly unfunded retirement and health systems, is comparable or even worse.

The third area crying out for Heller's approach is the work of the IMF and the World Bank in the poorest countries, as those countries strive to meet the Millennium Development Goals of poverty reduction. Heller's approach would call upon both institutions to take a much more detailed look at the medium- and long-term fiscal implications of ambitious programs of poverty reduction. The world has committed to helping the poorest countries escape the trap of extreme poverty. That will require massive public investments in roads, energy systems, water treatment facilities, health systems, and education—investments far exceeding any currently being undertaken (thus helping explain why many countries are still mired in extreme poverty). Indeed, the investments required will far exceed the capacity of these governments to finance them out of national revenue. A greatly increased transfer of fiscal resources from the richest countries to the poorest is needed, much closer to the internationally accepted and lauded target of 0.7 percent of donor GNP each year in development aid (the current level is roughly 0.22 percent).

Heller's approach would urge the IMF and the World Bank to prepare fiscal scenarios in line with these required increases. In doing so, these institutions would gain much more clarity about the need to finance such transfers in the form of grants as opposed to loans, and about the need to support much deeper cuts in existing debt. The longer-term implications of bold poverty reduction programs are obscured by the typical three-year framework in which such programs are discussed, and by the lack of recognition so far by many of the richest countries of the need for greatly increased transfers to the poorest. Yet that recognition is likely to come, and Heller's admonitions for long-term planning will then be exactly what is needed.

In short, this is a book to be read, and then to be applied. Thinking ahead is a first and critical step to building a sounder economic future.

Jeffrey D. Sachs
Director
Earth Institute of Columbia University
New York City
August 2, 2003

Acknowledgments

This book has benefited from the comments and the perspectives of many. Particular thanks for many insights and useful references during its formative stages go to Barry Anderson, Orazio Attanasio, Ian Ball, James Banks, Nicholas Barr, Charles Bean, Peter Birch-Sørenson, Richard Blundell, Roger Bootle, Ralph Bryant, Robert Buckles, Marco Buti, Wendy Carlin, John Creedy, Thomas Dalsgaard, Nick Davis, Michael Devereux, Andrew Dilnot, Richard Disney, Frank Eich, Carl Emmerson, Neils Kleis Frederiksen, Richard Hemming, Richard Higgott, William Hsiao, John Janssen, Kirsten Jensen, Giles Keating, Andrew Kilpatrick, Mervyn King, Joslin Landell-Mills, Pierre Landell-Mills, Ben Lockwood, Warwick McKibbin, Costas Meghir, David Miles, Marcus Miller, Carin Norberg, Jonathan Ostry, David Pearce, Barry Potter, Lionel Price, Grant Scobie, Andrew Scott, Stephen Smith, Tim Swanson, Vito Tanzi, Carl Tham, Robert Watson, Nigel Wicks, and Martin Wolf. Valuable comments were received on early drafts of the manuscript from Henry Aaron, George Abed, Montek Ahluwahlia, Mukul Asher, Tamim Bayoumi, Elliot Berg, Steven Dunaway, Robert Gillingham, Edward Gramlich, Leslie Harris, Oleh Havrylyshyn, Yusuke Horiguchi, Edward Packard, Rudolph Penner, Lorenzo Perez, Murray Petrie, Stanford Ross, Allen Schick, Marcelo Selowsky, Eugene Steuerle, Alan Tait, Teresa Ter-Minassian, and Sarah Walton. The manuscript also benefited from the insightful editorial assistance of Michael Treadway, the vital secretarial assistance of Barbara Lissenburg, and source checking by Deidre Shanley.

The author acknowledges with great appreciation the support of the International Monetary Fund in providing financing, under its Independent Study Leave Program, for carrying out this research. Substantial intellectual and logistical support was provided by the Economics Department of the University College, University of London; The Centre for the Study of Globalisation and Regionalisation, University of Warwick; The New Zealand Treasury; the Economic Policy Research Unit, University of Copenhagen; and The Ross Institute, East Hampton, New York. I am also indebted to the External Relations Department of the IMF and, in particular, Jeanette Morrison and Sean M. Culhane, for their vital encouragement in the transformation of a manuscript into this volume.

List of Abbreviations

AIDS	Acquired immune deficiency syndrome
CSIS	Center for Strategic and International Studies
EC	European Commission
EcoFin	Economic and Financial Council of the European Union
EU	European Union
GA	Generational accounting
GDP	Gross domestic product
GPF	Government Petroleum Fund (Norway)
HIV	Human immunodeficiency virus
IFAC	International Federation of Accountants
IMF	International Monetary Fund
IPCC	Intergovernmental Panel on Climate Change
NGOs	Nongovernmental organizations
NIC	National Intelligence Council
NZSF	New Zealand superannuation fund
OECD	Organization for Economic Cooperation and Development
OLG-GE	Overlapping-generation multicountry general-equilibrium modeling
PAYGO	Pay-as-you-go pension scheme
SARS	Severe acute respiratory syndrome
SCP	Stability and Convergence Programme
SGP	Stability and Growth Pact
SWF	Social welfare function
UN	United Nations
U.S. CBO	United States Congressional Budget Office
U.S. CIA	United States Central Intelligence Agency
U.S. EPA	United States Environmental Protection Agency
U.S. GAO	United States General Accounting Office
VaR	Value at risk
WMD	Weapons of mass destruction

1

Introduction and Overview

The art of prophecy is very difficult—especially with respect to the future.

—Mark Twain

To understand long-range predictions is Promethean: The fate of the predictions, if not of the predictor, is likely to be unhappy. Still the challenge is hard to ignore.

—John Holland (2002)

At the outset of this 21st century, policymakers confront a number of profound developments, in their societies and in the natural world, whose significance is certain to increase over the next several decades. Some can be seen as dangers, some as opportunities, and some as both. One of the most important of these developments is demographic in nature. The proportion of the elderly in the populations of many industrial countries and some emerging markets will rise sharply, in some cases even as total population shrinks. Aging populations will become a growing burden for these countries and possibly for the world economy as well. In other countries, in contrast, a significant youth bulge will emerge, and in still more, HIV/AIDS and other infectious diseases will continue to lower life expectancy and retard economic growth.

Another long-term challenge is climate change. Now almost universally recognized as inevitable, global climate change will result in changes in temperature, precipitation, and the frequency and intensity of extreme weather events around the world, although with varying effects in different countries and on different industries. The only uncertainties are how quickly this warming will occur, how it will manifest itself in different regions, and whether human intervention can

1

moderate the extent of warming and its effects during the next century. Competition for some natural resources, particularly water and energy but including others as well, will also become an increasing concern for many countries and regions.

Other structural issues, already emergent, will continue to transform the world economy and the economies of individual countries in coming decades. The forces of globalization will continue to intensify, reshaping economies, promoting the movement of capital and labor as well as of goods, and influencing public policy while limiting its options. Rapid technological change—in biogenetics, information and communications, the science of new materials, cognitive science, and many other areas—will stimulate productivity growth, recast whole industries, and further spur globalization. The century may also see a further divergence in countries' incomes per capita, with many of the world's people still among the absolute poor, particularly in sub-Saharan Africa, South Asia, and Latin America. Finally, the events of September 11, 2001, as well as the situations in Iraq and Korea, have demonstrated the political tensions and security risks that can accompany these other developments.

All of these developments have one thing in common: although in each case the details of what will happen remain highly uncertain, few would question that the effects will be of considerable importance. Two other common features are also well worth noting. First, each of these developments is likely to have an important long-term fiscal dimension: each can be expected to have consequences for government budgets far into the future. In part, these consequences reflect the fact that governments have already *predetermined* their future budgetary priorities to an extent unprecedented in history. Many have committed themselves explicitly to a host of future spending obligations and policy initiatives, including increased outlays for social insurance and for the reduced emission of greenhouse gases. Governments have also repeatedly demonstrated an implicit commitment to respond, through increased spending, to extreme weather events or security risks. Some also face pressures on the revenue side, from international tax competition. For many countries the potential for fiscal disaster is quite real: the prospect of much larger fiscal deficits will require, in the absence of early policy change, either a large increase in tax burdens, a sharp cutback in public services and transfers, or a dramatic reneging on other government policy commitments or on government debt. Second, not just one or a few but *all* of these developments are likely to occur concurrently, if with varying degrees of intensity, in coming decades. To focus narrowly on the fiscal consequences of only one of these issues, in isolation from the rest, would be to ignore the *combined* pressure that may be felt on national budgets.

This study will argue that governments need to do much more, *now*, to take account of the potential fiscal consequences of these developments. The issues they raise need to be the subject not only of more analysis but, perhaps more importantly, of public debate over governments' budget policies. Although their full impact may be felt only in the long term, it would be a grave mistake to defer consideration of these developments and their fiscal effects. Rather, an awareness of these effects should influence the specification of governments' fiscal policy frameworks for the short to the medium term. It should also affect the design of specific policy programs. Five principal arguments can be marshaled to support this assertion.

First, although the fiscal costs of some of these developments may not come due for the next decade or so, capital markets are likely to anticipate the consequences of long-term fiscal weaknesses far sooner. If they do, they will make countries pay a penalty if they have done nothing to address the markets' concerns about the long-term sustainability of fiscal policy. These penalties may be exacted not only by credit markets, in the form of higher interest rates or refusal to lend, but also by long-term equity investors, including multinationals and other direct investors. Households, too, may in effect punish their government's perceived failure to address long-term fiscal concerns, by changing their saving behavior in ways that work against, or even completely offset, the government's macroeconomic policies.

Second, failure to address long-term risk factors sufficiently early may force future governments to adopt policies whose costs to the population living at that time will far exceed those borne by the same country's taxpayers today. That does not mean, however, that only future generations will bear those costs: part of the greater burden will fall on *current* generations, in their old age or even in their later working years.

Third, if they neglect the long term, governments will miss the chance to consider a structured approach by which *present* policies can facilitate the achievement of a long-term fiscal policy outcome that is both sustainable and equitable in sharing risks across generations.

Fourth, it is usually poor budget policy to set in stone today what a country's priorities will be in the future; some flexibility must be retained to meet unexpected challenges or new needs. There is a risk that, by failing to act far enough in advance on those issues that it can anticipate, the state's capacity to respond to other, less predictable problems, or to pursue appropriate macroeconomic policies, will be weakened.

Finally, there is an asymmetry in the ease with which fiscal policy adjustments can be taken. It is relatively easy, from a political perspective, to adjust policies that have erred on the conservative side, by reducing taxes or increasing expenditures. In contrast, fiscal overoptimism is far harder to correct, requiring politically difficult tax increases and expenditure contractions. This is not to minimize the cost or the political pain associated with early fiscal adjustments made in anticipation of long-term risks; indeed, such adjustments may be especially difficult when the corresponding benefits will accrue several generations hence.

Given the significant uncertainties about the likely state of the world decades into the future, taking accurate account of long-term issues is obviously difficult. Who in 1903 could have predicted the mid-century baby boom? Virtually no one foresaw, in 1953, the threat of worldwide climate change. Even if the world leaders of those times had anticipated these developments, could they have convinced their governments and peoples to take the policy actions that would have made a difference? The situation is little changed today. No one can claim to see clearly all the changes that lie in store for humankind in the decades ahead. Nevertheless, this study will argue that we have *sufficient* knowledge about *some* long-term developments for their plausible consequences to be taken into account in formulating fiscal policy frameworks today. The rest of this book will seek to make the case for such enhanced attention and propose ways in which that attention can lead to meaningful action.

Chapter 2 will identify some of the long-term developments that can be foreseen, at least in broad outline, and examine why they are likely to produce significant changes in the underlying fiscal positions of many countries. Of course, the importance of most of these issues will differ greatly from country to country. Not only do the underlying sources of change—geological, demographic, cultural—affect each country differently, but also, as a historical matter, each government has already made certain specific policy commitments, and these, too, differ. The chapter will also explore the nature of the uncertainties surrounding these prospective developments and the issues associated with taking these uncertainties into account in fiscal decision making. It concludes by emphasizing the importance of incorporating risk management in the formulation of fiscal policy.

Chapter 3 will examine how countries presently take account of long-term issues in their short- to medium-term budget frameworks. It reviews the analytical indicators used to assess long-term fiscal sustainability as well as the way in which long-term issues are treated both in the domestic budget process and in the surveillance of government budgets by multilateral institutions. Equally interesting is the question of how governments' policy frameworks today focus, if at all, on long-term risk factors. It emerges that governments rely partly on a strengthening of the aggregate fiscal policy stance—the achievement of budget balance or fiscal surpluses—and partly on specific policy reforms to shrink or expand their long-term commitments. For the former, fiscal rules have been a particularly common choice of policy instrument. The chapter also considers the role of the market as an independent force affecting fiscal policy.

Ultimately, Chapter 3 argues that current approaches to addressing long-term risks in fiscal policy formulation are deficient. Analytical processes are only beginning to include measures of the size of potential long-term imbalances. Meanwhile, budget processes in most countries do not go beyond a medium-term framework. Countries also rely too heavily on an aggregative approach to fiscal sustainability in an attempt to reduce government debt and raise the national saving rate. Ricardian equivalence effects—the potential for households to offset fiscal initiatives by increasing or reducing their own saving—are not adequately considered. Finally, issues of risk tolerance do not appear to be adequately addressed, particularly in terms of the need to create adequate room in the budget for less easily identifiable pressures that may arise in the future.

Chapter 4 will examine some of the conceptual issues that governments and citizens must confront in considering whether and how to address long-term fiscal challenges. Why should a government incur short-term costs to address issues that seemingly will yield benefits only in the very long term? What factors should be taken into account in assessing such trade-offs? Might failure to address long-term issues impinge on a government's capacity to act in the short run? What factors might make it difficult for a government to act on long-term concerns? Normative issues inevitably come into play. In part, this relates to the difficulty of making trade-offs between the welfare of different generations. In part, it mirrors the problems faced by a government and a society in deciding on a posture toward risk. Political economy issues are also critical to this discussion. Politicians are legendarily myopic, focusing mainly on the next election. But the citizenry in most

countries may be equally myopic, whether because people do not recognize the possible impact of long-term developments, or because they
see no way to deal with them, or because they attach far greater value
to consumption today than to consumption in the future. The chapter
examines the various factors—the legacy of past policies, concerns
about the sustainability of policies, concerns about allocative efficiency,
and the desire to achieve distributional goals, as well as political economy factors, feasibility constraints, and the need to maintain the legit-
imacy of the state—that are likely to influence the approach taken by a
government and society in addressing long-term issues.

Chapter 5 will suggest a number of concrete ways to strengthen
countries' current approaches to addressing the fiscal consequences of
long-term developments. It argues that a multipronged strategy is
vital, comprehensively blending changes in analysis with changes in
process and in specific policies. At the analytical level, this requires an
explicit focus on long-term fiscal sustainability and innovative techniques that allow a quantitative assessment of the risks associated with
alternative outcomes. Strengthened budget procedures and processes
are needed to counter the myopic incentives of politicians and citizens.
At the policy level, adjustments in the aggregate fiscal stance will in
most cases be insufficient *alone* to rectify long-term fiscal imbalances.
Rather, reductions in policy commitments, in ways that affect the time
path of expenditure, and a more cautious approach to taking on new
expenditure commitments are also necessary. In other words, more
weight needs to be placed on policy reforms that ensure that governments have an adequate fiscal cushion to face the challenges associated
with looming structural and political trends. Globally, enhanced policy
coordination among countries would also be desirable. Chapter 6 provides some concluding thoughts.

Before beginning, it is worth being explicit about what this study will
not do. It will not address the specifics of how governments might wish
to restructure their existing policies—whether in terms of particular
programs or in terms of the regulation of the private sector—on the
many complex issues that pertain to the long term. Such issues include
pension reform, medical care, climate change adaptation and mitigation, hazard insurance, and overseas development assistance, to name
a few. Each of these issues is vast and complex and warrants its own in-
depth analysis. Although this study certainly emphasizes the importance of governments reconfiguring the scale of their obligations in
each area—reducing the extent of their commitments and considering

initiatives that would limit future outlays—how to do so is another large topic indeed.

It is also worth noting that there are some who would question the importance and relevance of this topic. Perhaps three schools of thought can be identified. The first (to which this study belongs) holds that it is important for policymakers to begin, at least, to grapple with the challenge of ensuring long-term fiscal sustainability in the face of clearly anticipated risks and great uncertainties.[1] A second school, while not denying the importance of some of these issues, would nonetheless contend that, even under conservative assumptions about productivity growth, living standards by the mid-21st century will be so much higher than today that the fiscal consequences of potential risk factors can be reasonably accommodated.[2] A third school, reflecting the views of experienced budget planners, may be described as skeptical. It notes the considerable uncertainty of any budget forecast that looks beyond two to three years. It also suggests the need for considerable caution in any effort to formulate a fiscal policy stance that is meant to affect the fiscal outcome long into the future.

The perspectives of the latter two schools are important for the light that they shed on the basic questions posed by this study, and it is worth responding to them. In some respects, the advocates of the third school themselves offer the best argument for why a concern with the long term is important, uncertainties notwithstanding. Aaron (2000, p. 193), for example, has noted that

> Forecasts...are notoriously unreliable. In fact they almost always are wrong.... Nonetheless, ...without forecasts, we would be totally at sea. That we have to use forecasts or projections that we know will be wrong and that usually are wrong raises some difficult questions for policy

---

[1] The final communiqué of the March 2001 Stockholm European Council (2001, p. 11) emphasized that the Council "should regularly review the long term sustainability of public finances, including the expected strains caused by the demographic changes ahead." Auerbach and Hassett (2001, p. 91), in a recent paper, emphasize that "the presence of uncertainty about the future offers little apparent justification for waiting to act in response to an anticipated fiscal imbalance."

[2] For example, Schelling (1992) and, more recently, Beckerman and Pasek (2001) argue that although global climate change may entail significant costs for future generations, absolute incomes will be well placed to afford policy solutions, even under the most conservative assumptions about growth in income per capita over the next 30 to 50 years. Similarly, Guest and McDonald (2001a, 2001b) argue that consumption per capita should almost double over the next 50 years in real terms, so that the cost of aging populations will reduce only modestly the anticipated rise in living standards.

analysts and policy-making. Regrettably, in my view, they receive too little attention. My purpose today is to urge that they receive more.

Similarly, Penner (2001, p. 20), a past director of the U.S. Congressional Budget Office, has argued that

> Because budget projections tend to be highly inaccurate and are unlikely to get better soon, policymakers...must live with tremendous uncertainty. That uncertainty should be recognized more explicitly than it has been in the past, and the dialogue regarding policy decisions should pay more attention to the risks of being wrong.

The views of John Holland (2002), who is not an economist but a scientist specializing in complex adaptive systems (and widely known as the "father of genetic algorithms"), are also relevant in this context:

> The common way of making predictions is to examine extensions of current trends.... Such predictions can be valuable in the short term, but trends are fallible guides for longer periods, *unless the underlying processes have great "inertia,"* as in the case of population growth or the buildup of greenhouse gases. (p. 171, italics in original)

> Much of our social agenda is influenced by problems that are not subject to a quick fix. Fixes in this realm require plausible predictions of the long-term effects of current actions. (p. 175)

In effect, despite a poor record of projections, and despite the wide fan of uncertainty that characterizes projections even 5 years out, let alone 30 or 50, the issues that are likely to pose challenges are nevertheless real, and their consequences for future welfare potentially significant. Policy reforms, both those aimed at the program level and those addressing the aggregate balance, can limit the extent to which long-standing policy commitments leave a society exposed to an excessive risk of a government defaulting on its debt, reneging on its obligations to society, or seeing its fiscal capacity weakened to the point where it cannot cope with unpleasant surprises.

The issues posed by the second school are equally challenging. Why worry about a higher tax burden on future generations—a burden that in any case is, at most, probable rather than certain—if those who would have to bear it will be so much better off than we are today?[3] Two answers are possible. First, high marginal tax rates always create

---

[3] In effect, Robert Nozick (1989) would argue that this approach is equivalent to a social welfare framework that treats the resources of citizens as a common property resource that the government may extract, subject only to constraints imposed by administrative feasibility and potentially adverse incentive effects. Kotlikoff and

disincentives to work, save, and invest, independent of income. They did so for the working generation in many countries 30 to 40 years ago, and they do so for the working generation of today, whose incomes are significantly higher. If today's working generation leaves long-term issues unaddressed, with the result that future generations are confronted by exorbitant tax rates, the latter will react adversely in their economic behavior no matter how high their incomes have risen. The result could be stiff political resistance to a higher tax burden "imposed" by previous generations.

Second, although today's generations may perceive a doubling of their income per capita as representing a significant improvement in the standard of living, it is not clear whether the future generations that will earn those doubled incomes will be any more satisfied than we are with ours, and therefore any more complacent about higher tax rates. Their perception of relative needs, and of what can be purchased from a given income, will undoubtedly be different from ours today. In other words, it would be risky for present generations to assume, myopically, that they can rely on future generations to honor in full the commitments made today, long in advance of when the bills come due. Most likely, all would lose as a result—in the form of a diminished capacity for action by the state, sharply curtailed public services, and large and unanticipated cutbacks in benefits to many elderly whose capacity to offset these losses is diminished.

In sum, despite contrarian views, governments can ill afford to remain complacent about the fiscal consequences of recognizable long-term trends. Governments owe it to future generations to take stock of the potential consequences of their current policy frameworks and to prepare responsibly for an uncertain future.

Raffelhuschen (1999) have noted that one potential theoretical justification for efforts to achieve fiscal sustainability derives from the concept of the welfare state as a social contract, which is transacted between generations. By each generation honoring its part of the contract, current and future generations carry out exchanges that are expected to benefit everyone.

2

Why Consider Long-Term Issues in Thinking About Fiscal Policy?

A forward-looking perspective is always useful in policymaking, and it is especially useful for fiscal planners. The capital outlays of governments are large and discrete, and their benefits are realized only over time. Policy commitments that may cost little in the short term may become more costly over time as their full ramifications are felt. In addition, governments often borrow to finance today's outlays, whether for current or for capital spending. Policymakers should always be mindful of the capacity of their government to service both its public debt and its policy commitments in the future. The consequences for a government that incurs excessive debt or accumulates exorbitant policy commitments, and therefore risks defaulting on that debt or reneging on those commitments, can be stark. Private credit rating agencies may downgrade its sovereign debt, thus raising the risk premium the country will have to pay on subsequent borrowing. This in turn may force abrupt cutbacks in politically popular government programs in order to reduce the fiscal deficit and restore fiscal credibility.

Today, at the beginning of the 21st century, many governments need to take account of long-term issues in their fiscal policy analysis and planning far more explicitly than they have done up to now. A number of specific major developments can be readily anticipated to happen *concurrently*, over the medium to long term, which will have important fiscal dimensions, even if their magnitude is still uncertain.[1] Among others,

---

[1] The recent U.S. Climate Action Report (U.S. Environmental Protection Agency, 2002) highlights this concurrent nature of future long-term developments, noting that "climate change is only one among many potential stresses that society and the environment face; ... an ageing national populace and rapidly growing populations in cities, coastal areas, and across the South and West are social factors that interact with and in some ways increase the sensitivity of society to climate variability and change. In both evaluating potential impacts and developing effective responses, it is therefore important to consider interactions among the various stresses" (p. 88). Also see Schwartz (2003).

these developments include the aging of populations, global climate change and other environmental pressures, globalization and the greater interconnectedness it brings, the growing disparities between rich and poor nations, the explosive growth of massive urban centers, continued rapid technological change, and potential resource scarcities. All of these are likely to imply important structural changes for the economies of individual countries as well as for the global economy. Certain structural assumptions that heretofore may have been reasonable in making long-term projections can thus no longer be readily made. The prospect of disruptive events that are even more difficult to foresee—like those of September 11, 2001—adds a further layer of uncertainty.

This chapter begins by identifying a number of developments that are likely to have significant fiscal ramifications for many countries, and in some cases worldwide, over the long horizon. The chapter then examines the case for a more proactive consideration of these long-term issues in formulating today's fiscal policies, despite the considerable uncertainty that surrounds each of them. The chapter goes on to discuss the nature of the uncertainties characterizing the long term and the problems posed for fiscal policymakers in taking account of such uncertainties.

Transformative Issues in the 21st Century

Demographic Change

There seems to be little doubt that most of today's industrial countries will face a dramatic shift in their demographic structure in coming decades. These countries have already experienced an unprecedented and continuing rapid growth in life expectancy, a surge in fertility rates (the baby boom) from the late 1940s through the early 1960s, and a subsequent sharp and sustained decline in fertility. Together these trends have set the stage for, in the near future, a sharp increase in the share of the population that is elderly (Figure 2.1), an even more rapid growth in the number of very elderly (those over 85 years of age), a corresponding decline in the population share of the young, a stabilization in the absolute size of the population (or a decline, depending on immigration patterns), and, on balance, some increase in the overall dependency rate, defined as the ratio of children (those under age 16) and elderly (those aged 65 and over) to the total population. As this transition occurs,

Figure 2.1
Projected Shares of Elderly in Total Population by World Region
(In percent)

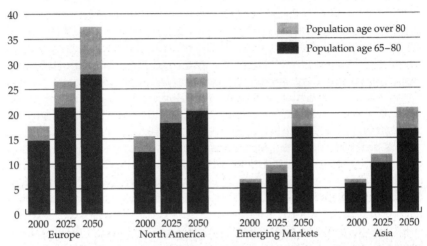

Source: United Nations Population Division (2003).

coming decades will witness significant changes in the size and age composition of the labor force in these countries.[2]

These demographic shifts are not limited to the industrial countries, however. Many emerging market economies as well as some of the economies in transition from central planning have experienced similar trends, albeit with a lag of years or decades. They, too, can anticipate a graying of their populations during this century. China, in particular, will face a marked change in its age structure: its population aged 60 and over is projected to increase to 420 million by 2050, at which point it will exceed the entire population of the United States (United Nations Population Division, 2003).

At the same time, despite signs of declining fertility rates in many countries that now have high fertility, the world's population will continue to rise, with the increase heavily concentrated in some of the poorest regions of the world: sub-Saharan Africa, South Asia, North Africa,

---

[2]The recent EC report (European Commission, 2002b) on economic trends in the European Union suggests that the population of the current 15 EU countries is leveling off at less than 400 million, and that the share of the population of working age will fall. The U.S. population, in contrast, will have grown by 40 million by 2050, and many more will be of working age. Both regions will see an increase in the dependency ratio, but this increase will be sharper in the European Union, resulting in an economic growth rate less than half that in the United States.

and the Middle East. Recent UN projections (United Nations Population Division, 2003) suggest that the largest absolute increases in populations in the next half century (2000–50) will occur in India (an increase of 514 million), Pakistan (206 million), Nigeria (144 million), the United States (123 million), Bangladesh (117 million), Ethiopia (105 million), and the Democratic Republic of Congo (103 million). The populations of some countries may explode—more than doubling in Ethiopia, Pakistan, Nigeria, Bangladesh, the Democratic Republic of Congo, and Egypt. In some countries the population will *quadruple or quintuple*, for example in Yemen from 18 million to 84 million, and in Niger from 11 million to 53 million.

Most of these countries now have a large share—from a third to as much as a half—of their population in the under-15 age group. Because UN projections suggest a significant decline in fertility rates over the next half century, this youth bulge will be transformed into a bulge in the share of the population that is of working age (15–59), with a heavy concentration in coming decades in the younger component of the workforce. For example, in India and Pakistan the shares of the young will fall from 34 percent and 42 percent of the population, respectively, to 19 percent and 24 percent. Reflecting high fertility rates, many African countries will still see a significant youth share, at about 30 percent of the population.

Many of the countries that will see a large growth in population will also see a dramatic increase in the population share of the elderly, even though such shares will be far less than in the aging industrial and emerging market countries. But the political and economic effects of a tripling of the share of the elderly will surely be felt. Population shares of the elderly will rise from about 5 or 6 percent to the 14 to 25 percent range in Algeria, Egypt, Iran, Iraq, Libya, Morocco, South Africa, Sudan, and Tunisia; most strikingly, the population share of the elderly in the United Arab Emirates is projected by the United Nations to rise from 2 percent to 28 percent by 2050.

A vast literature addresses the fiscal implications of aging populations.[3] Most studies suggest that the aging of industrial country

---

[3]Studies include those carried out by the European Commission (EC Economic Policy Committee, 2000; EC Directorate-General for Economic and Financial Affairs, 2001; EC, 2002a), the Organization for Economic Cooperation and Development (2001a), the Group of Ten (1998), the International Monetary Fund (Chand and Jaeger, 1996), international commissions such as the CSIS Commission on Global Aging (see Hewitt, 2002), and many individual countries, including Australia, Commonwealth of (2002), New Zealand (Janssen, 2001), and the United States (U.S. Congressional Budget Office, 2000, 2001b), not to mention many academic studies (Bohn, 1999; Börsch-Supan and Winter, 2001; Cutler and others, 1990; Lee and Tuljapurkar, 2000; Lee and Edwards, 2002; Sinn and Uebelmesser, 2001).

Figure 2.2
Projected Government Pension and Health Spending,
Selected OECD Countries
(In percent of GDP)

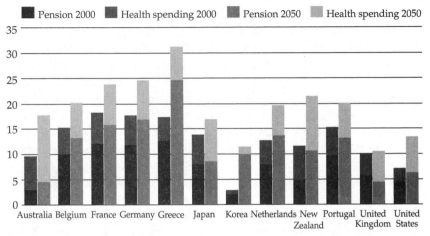

Sources: OECD (2001a); European Commission, Economic Policy Committee (2001).

populations will add greatly to the burden of public expenditure, principally through a sharp growth in real spending on pensions, health care, and long-term residential care, offset only minimally by a decline in education expenditure (Figure 2.2). It is this issue, perhaps more than any other, that has triggered popular concern about the long-term sustainability of government budgets.

Although some of this rising burden can be attributed to the underlying dynamic, in many countries, of slowing real economic growth accompanied by a shrinking labor force (not to mention a possible slowdown in productivity growth), the fiscal pressures in fact originate mainly from the existing framework of social insurance commitments in most industrial countries. One dimension of this, in many countries, is the comprehensive role of the government in the provision of medical care. A second is the commitment to generous public pensions: with few exceptions (such as Australia, New Zealand, and the United Kingdom), public pension systems in the industrialized world are structured to facilitate retirement at or around age 65, if not earlier (despite rising longevity), and starting pension benefits are roughly indexed to the wage at retirement (thus rising with average earnings in the economy). A third dimension is the commitment to public welfare systems, which in some countries provide outlays to support at least the neediest of the very elderly, if not others as well.

The precise dynamics of potential expenditure growth in any given country depend very much on the characteristics of its social insurance system, including the tax treatment of pension savings and benefits, and on assumptions made about a number of economic and demographic variables.[4] Among others, these variables could include future rates of fertility, life expectancy, migration, productivity growth, labor force participation (particularly of the elderly), and medical care cost inflation. The magnitude of the potential fiscal challenge posed by the aging of a country's population is also very much related to that country's starting fiscal position, as measured by its primary fiscal balance (the total fiscal balance less interest outlays) and its public debt. It is also related to assumptions about the likely pace of expenditure adjustment in areas not related to aging, and to future revenue performance.[5] But the basic conclusion of most studies is that, for most industrial countries, population aging will either impose a significantly higher tax burden in the future or require the adoption of specific policy measures to limit future spending and the implied increase in the public debt. Box 2.1 summarizes the conclusions of a number of recent studies on the fiscal impact of aging populations.

Population aging may also have important economic effects beyond the government budget: on output, on saving and investment, on productivity, on capital markets (including interest rates and asset prices), on labor markets, and on migration. In a country with a growing retired population and a declining labor force, only faster productivity growth, increased labor force participation among those of working age, or reduced unemployment will support an increase in output and an improvement in real living standards. Even strategic and military weakness has been flagged as a potential consequence of the aging of industrial country populations (U.S. Central Intelligence Agency, 2001b). These effects, which would be of serious concern to any single economy, are likely to be magnified and take on global importance to

---

[4]For example, in countries with substantial defined-contribution pension systems, the practice of exempting from income tax both pension contributions and the investment returns associated with those contributions has important fiscal implications. Significant fiscal costs in terms of forgone tax revenue are incurred in the present, but there is an offsetting fiscal payback in the future, when retirees receive distributions from their accumulated assets and pay taxes on those distributions (see Frederiksen, 2000, 2002).

[5]Beyond demographics, in many countries the active role of the state continues to fuel an increasing demand for either publicly produced services or subsidies to privately produced services. Although governments are increasingly constrained in their ability to respond, the fact of these pressures makes it difficult to realize significant adjustments in the share of government expenditure in total output.

Box 2.1. Conclusions of Recent Studies on the Fiscal Impact of Aging Industrial Country Populations

Directorate of Economic and Financial Affairs, European Commission
"...[M]ost Member States included a specific section on the sustainability of public finances in their programme, presenting long-term budgetary projections. This information shows that ageing populations will have a considerable budgetary impact. Public spending is projected to rise by between 4% and 8% of GDP in the coming four decades, although much higher increases are projected in several Member States. Increases in public spending due to ageing populations will start as of 2010 in some countries as the baby-boom generation enter into retirement, and the steepest rise will occur between 2020 and 2035 in most Member States.... In brief, ambitious and comprehensive strategies of a few Member States contrast with as yet rather piecemeal approaches in other countries which are not commensurate with the seriousness of the policy challenge." (European Commission, 2002a, pp. 48–49)

Organization for Economic Cooperation and Development
"The projections point to a generalized deterioration in the public-sector primary fiscal balance over the projection period [2000 to 2050] reflecting:
• The increase in old-age pension spending.
• Changes to other age-related spending in countries providing such information.
The projected deterioration in the primary balance is likely to be substantially larger than the impact of old-age pension spending alone in the countries which project only the latter.... For the 'stylized' country, the accumulated impact on the public debt of aging is large, approximately 200 percentage points of GDP." (OECD, 2001a, pp. 158–62)

The Treasury, Commonwealth of Australia
"The projections in this [Intergenerational] report suggest that, if policies are not adjusted, the current generation of taxpayers is likely to impose a higher tax burden on the next generation. The required adjustment in taxes and spending is about 5.0 percent of GDP by 2041–42.... Although the aging of the Australian population is not expected to have a major impact on the Commonwealth's budget for at least another 15 years, forward planning for these developments is important, to ensure that governments will be well placed to meet emerging policy challenges in a timely and effective manner." (Australia, Commonwealth of, 2002, p. 1)

Moritz Kraemer, Standard & Poor's
"After 2020...additional age-related expenditure would, on average, outweigh savings on debt service, and the EU–15 debt ratio would...eventually top currently observed levels.... As the fiscal implications of aging become

more pronounced and debt levels start to pick up again...the average EU–15 fiscal balance deteriorates and reaches a deficit of 5 percent of GDP by 2050. For a subset of countries, including Germany and France, the results would be much more severe, as these countries have made little progress in fiscal consolidation and structural reform. Left unchecked, their debt levels would exceed 200 percent of GDP by 2050, bringing about double-digit deficits. By contrast, other countries such as the United Kingdom and Sweden would by 2050 have accumulated net general government assets exceeding their respective GDP." (Kraemer, 2002, p. 1)

Niels Frederiksen, Ministry of Finance, Denmark

"If OECD governments adopt a strategy of fiscal sustainability, they will over the next 3 or 4 decades all but eliminate government gross debt liabilities in order to make room for the spending increases driven by the interactions of population changes and welfare state programs. However, on average, actual current fiscal consolidation falls short of the required amount by about 5 percent of GDP." (Frederiksen, 2003, p. 10)

Robert England and Sylvester Schieber, Center for Strategic and International Studies

"The growing imbalance between the population of working people and those who are retired threatens to cause a future fiscal crisis in virtually every nation in the industrial world. This crisis will occur because virtually all social security systems, including elderly health and nursing care, operate on a pay-as-you-go basis. That is, they are not prefunded by contributions that are invested in liquid assets that earn a return on those investments. Current workers support current retirees through the payroll tax (sometimes called a 'contribution' in some countries, income tax, and other taxes.... The future imbalance between workers and retirees in industrial nations could lead governments to make sharp cuts in old-age benefits. Alternatively, it could lead to large run-ups in debt that could destabilize some currencies and financial markets. It also could lead to large tax increases that would dampen economic growth or cause what some economists call 'aging recessions.' All three outcomes—benefit cuts, higher debt, and higher taxes—could occur simultaneously or in succession in any given country over the next three decades, as the aging crunch begins to hit." (England and Schieber, 2001, pp. 9–10)

Paul Hewitt, Center for Strategic and International Studies

"Population trends in the developed world will challenge societies at every level: individuals, employers, governments, international arrangements and financial markets.... Rising old-age dependency in every industrial country could trigger budget turmoil with broad implications for global growth." (Hewitt, 2002, p. 9)

Center for Strategic and International Studies
Jackson and Howe (2002) have compiled an "Aging Vulnerability Index" to assess the vulnerability of industrial countries to rising old-age dependency costs. It is compiled from indicators in four basic categories, each of which deals with a crucial dimension of aging. These include public burden indicators, which measure the magnitude of the spending burden; fiscal room indicators, which track the ability of a country to accommodate the growth in old-age benefits through higher taxes, cuts in spending, or public borrowing; benefit dependence indicators, which track how dependent the elderly population is on public benefits; and elderly affluence indicators, which capture the relative affluence of old and young generations. From data on 12 industrial countries, the index suggests that the least vulnerable countries are Australia, the United Kingdom, and the United States. The most vulnerable are France, Italy, and Spain. In the middle are Belgium, Canada, Germany, Japan, the Netherlands, and Sweden.

Richard Davis and Nick Fabling, New Zealand Treasury
"[In New Zealand], studies of the fiscal implications of population aging consistently show that, in the absence of policy change, a significant deterioration in the fiscal position is inevitable.... The Treasury's Long-Term Fiscal Model (LTFM) projects government expenditure (excluding financing costs) increasing by approximately seven percentage points of Gross Domestic Product (GDP) over the next half century. First, a slower growing and eventually declining labor force is expected to lead to lower economic growth and tax revenue since unemployment and labor productivity are not projected to change significantly from historical norms. Second, increases in the average age of the population are expected to raise per capita health and superannuation expenditure." (Davis and Fabling, 2002, p. 1)

the extent that they are taking place at roughly the same time in virtually all of the major industrial economies of the world. The ripple effects of such aging in the industrial world may also have economic consequences, through changes in world interest rates and in global economic growth rates, that will affect fiscal policy management.

For those countries where rapid population growth continues, the direct fiscal policy challenges will prove very different. On the one hand, a rising share of the population that is of working age presents an opportunity for more rapid economic growth (like that enjoyed by many Asian countries in the 1970s and 1980s) and a more buoyant fiscal position. On the other hand, serious political and economic risks can emerge if, instead of rapid growth, there is widespread and rising unemployment among younger workers. The pressures on the fiscal regime to finance the provision of education and health services as well as additional urban infrastructure will also be substantial.

Moreover, many emerging market and other developing countries, even those experiencing significant population increases, will see a dramatic increase in the share of the elderly. The absence of well-developed and broadly based social insurance systems in these countries may limit the adverse effects on government budgets observed in industrial countries. Extended family structures may offer some mechanism for absorbing the costs of providing for the elderly through private channels. But make no mistake. The aging of these countries will give rise to pressures for an expansion in publicly provided social insurance that, if not directly confronted, could begin to mirror the fiscal pressures faced by industrial countries.

Global Climate Change

The change in the global climate that is expected to occur over the next century will have a number of different impacts. Apart from the central question—how much warming will take place globally—important considerations include the extent of warming in different world regions and subregions, changes in precipitation rates, changes in the frequency and intensity of extreme weather events (such as cyclones, hurricanes, and heavy rainstorms and snowstorms), a rise in the sea level (which will result in higher storm surges from cyclones and other storms), and the very small but real possibility of abrupt and drastic climatic change (Committee on Abrupt Climate Change, 2002).[6] The probability of each of these potential outcomes is unknown. Even the precise probability distribution of alternative outcomes is still unclear.[7]

What we do know to a high degree of statistical confidence is that the concentration of greenhouse gases already present in the atmosphere will give rise to a warming of the earth's atmosphere in the range of 1.9° to 5.8°C (roughly 3° to 10°F) over the next century (Figure 2.3, top

---

[6]The threat of abrupt change is associated with changes in the thermohaline circulation in the North Atlantic or in the El Niño/Southern Oscillation patterns in the tropical Pacific. These changes could have implications for the tropical Atlantic and Indian Oceans, the southern Pacific Ocean, and the middle to high latitudes of the Northern Hemisphere.

[7]The U.S. Environmental Protection Agency (2002) in its U.S. Climate Action Report notes that it cannot present absolute probabilities, but rather "only...judgments about the relative plausibility of outcomes in the event that the projected changes in climate that are being considered do occur" (p. 82).

panel). Efforts at mitigation on the order of those presently being considered are unlikely to reduce significantly the amount of climate change already embedded in the system.[8] Gerhard Berz of the insurance company Munich Re has stated, "To put it bluntly, the climate will not notice the Kyoto Protocol, even if it is implemented in full" (Munich Re Group, 2002, p. 78). Similarly, the U.S. Environmental Protection Agency (U.S. EPA, 2002, p. 82) reports that, "Because of the momentum in the climate system and natural climate variability, adapting to a changing climate is inevitable. The question is whether we adapt poorly or well." The Intergovernmental Panel on Climate Change (IPCC) has produced several reports (IPCC, 2001a–d) that give a sense not only of the expected incidence and impact of the various dimensions of climate change on a global and regional basis, but also of the considerable uncertainty that still exists. It is also widely recognized that the likelihood of adverse economic effects rises as one moves to the upper end of the forecast statistical confidence interval, but even smaller changes could have significant economic effects (Swiss Re, 2002).

Accompanying global climate change will be a continued rise in global population and, most likely, continued (although perhaps slower) economic growth in most regions of the world. Even in the absence of climate change, pressure on natural resources (including water, energy, forests, fisheries, and arable land) will increase, and the world's large population centers will continue to grow. The consequences of global climate change, even if it occurs only gradually, will be intertwined with these intensifying economic and population pressures. Climate change will require adaptation in agriculture and will affect the regional availability of water, arable land, and forest reserves. Extreme weather events and rising sea levels will have greater economic and social consequences than they would otherwise, if only because of the rising economic value of exposed infrastructure and human settlements, and because most of the world's largest cities lie in coastal zones.

The possible *fiscal* implications of global climate change, particularly as it interacts with these other pressures affecting the global environment, have been studied far less than these other effects. In part, this may reflect the expectation that, for some of the industrial

---

[8]This is the principal reason that some important academic efforts to evaluate the net present value of mitigation investments are likely to have only small returns (see Nordhaus and Boyer, 2000). The costs would be large, and the probability of a significant reduction in consequences small, at least within this century. The principal climatic benefits would be realized only in the following centuries.

countries (including notably the United States and Canada), climate change may have a net positive economic impact (although negative net effects are projected for much of Europe). Also, and quite importantly, the mainstream view is that whatever climate change will occur will take place gradually and over a long period, allowing enough time for adaptation.

These are not sufficient grounds for complacency. Even for industrial countries, the consequences of climate change are recognized to be important and damaging: aside from greater susceptibility to extreme weather events, loss in biodiversity, shifts in agricultural and forestry patterns, and increased health hazards, there are the particular, industry-specific economic effects associated with even modest changes in average temperature and weather conditions.[9] For developing countries, including emerging markets, the impact is likely to be far more adverse, for several reasons. First, for any given *global* climate outcome, developing countries as a group are expected to suffer a greater degree of climatic change than the industrial countries as a group, simply because most developing countries are in the tropics. Second, the developing world relies more on those economic sectors, such as agriculture, that are more sensitive to changes in precipitation and temperature. Third, these countries are likely to be particularly exposed to the impact of changes in sea level, given the number of coastal megacities likely to be affected (Figure 2.3, bottom panel).

Moreover, even if the upward trend in average global temperature proves gradual, that trend may be punctuated by more frequent extreme weather events. In addition, there is a small but real possibility that the assumption of gradual, linear climate change may be in error—that abrupt climate changes, with severe economic consequences, may

---

[9]This has been set out clearly in recent national reports on climate change by Denmark (Denmark Energy Agency, 2000), the Netherlands, the United States, and the United Kingdom. The recent *National Communication* of New Zealand on climate change (New Zealand Climate Change Programme, 2002) notes that "While on-going research will lead to a greater understanding of the possible impacts of climate change on specific sectors, there are still large uncertainties, [which have]...made it difficult to mandate or implement specific actions at a national scale aimed at adaptation to climate change. However, it is recognized as important that policymakers at both the national and local level...take account of the possible effects of climate change in formulating policy and developing strategic plans" (p. 75). "Climate change may result in more frequent occurrence of 'unusual' climate events, and greater extremes, such as high rainfall and periods of drought. Coastal and low-lying land is particularly vulnerable to...climate change" (p. 75). The experience of Australia, which recently suffered its worst drought in a century, illustrates the importance of considering the implications of climate change.

Figure 2.3
Projected Climate Change Indicators

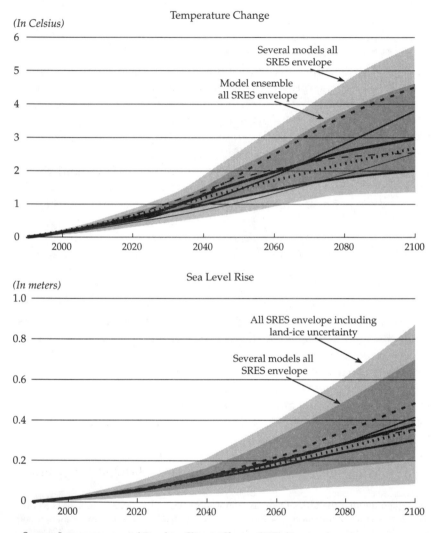

Source: Intergovernmental Panel on Climate Change (2001a).
Note: The different lines represent alternative projection scenarios carried out by the IPCC (2001a) (from a Special Report on Emission Scenarios (SRES)). These scenarios seek to characterize possible future states of the world in terms of the magnitude of forcing agents emitted into the atmosphere (greenhouse gas and sulphur emissions, aerosols, etc.). They reflect the impact of alternative economic, technological, and environmental policy choices, with potential effects in terms of such greenhouse gas emission drivers as population growth, the rate and structure of economic development, and the rate of usage of alternative energy sources. The shading represents overlapping confidence intervals of the projections shown.

lie ahead.[10] This discussion will highlight a number of issues related to climate change that are worthy of consideration for their potential effects on the future fiscal positions of many countries.

Adapting to Climate Change

The extent to which a given country will have to adapt to climate change will depend on how much its own climate changes, what forms that change takes, and how those changes affect the country's economic and physical assets (including biodiversity). Although much of the burden of reallocating resources and financing new investment will undoubtedly fall on the private sector, it is unlikely that the public sector will remain unscathed, especially in countries, such as many developing countries, where the net economic impact of climate change is expected to be negative. Areas of potential public sector involvement include outlays on infrastructure (for example, for urban water control and irrigation systems), other public goods in the areas of disease prevention and agricultural extension and research (to address public health risks and to help the agricultural sector adapt), and subsidies (to facilitate the resettlement of populations).

The economic consequences of potential losses in biodiversity are far more difficult to anticipate, but one can imagine that many localized industries may be seriously affected, and pressures for subsidies, however temporary, may emerge. Even in countries like the United States, where climate change is expected to have a net benefit, some important regions will be adversely affected. Public sector subsidies and transfers may be demanded to compensate for losses, to facilitate the relocation of infrastructure and of resources, and to provide relief and rehabilitation for those most severely affected.[11] There is already ample precedent for such transfers. In the recent past, for example, the United States has compensated farmers in the U.S. Midwest for weather-

---

[10]Again quoting the U.S. Climate Action Report (U.S. EPA, 2002, p. 83), "it is important to recognize that there are likely to be unanticipated impacts of climate change that occur. Such 'surprises,' positive or negative, may stem from either (1) unforeseen changes in the physical climate system, such as major alterations in ocean circulation, cloud distribution, or storms; or (2) unpredicted biological consequences of these physical climate changes, such as pest outbreaks."

[11]Even in the United States, the recent Climate Action Report notes that although many "U.S. communities and industries have made substantial efforts to reduce their vulnerability to normal weather and climate fluctuations...adaptation to potential changes in weather extremes and climate variability is likely to be more difficult and costly" (U.S. EPA, 2002, p. 87).

Figure 2.4
Global Costs of Extreme Weather Events
(In billions of constant U.S. dollars)

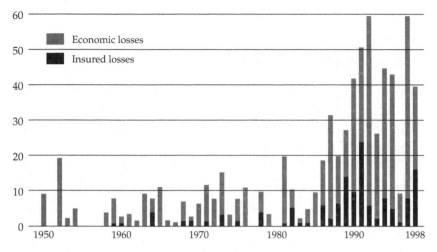

Source: Intergovernmental Panel on Climate Change (2001d).

related losses, including those from massive floods in 1993 and from drought in 2002.

Extreme Weather Events

A recent IPCC report (IPCC, 2001b) suggests that both the frequency and the intensity of extreme weather events will increase in coming decades, and worldwide trends over the past decade bear witness to this possibility (Figure 2.4). Such events will produce significant economic losses that may be difficult to insure against fully. Public expenditure may be required to provide emergency assistance, to rebuild damaged infrastructure, and to build new infrastructure (such as dikes) to prevent future losses.[12] Increasingly, the global insurance industry is reevaluating what risks it can realistically cover and what premiums will have to be charged, in view of changing risk patterns. The role of governments as ultimate sources of reinsurance will become the subject of more pressing debate in the future, in which moral hazard

---

[12]For example, in the Republic of Korea, the typhoons of 2002 were the worst in 40 years. The government appropriated $3.4 billion (about 85 percent of total estimated damage costs) to finance relief efforts and repair damage (Reuters World Service, 2002).

will be a prominent issue (Munich Re Group, 2002; United Nations Environment Programme, 2002).[13]

Mitigation

Much effort will be devoted to reducing emissions of greenhouse gases, and much of the increased expenditure toward this effort will come from the private sector. Here public sector involvement may involve replacing existing taxes with new ones that promote reduced emissions. Or there may be more active use of regulation, whether of the command-and-control or the market-based type (such as tradable permits), in which case the fiscal consequences are likely to be more limited. However, even greater efforts at mitigation may be necessary in the future. Studies are under way to assess whether even more dire consequences than are currently expected could result from the existing concentration of greenhouse gases or from the increases that are likely to occur as development proceeds in many countries in the developing world that today have low emissions. If the findings are unfavorable, more expensive programs may be needed to overhaul existing energy-using technologies and infrastructure.

Low-Probability, High-Consequence Climatic Events

In a recent paper, Alley and others (2003) note that all research on climate change has relied on scenarios with slow and gradual changes. This assumption reflects "how recently the existence of abrupt climate change gained widespread recognition, and how difficult it has been to generate appropriate scenarios for abrupt climate change for impacts assessments" (Alley and others, 2003, p. 2007). Abrupt climate change would be associated with unprecedented changes in temperature and precipitation patterns, such as would result from a shift in the Gulf Stream. This could require major adaptations in infrastructure and would likely result in significant structural adjustment in weather-dependent economic sectors such as agriculture and tourism. Among produced capital stocks, buildings and infrastructure specific to particular locations and adapted to particular climates with lifetimes of 50 to

---

[13]Munich Re Group (2002) notes the dangerous exposure arising from the insurance industry's reliance on retrospective underwriting approaches, based on historical claims development. If a significant structural change is taking place, premiums will lag behind claims. "The insurance industry must think about how risk-commensurate fluctuation loadings can be calculated for the risk of change inherent in climate change" (p. 43).

100 years are especially vulnerable to abrupt climate change. These changes would undoubtedly entail far more significant fiscal interventions to help the private sector adapt to and address the economic and social consequences.

In sum, the global climatic environment will certainly be influenced by both demographic and economic change, but at the same time it will evolve in ways that affect the nature of consumption and production decisions and the quality of economic and natural resource assets. Much has been written about the fiscal impact of demographic change, but the potential fiscal consequences of global climate and other environmental change have received less scrutiny. Yet it is difficult to imagine that the impact of climate change will be inconsequential, especially if climate change itself proves to be greater than currently estimated.

Globalization

Globalization has been the subject of extensive discussion and debate in recent years. Yet the evidence on its effects, including its influence on public policy, remains highly debatable. Many hypotheses have been offered, but most remain empirically unproven. Some suggest that globalization will constrain governments' capacity to tax the more mobile factors of production, especially capital, and that this will shift the burden of taxation increasingly to labor (see Devereux, Griffith, and Klemm, 2001; Devereux, Lockwood, and Redoano, 2001; Asher, 2002; Tanzi, 1995). However, many countries, especially in the developing world, are keenly aware that their skilled labor is increasingly a mobile resource as well.[14] Both tax competition between national jurisdictions and the rise of electronic commerce may also limit countries' ability to rely on general sales taxes, especially on services and on goods that can be digitized and transmitted electronically. Figure 2.5 illustrates the extraordinarily rapid growth of Internet use in recent years, as proxied by the number of Internet hosts worldwide (top panel) and by growth in e-commerce, defined as the number of commercial transactions conducted over the Internet (bottom panel).

---

[14]For example, some have expressed the concern that countries with relatively high taxes or low incomes may suffer a brain drain to industrial countries with higher wage rates. Many developing countries are concerned about the brain drain associated with the active efforts by industrial countries to recruit medical and paramedical personnel from abroad. Virtual migration of labor may also occur, with outsourcing over networks to developing countries.

Figure 2.5a
Measures of Global Interconnectivity

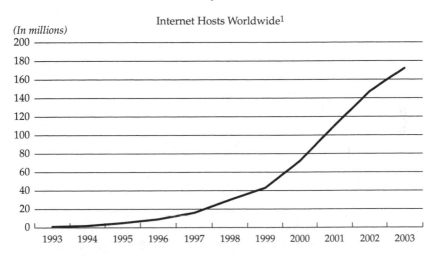

Internet Hosts Worldwide[1]

(In millions)

Source: Internet Software Consortium (2003).
[1]Number of hosts advertised in the domain Name Server.

Figure 2.5b
Value of Business Conducted by eCommerce by World Region
(In trillions of U.S. dollars)

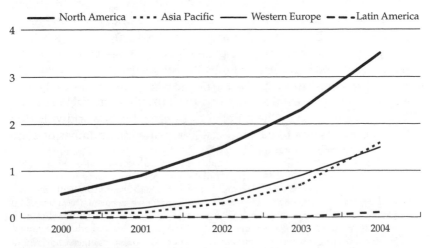

Source: Global Reach (2003).

Countries may also increasingly find that economic policies and models that deviate significantly from world norms prove politically unacceptable. The Internet now affords greater opportunity for "comparison shopping," whereby citizens of one country can learn what social insurance benefits and other public services are offered in other countries.[15] Across the board, government policy regimes—including approaches to budgeting, regulatory policy, accounting techniques, and labor standards—are now more readily compared, and questioned when they differ substantially from what is perceived as the international norm or as best practice. The pressures to conform arise not only internally but also from membership in global organizations and regional bodies, from criticism by international nongovernmental organizations, and from forces in the financial markets, which assign a higher risk premium to countries with inferior macroeconomic policy frameworks.

Pressures to join regional customs and other economic unions may exert an independent source of pressure for standardization. For example, for the existing member countries of the European Union, as well as for those countries in Central and Eastern Europe seeking accession, a variety of standards and norms constrain many aspects of fiscal policy. Not the least of these relates to the overall policy stance (through the Stability and Growth Pact, tax harmonization, agricultural and industrial subsidies, and various aspects of regulatory policy). These constraints are likely to become even more binding in future years.[16]

The quality of a country's infrastructure is also likely to matter increasingly to its competitiveness. Globalization will thus intensify pressures for public infrastructure investment precisely at a time when budgetary rules in some regions, notably Europe, are biased against public investment outlays.[17] These competitive pressures may be seen to some extent as a means by which the market limits the role of the state. Although the nature of such pressures will likely differ across countries, depending on

---

[15]Policymakers in New Zealand, for example, are keenly aware of the social insurance programs of neighboring Australia and recognize that there may be difficulties if benefits in the two countries diverge too sharply.

[16]The Stability and Growth Pact in particular is a difficult constraint on fiscal policy options. Difficulties in meeting the terms of the agreement are already in evidence in some of the larger EU countries, but the problems are likely to become particularly acute for the accession countries. For them, fiscal adjustments must occur in the face of both significant prior commitments on social benefits and the need for heavy infrastructure investment to modernize their economies.

[17]Balassone, Momigliano, and Monacelli (2002) note the pressures faced by Italy in seeking to meet the pact's budgetary requirements at a time when many of Italy's regions are seeking to catch up in the building of their network infrastructure.

the region or subregion to which a country's policies are effectively linked, the increasing need to take them into account is already evident.

Other global linkages, arising from labor flows, may also give rise to public expenditure pressures that are not obvious today. For example, many argue that the increased population pressures for migration from developing countries, combined with warming temperatures in the world's northern latitudes, may give rise to infectious disease outbreaks in countries in the Northern Hemisphere. The public health sectors of most of these countries have little experience with such problems.

In many respects, however, it is the ever-deeper interconnectedness of the global economy that may bring the most important ramifications for the management of fiscal policy in coming years.[18] Movements of capital can be both large and swift, influenced by a wide range of factors reflecting shifts in underlying perceptions of country risk. Limiting the impact of excessive capital mobility may require greater fiscal conservatism (Heller, 1997; Kopits, 2002). More directly, any shocks to the larger industrial economies can induce rapid and demonstrable demand shocks on other economies. The events of September 11 had demand effects on economies quite far removed from the United States, both from the overall softening of the U.S. economy that ensued and from the impact on specific industries such as tourism, the airlines, and insurance. Weakened fiscal positions and reduced progress in reducing public debt can be obvious consequences of such shocks. Although such temporary setbacks to fiscal rationalization can in principle be ignored, the world may now be facing a greater frequency of such setbacks, which can have more durable effects.

Finally, the external spillovers from bad policies in one country are also likely to be greater in a globalizing world. Should the major industrial economies fail to address their own key underlying vulnerabilities (including their own unsustainable fiscal positions), the global ramifications can be great, both in terms of aggregate economic activity and in terms of the effects on capital markets. A slump in equity prices in the major financial markets would have serious implications for wealth and financial balances around the world.

---

[18]At a recent RAND conference on the information technology revolution (Hundley and others, 2000), globalization was defined as "more information flowing with less obstruction; information flowing independent of distance; increasing opportunities for economic cooperation across borders; and greater opportunities to profit globally." Buiter (2001, pp. 2–3) has coined the term "pathological globalization" to refer to the risks from the spread of disease, international financial contagion, global crime, terrorism, and the threats to national or regional cultures and identities.

Figure 2.6
Projected Population of World's Largest Megacities
(In millions)

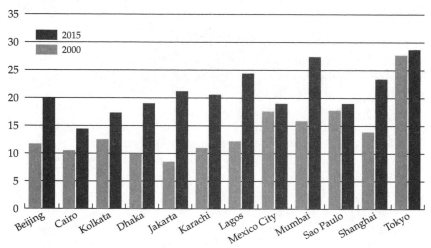

Source: U.S. Central Intellience Agency (2001).

Urbanization Pressures

For many developing countries, including some emerging market economies, fiscal pressures will mount as governments seek to cope with an increasingly younger population and with expected growth in large urban agglomerations. There will be a dramatic expansion in the number of giant metropolises in developing countries (Figure 2.6). By mid-century even many of the world's smaller cities will be equivalent in size to some of today's largest urban centers. The capacity of governance and fiscal systems to keep pace with these pressures will be sorely tested.

Shrinking Agricultural Land

Some have recently expressed concern about the capacity of the world's agricultural producers to meet the demands of a world population that will rise from 7 billion to 10 billion in the next half century. Such concerns are highlighted by projections that total land under cultivation will diminish as a result of urbanization and desertification, increased pressures on limited water supplies (Figure 2.7), and inadequate outlays for agricultural research (Mason, 2002).

Figure 2.7
Shares of World Population in 2025 in Countries with Physical or Economic Water Scarcity

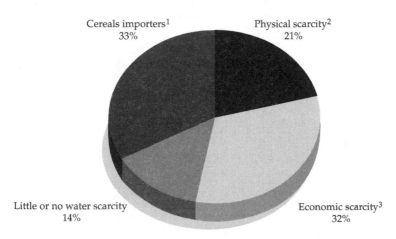

Cereals importers[1]
33%

Physical scarcity[2]
21%

Little or no water scarcity
14%

Economic scarcity[3]
32%

Source: World Bank, *World Development Report* 2003.
[1]Countries projected to import more than 10 percent of their cereals consumption, typically an indication of water scarcity.
[2]No reallocation of water or construction of water supply structure will satisfy all water needs in these countries.
[3]Countries must increase primary water supply by more than 25 percent through additional storage and conveyance facilities.

Rapid Technological Change

The coming decades are also likely to see the dramatic realization of technological advances either now on the drawing board or still only imagined—in genomics, medical therapies and drug treatment, biomedical engineering, materials engineering, smart materials (including nanotechnology), and the information sciences (broadly defined to include nanotechnology, biotechnology, information technology, and cognitive science).[19] A recent RAND Corporation study (Antón,

---

[19]An article in the *New York Times* (Brown, 2002) notes that "the whirlwind convergence of science fiction and fact raises the question of whether a sense of the impossible is becoming passé.... 'Science fact is rapidly outstripping science fiction,' said Neil Gershenfeld, head of the new Center for Bits and Atoms at M.I.T.'s Media Laboratory.... 'Things that clearly seemed impossible a few years ago, like nanotechnology, have moved from the lunatic fringe to core doctrine more quickly than at any time in history,' said Stewart Brand, a founder of Long Now. 'The downside has become taking the long term seriously. We need to develop civilizational patience.'"

Silberglitt, and Schneider, 2001) examines what technological break-throughs could plausibly occur over the period through 2015, and it emphasizes that many of these are likely to have important economic, political, demographic, and ethical consequences. In addition to further intensifying existing trends toward global interconnectedness, they will offer dramatic opportunities for improving health, by reducing morbidity from infectious and other diseases, and extending life spans. The possibilities are illustrated in Box 2.2, which reports the speculations of a number of distinguished biologists and computer scientists.

Yet these advances in health care will also raise public expectations about treatment possibilities, which in turn may lead to greater demand for such technologies from public and private medical care systems. The consequences for the cost of new medical care options and the impact on medical care costs overall could be both positive and negative. One recent survey for the United States (Glied, 2003) suggests that, on balance, technology will contribute to a faster growth of health care costs over the long term. Indeed, it is argued that "Expenditure-increasing technological improvement is likely to continue into the future and does not appear highly responsive to policy changes" (p. 145). The effects on life span are also likely to bolster the gains already anticipated, which are increasingly feeding growth in pension cost projections.[20]

Rapid technological change may also have an impact on the extent of government involvement in the medical care sector. Moss (2002), in his recent study on the approach to risk management in the United States, speculates that the emerging capacity to use DNA tests to identify the degree of genetic risks of major diseases may result in sufficiently large adverse selection in medical insurance pricing as to render private medical insurance unaffordable for many. This might force the government to provide national medical insurance in order to broaden the risk pool for insurance purposes.[21]

---

[20]Australia's recent Intergenerational Report notes that "technological advancement... and the community's expectation of accessing the latest health treatments will continue to place increased demands on taxpayer funds.... Australians expect to access more expensive diagnostic procedures and new (and more expensive) medications listed on the PBS [Pharmaceutical Benefits Scheme]" (Australia, Commonwealth of, 2002, p. 9).

[21]This assumes that the present efforts to cast a "veil of ignorance" over such genetic attributes, by prohibiting insurance companies from having such information, is likely to prove ineffective. "Compulsory community-rated insurance, which has long been the norm in most other developed economies, would prevent not only market fragmentation along genetic lines but also market breakdown as a result of adverse selection (since no one would be allowed to opt out)" (Moss, 2002, p. 334). Alternatively, in the United States the result may be higher costs being borne by the public sector for its existing beneficiaries, thus limiting the capacity of the public system to extend coverage to those uninsured (Glied, 2003, p. 145).

Box 2.2. Speculating on Technological Change in Medicine in the Next Half Century

Richard Dawkins

"Technological advances in medical care in coming decades will also allow physicians to construct a complete individual human genome at small cost. While this will be enormously useful in the provision of medical care—allowing doctors to prescribe based on the prescription that suits the individual's genome—it will also create enormously difficult privacy issues with respect to the problem of adverse selection by the medical insurance industry." (Dawkins, 2002, p. 151)

John H. Holland

"By the mid-twenty-first century, much of medicine as it was practiced in the latter part of the twentieth century—for example, using surgery, chemotherapy, and radiation to treat cancer—will look as ineffective as the bloodletting of earlier centuries. We will be able to produce life in a test tube by starting with simple, nonliving biochemicals, with all that implies for engineered solutions to diseases. And we will almost certainly be able to produce artificial immune systems that can counter both living viruses and computer viruses." (Holland, 2002, p. 177)

"Artificial immune systems constitute powerful protection for both natural and artificial systems. The ability of artificial immune systems to discover biomolecules that counter unusual antigens, combined with the technological automation of drug design and production, will finally bring drug costs down, even in small markets (rare diseases).... This reduction in treatment costs, combined with the diagnostic capabilities of artificial immune systems, should at last reverse the ever increasing costs of medicine." (Holland, 2002, p. 181)

Rodney Brooks

"Over the next ten to twenty years, there will be a cultural shift, in which we will adopt robotic technology, silicon, and steel into our bodies to improve what we can do and understand in the world.... And then, approximately a quarter of the way through this century, similar enhancements of a more biological nature will begin to be available to use. In that time frame, the really large-scale use of genetic engineering will be common—beyond agribusiness and medicine, where it is currently being explored. Genetic engineering will be used in the petroleum industry, in the production of plastics and other materials, in recycling, in batteries, in renewable energy sources, and in other applications hard to imagine from this vantage point. By 2025, we will also have achieved enough explicit control to apply these technologies with confidence to our own bodies." (Brooks, 2002, p. 190)

Paul W. Ewald

"Over the next five decades, the development of vaccines against infection-induced chronic diseases should follow closely our discovery of the causal agents. When a pathogen is not particularly mutable, vaccines can be particularly effective.... [There is a promise] of a third major approach to controlling infectious disease; that is, in addition to curing infection and controlling the spread of infection, we should be able to control the evolution of the pathogen.... During the next quarter century, I expect that the first of these evolutionary success stories will be demonstrated, probably through the clever use of vaccines or by inhibiting waterborne transmission of diarrheal pathogens in poor countries.... [Moreover], if we can control the evolution of virulence we should also therefore be able to control the evolution of antibiotic resistance.... By mid-century, we will probably have enacted the evolutionary transition from virulence to benignity for a few diseases, such as the damaging diarrheal disease, but we will still be in the midst of the testing process for most of the rest." (Ewald, 2002a, pp. 297–99)

Technological advances should also at least raise the *potential* for faster productivity growth in manufacturing and agriculture (and help the latter respond to climate change). Even the approach to revenue mobilization may be influenced both positively and negatively, as technological progress affects the capacity of governments to collect taxes (Treverton and Mizell, 2001).

On the downside, society's reliance on technologically advanced networked systems in the financial sector already implies greater exposure to the risk of a software or hardware breakdown, whether malicious in origin (from a virus) or not. Munich Re Group (2002) notes that "even tiny programming errors can lead to catastrophes, and minimal tolerance exceedances can make robots and control systems go haywire." This vulnerability will only increase in the future as the degree of interdependence further intensifies. A RAND Corporation study (Hundley and others, 2000, p. 60) warns that

> As society becomes increasingly dependent on the Internet working to conduct a vast range of political, social, and economic activities, the risks posed by potential instability and disruption (whether intentional or inadvertent) become great. Major chaos, for example, could ruin even large banks. System vulnerability should therefore be probed in future work.

Technological progress may also make it easier for nonstate actors to carry out acts of destruction, whether by means of computer viruses or by chemical, biological, or nuclear attack. Assessing the potential economic and fiscal consequences is a challenge, but the likelihood of such attacks is sufficiently high to warrant their consideration in evaluating overall risks.

HIV/AIDS and Other Infectious Diseases

The HIV/AIDS epidemic is but one manifestation (tuberculosis is another) of a resurgence in life-threatening infectious diseases around the world. The outbreak of SARS further illustrated the potential risk and economic impact. The threat of HIV/AIDS to world health may shape both the demographics and the public expenditure needs of many countries—from countries in transition such as Ukraine and Russia to Brazil, China, and the countries of sub-Saharan Africa and South Asia. The economic ramifications of these crises, including reduced productivity and slower growth, the loss of human capital, and an expanding need for public services, are likely to create pressures for greater public sector involvement even as they weaken the economic base of these countries (Eberstadt, 2002). Although much effort is being invested in the development of a vaccine for HIV, the mutability of the virus has led some to speculate that this will prove impossible.[22]

Global Political Tension and Heightened Insecurity

A hopeful but realistic look into the crystal ball would find, in the next several decades, significant economic growth occurring in Asia, with growth in incomes per capita in the heavily populated countries of India and China further outpacing that in the industrial countries. For other regions of the world, however, it is harder to be so optimistic. Sub-Saharan Africa faces tremendous challenges and obstacles as it seeks to break out of its profound poverty. Even in the best of likely scenarios, dramatic differences in incomes per capita will persist between this region and most other parts of the world. Latin America confronts

---

[22]Paul Ewald, a biologist at Amherst College, has argued that in the next 50 years, "Unless some fundamentally new measure is brought to bear on HIV, it will still be a problem suppressed but not solved by the patch jobs...the antivirals and vaccines that constrain but do not decisively control the virus.... The best hope is to buy time—a decade or so of AIDS-free life from antivirals, perhaps a decade or so from therapeutic vaccines administered soon after infection, and perhaps a decade or so by controlling the evolution of virulence" (Ewald, 2002a, p. 299).

a similar, if less daunting, set of obstacles. In the Middle East and parts of South Asia, inequalities in income could remain wide.

The share of the world's population living in the aging industrial world is projected to shrink from 20 percent in 2000 to 14 percent by 2050 as the populations of many of these nations decline in absolute terms. By 2025 more people will be living in Africa than in all of today's industrial countries taken together (Eberstadt, 2001). Even on conservative assumptions about productivity growth, incomes per capita in the industrial countries will dramatically exceed those of at least half the world's population.

In contrast, the populations of many developing countries will continue to expand—in South Asia and the Middle East particularly. Their demographic structures will remain heavily weighted toward the young, and their populations will be increasingly urbanized.[23] Unemployed youth, concentrated in major urban centers, may be a source of political instability in some of the larger countries. In a world that already is intensely integrated, it is difficult to imagine that the projected future income disparities can be maintained without, at a minimum, occasional outbursts of tension.[24]

Moreover, forecasts of serious demand pressures on some critical resources—most notably, clean water and crude oil—lead analysts to see the potential for a flare-up in tensions in those regions where competing demands are most pressing (Klare, 2001; World Panel on Financing Water Infrastructure, 2003). Tensions surrounding the demand for water

---

[23]Bräuninger and others (2002) note that "48 states regarded as least developed countries under UN definition will see their population triple to exceed 1.8 billion by 2050 while others in the less developed regions will see an increase of 'only' 50 percent; the number of people per square kilometer in least developed countries will rise from just over 30 today to 90 by 2050 (now France is 135; Germany, 225). But these are already countries now suffering from food and water shortages and environmental destruction." By contrast, most countries in Eastern Europe will see a sharp decrease in their population: Bulgaria is expected to see a decline in its population by 43 percent, Poland by 14 percent, Russia by 28 percent, Hungary by 35 percent, Romania by 20 percent, and Ukraine by 40 percent.

[24]In the light of the events of September 11, it is striking to read the early 2001 report of the U.S. National Intelligence Council (U.S. CIA, 2001a): "Regions, countries, and groups feeling left behind will face deepening economic stagnation, political instability, and cultural alienation. They will foster political, ethnic, ideological, and religious extremism, along with the violence that often accompanies it. They will force the United States and other developed countries to remain focused on 'old-world' challenges while concentrating on the implications of 'new-world' technologies at the same time" (p. 10). Also, "disaffected states, terrorists, proliferators, narco-traffickers, and organized criminals will take advantage of the new high-speed information environment and other advances in technology to integrate their illegal activities and compound their threat to stability and security around the world" (p. 18).

will be most intense in the Jordan, Tigris-Euphrates, Nile, and Indus River basins. Conflicts may arise over reserves of petroleum in the Persian Gulf, the Caspian Sea, and the South China Sea. The potential for outbreaks of armed conflict will be a particular concern where resources lie in shared border areas or in disputed offshore waters.[25] Climate change is likely to heighten competition for access to water. A decrease in rainfall and increased evaporation rates in dry inland areas are likely to reduce the flow of water into vital river systems.

One implication of all this is the following: any expectation that past trends of declining public outlays for military and security purposes can be continued in the future, providing fiscal breathing room for outlays on aging populations, is likely to be dashed, if the events of September 11 have not dashed them already. Indeed, it is not difficult to envisage a scenario in which such outlays rise significantly. Moreover, pressure on the industrial countries to raise their level of overseas development assistance on a sustained basis is already evident.[26] Governments in developing countries may also experience increasing pressure to absorb some of their unemployed youth into the military, and this will limit their capacity to spend on other, more productive fiscal needs.

Terrorist Attacks and Other Catastrophic Events

The U.S. National Intelligence Council's report, *Global Trends 2015*, written in late 2000 (U.S. Central Intelligence Agency, 2001a), notes that the United States will face three main types of threat in the future, one of which is attack using weapons of mass destruction (WMD):

---

[25]Klare (2001) has noted that governments have historically gone to war over vital national interests associated with natural resources, rather than seek market solutions.

[26]Sandler (1998) has argued that if the world's income distribution becomes more unequal, industrial nations may be led to shift from traditional aid toward the provision of public goods that eliminate threats to world peace, provide much needed information, and accomplish scientific breakthroughs. "If the trend toward income inequality continues...then the rich nations may have little choice but to underwrite these free riders in order to ensure their own well-being. This anticipated change in foreign aid will circumvent foreign aid fatigue and the reluctance of countries to give aid that ends up in the hands of corrupt officials" (p. 223). In fact, what one might observe is pressure for *both* expanded traditional aid—out of moral concern for continued high levels of poverty—and greater outlays on global public goods of the type mentioned by Sandler. This recognizes that some events now thought of as exogenous should perhaps be considered endogenous, to some degree, to possible policy actions by governments.

> Strategic WMD threats, including nuclear missile threats, in which Russia, China, most likely North Korea, probably Iran and possibly Iraq have the capability to strike the United States, and the potential for unconventional delivery of WMD by both states or non-state actors also will grow. ... The likelihood will increase over this period that WMD will be used either against the United States or its forces, facilities, and interests overseas. (U.S. Central Intelligence Agency, 2001a, pp. 11–12)

Other countries, whether industrial or developing, whether confronted by regional adversaries or by terrorist threat, may be equally subject to such risks. An attack with such weapons could wreak enormous economic damage and would obviously have major fiscal implications.

It would not be unreasonable to argue that the probability of terrorist acts of global economic import is greater in the wake of September 11 than ever before. Months before September 11, the former U.S. National Security Adviser Anthony Lake, as well as the U.S. Central Intelligence Agency, had emphasized the multiple risks from bioterrorism, cyberterrorism, nuclear threats, and other acts of terror (Lake, 2000). The simple fact that September 11 happened has surely heightened awareness on the part of potential terrorists of what is possible and of how much economic and political disruption can be caused. This is itself an important risk factor. The probability of such global shocks weakening government revenue and fueling unplanned expenditure is consequently higher. It is difficult to see how this change can be reversed.

The fiscal ramifications of a world menaced by terrorism can be seen in the response to September 11. In addition to bearing the costs associated with the immediate economic losses from the attack—which were themselves substantial, both for the United States and for the global economy—governments have moved to create new fiscal liabilities contingent on future terrorist acts. In the United States, the passage in late 2001 of legislation on terrorism risk insurance is a notable example: the federal government committed itself to cover 90 percent of future terrorism-related insurance claims when losses to private insurers exceed certain levels ($10 billion being the initial threshold). Like flood insurance, terrorism risk insurance may have fiscal implications beyond those immediately recognized; for example, such insurance could create a moral hazard, deterring households and businesses from adopting their own security measures sufficient to prevent terrorist attack (see *New York Times*, 2002).

Taking a broader perspective, Martin Rees (2003), the Astronomer Royal of the United Kingdom, has argued that "technical advances will in themselves render society more vulnerable to disruption" (p. 21).

"Prospects are so volatile that mankind might not even persist beyond a century—much less a millennium—unless all nations adopt low-risk and sustainable policies based on present technology" (p. 24). Indeed, he asserts that "the odds are no better than fifty-fifty that our present civilization on Earth will survive to the end of the present century" (p. 8).

Do Long-Term Fiscal Issues Matter Only to Aging Industrial Countries?

There is little doubt that issues of long-term fiscal risk are an increasing source of concern in many industrial countries, primarily because of the anticipated effects of an aging population on the viability of social insurance systems. However, many of the risk factors identified above may prove just as relevant for the fiscal situation of developing, transition, and emerging market economies.

For example, climate change may, in net terms, be beneficial to the United States, China, and some other countries in the Northern Hemisphere. But for countries in the tropics, for southern Africa, and for certain island states, even the most conservative climate change projections suggest serious economic harm, and the impact of both increased temperature and increased precipitation cannot be ignored. In a similar vein, limited natural resources, particularly water for drinking and agriculture, loom large as a potential source of economic and political pressure in a number of heavily populated countries, particularly in the Middle East and South Asia. Such pressures will arguably give rise to future burdens both on countries' revenue bases and on their potential expenditure requirements.

Demographics is another area of concern. Some transition economies face a dramatically different demographic picture than the industrial countries, with declining fertility and life expectancy rates and with shrinking populations. If these trends continue, they will have important implications for the revenue base of these countries. Moreover, in some transition economies, social insurance systems remain excessively generous (although others have been seriously eroded by inflation). If the benefit structures of these systems remain unchanged, the tax rates that would be needed to support them appear excessive and possibly unsustainable.

In contrast, as previously noted, demographic forecasts in some developing countries suggest a further explosion not only of youth populations but also of urban agglomerations. The resulting pressures for delivery of public services—education and health services, in particular—may overwhelm the financial capacity of the fiscal sector. A number of emerging market economies and other developing countries may also face, with respect to their social insurance and civil service pension schemes, rising financial burdens analogous to (although not of the same magnitude as) those confronting the industrial countries. Many emerging market economies, particularly in Asia and some parts of Latin America, have already undergone the demographic transition that has contributed to the aging of populations in the industrial countries. Social insurance commitments are less pervasive in these countries, but the combination of pressure to introduce Western-style social insurance systems and the prevalence of generous civil service pension schemes (Heller, 1999) will add to the cost burdens on their governments in the future.

The demand for sophisticated medical care from politically influential middle- and upper-income groups is also likely to be strong. Two examples will suffice in the sphere of medical insurance. In recent years both the Republic of Korea and Singapore have had difficulty restraining the rising costs of medical care. Although Korea's health care system is largely in the private sector, the mandatory nature of the scheme suggests that it may be difficult to insulate the government fully from the consequences of cost pressures. Rising costs have also been a problem in Singapore, despite the emphasis on market-oriented reforms.

Even in some developing countries where aging of the population is not a prospect, the fiscal sector may be confronting pressures from unsustainable commitments in the social insurance sphere, which may compromise other public service needs and the revenue base. In a number of poor countries, pension schemes for public employees have been fairly generous, are typically financed on a pay-as-you-go basis, and effectively target precisely those groups (educated civil servants) that are likely to have the highest life expectancies. Egypt is one country where these pressures are already emerging. Recent work by Holzmann, Palacios, and Zviniene (2001) underscores that significant implicit pension debt levels relative to GDP are not unique to industrial countries.

The starting point for any country in adopting a long-term fiscal perspective is thus to identify the country- or region-specific risk factors, the sources of fiscal pressures, and the key uncertainties to which it is susceptible. Tables A.1 through A.9 in the appendix are a highly speculative effort at illustrating the different ways in which each of the various regions of the world is likely to be affected by readily identifiable sources of long-term fiscal risk. Some potential long-term developments may have common effects on all countries or, through their repercussions on one important group of countries, may move global markets, and thus affect all. Others are specific to a single region or country. This effort obviously paints with a broad brush. It ignores the widely varying effects of climate change, political risk, and demography across and even *within* countries in a given region. It also necessarily *understates* the risks, because it does not take account of the external effects that adverse shocks or developments in one region may have on other regions. The tables are thus meant solely to stimulate more careful thought and speculation at the country level about the implications of such future developments for fiscal policy.

Why Is More Long-Term Fiscal Policy Planning Needed?

What is different about this moment in history that makes it especially important to take long-term risk factors into account in considering countries' short- to medium-term fiscal frameworks? Is the cataloguing of risk factors attempted above needlessly alarmist? Are the risks and uncertainties really any greater today than they were 50 years ago, at the onset of the Cold War, or 75 years ago, before the Great Depression and World War II, or even 25 years ago, before the collapse of the Soviet Union and of superpower rivalry? Has something changed about our understanding of potential future outcomes, or about the nature of the government's role in the economy, in a way that argues for a different approach to fiscal policy planning?

The simplest part of the answer is that the nature of government involvement is indeed more activist today, in almost all countries, than it was even 30 years ago, and far more than it was in the late 1920s or the 1940s. Even setting aside the *implicit* challenges to which a government of today may feel compelled to respond, *explicit*, legislated policy commitments in the social insurance sphere are far greater, and these are keyed to demographic or economic variables that can be readily projected. In the past, projections of unfavorable demographic outcomes would not have given rise to the same level of concern, simply because governments were not as committed, in terms of their legislative obligations, to dealing with them. Nor can the implicit commitments be readily ignored.

This does not mean that governments can or should automatically compensate their citizens for every unanticipated or uninsured event that may do them harm, such as a terrorist attack. But it cannot be argued that governments are not politically responsive at some level to significant adverse events. The events of September 11 illustrate this well: governments quickly stepped in to cushion the economic impact on adversely affected sectors, regions, and households. Thus the extent of a government's commitments has an important bearing on how much it should take account of potential long-term developments. (See Box 2.3 for a discussion of the various factors that may underpin a government's commitments.)[27]

But other factors make the consideration of long-term fiscal issues a more compelling and important exercise today than in the past. First, there is obviously still great uncertainty about the future. Recent events and security warnings by political leaders (starting, in the United States, from the president, the secretary of defense, the secretary of homeland security, and the head of the Central Intelligence Agency in late 2002 and early 2003) suggest that events unthinkable (at least to the broad public) even a year ago might indeed happen in coming months and years, with dramatic consequences for the global economy and for society.[28] It might even be argued that the probability of such previously unthinkable events is greater today than in the past, reflecting the breakdown of government control in many parts of the world, but again the level of uncertainty is considerable.

Equally, much is unknown about the possible impacts of climate change. One can imagine global warming leading to events with significant social ramifications: for example, the emergence of unanticipated disease vectors that threaten life expectancy gains, or an epidemic on the scale of the Spanish influenza of the early 20th century. Thus it is not the case that policymakers are in a better position today to predict or to rule out catastrophes, whether caused by human malice or by unforeseen natural events. Even at the more mundane level of changes in interest rates, fertility, or productivity, society's capacity to forecast long-term developments is not dramatically better than it was in the past.

On the other hand, we do have a greater awareness than before of the range and character of possible outcomes, for better or for worse. Many possibilities are at least recognized, and their probabilities,

---

[27]See Brixi and Mody (2002) for a useful discussion of the differences between explicit and implicit commitments associated with direct and contingent liabilities.

[28]As an example, in June 2002 it was noted that a meteorite the size of a soccer field had passed between the earth and the moon. (The meteorite that hit Siberia in the early 1900s was of comparable size.) Had it struck the earth, the consequences could have been devastating, particularly if it had fallen in the ocean (triggering a tsunami) or near a populated area.

Box 2.3. What Constitutes a Fiscal Commitment?

Any assessment of a country's fiscal sustainability requires an understanding of the extent of the government's fiscal commitments. It is useful to distinguish between explicit and implicit commitments. *Explicit* commitments are those for which the government has, through legislation or contractual undertaking, expressly accepted responsibility for disbursing funds in the future. This disbursement may be in exchange for some previous payment (whether in kind, in fees, or in taxes) or service, or it may be conditional on the occurrence of a defined event (for example, the retirement of a civil servant enrolled in a public pension scheme, or the presentation of a citizen with a medical complaint). The amount to be disbursed may be agreed upon in advance or may depend upon the future price of some good or service. Alternatively, it may only be related to the nature of the event and the exigencies it imposes, as interpreted by the government or the recipient, or both.

Government contracts for the purchase of goods and services and government agreements to pay scheduled debt service are among the most obvious types of explicit commitments. Pension and deposit insurance commitments would appear equally explicit. Typically, in exchange for payroll contributions or the payment of payroll taxes, workers or their survivors can expect to receive a lump-sum payment or an annuity, contingent on such factors as the amount of their prior contributions, the age at which they retire, their earnings history, their family situation, or their health status (in the case of disability pensioners, for example). Welfare payments may be means-tested or subject to an assessment of a potential recipient's efforts in the job market. Unemployment insurance payments are typically conditional on the loss of a job after a previous period of employment. Subsidy payments (for example, in agriculture) may be contingent on price or production (or nonproduction) decisions.

Even commitments viewed as explicit may be subject to considerable discretion on the part of a government, even apart from its ability to renege or default. The decision about what constitutes a disability is one example. For pensions, governments may have discretion in choosing the inflation indicator to be used in indexing benefits. In government-operated medical units, the obligation to provide medical care may be unconditional, but the terms of that care—the timing, quantity, and quality—may be quite conditional. Similarly, for public medical insurance schemes, the government's co-payment and the extent of qualified goods or services that will be paid for may be subject to administrative guidelines rather than set specifically by legislation. Governments may also have leeway in modifying their explicit commitments, particularly when the individuals or groups affected have not yet satisfied the conditions for eligibility. Reforms of public pension or health insurance schemes are often in this category.

The "hardness" of an explicit commitment is not independent of whether a government's aggregate fiscal position is sustainable in the long run. If a government's liabilities are truly unmanageable, either the law will *have* to change, or the country will face bankruptcy. How governments account for their explicit commitments in their public budgeting is thus an important and sensitive issue (see Chapter 5).

In a recent study, the U.S. General Accounting Office (2003) defines "implicit exposures" as those stemming "not from a legal obligation of the federal government but rather from implied commitments embedded in the government's current policies or in the public's expectations about the role of government" (p. 3). One type of implicit commitment relates to "contingent liabilities" or "state guarantees." These are implicit in that the obligation to disburse funds may or may not be realized, depending on the nature of the contingency. Schick (2002c) notes the various ways in which some governments have sought to measure and account for such contingent outlays. But there is another class of implicit commitment. In some situations the government has no formal commitment to provide any form of fiscal compensation, yet the political authorities recognize the need to respond in some way. These implicit commitments may arise from the government's failure to exercise its regulatory responsibilities effectively. Such failures may lead to private sector losses for which political decision makers feel obliged to provide some form of compensation. An obvious example is the bank recapitalizations effected by many Asian countries during the crisis of 1997–98.

Equally, such commitments may arise from the government's role in supporting the general public welfare, for example, by authorizing transfers or spending on relief and rehabilitation in the event of a natural disaster, a serious economic collapse, a failure in the government's policing and security efforts, or the emergence of a perceived social crisis, when it is recognized that the amounts available under current welfare legislation are inadequate. A concrete example of the latter is the recent scaling up of minimum pension benefits in the United Kingdom. Similarly, during the Asian crisis, governments to some extent bailed out both private sector debtors and creditors, out of concern for the systemic and welfare damage that might otherwise have occurred. Finally, in some circumstances where private sector reinsurance agencies prove unable or unwilling to provide insurance cover, the government may essentially undertake to be the ultimate source of reinsurance.

Clearly, governments have far more leeway *not* to recognize a responsibility to disburse funds in cases where there is no formal legislative mandate to do so, or where the decision to respond is one over which the government has total discretion. And of course, political considerations may weigh as heavily, both in the decision to respond and in the nature of the response, as the underlying merits of the situation.

The flexibility that governments have in interpreting their implicit commitments is shown by the U.S. government's response to the events of September 11. Although no law specifically directed it, the federal government quickly agreed to provide compensation to those immediately affected—both those who suffered financial and property losses (including the insurance and airline industries) and those who lost family members. Equally interesting was the extent to which, according to reports, the actual compensation provided by the Federal Emergency Management Agency to directly affected individuals proved to be considerably less than had been expected; this suggests that considerable discretion was used in making administrative judgments about disbursements (see Henriques and Barstow, 2002). Indeed, it appears that different criteria were used in deciding the amounts to be provided to the different industries that were directly or indirectly affected by September 11. It is also interesting to contrast the compensation provided to those affected by the 1995 bombing of the Oklahoma City federal building with the much larger amount paid following the September 2001 attack on New York's World Trade Center.

consequences, and potential remedies at least considered and reckoned with, particularly at the global level. Equally, there is greater awareness of the nature of limits—technological, geological, demographic, and economic. For many issues the range of uncertainty is also far narrower.

Moreover, society's understanding of the world and beyond—of the size and dynamics of populations, of the nature of the physical and biological resource base, of the characteristics of climatic forces, and of the earth's geology and terrain—is far more profound than it was only a few decades ago. Our capacity to model and simulate potential trends in and impacts of natural, social, and economic forces, and at least to come to grips with the range of possibilities, is likewise far greater. Although much remains unknown, the capacity of scientists to discern changes in the physical and economic environment, and sometimes to prompt a speedy response by policymakers, is breathtakingly different from what it once was.[29]

Indeed, it can be seriously argued that, compared with even 50 years ago, humankind is closer to an understanding of the limits of technological possibility than ever before. Some (such as Horgan, 1997) have

---

[29]A simple example can be offered. To minimize damage from earthquakes, it is now possible to put in place diagnostic sensors to pick up the first signs of a tremor. These sensors can trigger a shutdown of electricity and gas lines within 10 to 15 seconds, so that if these lines are disrupted by a quake, the damage will be minimized.

seriously raised the question of whether we are nearing the frontiers of knowledge in the fundamental disciplines of biology, physics, and chemistry. Although, again, much obviously remains unknown,[30] the broad parameters and characteristics of physical and biological phenomena are understood with far greater clarity than before. It follows that the capacity of governments to address and at least partly manage risk is far greater than ever in the past.

There is a second dimension to the argument that issues of the long term are perhaps more important now than they were several decades ago. There appears to be a consensus (if not unanimity) on the proposition that the impact and relevance of global externalities are far greater today—that the scale of global economic activity is having much more serious consequences for the environment. The capacity of many elements of the global environment to absorb, without significant harm, the impact of economic activity appears lessened.[31] Equally, the sense of limits on the availability of resources is resurfacing as an issue (see World Bank, 2002). Some might argue that this is a familiar refrain, and that a resuscitation of the Club of Rome's worries during the 1970s about the limits to growth would still be in error. But the concerns described earlier about competition for water in a number of key river basins—a consequence of both population growth and climate change—would appear difficult to ignore, as are the melting of the Andean glaciers and the thinning of the polar icecaps.

Third, policymakers today operate in a far more constrained and transparent environment. The limits to their action are not simply physical. In the past just as today, external constraints mattered and influenced economic policy decisions, but the time frame during which there was scope for independent action on monetary or fiscal policy was far longer. Today all policy actions must be considered through the filter of their potential ramifications for external markets. The speed with which faulty policies are punished is far greater. Equally, both the nature of the policy actions being pursued and their likely quantitative implications are far more rapidly transmitted into the public domain. Again, the limits confronted by policymakers are more confining.

One final question in this vein: Are policymakers today confronting relatively predictable events, such that indicators of fiscal unsustainability or threats to the future fiscal position reflect a failure by *past*

---

[30]For example, in a recent book, Rees (2003) takes issue with Horgan, arguing that ideas as revolutionary as any that were discovered in the twentieth century remain to be disclosed.

[31]For a contrary perspective, see Lomborg (2001).

policymakers to pursue appropriate policies? Or do fiscal policymakers today have to formulate policies in the context of larger uncertainties, even with the best of will and political support? The answer is both. Much of what can be forecast and imagined as likely to happen in coming decades is very predictable. Failure to position government policy prudently, to address these issues, could be considered irresponsible. The more difficult challenge is to assess how much more prudent fiscal positions should be for the *truly unpredictable* events. Should government policies be pursued both at a microeconomic level, to narrow and reduce the likelihood of the more adverse possibilities coming to pass, and at the macroeconomic level, to limit the prospect of a government being forced to renege abruptly on its commitments?

Grappling with Forecasting Uncertainty in the 21st Century

The discussion thus far in this chapter has suggested that the world of even 20 years from now, let alone 50 or 75, is likely to be quite different from what it is today, but reasonable speculation is possible about the broad dimensions of what will make it different. Economic forecasting that simply extrapolates from a linear model and stable systems is not likely to be very useful or accurate as a basis for fiscal planning or for analyzing the fiscal implications of public policy commitments. It is equally important to understand the nature of the uncertainties associated with forecasting the impact of developments like those described above. The still-significant uncertainty about the dimensions of climate change has already been flagged. But even for a more predictable phenomenon like population aging, the range of potential outcomes is wide, judging by how far demographers in recent years have underestimated growth in life expectancy or have been too optimistic about a rebound in fertility rates.[32]

This suggests the importance of recognizing the different characteristics of the multiple uncertainties facing policymakers today as they make decisions that are likely to have long-term consequences. Seven broad types of uncertainty can be posited. The first three are uncertainties that policymakers have long had to address as a matter of

---

[32]See Lee and Tuljapurkar (2000); see also Oeppen and Vaupel (2002), who provide international evidence on the extent to which life expectancy forecasts have typically underestimated reality.

course in carrying out medium- to long-run forecasting and in designing policies. These kinds of uncertainty will be even more relevant in considering the probability of alternative scenarios in the future. However, there are additional types of uncertainty, which appear very much a product of the kinds of changes that can be anticipated in coming decades. The implication is that long-term forecasting will be an even more complex undertaking in the coming years.

Uncertainty *Within* Existing Economic and Demographic Models

Most fiscal forecasts or aggregate economic scenarios assume that the key underlying causative variables—be they economic (productivity growth rates, labor force participation rates, interest rates), demographic, or even meteorological—can be modeled and predicted on the basis of past trends, and that the underlying model structure is not likely to change. Forecasting models and statistical confidence intervals can thus be determined from historical data.

For some variables, although one may not necessarily anticipate any structural shift in their underlying probability distribution, it may not be easy to judge what target rate of change should be used for projection purposes. For example, some contend that the official demographic community tends to underpredict gains in life expectancy (U.K. Government Actuary's Department, 2001; Lee, 2001; Oeppen and Vaupel, 2002). The outcome of this debate can have important implications for estimates of the financial sustainability of public pension schemes.[33]

Demographers are similarly uncertain as to what to assume about future fertility rates. Should they assume that these rates will remain at the low levels currently observed in many industrial countries? Or has the decline in fertility rates simply reflected a shift in the desired age of childbearing, so that some rebound to replacement levels may be anticipated? Although economic demographers have focused on the implications of longer life expectancy, assumptions about fertility rates will have an equally important bearing on economic outcomes several decades into the future.

---

[33]It is also a matter of concern for the life insurance industry, where mispricing of annuities, as a consequence of underestimation of longevity risks, can prove a source of financial weakness (U.K. Financial Services Authority, 2002).

Uncertainty about the future of functional status and disability in an aging population is also an important issue confronting policymakers, with varying degrees of optimism in the United States and Europe (see Manton and Waidmann, 1988; Manton and Gu, 2001). Views on this issue are important because of what they imply for the possibility of rescaling the economic life cycle as life expectancy rises, and in particular raising the age of retirement (see Lee and Goldstein, 2003).

Another key variable about which there is considerable uncertainty is the impact of an aging population on outlays for medical and long-term residential care for the very elderly. Early studies on the fiscal effects of aging populations simply used estimates that applied the higher average outlays per capita on medical care of the over-65 age group to this entire group in the population. With the size of this group forecast to rise sharply (in part reflecting increasing longevity), the effect was to project substantially higher medical expenditure for industrial countries as their populations aged. Critics of this approach, however, have noted that the higher relative spending of the elderly on medical care reflects the well-known fact that medical spending is typically high in the last two to three years of life; in contrast, for much of the rest of life beyond age 65, health expenditure is typically closer to the average for the working-age population. Thus, these critics argue, what is relevant to spending projections is not the total size of the elderly population, but rather how many of the elderly are in those last few years of life. With increasing longevity, these years occur at progressively older ages. Applying this assumption would result in projections in which an increase in the population over age 65 does not have an explosive effect on total medical care expenditure.

But there is still considerable uncertainty. In carrying out fiscal forecasts, should one still assume higher medical expenditures for those over 65 than for the working-age population (even if perhaps not as high as previously thought)? Moreover, might it still be the case that increased longevity and an increasing population share of the very old (those over age 85) are associated with significantly higher outlays for long-term residential care? This is what one might expect given both the larger size of this population group and the possibility that, for this type of expenditure, increased longevity would indeed mean a longer period during which such outlays may be necessary (although it might also mean better health and reduced medical outlays). Again, experience with the health status of a large population of the very elderly is still too new for fiscal planners to have understood clearly the nature of the likely costs.

Uncertainty also still surrounds assumptions about the rate of medical care inflation. Efforts to control the pace of this inflation have had mixed results, as recent cost data have revealed (Cutler, 2002). Some authorities (see, for example, Australia, Commonwealth of, 2002) have noted that higher expectations about the standard and quality of care will boost demand, particularly for pharmaceuticals, and make it difficult to contain costs. In many countries there is an expectation that government will finance the provision of additional medical services as well as drugs.

Finally, one other element of uncertainty is particularly important, given its central influence on any long-term policy assessments that affect the future: uncertainty about the appropriate discount rate. Weitzman (1998) and Newell and Pizer (2002a, 2002b) have called attention to the consequences of uncertainty about future long-term interest rates.[34] Weitzman argues that, if there is uncertainty as to the appropriate interest rate that will apply far into the future, the optimal choice of policy instruments "may well be skewed toward what would be optimal for a low interest rate situation because, other things being equal, that situation will carry relatively more weight in determining the expected difference between present discounted costs and benefits" (Weitzman, 1998, p. 207).[35] Box 2.4 expands on the important implications of this line of thinking. This approach does not touch on the equally relevant issue of the appropriate social time preference rate to apply when weighing intergenerational trade-offs (a subject discussed at greater length in Chapter 4).

Uncertainty about Expected Changes in Underlying Models

Assume that the policymaker knows, with reasonable certainty, that important changes in the underlying demographic, economic, or climatic structure can be expected, and indeed that some of the key variables that are likely to change can be explicitly identified. Even with

---

[34]Weitzman (1998, p. 207) argues that "uncertainty about future discount rates provides a strong generic rationale for using certainty equivalent social discount rates that decline over time...to the smallest imaginable rates for the far distant future." At a minimum, he argues that it is worth assessing net present values using the lower rate.

[35]This argument is based on the fact that if the probabilities of alternative outcomes for the net present value of a stream of benefits are weighted using high and low discount rate factors, the net present value arising from the low discount rate factor will dominate (with the former falling to a low value, given the effect of discounting higher interest rates far into the future).

Box 2.4. The Implications of Uncertainty about the Discount Rate

Economists routinely apply a discount rate as a method of placing the value of present consumption and that of future consumption on the same basis. But the choice of discount rate to use is seldom straightforward. Indeed, as Weitzman (1998) notes, "while there is uncertainty about almost everything in the distant future, perhaps the most fundamental uncertainty of all concerns the discount rate itself" (p. 205). Weitzman argues that, beyond a given time horizon (which could be construed as the longest maturity period—for example, 30 years—for which current financial markets are willing to provide financing at market-based interest rates),[1] it would be reasonable for discounting to take place at a certainty equivalent interest rate that declines over time.[2] The key insight is that "what should be averaged over states of the world is not discount rates at various times, but *discount factors*. In the limit, the properly averaged certainty equivalent discount factor corresponds to the minimum discount rate" (p. 206).[3]

Newell and Pizer (2002a, 2002b), drawing on historical interest rate data, further demonstrate that it is unnecessary to apply an arbitrarily low discount rate to ensure that the interests of future generations are adequately taken into account. If it is assumed that interest rates follow a random walk from a given starting point, the average effective interest rate that emerges from thousands of stochastic simulations would yield a discount rate significantly lower than if one simply assumed a constant discount rate far into the future. The difference in the relative valuation attached to benefits received far in the future becomes clearest when a higher starting discount rate is assumed.

The consequence of the Weitzman-Newell-Pizer results is to significantly improve the net present value of policies, such as climate change policies, that realize their benefits in the distant future (for example, beyond a century). But what is equally important in the Newell-Pizer results is that, even for policies that will yield benefits within the next 40 years, the difference in the discount factor can be 10 to 30 percent greater (depending on the initial starting discount rate, with the difference positively correlated with the initial rate).

---

[1]During this time period, Weitzman would argue that market-determined rates would be appropriate.

[2]In effect, this would be equivalent to weighting the discount factors associated with alternative plausible discount rates by the probability of each rate occurring. Given that, over long periods, the discount factors associated with high rates become quantitatively insignificant, only the discount factors associated with low rates end up being relevant.

[3]Note this is *not* an argument that discount rates in the future should necessarily be lower. Indeed, one can think of various reasons why they might be higher (for example, greater uncertainty or lack of altruism toward future generations who may be expected to have higher incomes). Rather, if there is uncertainty about what interest rates should be used, a probabilistic approach effectively results in the lower rate being used (weighted by its probability).

this knowledge, there may be considerable uncertainty about both the mean and the variance of the future probability distribution of these key variables. Thus, for example, it may be clear that there will be an improvement in life expectancy, but even when fully informed by historical experience, experts may differ on the mean improvement to be forecast, let alone on the variance.[36] Similarly, all the best models may suggest inevitable global warming within a 95 percent confidence interval, but the nature of the probability distribution of the temperature change within that interval may be difficult to assess. Climate change models may also be too weak in their capacity to predict the likelihood of extreme weather events, particularly at a sufficiently detailed regional level, to be relevant to policymakers in a given country. And, of course, beyond the issue of estimating the probability distribution of these key structural variables is the need to link the possible range of such estimates with the corresponding economic or fiscal impact (as discussed above).

Uncertainty about General-Equilibrium Effects

Many countries do not expect any significant aging of their population. Yet in a world where the dominant share of total output derives from those countries where aging is likely to be important, shifts over time in the saving and investment rates of these countries will have an impact on global capital markets. Thus, if one accepts the hypothesis of a life cycle approach to saving, one might expect an increase in saving rates with population aging in industrial countries before 2010, but a gradual decline in saving rates thereafter as the population share of the elderly rises. As the populations of these countries stabilize and then decline, a corresponding drop in their investment rates is also likely. In contrast, many important emerging market countries will experience a further increase in their labor force for a decade or so beyond 2010, suggesting both higher saving and higher investment rates for another 15 years, but with declines thereafter, reinforcing the pattern observed in the industrial countries.

---

[36]A recent study compared population projections made over the last decade by the OECD (in the mid-1980s), the World Bank (in the early 1990s), the United Nations (in the late 1990s), and the OECD/Eurostat (in the late 1990s). All projections indicated a rise in the elderly population, but the "extent of change differs substantially across the four sets of projections. In nearly all countries, the old age dependency ratios are higher, the more recent the projection" (U.S. CIA, 2001b, p. 24).

The net balance between saving and investment in the global economy will reflect the relative weights of these different economies and will have a corresponding effect on global interest rates. Exchange rate patterns may also be affected. To the extent that there are significant capital flows from the industrial economies to emerging markets and other developing economies during the period through 2010 or 2015—reflecting efforts of pension funds to diversify their investment portfolios—one might observe pressures for the currencies of these economies to appreciate. Correspondingly, to the extent that this flow of funds reverses itself after 2010 or 2015, with reduced saving associated with pension consumption in the industrial economies, the currencies of the industrial countries might tend to appreciate and those of emerging market economies and other developing countries to depreciate (see Heller and Symansky, 1998). This description is obviously simplistic; however, complex general-equilibrium models can be used to estimate the balance of prospective pressures on global interest and exchange rates in coming decades (see Turner and others, 1998; Attanasio and Violante, 2000). The use of these models is described further in Chapter 3.

Uncertainty about Interactions Between Policy Variables and Economic and Demographic Variables

Policymakers often confront uncertainty about the impact of specific policy changes on key economic (and demographic) variables. This can make assessment of the long-term fiscal situation particularly problematic. Efforts to redress potential disequilibria in the long-term fiscal balance rely on assumptions about the impact of particular policy changes. Yet if there is uncertainty about how labor force participation rates, saving, the demand for health care, or decisions about fertility will react to changes in specific policy instruments, it will be difficult to evaluate the effectiveness of alternative policies. Moreover, if the choice is between marginal and fundamental reforms, the latter are far more likely to have unintended consequences.

Uncertainty Due to Possible Shifts in Political Regime

Policymakers cannot rule out the possibility that future shifts in the political regime will result in a change in the basic philosophical perspective on the appropriate policy regime, which in turn will affect the

direction of tax or expenditure policies. Whether health costs rise by
more or less than the rate of productivity growth in the sector is not
wholly exogenous to the policy regime chosen. Decisions on the extent
of allowable immigration into industrial countries could, over time,
make a significant difference in fiscal outcomes. Regulatory decisions
concerning land management and zoning could influence the extent of
economic losses associated with climate change-induced changes in
mean sea level.

Uncertainty about the Probability Distribution Itself

As noted earlier, climate change scientists recognize that the "climate
forcing" associated with the increased concentration of greenhouse
gases that has already occurred has a small but real likelihood of giving rise to abrupt, potentially catastrophic, climate changes—a shift in
the El Niño pattern, for example, or in the Gulf Stream. Estimates of
even the mean probability of such "low-probability, high-consequence
events" may differ dramatically—say, by a factor of 6 (from 0.5 percent
to 3 percent) over the next 100 years—and estimating a variance or
probability distribution is even more difficult. Yet the economic consequences of such an event could be enormous.[37] Some climate change
experts have argued that any decisions about substantial investments
in climate change mitigation should be deferred for 15 to 20 years until
more evidence is accumulated and better models of climate change are
developed. It is thus difficult, within a reasonable long-term framework, to judge the probability of large costs (some of which would
surely affect government budgets) being incurred.

At a different level, the events of September 11 illustrate that there
may be a real counterpart to the types of qualitative forecasts made by
such agencies as the U.S. Central Intelligence Agency (CIA), through its
National Intelligence Council (NIC), in its long-term assessments (U.S.
CIA, 2001a). The NIC study, written in late 2000, suggested a significant risk of a terrorist attack, but in the absence of an assessment of the
probability of such an attack, political decision makers at the time did
not appear to view it as likely to happen. Thus the possibility of such
high-cost future events or trends cannot be dismissed. If they occur,
they can give rise to a policy regime shift (for example, a sustained

---

[37]Indeed, in a paper by Nordhaus (1998) on the economic impact of climate change
in the next century, the most important cost was associated with such low-probability
events.

higher level of military outlays), with significant associated fiscal costs of possibly long duration. Thus the U.S. CIA (2001b) has identified a number of possible situations that are sources of economic and political concern, some of which have been noted above. In a qualitative sense, probabilities might be subjectively attached to such occurrences. Should this feed into a long-term fiscal forecast?

Within the economic domain more narrowly, this type of uncertainty also relates to whether the underlying structural model on which economic assessments are being made is itself undergoing change. Certainly, the idea that the celebrated technology revolution of the late 1990s (Hundley and others, 2000) is contributing to a structural shift in the rate of productivity growth is now being revisited. Similarly, many have hypothesized that the forces of globalization will give rise to international tax competition—a "race to the bottom"—as countries lower their tax rates in an attempt to retain footloose capital within their borders. The typical long-term modeling assumption that the tax revenue share will remain unchanged becomes subject to question in such a world, but whether the estimated probability distribution around future fiscal revenue should be changed remains uncertain.

Uncertainty about Unforeseeable Events

The events of September 11 also illustrate the biases associated with a focus on those significant "structural breaks" that one can identify and that are perceived to have important fiscal implications. This can give rise to an inevitable bias—which could work in either a positive or a negative direction—toward focusing exclusively on a limited set of issues while other possible shocks, which may prove of equal importance, are ignored or not anticipated. (This is often termed the "lamppost" approach: analysis is focused on certain areas that are better understood than others—the light is better under the lamppost.) Certainly, even a decade ago, any long-term forecast for many developing countries would not have identified HIV/AIDS as an important factor affecting their macroeconomic landscape.

Summing Up

The discussion thus far has sought to highlight two principal points. First, a number of potential developments over the next several decades could have serious ramifications for the fiscal positions of governments around the world. Revenues may be constrained even as expenditure pressures intensify. The degree to which any government is sensitive to these pressures in part reflects the nature of its policy commitments to its citizens. Second, although much can be deduced about the principal forces that may play out in the future, considerable uncertainty remains about how each of these (and other) forces may unfold. One can envisage a relatively benign outcome, where only a few of the risk factors discussed above have major impacts. But one can also readily imagine how a number of these risk factors could simultaneously come into play. For example, it would not be unreasonable for policymakers in Northern Europe to assume that the aging of their populations will take place precisely at a time when global climate change is also buffeting their economies.[38]

The question that then arises is how governments should take these issues into account in determining fiscal policies today. Economists have increasingly emphasized the importance of assessing the long-term sustainability of a government's fiscal position. They have recognized that this entails going beyond an assessment of whether a government will be able to service its outstanding debt obligations, to require consideration of its capacity to meet its social insurance obligations (principally pensions) as well. This chapter suggests that an even broader perspective may be required, one that assesses the multiple long-term risks to which a government is exposed and the considerable uncertainty surrounding judgments about the fiscal consequences of these risks. Governments may be forced to address a number of adverse developments simultaneously, raising the specter of governments being forced to renege on their obligations to their citizens.

Confronting these issues will require that governments assess the long-term sustainability of their fiscal position in a broad and probabilistic way. By "broad" I mean that the authorities consider both the nature of the government's commitments—of its political contract—with its citizens and the possible scope of developments that can be reasonably anticipated in the future. By "probabilistic" I mean that attention is paid to the likelihood of adverse outcomes for each of a number of risks, and that some "insurance factor" is built into fiscal policy

---

[38]Moreover, Lee and Tuljapurkar (2000) have noted that if these relevant independent variables are log normally distributed, then their joint probability distribution is likely to be asymmetrically distributed, with a higher probability associated with adverse outcomes around the mean. Their work focused principally on demographic variables: fertility and life expectancy. Adding the potential stochastic distribution of other significant variables may render the probability distribution more adverse.

planning. Ensuring sustainability for the long term may thus require that policies be put in place in the near term that will ensure a greater robustness of the future fiscal position to alternative risk factors.

The obvious question is whether and how governments are already taking account of potential long-term developments in the analysis and formulation of their fiscal policies. This will be the focus of the next chapter.

3

How Governments (and Academics) Address Long-Term Issues in Fiscal Policy Planning

This chapter examines how long-term issues are presently brought to bear in the analysis, formulation, and implementation of aggregate fiscal policy and the budget. It starts by reviewing the various analytical approaches that governments and academics have used to appraise long-term fiscal viability. Specific attention is paid to the way in which developments that might affect the future fiscal position are integrated within the analysis and considered, if at all, in assessing the short- to medium-term fiscal stance. The discussion suggests that budget agencies, academics, and financial analysts have begun to pay at least some attention to the implications of the aging of the population that is projected to occur in many countries. But this focus has not been appreciably extended to include other potential developments over the long term that could also influence the viability of the fiscal regime.

The chapter then turns to a review of how these analyses are integrated into the formal domestic budget process. It finds that such efforts remain limited to only a few countries. Multilateral surveillance is shown to be an independent source of pressure on governments' approach to fiscal policy. Long-term issues are also starting to appear in this context as points of concern.

The chapter then examines some of the policy approaches that governments are pursuing to address long-term issues. One approach relies on aggregate fiscal policy—the size of the fiscal surplus or deficit—to achieve a more robust financial position in anticipation of potential long-term developments. The chapter thus examines the various aggregate fiscal policy "rules" that governments have adopted in recent years. Rules can be seen as a mechanism for taking account of political economy factors, since they seek to constrain the short-term biases of political leaders in their approach to fiscal policy. The chapter then assesses the complementary institutional approaches that have been adopted to support aggregative prefunding of future obligations. In particular, it reviews the policy, adopted by several governments, of accumulating resources in an earmarked financial "lockbox."

Many governments have sought to complement an aggregative fiscal policy approach with specific policy reforms that act directly on the sources of future financial pressures. The chapter characterizes the different types of policy reforms that governments have adopted to narrow the extent of their long-term commitments and potential future fiscal obligations. The decision to defer reform may also constitute a legitimate approach to addressing long-run concerns, particularly if the costs of immediate action in the face of uncertainty are very high, or if investments, once undertaken, are both costly and irreversible.

The chapter then examines whether capital markets have constituted an effective independent force pressuring governments to address long-term fiscal issues. It argues that although financial market institutions such as credit rating agencies are often in the forefront of signaling the importance of policies to address long-term pressures, it is unusual for a credit rating agency to look far into the future in assigning ratings to government debt instruments. Capital markets may also help not only in diagnosing but also in dealing with long-term fiscal problems, as financial engineering develops new ways to address risks (an example is the recent innovation of catastrophe bonds). Finally, the chapter examines recent proposals to rely on public debt risk management as a means of limiting the fiscal impact of unanticipated shocks.

Analytical Approaches

It has become increasingly common in assessments of fiscal policy to consider the issue of sustainability (Cheasty and others, 2002; IMF, 2001a; United Kingdom, H.M. Treasury, 2001a). In the mid-1980s a common starting point for such an assessment was an examination of the potential dynamics of a country's public debt position. A simple analytical approach was applied to determine whether the current primary fiscal balance—the deficit or surplus exclusive of interest payments—if sustained into the future, would lead to an increase or a decrease in the ratio of public debt to national output. Given the difference between forecast nominal interest rates and the nominal growth rate of the economy, estimates could then be made to determine whether an adjustment in the primary balance would be needed to maintain the present debt ratio at a constant level.[1] This approach was further elaborated to take account of the possibility that a high debt ratio might lead credit markets to exact more of a risk premium, which would then increase the corresponding primary surplus required (Blanchard, 1984). Obviously, with a high debt ratio, an assessment that a government's primary fiscal balance position was insufficient to lower that ratio would raise questions about that government's long-run solvency.

However, this approach had its limitations. First, it was highly aggregative, offering only a shorthand basis for judging aggregate sustainability. Second, even if a government's overall debt position appeared sustainable on this basis, this would not indicate what primary balance target should be pursued, particularly in situations where a government's debt ratio was either low or likely to be declining. (For example, for some countries, additional investment in public infrastructure, funded by public debt, might be desirable.) Third, and more fundamentally, this approach largely involved extrapolating the implications of the current fiscal position, in stock and flow terms, given expectations about future interest rates. It neither took account of any additional specific long-term factors that might influence the fiscal position nor considered the degree of risk to which a government was exposed. The first of these deficiencies was recognized quite early, as governments and academics became seized with the concern that the "baby bust" of the industrial countries, following the baby boom of the early postwar period, threatened to create financial problems for government pension systems, almost all of which were on a pay-as-you-go (PAYGO) basis.

The awareness of the inadequacy, then, of a government's explicit debt ratio for conveying the full sense of a government's true liabilities also implied that previous measures of sustainability were likely to be misleading in terms of their policy implications. This recognition has led to a number of strands of work, all of which seek to provide a perspective on the nature of the government's fiscal position in coming years. Most flow out of an awareness of the need to take account of the impact of aging populations, although to some extent the Asian crisis extended this concern to include the possibility of contingent liabilities associated with financial and corporate recapitalizations.

---

[1]The greater this difference, the more the primary surplus would need to be increased. If d is the ratio of debt to GDP, r the nominal interest rate, g the nominal growth rate, and p the ratio of the primary surplus to GDP, then $p = (r - g) * d$ is necessary to maintain the debt ratio at its existing level.

The principal strands of this research, described below, include efforts to come up with a more comprehensive measure of the government's balance sheet, to develop alternative measures of the scale of fiscal adjustment required to put the government's long-term financial position on a sustainable footing, to identify the intertemporal phasing of the government's fiscal balance, and to assess the distribution of the burden of fiscal commitments across different generations, present and future. New strands of the literature have sought to quantify the likelihood of alternative fiscal scenarios coming to pass, as well as to take account of how the global dimensions of aging populations are likely to affect key variables, particularly exchange and interest rates, that influence fiscal scenarios in individual countries.

Balance Sheet Approaches

Surprisingly, the notion of presenting the government's financial position in the form of a balance sheet and operating balance is fairly recent. Even today, few countries have adopted this approach, originally pioneered by New Zealand in the late 1980s. Only recently have the principal methodological frameworks for government finance (as laid out in the IMF's *Manual on Government Finance Statistics*) formally adopted such an approach (Blejer and Cheasty, 1993). Even within this perspective, only explicit debts are formally included in the balance sheet, primarily out of recognition that a number of important issues remain to be resolved (as briefly discussed below) on how to take account of the impact on the balance sheet of such factors as demographic trends, the depletion of natural resources, and environmental costs.

Nevertheless, at a research level, some analysts have sought to extend the measure of a government's debts beyond its outstanding formal debt instruments (that is, short-term bills and medium- to long-term bonds) to include estimates of implicit debt obligations. Almost exclusively, the principal focus of such analyses has been the expected public pension outlays of industrial country social insurance systems in the face of projected population aging. Most public pension systems are PAYGO systems, with benefit payments funded from the contributions of the current workforce.

Under current policies with respect to the age of pension eligibility, aging populations will imply shrinking or constant labor forces and a rising ratio of retired beneficiaries to workers. Without an increase in the contribution rate or a reduction in benefit payouts, PAYGO systems would begin to incur financial deficits, which would add to the explicit debt of governments. Estimates of such implicit debt (see Chand and Jaeger, 1996)[2] normally require assumptions about economic and de- mographic developments in the long run, particularly with respect to rates of fertility and life expectancy, productivity growth, interest, and labor force participation and employment. Critically, they are based on the assumption of no further rise in the social insurance contribution rate or the tax burden.

Alternative approaches to such calculations may be made, depending on the perspective of the analyst. If the objective, for example, is to re- form an insolvent public pension system, one might wish to estimate how much the government would owe participants in the scheme were it to be terminated immediately. Because, under a PAYGO system, only negligible assets are maintained, such an accounting would reflect the value of future benefits, discounted to the present, that have accrued to current participants (whether retired or currently working).[3] In contrast, under the assumption that the public pension scheme will be continued without policy change, assumptions would need to be made about the flow of future contributions and benefit accruals long into the future.

Recent work by Holzmann, Palacios, and Zviniene (2001) suggests that large, unfunded, pension-related debt is a problem not only for in- dustrial countries, but also for many emerging market economies and other developing countries. In some cases the large implicit debt may arise independent of demographic considerations, as a consequence of excessively generous pension promises. This has been the case in some Eastern European countries, where pension commitments have arisen less from any change in the population share of the elderly than as a consequence of the use of these public pension systems to finance early retirement associated with the restructuring of these economies.

However, judging the true magnitude of a government's implicit debt requires looking beyond unfunded pension liabilities alone. The last few years have seen increased efforts to clarify the nature of any explicit

---

[2]The term derives from the fact that such deficits would formally not occur if gov- ernments maintained the PAYGO system by raising the rate of contributions of partici- pants in the system.

[3]Under a defined-benefit system, this would reflect both the existing pension entitle- ments of current retirees and some judgment about the pension replacement rate (the ratio of the pension benefit to the final wage rate) for future retirees, based on estimates of future earnings and the length of time participants have been in the scheme. For a de- fined-contribution scheme managed on a PAYGO basis, it would relate to the amount of contributions that current workers have made in the past, scaled up to the present by some assumed rate of return on these past contributions.

or contingent liabilities that may emerge from the government's involvement in the economy, whether in the real or the financial sector. Such involvement may include state guarantees of public enterprise debt or deposit insurance, or the public recapitalization of businesses in the financial or the corporate sector. Estimating the government's potential debt exposure from such policy initiatives is obviously not easy, because it may not be clear to what extent the government is legally obligated to meet such potential obligations, and to what extent the justification for assuming those obligations is "merely" moral or pragmatic.

These approaches are not without their hazards and complexities. First, should the focus be exclusively on pensions? Is not the government's commitment to provide education or, in some countries, medical care just as important in considering the scope of the government's policy commitments? Although it could be argued that a government's future pension obligations to an individual worker can be more directly linked to that worker's past earnings and contribution history, governments providing publicly funded medical care have no less of an obligation to provide care of a certain quality and quantity to the average retiree or citizen; the same applies to the obligation to provide education.[4] Second, critical to any such estimate is the assumption that government revenue cannot be increased commensurately with the expected growth of expenditure. Indeed, it is the difference between the future expected growth of expenditure and that of revenue that is the basis for estimating the net present value of such implicit debt measures. If revenue could indeed be raised instead, it would be inaccurate to treat some of the future commitments as being debt financed.

Third, adding further to the complexity of any judgment about sustainability is the fact that governments are unlikely to question the "political" sustainability of an existing policy commitment. A case in point is the U.K. pension system. In the 1980s the U.K. government changed the system so that the basic state pension at retirement was held constant in real terms, rather than indexed to a measure of average real earnings in the economy. The consequence is that the basic pension is progressively shrinking relative to the average wage. Most projections of the government's pension obligations thus suggest that government pension outlays will remain quite limited as a percentage

---

[4]Indeed, from the perspective of government accountants grappling with how to measure such liabilities on the balance sheet, there are serious problems in quantifying or even accepting such commitments as obligations until the actual liability-incurring event has taken place.

of GDP. Yet it is difficult to imagine that a growing disparity between the average wage and the initial minimum pension can be sustained politically for very long.[5] Indeed, recent adjustments by the government to its minimum means-tested welfare payment suggest that this transfer mechanism may end up supplanting the state pension. Again, an increase in the long-term financial implications of the government's likely spending on pensions or welfare would not show up in any government financial projection, since neither benefit is legally required to be adjusted.

Thus, attempts at estimating implicit debt arising from future policy commitments ultimately revolve around the definition of whether a policy commitment has an explicit legislative underpinning to give it a semblance of equivalence to explicit debt. Most estimates of implicit pension debt are normally qualified by the recognition that future policy changes are inevitably likely to temper their magnitude (which is indeed often the motivation for making the estimates in the first place). Yet the same is likely to be true for *other* commitments that do not have the same formal legal underpinning as pensions, but for which it would be hazardous to assume the absence of further reforms that might either contain or increase outlays.

Despite these concerns, these various efforts at measurement represent an important step toward a more comprehensive picture of a government's overall potential debt exposure—explicit and implicit. Such analyses would need to be taken into account in qualifying the results of the more basic assessments of public debt sustainability described at the outset.

Medium- to Long-Run Projections

In an operational sense, recognition of the need to look beyond the current fiscal year position has led governments to construct aggregate fiscal scenarios that extend at least to a medium-term horizon of three to five years and sometimes longer. This is an increasingly common approach, pursued today by many governments (Schick, 2002a). Normally

---

[5]Witness a recent editorial in the *Financial Times* (Ewald, 2002b), which states, "Britain...[is] the only EU country where public pension spending is projected to fall by 2050. Private provision is falling short, as employers back away from commitments and savers lose faith in a pension industry hit by scandal and falling investment returns. Governments can scale down public pensions only if people at work can invest with confidence over the time necessary to replace state provision."

these are straightforward projections that take account of expected revenue buoyancies and known expenditure commitments and make basic assumptions about underlying real growth rates and inflation.

IMF fiscal economists frequently construct such medium-term fiscal scenarios (Chalk and Hemming, 2000), particularly for countries where the debt dynamics appear unfavorable. Fiscal projections are made, starting with the assumption that no changes will be made in the underlying policy regime. Estimates are then made of the magnitude of fiscal adjustment required to arrive at a more sustainable fiscal position over the medium term. Consideration is given as to what broad strategy, in terms of increased revenue or cutbacks in expenditure, would appear most plausible. Best-practice analyses of this sort usually include stress tests, to assess the robustness of alternative fiscal adjustment paths to adverse economic scenarios. They also seek to take account of any obvious potential feedback that the fiscal adjustment itself might have on interest or growth rates. Most such analyses incorporate any obvious expenditure or revenue developments that are seen on the horizon, due either to exogenous factors or to the effects of past policy changes. As these are typically medium-term assessments, they do not typically consider whether factors that may influence the long-run fiscal situation should also be taken into account in deciding on the appropriate short- to medium-term fiscal stance.

For a number of industrial countries, long-term quantitative projections of revenue, expenditure, and the overall fiscal balance have been undertaken. In general, this is rarely a routine or a required component of most governments' budget processes (see below). When undertaken, such projections are made for periods of 10 to 30 years, although occasionally they go as far out as 75 years. Heavily motivated by the recognition of the interface between likely demographic developments and legislated social insurance commitments, such projections usually include both actuarial best guesses and alternative scenarios for critical demographic variables such as fertility, life expectancy, and immigration. Assumptions are normally made about a number of key economic parameters and variables: the projected real growth rate, wage and labor productivity growth rates, the real interest rate, labor force participation rates of different age cohorts, and employment rates.

Projections typically include a baseline representing a continuation of the status quo policies, particularly with respect to such elements of social insurance and other welfare or transfer-type schemes as the age of pension eligibility and the benefit replacement rate.[6] But normally such projections also make sensitive assumptions about such issues as the likely relationship between the growth rate of income per capita or productivity and the growth of outlays per capita on health, education, and other programs. Taxes and other revenues are usually assumed to remain constant as a share of GDP. Unit-elasticity assumptions are typically made for other expenditure categories that are not age related and not readily forecast as subject to any obvious structural developments.[7] Projections of the interest bill are based on assumptions about interest rates, the initial public debt, and the projected pattern of government deficits or surpluses.

Such projections are normally exogenous and rarely include any endogenous or general-equilibrium feedback. Thus a growing (or a declining) fiscal deficit and a rising (or falling) public debt would not be assumed to have consequences for the interest rate at which a government can borrow or invest, or for any effects on investment and growth that might arise from the government's crowding out (or crowding in) the private sector in financial markets.

Often such long-term scenarios are undertaken only for those programs whose long-term financial viability has come into question. For example, in recent years the IMF, the European Union, and the Organization for Economic Cooperation and Development (OECD) have undertaken a number of long-term forecasts of country outlays on age-related social expenditure programs. These studies take account of anticipated changes in the demographic structure, all for the purpose of assessing future expenditure pressures (OECD, 2001a; Dang, Antolin, and Oxley, 2001; European Commission, Economic Policy Committee, 2001; Chand and Jaeger, 1996; Creedy, 1999; Guest and McDonald, 2000). In some countries, governments are legally required to present long-term actuarial assessments of their social insurance schemes. The U.S. Social Security Administration is a case in point: it is mandated to present 75-year projections that assess the adequacy of current payroll contribution rates in financing the scheme.

Such projections often suggest that a government's finances may be imbalanced over the long term, in the sense that they indicate either a

---

[6]Unlike projections made under a medium-term framework, these may not be based on the assumption of unchanged legislation, but rather may assume a continuation of the basic policy framework, thus implying the need for legislative changes.

[7]Thus, in the United States during the 1990s, the assumption was most likely made that military outlays would diminish somewhat as a share of GDP from their levels during the Cold War period.

rising or a falling debt level that is recognized as unlikely to be realized. Tax rates are sometimes used as the equilibrating factor that will keep the debt stable, but such forecasts might suggest the need for tax rates to rise or fall to unrealistic levels. Typically, stress tests are undertaken and multiple scenarios presented, often as optimistic or pessimistic variations around a central scenario. These account for the inevitable uncertainty surrounding the appropriateness of alternative assumptions about key economic or demographic parameters. Projections may also seek to gauge the impact of specific policy adjustments or of alternative policy assumptions (for example, changing the age of pension eligibility or adjusting the differential between productivity growth and the growth of health outlays).[8]

Projections tend to be highly sensitive to the underlying assumptions, both about the starting point and about the end date or terminal point of the projections. There can be significant swings in the amount of debt forecast decades in the future, depending on the starting level of the public debt and the deficit or surplus position. Similarly, the choice of the terminal point can affect the underlying results in ways that are not trivial. For example, actuarial estimates may be made of the contribution rate required to yield financial viability through the period under consideration. If the underlying demographics of a social insurance scheme suggest deficits beyond the end date T (as a consequence perhaps of a continued adverse dependency rate or increasing life expectancy assumptions), then extending the terminal point to year $T+1$ would result in a larger debt and require a correspondingly higher contribution rate (see Lee and Yamagata, 2003; Lee, 2001).

A similar type of result emerges in projections that estimate the net present value of the stream of fiscal balances over time. Such projections may show a significantly higher net present value of accumulated debt when the time horizon is extended. For projections with an

---

[8]There remains the interesting question of why governments fail to act on analyses that seem to demonstrate a lack of long-term fiscal sustainability. One obvious explanation is that governments have a healthy skepticism about the accuracy of economists' forecasts. Most retrospective assessments of even the best economic forecasters find that they have often been inaccurate. Structural variables have moved in ways that were quite unexpected at the time the basic parameters for a policy were originally formulated. A second answer may be that political decision makers prefer to rely on optimistic long-term scenarios in making policy decisions. A third is that policymakers may be slow to adapt policy commitments to resolve perceived inconsistencies in financial balances. Finally, policymakers may simply make the intergenerational assessment that future generations will be able to absorb an increased burden in financing future public policy commitments. Thus they might not perceive the fiscal forecasts as unsustainable.

infinite time horizon, even though the discounted value of deficits far in the future may be relatively small, the cumulated debt arising from an infinite stream of such future discounted deficits can nevertheless prove quantitatively significant (particularly if uncertainty about the discount rate is assumed).

A recent example of such an approach by Gokhale and Smetters (2003) estimates, for the United States, a measure of the long-term fiscal imbalance. Their measure is calculated as the current federal debt held by the public plus the present value of all future federal noninterest spending, minus the present value (without a terminal point) of all future federal receipts. To gauge how much of that imbalance arises as a consequence of policy commitments from past and current generations, they decompose their fiscal imbalance measure into a component that they call the generational imbalance and a residual, which equals the imbalance due to the spending arising from future generations. They estimate that the U.S. fiscal imbalance may range from $29.5 trillion to $63.9 trillion, depending on the assumed rate of growth in medical care spending, with a midpoint of $44.2 trillion (in contrast, the current federal debt is about $5.1 trillion).

Finally, the problem of false precision in such long-term projections underscores the caution with which they should be regarded. Moreover, because they are *deterministic* projections, each forecast, even when accompanied by stress tests, confers no sense of the likelihood of any specific scenario. Indeed, one often observes a pairing of assumptions that might yield the most optimistic or the most pessimistic case, but that may be unlikely to occur together.[9] Certainly, fiscal forecasters are aware of the high degree of uncertainty associated with long-term projections.

Synthetic Indicators of Sustainability

Another approach to characterizing the fiscal sustainability of current policy commitments over the long run has developed as a natural

---

[9]Lee and Tuljapurkar (2000) have noted the divergent treatment by the U.S. Social Security Administration and the U.S. Bureau of the Census in their construction of demographic scenarios. The Social Security analysts provide optimistic and pessimistic forecasts that assume, respectively, a scenario of high fertility and low life expectancy versus one of low fertility and high life expectancy. The Census Bureau, in contrast, in its high and low population forecasts, pairs high fertility with high life expectancy in the former scenario and low fertility with low life expectancy in the latter. Given their differing objectives, each agency's approach may be sensible. For the purpose of a budget forecast, however, neither set of scenarios indicates what demographic forecast is most likely to be correct.

outgrowth of long-term forecasting. Both Blanchard (1985) and Buiter (1985) have developed ways of characterizing the amount of sustained fiscal adjustment required to equilibrate the present value of the long-term budget constraint faced by a government (also called the intertemporal budget constraint). Both authors start from the assumption that a government with a stock of existing public debt should be able to repay any new debt incurred by deficits through the accumulation over time of net surpluses, the net present value of which would equal the net present value of the deficits. In other words, any anticipated future deficits must, at some point, be offset by surpluses.[10]

Blanchard's "tax gap" indicator is a measure of the adjustment in the ratio of taxes to GDP needed in the present, and to be sustained until some terminal point in the future, to allow the debt ratio to return to its initial level. Calculation of this indicator requires assumptions about the level of nominal interest rates and the growth rate likely in the future (and thus the difference between these two rates). Buiter has developed an analogous indicator, the "primary gap," which is the amount of immediate adjustment in the primary balance (as a share of GDP), whether derived from tax increases or expenditure decreases, that would allow for the ratio of net worth to GDP to be maintained at its current level at some terminal point. Reflecting the concern noted above about the sensitivity of such measures to the choice of terminal date, other authors have sought to estimate these indicators assuming an infinite horizon (thus requiring specific assumptions about the nature of the fiscal gap or policy requirements beyond a terminal point in the future; Lee and Yamagata, 2003; Auerbach, 1994; Auerbach and Gale, 2000). Studies also differ as to whether the required fiscal adjustment needs to be sufficient simply to maintain the debt ratio at its current level, or whether it would need to be able to repay existing debt in full. Indeed, they offer no judgment on what should be the target debt or the net asset ratio at the terminal point.[11]

These so-called synthetic indicators have since been elaborated and based less on highly simplified models and more on more detailed empirical projections that take account of age-related trends in public expenditure (see Balassone and Franco, 2000b). Thus Delbecque and Bogaert (1994) define a measure of the "recommended primary

---

[10]Under a sustainable fiscal policy, public debt is used to smooth intertemporal variations in the primary balance.

[11]Chalk and Hemming (2000) note that highly indebted countries should probably target a reduced level of debt, but that it might be optimal for countries with low starting debt levels to allow for an increase in debt.

surplus," which indicates the amount of adjustment in the primary surplus needed today to achieve a sufficiently lower public debt, and thus lower future interest spending, to offset projected increases in pension expenditure due to the aging of the population.[12] Similarly, Chand and Jaeger (1996), examining the unfunded pension liabilities of several industrial countries, estimate the tax adjustment required to fund the anticipated shortfall in receipts relative to pension liabilities.

The European Commission's Economic Policy Committee (2001), in its study on the long-run challenges facing countries with aging populations, suggests two indicators, which in part derive from the fiscal rules associated with the 1997 Stability and Growth Pact (SGP). The first is analogous to the tax gap indicator, but with a focus on the amount of tax adjustment required "to reach the same debt level in 2050 as would result from a continued balanced budget position over the projection period" (p. 68). This represents what would happen in the event of a sustained realization of the SGP over the period. The second indicator is measured as the difference between projected primary surpluses, based on projections of budgetary pressures associated with population aging, and the primary surpluses that would be required "to ensure a balanced budget in all years of the forecast exercise" (through a terminal point in 2050).[13]

In a recent application of the concept to New Zealand, Janssen (2002) estimates the fiscal gap adjustment that would be required to maintain that country's ratio of public debt to GDP at 30 percent through 2050. He explores how the size of the gap is affected by alternative assumptions about tax and expenditure policies or by delays in policy implementation. Frederiksen (2003) similarly provides estimates of the adjustment in the primary balances needed in 19 OECD countries to achieve sustainability; his most recent update (reproduced in Table 3.1) suggests that, on a GDP-weighted basis, the primary balance would, on average, need to be adjusted upward by 5.2 percent of GDP.

Synthetic indicators usefully quantify the imbalances facing the public sector over the long term. But their value perhaps derives more from their simplicity and their appealing policy symbolism—the fact that they indicate the increase in the taxes-to-GDP ratio needed to achieve intertemporal budget consistency. Because one can also calculate these

---

[12]The offsetting changes in explicit and implicit debt mean that total debt is constant (Buiter, 1985).

[13]The commission notes that, from this calculation, the net present value of the required primary surpluses over the period can be calculated, as can the average required primary surplus over the period.

Table 3.1. Fiscal Sustainability in OECD Countries:
Primary Fiscal Balance Approach
(In percent of 2002 GDP)

| Country | Adjusted Structural Primary Balance[1] | Net Government Debt | | | Adjustment in Primary Fiscal Needed to Achieve Sustainability[3] |
		Explicit	Implicit[2]	Total	
Australia	1.7	5	220	225	−2.8
Austria	0.8	50	199	249	−4.2
Belgium	6.1	98	207	305	0.0
Canada	3.0	44	376	419	−5.3
Denmark	3.7	23	155	178	0.1
Finland	4.5	−42	283	241	−0.3
France	−0.1	38	193	231	−4.7
Germany	−0.1	44	157	201	−4.2
Greece	4.0	107	490	597	8.0
Ireland	−2.1	36	260	297	−8.0
Italy	3.4	97	53	150	0.4
Japan	−6.0	58	78	136	−8.8
Netherlands	2.5	42	253	295	−3.4
Norway	12.7	−73	898	824	−3.7
Portugal	−0.2	55	178	233	−4.9
Spain	2.7	41	312	354	−4.4
Sweden	3.3	−1	183	182	−0.3
United Kingdom	0.5	29	75	104	−1.6
United States	−0.8	43	223	266	−6.1
Unweighted average, all countries	2.1	37	252	289	−3.7
GDP-weighted average, all countries	−0.5	46	187	233	−5.2
GDP-weighted average, EU countries only	1.4	49	163	213	−2.9

Source: Frederiksen (2003).

[1]Actual primary balance (the general government fiscal balance exclusive of interest payments) that would prevail if the economy were at full employment.

[2]Debt that is "embodied in current expenditure standards and benefit rules" (Frederiksen, 2003, p. 4).

[3]A negative number indicates that fiscal policy is unsustainable; the value of the index in such cases indicates the size of an immediate and permanent tax increase or expenditure decrease that would be needed to bring the fiscal balance to a level consistent with intertemporal solvency.

measures under the assumption that fiscal adjustment is delayed, they also provide some sense of the intergenerational trade-offs: how much of an increase in taxation on current generations today would reduce the burden that would otherwise be borne principally by future generations. For example, in the New Zealand case, Janssen's results suggest the need for a sustained fiscal adjustment of roughly 1 to 2 percent of GDP as of today, but if sustained adjustment were delayed until 2020, it would need to be more than 4 percent of GDP.[14]

As noted earlier, synthetic indicators are *aggregative* measures. They do not give any direct sense of the *pattern* of surpluses or deficits that would emerge in different periods, or of the likely economic consequences of any particular time path. The former can be readily calculated, given the underlying data and assumptions used to estimate the indicators. But the latter raise far more complex issues, requiring a broader macroeconomic model, not to mention many assumptions about the political economy of the public sector. Particularly for countries with aging populations, in many ways the gap indicators assume a model for the aggregate fiscal sector that is analogous to the underlying rationale of a prefunded pension scheme, namely, a buildup of surpluses and a reduction in debt (or the accumulation of assets), followed by a drawdown of assets or a buildup of debt in the future.

Gap indicators are also subject to many of the same deficiencies and weaknesses as long-term fiscal forecasts, given that they rely, essentially, on the same things: an underlying set of economic assumptions, a basic starting point for public debt and the fiscal balance, and a set of assumptions about potential expenditure developments. They also are sensitive to the more critical, and ultimately policy-based, assumptions about how much expenditure will be allowed to increase in response to uncertain future changes (notably, for example, in spending in the health sector) or about the sustainability of particular policy assumptions.[15] They handle uncertainty in analogous fashion, being essentially

---

[14]The increase in the fiscal gap under delayed adjustment can thus be very large, growing by the growth-adjusted rate of interest (Blanchard, 1985).

[15]For both long-term forecasts and gap indicators, implicit assumptions are normally made as to the role of the public sector and the nature of its commitments that may not themselves be sustainable. For example, the question was raised earlier whether the United Kingdom could sustain its presently modest public sector commitments with respect to the basic state pension. Or would the implied low replacement rate be adjusted upward or substituted by a more generous minimum income guarantee (a trend already emerging)? The treatment of the health sector in most projections of this type is particularly problematic, and not only with respect to assumptions about the nature of health demand pressures associated with population aging (especially regarding the sensitivity

deterministic scenarios that give no sense of the probability that measures to close a specified gap will result in a fiscally sustainable solution. Thus they do not give any sense of the relative variance associated with the projections for different sectors. The gap measure may include forecasts for sectors where there may be a relatively high degree of certainty (for example, pensions) and forecasts for other sectors (for example, health or education) where the uncertainty may be considerably greater. Finally, like the long-term forecasts, they do not provide for any feedback from fiscal adjustment itself to the underlying variables.

As a representation of the "needed" policy adjustment, gap measures may create a biased perspective, focusing only on the tax increase or expenditure decrease presently required to produce intertemporally consistent fiscal budgets. But many alternative policy reforms could equally result in reduced expenditure or increased tax commitments in future years, leading to a reduced fiscal gap indicator.

New Approaches to Assessing the Long-Term Fiscal Situation

Three other analytical approaches have emerged in recent years to address some of the issues that arise in assessing the fiscal impact of long-term developments. Although all focus principally on the problems associated with aging populations, each could be used to address a broader set of issues. The first, *generational accounting* (GA), provides a perspective on how age-related transfers and outlays might impose different burdens across generations, both those alive today and those yet unborn. The second, *stochastic forecasting*, seeks to gauge the likelihood of each of several alternative forecast outcomes. The third, *overlapping-generation, multicountry general-equilibrium* (OLG-GE) *modeling*, seeks to examine the potential ramifications of aging populations for living standards, wage rates, asset prices, and interest rates within a global framework. Such models recognize that most of the industrial world and some large emerging market economies will all experience aging of their populations over the next several decades.

---

of health spending to an increased population share of the elderly). For example, there is considerable uncertainty about what to assume concerning the responsiveness of health care demand to the availability of new technological innovations, about the degree to which increased demand for newly developed pharmaceuticals will be accommodated, about the cost-reducing effects of new technologies, and about the impact of health care costs on cost pressures in other sectors (that is, a Baumol effect).

Generational Accounting

Pioneered by Kotlikoff and Auerbach in the 1980s (Auerbach and Kotlikoff, 1999), the GA methodology estimates the fiscal burden that current age-related tax and transfer policies imply for future generations, and the fiscal adjustment that would be needed to produce generational balance, so that "future generations face the same fiscal burden as do current generations when adjusted for growth (when measured as a proportion of their lifetime earnings)" (Kotlikoff and Raffelhuschen, 1999, p. 161).

Applying this methodology, a number of country-specific studies have measured the intergenerational imbalance, that is, the difference between the net transfers to the public sector (taxes paid less transfers received) paid by generations that are alive today and those paid by future generations (those born from tomorrow onward).[16] The calculation of the imbalance takes account of current levels of net public debt that must be serviced in the future (netting out the financial and real assets of the government), projected demographic developments, and projected government purchases (exclusive of transfers). It also assumes that future generations must pay all debt that is not paid by current generations. The estimates also require assumptions about the allocation per capita of benefits across generations for other government purchases of goods and services (for example, all public goods). The age profile—the different ages at which taxes are paid and transfers received—is assumed to be constant. GA estimates are deterministic (that is, they do not take account of uncertainty) and lack any endogeneity (government policies are assumed to induce no change in economic behavior).

Not surprisingly, the interaction between the existing public policy framework on age-related transfers and future demographic developments drives the results on intergenerational balances. For most industrial countries with aging populations, current policies imply that much larger net transfers will be needed from future generations in order to pay for the larger flows to present generations as they age, with the older cohorts among the latter being the greatest beneficiaries. However, Kotlikoff and Raffelhuschen (1999, p. 162) note that

---

[16]The basic identity is that the present value of net transfers by future generations must equal the sum of three quantities: the present value of net transfers to the present generation, current public debt, and the sum of future government purchases valued in the present. If the latter two are held unchanged, there is an obvious trade-off between what future generations must pay and what the current generation must pay.

The calculation of generational imbalance is an informative counterfactual, not a likely policy scenario, because it imposes all requisite fiscal adjustments on those born in the future. But it delivers a clear message about the need for policy adjustments. Once such a need is established, interest naturally turns to alternative means of achieving generational balance that do not involve foisting all the adjustment on future generations.

Thus estimates are typically made of the tax increases or cuts in transfers needed for all generations in order to service the intertemporal liabilities of the public sector.[17]

The GA framework offers a useful perspective on how different cohorts—existing generations and future generations—are differently affected by prospective structural developments that affect the budget, or by alternative policy reforms. However, the GA results, which rely very much on the same type of economic and demographic assumptions and data used in long-term forecasts, do not appear to yield significantly different or fuller insights than do gap analyses or long-term forecasts. Indeed, the GA results, even in terms of their perspective on alternative generational burdens, are as likely to mislead as to offer new insights. The GA methodology is also empirically cumbersome.

Banks, Disney, and Smith (2000) note several principal analytical difficulties with the GA approach.[18] First, it assumes constancy in the relative tax and transfer profiles of different cohorts derived from historical data. But, looking forward in time, the anticipated demographic changes may lead to underlying structural changes in both age-earnings profiles and household composition. These factors may have important effects on the tax-transfer pattern observed for different age groups in future cohorts. Stability in these relationships cannot be readily assumed (indeed, even their appropriateness as representative of all individuals in a cohort can be questioned). In using household economic surveys to capture current patterns of net transfers of age groups, the GA approach "may conflate age (life cycle) and cohort effects." Such changes could significantly alter the results.

Second, the GA approach applies arbitrary assumptions to the distribution of benefits associated with the government's purchases of goods and services. Although there is no obvious alternative, this arbitrariness nevertheless raises issues about the significance of the results.

---

[17]Although most GA analyses have focused on tax adjustments to resolve generational imbalances, reform of transfer benefit policy is an equally plausible solution.

[18]See also the critique by Buiter (1997) and the response by Kotlikoff and Raffelhuschen, (1999).

Third, like the measures discussed earlier, GA estimates are highly sensitive to the starting point estimate for the fiscal deficit and the public debt, as well as to the underlying economic (real interest rate and growth) and demographic assumptions.

Fourth, in assessing relative generational balances, the GA approach ignores the taxes and contributions made by existing generations in the past, thus potentially distorting judgments about the relative burdens of different generations. Nor does it provide a means of assessing fairness, however that is defined. To the extent that future generations' higher income and living standards are directly attributable to the investments of past generations, a higher overall tax burden on the former may be reasonable.

Finally, GA estimates typically accept present levels of taxes and primary surpluses as given. Thus, such estimates might find that a country with a high public debt ratio and high tax rates would require a much smaller tax adjustment than a country with low or negative public debt and consequently a smaller primary surplus. This might suggest that the former country is better off in terms of the extent of its generational imbalance than the latter—a questionable conclusion. A negligible generational imbalance that is predicated on high tax rates may prove unsustainable.

Stochastic Long-Run Forecasts

The second approach, developed by, among others, Ronald Lee and colleagues, introduces a stochastic element into long-run fiscal scenarios (Lee and Tuljapurkar, 2000; Lee and Edwards, 2002; Lee and Yamagata, 2003; Lee and Miller, 2002). The objective is to provide policymakers with an estimate of the probability of alternative long-run fiscal scenarios coming to pass. Lee's earlier work highlighted both the extent of the uncertainty associated with demographic variables and, in particular, the magnitude of underestimation of life expectancy that has characterized most official demographic forecasts in the last 20 to 30 years.[19] His more recent analyses take account of historical data on fluctuations in some of the principal variables likely to affect long-run fiscal forecasts—in particular, life expectancy and fertility.

The methodology can be described simply. Estimating stochastic time-series models for the principal demographic variables for the

---

[19]More recently, Oeppen and Vaupel (2002) have underscored past errors that contributed to an underestimation of longevity.

United States, Lee develops stochastic structural forecasting models for the key demographic and (more recently) economic variables, with the principal focus on capturing the historic variance in the error term for each variable. For the structural forecasts, Lee relies in most cases (the exception being mortality rates) on exogenous estimates of the central trend (or mean) of these variables made by authoritative agencies, including the Social Security Administration, the Congressional Budget Office, and the Health Care Financing Administration (now the Centers for Medicare & Medicaid Services). Given this information,

> The actual stochastic forecast is then carried out through stochastic simulation. A single stochastic trajectory is calculated by drawing random numbers to determine the forecast errors for the first year, which are then inserted in the appropriate equation for each input, along with the previous years' values, leading to a one step forecast. Then the forecasts of population and benefit costs are derived mechanically from these forecasts of inputs. Then a second round of random numbers is drawn to generate the second year of the forecast, and so on. In this way, one stochastic trajectory is forecast. We generate many such trajectories, generally at least a thousand, and then use the frequency distribution for outcomes of interest to estimate the probability distribution of the forecast. (Lee and Edwards, 2002, p. 164.)

Relying on formal demographic relationships allows for the generation of a population structure that evolves over time, characterized of course by the evolution of various key indicators relating to the age structure. Fiscal variables are then linked to these population estimates according to current data on expenditure per capita by age group. These are modified to the extent that expenditure per beneficiary is assumed to rise in some specified way. For example, this expenditure might rise in tandem with productivity growth, or perhaps at a higher rate based on historical experience, legislated policy, or best policy guesses by authorities (for example, with respect to the growth of medical costs per enrollee). Lee is thus able to link a given demographic outcome with a fiscal outcome for at least the age-sensitive fiscal variables. In more recent work, Lee and Miller (2002), Creedy and Alvarado (1998), Creedy and Scobie (2002), Davis and Fabling (2002), and the U.S. Congressional Budget Office (2001b) have extended the stochastic approach to include both empirical and Bayesian estimates of the variance of the error term, both for some key economic variables (productivity, the real interest rate, stock market returns) and for the gap between the rate of growth of medical care costs per enrollee and the rate of productivity growth. The U.S. CBO study assessed the long-term finances of the U.S. Social Security system using this technique.

The multiple outcomes associated with the many simulations allow the estimation of a probability distribution of fiscal outcomes. In effect, this allows for an assessment of outcomes associated with a specified confidence interval. Like deterministic long-term fiscal forecasts, this type of analysis lends itself to an evaluation of the impact of particular policy reforms on the estimated fiscal outcome, but with some sense of the range of outcomes that can emerge with a given confidence interval. Thus Lee is able to assert that, in the context of demographic uncertainty, one might observe the aging of the U.S. population to lead, by 2075, to the equilibrium payroll tax rate of Social Security (presently 12.4 percent) ranging from 14.6 percent to 36.5 percent within a 95 percent confidence interval, with a median of about 21.2 percent. Similarly, Lee's results suggest that the cost of Medicare as a fraction of GDP may vary, in 2075, between 5 percent and 26 percent, within a 95 percent confidence interval, with far greater uncertainty in the upward direction than in the lower (reflecting the asymptotic characteristics of log-normal probability distributions). Thus, policies that may work at the median or the mean may still have a high probability of being inadequate.

The strength and importance of the stochastic approach is that it allows the policymaker to obtain some handle on the likelihood of a particular fiscal outcome,[20] or, put another way, it facilitates an assessment of how much risk might be reduced *through policy*.[21] Thus it gives the policymaker a tool to judge how much of a policy adjustment might be necessary to provide a high degree of confidence that fiscal sustainability will be achieved, at least with respect to demographic variables. McFadden (2001, pp. 66–67) puts it well:

> Even more striking than the rapid rise in the elderly dependency rate and shift in economic resources to the elderly that are implied by expected patterns of fertility and mortality in the next fifty years is the uncertainty with which any of these forecasts can be made. A major contribution of Lee and Tuljapurkar is to provide machinery that quantifies that uncertainty and makes it clear that public policy on Social Security and Medicare must do more than just achieve positive expected balances. Their redesign must be sufficiently flexible and adaptive to ensure feasibility under a broad range of demographic outcomes.

---

[20] Lee and Tuljapurkar (2000, p. 53) suggest "that policies be viewed as filters which attenuate or amplify the consequences of variance and uncertainty...it should be straightforward to evaluate the success of different policies in dealing with uncertainty."

[21] Thus it would reveal that relating retirement age to life expectancy would reduce the risk of being out of balance in the long run even for a given median estimate of future imbalances.

The stochastic approach also allows the policymaker to gauge what are the key sources of uncertainty that matter at different points in the future in terms of the outcome for particular fiscal variables. For example, Lee suggests that the potential variability of fertility rates begins to make an enormous difference in outcomes as one moves further out into the future. The fertility rate will fundamentally determine the size of the school-age population, and thus expenditure on education, as well as the size of the labor force, which will determine real output. It will also affect the size of the potential contributor base for financing support for the elderly.

However, much more work is required to enhance the relevance of stochastic approaches to long-term fiscal issues. First, these techniques rely principally on exogenous forecasts of the mean trend for most of the central demographic and economic variables, while accepting fully the historical variance.[22] It may also be necessary to do more to capture the uncertainty about the central forecast of the mean. This is particularly the case if the structural developments expected in the future are such as would raise questions about the relevance of historical experience as a basis for assessing either the mean or the variance of future outcomes. Second, more emphasis is needed on analyses that go beyond the uncertainties associated with demographic variables, to capture the potential variability associated with underlying economic variables or with such highly sensitive policy variables as the rate of escalation of health care costs (relative to productivity growth). Other sources of uncertainty may also significantly influence fiscal outlays in coming decades.[23] Third, as was discussed in Box 2.3 in Chapter 2, uncertainty about future interest rates would need to be reflected, particularly in any presentation of net present value estimates.

Finally, the stochastic approach raises the important question of how policymakers should weight, in terms of a social utility framework, the relative probability of adverse outcomes. For example, suppose the current policy regime suggests a 70 percent probability that a given policy target, such as the level of social security reserves,

---

[22] As noted by Smith (2001, p. 71), the Lee approach "loves the variance and hates the mean," in effect rejecting the historical demographic data that suggest the level of future means while accepting the same data for determining the plausible variance of the error term in the future.

[23] Lee and Tuljapurkar (2000) also note that other important and uncertain variables (future disability rates, defense expenditure, the trajectory of transfer programs) are treated deterministically: "We have no good response to this objection. Perhaps these stochastic forecasts should be taken as indicating a lower bound on uncertainty about the future."

will be above a minimally acceptable level at a predetermined point in the future. This means that there is also a 30 percent probability that reserves will be below that minimally acceptable level. In formulating policies, how should policymakers judge a policy with such a probability of an unacceptable outcome? What probability of an unacceptable outcome is sufficiently low as to warrant the risks of a given policy?

General-Equilibrium Models of the Impact of Aging Populations

Within the last decade, a number of closed-economy OLG-GE models have been developed to assess the impact of an aging population on capital-labor ratios, real wage rates, living standards, interest rates, and the fiscal position (see, for example, Cutler and others, 1990; Miles, 1999; Miles and Cerny, 2001a, 2001b; Bohn, 1999). More recently, such models have been usefully extended to a multicountry context (McMorrow and Röger, 1999; Turner and others, 1998; Attanasio and Violante, 2000). The phenomenon of sharp fertility declines and increasing life expectancy characterizes virtually all of the industrial countries and, with a lag, some of the larger emerging market economies in Asia. A high proportion of world income is thus being generated in these countries today. An aging population is likely to lead to changes in a country's aggregate macroeconomic relationships—particularly in terms of saving and investment rates, labor force participation rates, and, ultimately, the rate of economic growth. Concurrent shifts in the age structure for this group of countries might thus be expected to give rise to swings in capital flows and current account balances, with effects on living standards, capital markets, growth rates, and interest rates in other regions of the world (see Heller and Symansky, 1998). Exchange rates may also be strongly affected. Turner and others (1998, p. 18) note that

> Examining the macroeconomic consequences of aging populations for a single economy is problematic because nearly all of the major economies will be experiencing major demographic changes in coming decades. The process of adjustment for any single economy—in particular, whether it takes place through changes in net foreign assets and exchange rates or through interest rates—depends on the extent and speed with which aging is taking place relative to the rest of the world.

In general such models rely on relatively simplified groupings of the world economy. For example, Turner and others (1998) aggregate countries into three groups: the OECD region, a fast-aging non-OECD region, and the rest of the world; Attanasio and Violante (2000) focus on the United States and the European Union as one region and Latin America as a second. The models seek to capture the fundamental changes in factor supply and production that would arise from the different starting points and demographic developments of the different regions. The fiscal sector is modeled to take account of current levels of public debt and a baseline trend for the public sector, given existing tax and transfer systems, but with constraints placed on the amount of public debt that can accumulate. Basic macroeconomic relationships concerning saving and investment and current account variables are also built into the model, with factor prices affected by movements in capital-labor ratios and the possibility of capital flows across regions.

Obviously, the results are sensitive to the assumptions made about the relationship between shifts in the demographic structure and some of the key macroeconomic variables, particularly saving and investment. Changes in assumptions about the impact of aging on labor force participation rates and employment as well as on migration can also affect the results.

The model results suggest the importance of taking a global view on how the aging of populations in the industrial and some nonindustrial countries will affect economic welfare within and across regions and across generations. Interest rates in particular are sensitive to the assumptions made. For example, Attanasio and Violante (2000) suggest that real interest rates would fall in the closed-economy case over time, where aging takes place in the three separate, closed economic regions. However, when capital flows across these regions are allowed, the reduction in rates is moderated. Wage rates prove sensitive to how much of a shift in the capital-labor ratio takes place, and to the effects of capital flows. The degree to which the aging process is synchronized across countries also affects factor price movements.

In Turner and others (1998) the impact on interest rates is contingent on the movement of global saving and investment balances. They note the pressures that will lead to a decline in both investment (reflecting the slower growth of the OECD region) and saving (with the aging of populations, a drawing down of assets, and increased government deficits). Their reference forecast suggests slightly greater downward pressure on saving rates, leading to only a small increase in world real interest rates (of about ½ percentage point) by 2050. In contrast, to the extent that fiscal reforms moderate the decline in public sector saving, real interest rates might be expected to fall by as much as 2½ percentage points by 2050.[24] Turner and others also note the likely swing in current account balances over time, with initial OECD current account surpluses gradually reversed by 2025–40 (and turning to deficits) and with the earlier buildup in OECD net foreign assets reversed. There is also a likelihood that the currencies of the OECD countries will appreciate over time. They observe that

> The magnitude of the swings in net foreign asset positions in both the reference and higher savings scenarios is considerably larger than has recently been experienced. This partly reflects the assumption of near perfect capital mobility, which underlies the model projections. Nevertheless, there are a number of factors suggesting that the past may not be a reliable guide to future developments...and that future changes in net foreign assets might, indeed, be larger than previously experienced. (Turner and others, 1998, p. 15)

Finally, the studies also highlight the likely differences in welfare that may be experienced across generations, as a function of their relative dependence on incomes from capital as opposed to labor.

An important conclusion of the study by Turner and others is that coordinated policy reforms could moderate the projected diminution in the growth of incomes per capita, all else being equal. Within the industrial countries, such coordination relates principally to the introduction of labor market reforms, deferral of the pensionable retirement age, and sustained fiscal consolidation that restrains the public debt. Within non-OECD, nonaging regions, both the study by Attanasio and Violante and that by Turner and others emphasize the importance of policies that create conditions conducive to growth and, in particular, improve the capacity of financial markets to absorb saving (both foreign and domestic) and provide opportunities for remunerative investment.

From the perspective of long-term fiscal policy, these models can shed light on the potential feedback effects on critical fiscal variables,

---

[24]Not wholly comparable, but still worth considering, is an earlier study by Masson and Tryon (1990) using the IMF MULTIMOD general-equilibrium model. Although the authors focused narrowly on the impact of a change in the age structure and ignored the effects of a continued slowdown in population growth, they found that interest rates might rise progressively beyond 2015, by 3 percentage points for the United States and 5 percentage points for Japan.

because the aging of the population in any country does not occur in a vacuum. Such variables as interest rates, which are a critical element in any sustainability analysis, are thus influenced by these global trends, and possibly by the concurrent efforts in individual countries to address the fiscal consequences of their aging populations. The study by Turner and others clearly suggests that a coordinated effort by all countries with aging populations to increase fiscal balances and private sector saving rates may dampen interest rates on a global basis, in effect raising the bar on the amount of prefunding that might be needed to finance public retirement commitments or private funded schemes. Thus, these models would be relevant in clarifying long-term scenarios or in calibrating stochastic models in terms of their assumptions about interest rates. The studies also illuminate the impact that policy reforms might have if they were coordinated and implemented in a number of the industrial countries with aging populations.

Yet one must also emphasize that few studies of this kind are available. Moreover, the lack of clarity in the results on key variables, particularly interest rates, suggests that this is a line of research still needing further work. One ambitious effort, presently under way by Ralph Bryant, Warwick McKibbin, and a number of collaborators in Australia, Japan, the United States, and the United Kingdom, among others, may prove productive, not least because it has been extended to take account of climate change considerations (Bryant and McKibbin, 2001).

"Futures" Studies

Finally, another category of long-term analysis is typically qualitative in character but can yield interesting insights. "Futures" studies attempt to identify the key long-term forces that will bear on a country, whether those forces are of a security, demographic, economic, or even climatic nature. For example, every several years the U.S. Central Intelligence Agency carries out an exercise to consider the possible political, economic, security, and technology situation 15 years into the future (U.S. CIA, 2001a, 2001b). It also analyzes the nature of long-term demographic challenges. Such studies, which are carried out with much interdisciplinary input, can provide a useful forum for thinking about issues that may not yet be on the screens of fiscal economists, let alone budget analysts.

Domestic Budget Processes

Prevailing Practices

In recent years a number of industrial country governments have moved to incorporate a medium-term fiscal framework within the formal budget process. This may include the setting of aggregate budget targets for a three- and sometimes a five-year period. OECD sources suggest that the following governments have moved to or will soon place their budgets within such a framework (see the 2000 or 2001 *OECD Economic Survey* for each country; the number of years forward is noted in parentheses): Australia (4), Austria (2), Canada (5), Denmark (8), France (4), Germany (general government, 5), Japan (3), Korea (3), the Netherlands (4), New Zealand (10 and occasionally longer), Sweden (3 to 5), the United Kingdom (5), and the United States (5).[25] Such medium-term budgeting involves setting either broad objectives for the major budget aggregates (government spending, tax receipts, debt service, transfers, gross or net debt) or more explicit targets.

Most country authorities stress (often within their official budget documents) that population aging is a factor motivating policies to at least limit, if not reduce, the government's net debt. Yet in most countries the integration of long-term issues into the budget framework is implicit at best and absent more generally. Issues of uncertainty rarely enter the discussion. Longer-term projections are equally unusual in that there is no reconciliation between the prospect of an unsustainable long-term budget position and the short- to medium-run budget stance.

Four countries—Australia, New Zealand, the United Kingdom, and the United States—stand out for their consideration of long-term issues. But even in these countries the extent of integration is quite limited.[26] Only in Australia, New Zealand, and the United Kingdom is formal consideration of long-term factors, at least in principle, a minimal requirement in the budget process.

---

[25]Canada presents its five-year fiscal projections in the context of private sector forecasts, with a systematic downward revision of these forecasts to ensure a prudent stance (Blöndal, 2001b). However, budgetary spending decisions are not made within a medium-term framework. Sweden's multiyear budget framework is for three years, but agencies are expected to provide forecasts for four years beyond the current budget year (Blöndal, 2001a). For Japan see Japan, Ministry of Finance (2001).

[26]For example, long-term assessments of social insurance programs, when carried out at all, principally reflect actuarial requirements associated with funded schemes (the U.S. Social Security Administration being an exception, given its largely PAYGO character).

The United Kingdom, under its Code for Fiscal Stability, requires the government to publish illustrative long-term projections covering a period of at least 10 years. In recent years it has published 30-year projections (United Kingdom, Her Majesty's Treasury, 2000, 2001b). These are indeed illustrative, demonstrating what level of current consumption of goods and services would be compatible with an acceptable revenue share of GDP. The consumption path must also be consistent with the fiscal rules. These require both a balanced current budget—the "Golden Rule"—and a sustainable overall net debt limit (see below) and take account of the projected path of transfer outlays (principally for the social security program). Generational accounting estimates are also made on an occasional basis, as are long-term actuarial analyses of the government's pension funds. In late 2002, the U.K. Treasury (2002) issued its first *Long Term Public Finance Report*, providing a "comprehensive analysis of long-term economic and demographic developments, and their likely impact on the public finances" (p. 1). This report is envisaged to be published on an annual basis.

Under New Zealand's Fiscal Responsibility Act, the government is mandated, in its annual Fiscal Strategy Report (presented at the time of the annual budget; New Zealand Treasury, 1995, 2001b), to take account of long-term factors. In practice, the way in which long-term considerations are integrated within the short-term budget process is still evolving. For example, the legislation is not explicit as to the definition of the long term (Janssen, 2001). Explicit consideration is given to projections of at least 10 years, in order to demonstrate that the overall budget framework is consistent with long-term policy objectives. A long-term fiscal model has been developed within the New Zealand Treasury to make these projections.[27]

The New Zealand case illustrates well both an advanced approach to integrating long-term considerations into the annual budget process and the limits to such an approach. For example, one important development in 2001 was the establishment of the New Zealand Superannuation Fund (NZSF). This seeks to prefund in part the public pension scheme, building up a pool of financial assets separate from the government's gross debt target (McCulloch and Frances, 2001). The NZSF is deliberately flexible in its design, allowing for potential increases or decreases in the prefunding contribution rate, depending on evolving perspectives on its adequacy in relation to future

---

[27]As an analytical product, the long-term fiscal model is clearly evolving in complexity; presently it is a simple deterministic projection model without feedback.

public pension obligations. Other aspects of the long-term picture (notably the health consequences of an aging population) have not yet been integrated, however. Still less developed is a clear procedural linkage within the annual budget process to force the results of long-term projections to be explicitly considered in deciding on the annual budget target. Presently such issues are raised only on an ad hoc basis.

Australia's "Charter of Budget Honesty" requires the government to present a medium-term fiscal strategy with each budget. Also required is a longer-term intergenerational report "to assess the long-term sustainability of current Government policies over the 40 years following the release of the report, including by taking account of the financial implications of demographic change" (Australia, Commonwealth of, 2002). The focus is on prudent levels of debt and contingent liabilities, as well as on a reasonable degree of stability and predictability in the tax burden. One goal is to ensure that policy decisions take account of their financial effects on future generations and that "future generations do not face an unmanageable bill for government services provided to the current generation" (Australia, Commonwealth of, 2002, p. 2). A strong net worth position is also seen as an objective, again to address issues of aging.

The first intergenerational report was issued in 2002. With a heavy focus on the impact of demographic trends on pensions, health care, and long-term care costs, 40-year fiscal projections were carried out. Alternative scenarios were assessed, relating principally to demographic trends and rates of growth of health care costs. For other types of expenditure, constancy in the expenditure shares was assumed. No effort was made to consider the impact of fiscal deficits beyond the 40-year time horizon. Environmental issues received little attention, although the recent droughts and wildfires in Australia may indicate that such issues pose significant fiscal risks.

In the United States, aspects of the budget system at least "inform" the budget process, on an ad hoc basis, about long-term issues. However, these are not an explicit part of the process.[28] Specifically, the budget, as proposed by the executive branch, is set within a 5-year framework. Although not required by law, the president's budget includes 75-year projections in the stewardship section of the "Analytical Perspectives" volume; these assume continuation of current policies as well as a discussion of the government's balance sheet, which includes some liabilities not yet included in the primary budget

---

[28]See the World Wide Web site of the U.S. Senate Committee on the Budget.

data. The stewardship section of the financial statements contains information intended to facilitate the assessment of the long-term sustainability of social insurance programs (see U.S. General Accounting Office, 2003, p. 38). The U.S. CBO, as part of its mandate, routinely carries out baseline analyses for a 75-year fiscal projection period. This complements the regular reports carried out by the Social Security Administration and the Centers for Medicare and Medicaid Services.

Until recently, the congressional budget process (through its budget reconciliation procedures) included steps to ensure that budgetary and tax policies were consistent with targets set for the overall budget deficit over a five-year period, as prescribed by congressional resolution.[29] However, the expiration of the Budget Enforcement Act has meant that there is no longer a formal reconciliation of long-term goals in the congressional budget process.

Other countries are moving in similar directions in terms of extending the horizon of budget analyses. In Denmark targets have been set through 2010 relating to both the budget balance and growth in public consumption. Sweden's Multi-Year Budget Framework explicitly includes binding ceilings on expenditure, on a rolling basis, for three years. These aggregative ceilings are based on conservative economic assumptions, and any excesses in revenue that emerge are "made available" for a more accelerated reduction of debt rather than used to fund new spending measures. In addition, in setting the indicative level of funding for each of 27 expenditure areas, total funding is put at less than the maximum level of total expenditure, with increasing margins for the second and third years of the forecast.[30] The objective is to "provide a buffer against forecasting errors so that the maximum level of total expenditure approved by Parliament will not have to be amended" (Blöndal, 2001a, p. 31). In Canada the government has "established a significant contingency reserve," which may only be used to compensate for forecast errors and unanticipated events, and not for new policy initiatives. "Recourse has never had to be made to the contingency reserve funds and they have been applied to deficit reduction (surplus) in their entirety in each year" (Blöndal, 2001b, p. 46).

---

[29]This can have odd results, as Paul Krugman often noted in his *New York Times* columns in the course of 2001. Specifically, it can have knife-edge results where tax policies lapse at the end of a period, or where the choice of the first year or subsequent year of a projection period can mask many sins.

[30]The margin is programmed to rise from 1.5 percent in year 1 to 2 percent in year 2 and 2.5 percent in year 3 (Blöndal, 2001a).

Before concluding this section, a quite separate but potentially important exercise in long-term forecasting should be noted. Governments, as part of their obligations under the 1994 Rio Treaty relating to climate change, are expected to prepare national climate change assessment reports. In addition to reviewing the country's efforts at mitigating carbon emissions, the reports are expected to comment both on the potential impact of climate change on the various sectors of the economy and on policy actions taken to foster adaptation. A number of governments have begun to issue such reports, and to a limited extent these include a discussion on potential sectoral effects, corresponding to the alternative climate change scenarios discussed by the Intergovernmental Panel on Climate Change. Most are thus of a very hypothetical character—reflecting the considerable range of uncertainty in the panel's projections—and do not go beyond a qualitative characterization of the impact on particular economic sectors. None of the reports issued to date includes any significant discussion of the possible fiscal implications. However, this process offers the potential for the fiscal consequences of climate change eventually to be linked to budget projections.

Adaptations to Government Accounting Systems

Another trend that is very slowly developing momentum relates to the reform of government accounting practices to ensure that governments are forced to disclose the accrual of implicit as well as explicit liabilities. Such commitments may prove to be as substantial as the amount of government debt formally on the books. For example, the IMF's Fiscal Transparency Code calls on governments to provide, in their annual budgets, a statement of fiscal risks and, if possible, a quantification of the potential fiscal cost of such risks. Box 2.3 in Chapter 2 illustrated the number of ways in which governments may incur commitments that have the character of debt but are not recorded under prevailing cash accounting systems (see also Brixi and Mody, 2002). By moving to an accrual accounting system, governments would be forced to disclose these implicit obligations. The issues involved in providing such estimates are complex, given the varying forms in which commitments may arise, the extent to which they are implicit or explicit, and the problems that arise in determining when a commitment should be treated as binding. As a result, governments have adopted a patchwork of practices to address different elements of the problem.

For example, some countries have sought to quantify the cost of contingent liabilities or state-provided guarantees. Schick's (2002b, 2002c) recent surveys of such practices suggest that they differ, even within a country, according to the type of commitment. Certain kinds of contingent liabilities may be treated differently from others, and some forms of implicit debt may not be treated at all. For example, Schick notes that New Zealand appends to its budget a statement of quantifiable and nonquantifiable contingent liabilities. Although such costs are not recorded in the budget or on the balance sheet, they constitute an alert to the government of prospective payments arising out of contingent liabilities. The United States has taken a different approach, but only with respect to loans and guarantees, where the subsidy cost of a government guarantee is directly provided for in its budget appropriations (Schick, 2002c) at the time that a direct loan is obligated or a loan guarantee commitment is made. The focus of the Netherlands, in contrast, is on guarantees, with the full value of new guarantees (rather than expected payouts) treated directly as expenditure. Hungary limits state guarantees to a certain fraction of budgeted expenditure and publishes information on both estimated risk and the reasons for tendering the guarantee.

In the area of social insurance, there is a movement among public accounting experts to quantify the annual accrual of social benefit obligations by a government (for example, with respect to a defined-benefit, PAYGO type of scheme). Such an approach already appears to be the standard practice of some governments with respect to civil service employee pension schemes (OECD, 2001c).[31] Conceptually, broadening this treatment to social insurance programs appears straightforward. A nation's workforce may be accruing obligations from the government with respect to a statutory social pension scheme. For each year in which payroll contributions have been made, a worker would be entitled to assert that an obligation has accrued, upon the worker's reaching a predetermined eligibility age, to add to the amount of pension

---

[31] In fact, few central governments provide comprehensive data on such obligations. A *Financial Times* editorial on pensions in the United Kingdom (Ewald, 2002b) noted that "the figures are hard to come by, but the various unfunded (or 'notionally funded') plans—for the civil service, teachers, health service and so forth—were last revealed to Parliament as having liabilities of £350bn in March 2001. Accelerated inflation of public sector pay must be pushing the aggregate rapidly higher, to a figure which may soon exceed the published National Debt, which was £425bn at that date...." "The government has made sure that public sector funded schemes are not required to submit themselves to the solvency tests, such as the statutory Minimum Funding Requirement or the accountants' new pensions standards FRS 17" (Riley, 2002).

income to be received as a consequence of that year's contributions and work effort. Should not the net present value of that additional pension income, over that worker's retirement, be recorded in the government's balance sheet as a government debt obligation? Extending this argument, suppose a worker retires and begins receiving a social pension from the government. Should not the government quantify, as a debt liability, the net present value of the full pension obligations to this worker over his or her expected lifetime?

An even stronger case could be made where a government provides public medical insurance to retired workers. Should not those workers' annual payroll contributions be assumed to give rise to some quantitatively proportional obligation by the government to provide future medical care? Should this not be quantified in analogous fashion and included as an accrued obligation on the government's balance sheet?

Despite the logic of these arguments, governments do not typically account for such obligations on their balance sheets, in part because there remains significant disagreement among experts on public sector accounting about the appropriate treatment of such obligations. The complexity of taking account of such obligations arises from several factors: the fact that benefit formulas are often sufficiently complex so as not to lend themselves to measuring annual accrual values; the difficulty of making assumptions about the likely value of benefits (particularly in such areas as medical care); and the variability in the measure of the debt that arises depending on the assumed discount rate. For example, does the event that creates the government's liability occur when the individual meets the eligibility criteria for the benefit, or before? Similarly, should the amount of the government's obligation reflect an estimate of the current period's entitlement or the present value of all expected future benefits as determined on an actuarial basis? What interest rate is appropriate for discounting the future liabilities to current pension scheme participants?[32]

Perhaps because of these complexities, measures of contingent liabilities or provisions on the balance sheet do not presently include any estimates of such potential liabilities (International Federation of

---

[32]This issue became particularly relevant in 2001–02, when the decline in market interest rates sharply escalated the present value of private sector liabilities under defined-benefit schemes. With equity prices low, U.K. and U.S. corporations have found that their asset holdings are proving insufficient in value relative to their pension liabilities, forcing increased contributions to right these imbalances. This has led the U.S. Treasury to propose revised rules on what is the appropriate interest rate to use for discounting such long-term obligations (see Walsh, 2003).

Accountants, 2001),[33] although efforts are under way by the Public Sector Committee of the International Federation of Accountants to agree on an approach for treating public sector social benefit obligations in the public accounts. At most, some governments may include measures of such obligations as memoranda items in the presentation of the budget (or on the balance sheet if one is presented).

Even beyond these important accounting questions, issues of credibility remain in considering how to account for future obligations. When a government's formal obligations are clearly going to be excessive and unaffordable, should they nevertheless be measured as if they will occur?

For systems of social insurance that are on a defined-benefit basis, the financial viability of the system depends on the sources of income available to the government for financing its payments and on the demographic dynamics of the future beneficiary population. This rests on the capacity of a government to levy taxes and on the relevant tax bases, and these are very much contingent on the future size of the labor force and the growth of the economy. Such information will not be captured in a given year by simply estimating the growth in accrued obligations to the current working population. More specifically, for many social insurance schemes in many industrial countries, the "hardness" of the government's commitment to pay out benefits long into the future may be suspect, given the doubts that may surround the feasibility of higher tax rates or future growth in the payroll tax base. Enshrining the accrued obligations in the balance sheet has the benefit of signaling their size and the imbalances that may arise. But the cost of this is to harden the government's obligations and popular expectations, making reform of a financially unbalanced system more difficult.

Conversely, when a government's accounting of its commitments appears unrealistically low—for example, as would be implied if current

---

[33]Social benefits are defined by the International Federation of Accountants (IFAC) to refer to goods, services, and other benefits provided in the pursuit of the social policy objectives of government. These benefits may include the delivery of health, education, housing, transport, and other social services to the community, where, in many cases, there is no requirement for the beneficiaries to pay an amount equivalent to the cost of these services; they may also include payment of benefits to families, the aged, the disabled, the unemployed, veterans, and others to access services to meet their particular needs or to supplement their income. IFAC notes that the need for, and the nature and supply of, goods and services to meet social policy obligations will often depend on a range of demographic and social conditions that are difficult to predict. A key criterion in presently excluding these benefits is that the public sector entity providing the benefit receives no, or only nominal, consideration directly from the benefit recipients or, where there is no direct relationship, between the charge and the benefit received (IFAC, 2001).

U.K. state pension policies were to remain unchanged several decades into the future—a different problem arises. It would be inappropriate for a government to indicate that its policies are unlikely to be sustainable by valuing liabilities at a higher, perhaps more realistic level. But, equally, valuing liabilities under current policies probably understates the potential magnitude of future fiscal pressures. These issues already are posing difficulties in the private financial sector. The U.K. Financial Services Authority (2002, p. 6) recently emphasized the risks to insurance companies associated with the possible mispricing, on their balance sheets, of long-term annuity products, as a consequence of the possible understatement of longevity risks based on historical experience: "Any possible mismanagement or mispricing of this longevity and long term investment risk could pose a threat to firms' solvency." The same risks could be associated with a government's current provisioning policies.

Lessons to Be Learned

This discussion suggests that only a few countries have had experience with taking account of long-term fiscal issues in the annual budget process. It is thus difficult to draw many lessons about the value of doing this or of ways of doing it better. Several pragmatic observations can nevertheless be drawn, both from experience and from the small literature available. First, for some issues such as pension reform, forecasts in the public domain both catalyze public debate and crystallize issues in the formulation of fiscal policy. Witness the following quotation from a recent commentary on public finances by the European Commission Directorate-General for Economic and Financial Affairs (2001, p. 88):

> A broad concept of sustainable public finances is therefore needed which goes beyond simply avoiding structural deficits and the accumulation of public debt; sustainability also entails keeping the tax burden at reasonable levels and ensuring that non–age-related expenditures are not crowded out by increased spending on pensions and health care. Indicators could also be developed to identify whether current budget targets are sufficiently ambitious in terms of debt reductions and/or the accumulation of reserve funds to avoid future increases in the tax burden or cuts in non–age-related expenditures, measures which could be detrimental in terms of intergenerational fairness.

Second, forecasting results continue to be problematic. Studies that have compared actual with forecast medium-term outcomes suggest the high degree of error possible. In a recent budget outlook, the U.S. CBO (2001a, p. 93) noted that

> If the future record is like the past, there is about a 50 percent chance that ...errors [in the assumptions about economic and technical factors] will cause CBO's projection of the total budget surplus for the coming fiscal year to miss the actual outcome by more than 0.9 percent of GDP and its projection of the annual surplus for five years to miss by more than 1.8 percent of GDP...10 year projections are likely to be less accurate than five year forecasts.... The outlook for the budget can best be described...as a fan of probabilities around those [forecast] numbers. That fan widens as the projection extends.... [N]earby projections...have nearly the same probability as the baseline projections.... Moreover, projections...quite different from the baseline also have a significant probability of coming to pass.

The obvious question, then, is whether a forecast's accuracy should be the benchmark by which to judge its utility. The unsatisfactory quality of forecasts arises in part from the assumptions that are forced on them, such as the typical assumption of unchanged policies. Combined with sensitivity to the starting point, the likelihood of outcomes suggesting an ever-rising or an ever-falling debt is unavoidable.

A third lesson is the weak link between long-term projections and balance sheet assessments of a government's liabilities.[34] Projections typically force an evaluation of the possible magnitude of future expenditure, whether on age-related outlays or for other purposes. Most are presented on a "present policies" basis and do not anticipate the effect of policy reforms. In contrast, few governments today prepare a balance sheet. As noted above, current public accounting norms remain deficient in their treatment of many types of accrued liabilities, and a variety of practices can be observed.

A fourth observation is that governments find it difficult, in carrying out long-term forecasting exercises, to provide financially for events or developments that could have extremely important fiscal implications but that might have only a small probability of occurring. These developments may be political, or they may be related to climate change or to security issues.

Finally, lessons drawn by three experienced practitioners of long-run budget forecasting—Henry Aaron, Rudolph Penner, and Allen Schick—give pause for thought; these lessons are distilled in Box 3.1. Penner and Aaron, at least, argue that neither the uncertainty associ-

---

[34]This issue has been implicitly raised in a recent report to the IMF (2002b) on sustainability.

ated with forecasts nor the degree of error involved negates the need to carry out such forecasts and include them in the budget. Rather, the amount of uncertainty needs to be considered as an issue in itself. This relates both to the consequences of possible adverse outcomes and to the costs associated with deferring action in order to accumulate more information and reduce uncertainty. Penner and Aaron also emphasize that long-term forecasts should not blind policymakers to the need for policy reform. They emphasize that public authorities should be prepared to change, as needed, the methodology underlying their forecasts, even if doing so might result in frequent changes in the forecasts.

Multilateral Surveillance of Government Budgets

Countries that are members of the IMF, the OECD, or the European Union must, as a condition of membership, submit to an annual surveillance assessment of their economy. These assessments may include analyses of the medium- to long-run sustainability of the country's fiscal position.

Perhaps the most relevant fiscal surveillance to date is that conducted by the European Union, whose member countries are expected to submit each year their Stability and Convergence Programmes (SCPs) for consideration by the EU Economic and Financial Council (EcoFin). The objective is to assess whether a country is complying with the terms of the SGP. Since the meeting of the EU heads of state in Stockholm in March 2001, countries have been asked to provide information on long-term issues, although it is left to each member to decide how and even whether to do so. It was agreed that EcoFin:

> Should regularly review the long-term sustainability of public finances, including the expected strains caused by the demographic changes ahead. This should be done under the guidelines [that is, the Broad Economic Policy Guidelines] and in the context of Stability and Convergence Programmes. (Cited in European Commission, 2002a, p. 48.)

EcoFin has also recently asked member countries to participate in analytical exercises to obtain a uniform cross-country perspective on long-term issues, notably with respect to the likely consequences of aging populations for expenditures on health, pensions, and long-term care (using common demographic and economic assumptions).

In effect, a multilateral surveillance process provides a form of peer-group pressure to require countries to consider long-term issues within

---

**Box 3.1. Forecasting, Budgeting, and Addressing the Long Run:
The Perspectives of Henry Aaron, Rudolph Penner,
and Allen Schick**

The problems

- Forecasts are poor. Analyses are often based on different and, at times, inconsistent models. Delays in implementation are not correctly anticipated, and long lags occur between recognizing the need for policy change and implementing that change. Reversing incorrect policies can be costly. Politically, there may only be occasional windows of opportunity to initiate important policy reforms (Aaron, 2000).
- Budget forecasts and projections are always wrong, often significantly (in the United States, by as much as 2 percent of GDP). This is increasingly the case in the medium term, looking 3 to 5 years ahead, and is even truer for a 10-year period. Often there is serial correlation in the forecast errors, both for revenue and for outlays (Penner, 2001).
- Important structural changes in relationships among variables may go unrecognized for many years, during which forecasting errors are all likely to move in the same direction. Forecasters tend to assume that values will return to some historical norm, but that return to "normalcy" can take much longer than expected (Penner, 2001).
- Meaningful evidence is usually required before a significant change in forecasting techniques or assumptions can be introduced (in order to avoid erratic forecasts). Techniques and assumptions therefore change more slowly than the evidence would support, and errors persist (Penner, 2001).
- The failure to budget properly for contingent liabilities induces governments to substitute guarantees for conventional expenditures and to take risks that may imbalance future budgets (Schick, 2002a, 2002b).
- Although politicians are nominally in control of policies, they get blamed for matters over which they have little genuine control (Schick, 2002a, 2002b).
- An increase in the time horizon of the budget to five years or more might reduce the realism of budget projections. Expanding the time frame both extends the number of years and changes the perspective, transforming the central fiscal issue from current balance to future sustainability and the vulnerability of the budget to surprises and shocks (Schick, 2002a, 2002b).
- Rules matter when politicians are predisposed to act in a fiscally disciplined manner, by making it easier for them to resist spending demands. They fortify politicians who want to be fiscally prudent, but they do not stand in the way of those who are determined to spend more than the rules allow (Schick, 2002a, 2002b).

- National governments may be sandwiched between supranational and subnational governments and left with little room for action. They may be beholden to decisions made by others (Schick, 2002a, 2002b).

Policy suggestions
- Policymakers need to appreciate how prone to error forecasts actually are and to recognize that models may be wrong. They need to weigh the reliability of projections and take account of the time it takes to implement a new policy, the ease with which new policies may be reversed, the ease of future relative to current action, and the uncertain economic and political consequences of current action or inaction (Aaron, 2000).
- Formal analysis of how uncertainty in data and forecasts would affect policy recommendations deserves a high priority among policy analysts and academics (Aaron, 2000).
- Policymakers should not permit the availability of forecasts to obscure fundamental policy questions that are important in any policy scenario (Aaron, 2000).
- Policymakers should design policies with built-in flexibility that respond automatically to diverse possible outcomes (Aaron, 2000).
- Where built-in flexibility is impossible, complete analyses should consider the consequences of incorrect forecasts, of postponing action until information improves, and of other policies under the plausible range of outcomes (Aaron, 2000; Penner, 2001).
- Policymakers should take advantage of opportunities to experiment, particularly when the costs of error may be small and the potential gains quick and large (Aaron, 2000).
- When information about the current situation is not very good, and forecasts far into the future are unreliable, policymakers should delay action in order to establish whether or not the action is needed and, if so, to ensure that it can be justified to a skeptical population (Aaron, 2000).
- Policymakers should deemphasize forecasts produced for the second 5 years of a 10-year forecast period (Penner, 2001).
- Concerning contingent liabilities, the most sensible option is to provide for estimated losses from guarantees on the government's balance sheet (Schick, 2002b).
- If actual losses diverge from the estimate, the amount provisioned against such losses should be adjusted to reflect this (Schick, 2002a, 2002b).
- Class-based budgets will need to be prepared in the future covering major fissures in society: men versus women, rich versus poor, young versus old. National budgets will be flash points for social conflict (Schick, 2002a, 2002b).

- A rule that fortifies political will is one that bars actions, requires actions to be reviewed by an independent entity, or raises the political cost of acting relative to the benefits (Schick, 2002a, 2002b).
- Governments need to estimate systematically the risks they have incurred and to set aside funds for such contingencies. New systems will need to be devised to supplement conventional budget practices in this regard (Schick, 2002a, 2002b).

their budget process. For the European Union this pressure is stronger because it derives directly from a framework of fiscal rules, giving it a lever to strengthen budget processes that is not available to either the OECD or the IMF. Such a process has already gone beyond issues of demographics. The most recent European Commission report on public finances also emphasized the danger of the recent securitization of nonfinancial assets. It noted that, by advancing revenue flows earmarked for the future, such securitizations have the same effect as deficit spending, forcing larger budgetary adjustments in subsequent years to respect the medium-term balanced budget objective (European Commission, 2002a, p. 12).

The IMF has also attached increasing importance to the issue of sustainability. Although sustainability assessments have been undertaken in the context of the IMF's general surveillance efforts under Article IV of its Articles of Agreement, they have understandably been more intensely focused on those countries receiving IMF financial support, and on emerging market countries. Such assessments of fiscal sustainability have principally focused on medium-term (3- to 15-year) fiscal projections as well as on indicators of public debt and deficits. At times, longer-term assessments are made as well.[35] Stress tests are increasingly included. Also, calculations of the level of primary fiscal surplus that would stabilize the debt are often used as a benchmark to assess the sustainability of current fiscal policy.

Assessments of contingent liabilities have also received considerable attention, particularly in the context of IMF programs.[36] Although

---

[35]For example, see the recent analyses associated with IMF Article IV consultations in Belgium (Zhou, 2003) and Denmark (Eskesen, 2002).

[36]Such liabilities may be explicit, taking the form of publicly guaranteed debt. Also germane is debt of lower levels of government or of public corporations that has not been formally guaranteed. Such debt may become a contingent liability of the central government in a financial crisis. Equally, the central government may have to absorb other obligations of the private sector in the event of a significant financial shock (for example, when there is actual or implicit deposit insurance that extends beyond the public sector).

these assessments have been important elements of IMF program and surveillance analyses, it is recognized that there remains considerable room for improvement and that many past IMF assessments have proved overoptimistic. Box 3.2, excerpted from a recent IMF study, summarizes some suggested good practices for realistic fiscal sustainability assessments.

Recently, the IMF has recommended that its economists strengthen their approach to fiscal and external sustainability assessments by taking a more probabilistic approach (IMF, 2002b). Specifically, in addition

---

Box 3.2. IMF Views on Good Practices for Realistic Fiscal Sustainability Assessments

The following suggested good practices for realistic fiscal sustainability assessments are taken from a recent IMF study, *Assessing Sustainability* (IMF, 2002b, pp. 20–21):

"Sustainability analyses should not be based on assumptions that by themselves solve the debt sustainability problem...other than in the very exceptional cases.

"While the baseline projection may be predicated on policy actions and market outcomes, risks associated with exogenous variables should be balanced between the up- and downside. Moreover, sensitivity tests should be designed in such a way that risks on both sides are adequately examined.

"The sustainability assessment should be based on the fiscal measures needed to achieve the projected debt path. It is difficult to assess the feasibility of the primary surplus consistent with debt sustainability without first specifying the tax and expenditure measures that would be needed to achieve it, and judging whether these measures are sustainable over time, both technically and politically.

"Assumptions about fiscal policies should generally be in line with economic behavior. Revenue elasticities should be realistic.... Revenues from natural resources should be based on conservative long-term price forecasts.

"Large projected changes in revenue or expenditure ratios should generally be based on revenue and expenditure policy measures or tangible changes in the environment, and not on efficiency gains in tax administration or expenditure or on revenue windfalls.

"The assessment should include an examination of the authorities' planned financing policies.... Financing amounts from each source should be projected and associated risks assessed.

"Financing plans should be consistent with [reasonable] medium-term monetary and external sector projections.

"The impact of large real exchange rate changes on the level and dynamics of public debt needs to become a standard part of the core sensitivity test."

to a central medium-term scenario (with well-specified assumptions), it has proposed a number of sensitivity or stress tests to evaluate the implications of alternative assumptions about policy variables, macroeconomic developments, and costs of financing. Looking backward over the past 10 years, these assess what would have been the consequences if key parameters or variables either had been close to their previous historical averages or had experienced shocks of one or two standard deviations from the baseline for a limited period (say, one or two years). The impact of other possible shocks, either to the exchange rate or to the public debt ratio, is also expected to be explored. The objective would be to assess the effect of a major depreciation of the currency or an unanticipated exogenous increase in the debt ratio due to the realization of an unforeseen contingent liability. The framework calls for 10-year forecasts: "long horizons would help guard against excessive euphoria about a country's growth prospects following a growth spurt" (IMF, 2002b, p. 33).

Ultimately, this new approach seeks to judge whether current trends and policies are likely to be sustainable over a 10-year period, taking account of key macroeconomic and financial variables and possible risk factors. However, unlike the EU approach, the proposed framework does *not* attempt to assess whether longer-term factors might have a bearing in deciding what fiscal policy stance should be adopted over the medium term. Nor do the assessments consider the question of long-term sustainability.

The multilateral institutions have made another important contribution to stimulating consideration of long-term issues in the budget process. In developing standards and codes on fiscal transparency and budgeting, they have included elements that effectively encourage governments to address such issues. For example, the IMF's Code of Good Practices on Fiscal Transparency (IMF, 2001b) and, even more, its associated fiscal transparency manual (IMF, 2001c) provide a standard for good practice on fiscal transparency. The code calls for a clarification of the broad objectives of fiscal policy and, preferably, a quantitative characterization of the sustainability of fiscal policy over the long term. It notes the importance of assessing whether the buildup of debt has become excessive, calls for assessing contingent liabilities and implicit debt, and suggests the need to identify and quantify, if possible, the "major fiscal risks." More specifically, the manual suggests that countries should assess the budgetary implications of demographic change, looking 10 to 40 years ahead, and specify clearly the assumptions underlying the projections and the range of plausible scenarios.

The manual also identifies a set of best practices, which are principally used as a benchmark for fiscal transparency assessments in the more advanced economies. Specifically, it suggests that aggregate fiscal projections for 5 to 10 years ahead be provided in the budget documentation; that a full government balance sheet be published as part of the budget documentation; and that a long-term fiscal report assessing the sustainability of current fiscal practices be published every five years.

The OECD's code on budget transparency (OECD, 2001b) provides a "best practice approach" calling for governments to provide a long-term report at least every five years, with more frequent assessments if there are major revenue or expenditure changes. These reports would be expected to specify the assumptions underlying any long-term analysis and examine alternative scenarios. The OECD code advocates that, in addition to public debt, policy commitments with significant future financial impacts, including unfunded public pension liabilities, be taken into account in any budgeting exercise.

Presently, in the cases of the IMF and the OECD, the linkage between "surveillance" and the respective fiscal transparency code is indirect at best. Countries are urged to adhere to the codes on a *voluntary* basis. At most, each institution's surveillance exercise may urge governments to move in the direction of adopting the code.[37] Also of note, the private sector is producing fiscal transparency assessments of emerging markets against the IMF's code, with particular attention to whether information is disclosed on fiscal risks. Over time, these various assessment practices might help to bring about more focus by governments on risk and sustainability.

Addressing Long-Term Concerns Through Aggregate Fiscal Policy

A number of governments have begun to rely on aggregate fiscal policy over the medium to long term to address concerns about heavier fiscal burdens in the future, notably those associated with aging populations. The heart of the argument is that, by running balanced budgets or surpluses, governments would be able to progressively

---

[37]Almost 50 fiscal transparency assessments had been carried out as of March 2003 by countries in collaboration with the IMF. Among other things, these publicly assess how adequately countries are disclosing information on fiscal risks (and, to a lesser extent, fiscal sustainability).

reduce or eliminate their public debt, thus providing themselves additional budgetary leeway as a consequence of reduced debt-service costs. They would thus be able to accommodate the expected higher expenditure requirements associated with commitments with respect to pensions, medical care, and long-term care residential services. Beyond that, if after retiring the debt a government went on to accumulate assets, it would be able to supplement its revenue with investment earnings, thus in effect providing some prefunding of future outlays.

In some cases, "fiscal rules" have been devised and enacted to enhance the capacity of policymakers to maintain the necessary budgetary discipline to sustain such a strengthened aggregate fiscal stance. This section describes the principal fiscal rules that have been adopted and the institutional mechanisms used to support them.

The Concept and Application of Fiscal Rules

At the outset it is important to emphasize that, in many cases, long-term issues were not the motivation for the adoption of fiscal rules. Kopits and Symansky (1998) argue that the "pursuit of long-run fiscal sustainability" was only one among several reasons why some countries have introduced such rules. Other factors played a far more important role (which in part explains why existing rules often appear insufficient to close the intertemporal fiscal gap). One was the desire to apply some institutional brakes to the tendency, in the postwar period, for government expenditure to rise as a share of GDP. In the European Union an additional concern was that weak fiscal policies might jeopardize the prospect for maintaining a common currency: "It has been suggested (for example, in connection with EMU [European Monetary Union] and the SGP) that a rule that reduces budget deficits—while allowing the automatic stabilizers to work—tends to lessen the burden on monetary policy" (Kopits and Symansky, 1998, pp. 6–7). Countries have also sought to "ensure the credibility of government policy over time," thus providing a basis for capital markets to lower the risk premium associated with a government's borrowing. Yet increasingly, once in place, fiscal rules have been recognized as a mechanism that can contribute to long-run fiscal sustainability.

In the European Union, for example, the rule established under the SGP calls on countries to achieve "balanced budgets or surpluses over the medium term" (with a maximum allowable overall deficit of 3 percent in any given year). Over time, adherence to this rule should lead to the steady diminution of the net public debt-to-GDP ratio (assuming a comprehensive measurement of public sector fiscal operations). In effect, it supplants the criterion in the original 1992 Maastricht Treaty, which specified that gross public debt could not exceed 60 percent of GDP. In the context of a prospective increase in social insurance expenditure associated with a rising elderly dependency ratio, this rule should create additional budgetary room (as noted above).

Similarly, the Golden Rule of the United Kingdom, when paired with its Sustainable Investment Rule, was in part motivated by intergenerational concerns. The Golden Rule, which requires that current government consumption be at least matched, if not exceeded, by current revenue, seeks to achieve intergenerational fairness in the sense that, in the words of Fottinger (2001), each "generation [leaves] an unchanged or [greater] level of resources to the next generation" (see also Balassone and Franco, 2000a). The U.K. government thus indicated its intention, over the economic cycle, to borrow only to invest and not to fund current spending. The Sustainable Investment Rule provides the essential constraint on the amount of government debt that may be used to finance capital spending. It requires that "public sector net debt, as a proportion of GDP, be held, over the economic cycle, at a stable and prudent level" (Kilpatrick, 2001). Such a rule seeks to ensure that fiscal policy is prudent—that it can be sustained even in the event of adverse shocks. Of course, what debt level is prudent is open to debate. For the United Kingdom, a 40 percent net debt-to-GDP ratio is viewed as consistent with the Sustainable Investment Rule.

New Zealand's Fiscal Responsibility Act requires the government to define the quantitative targets consistent with long-run objectives. The approach is similar to that of the U.K. Golden Rule, requiring an operating surplus, on average, over the economic cycle. Gross debt is to be held below 30 percent of GDP, on average over the cycle, and net debt should be kept below 20 percent of GDP. In what might be construed as an additional rule, the latter target excludes the assets to be accumulated under the NZSF. The government is required to make annual contributions from its operating surplus in order to build up a stock of financial assets that can later be used to pay some of the costs of the government's superannuation (that is, pension) obligations. These contributions will be relatively modest at first, but they are scheduled to rise progressively over the next few years as a percentage of GDP, leveling off at about 1 percent of GDP (McCulloch and Frances, 2001).

The link to long-run objectives can also be seen in the fiscal rules of other countries. Some are aggregative, others sectoral. Several years ago the Norwegian government established the Government Petroleum Fund (GPF) for the purpose of investing its oil and gas royalties in external financial assets. The underlying objective was both to prevent the country's currency from appreciating excessively (thus avoiding a "Dutch disease" problem) and to accumulate resources to finance the large anticipated pension outlays associated with an aging population.[38] In the U.S. Social Security system both the payroll contribution rate and benefit amounts have, in principle, been set to yield actuarial balance over a 75-year period. Over this time frame the system is intended to be self-financing, building up assets today to finance future operating deficits.

In the United Kingdom and several Western European countries (such as Germany), the law requires that the social insurance payroll contribution rate be routinely adjusted to ensure the system's financing on a PAYGO basis. In principle this can be considered a sectoral fiscal rule. Finally, the Netherlands has a fiscal rule that applies principally to the budget over the medium term but also supports longer-term objectives. At the beginning of each four-year coalition government, an ex ante rule governs the use of any windfall in revenue, or addresses any shortfall that may arise, relative to the amounts targeted for the period. Expenditures are targeted on the basis of cautious economic assumptions, ensuring that extra revenue will not automatically be translated into extra expenditure (Blöndal, 2001c). Under these rules a specified share of any windfall is returned to the public through reductions in taxes, with the rest devoted to debt reduction (or asset accumulation).[39]

Another type of fiscal rule could be hypothesized, drawing on the analytical measures of the tax and primary financing gaps discussed earlier. Assume the requirement of a sustained adjustment in the fiscal balance equal to the amount of the calculated tax or primary gap. This would be a *variable* fiscal rule, wherein the targeted medium-term fiscal balance would be adjusted periodically to ensure, initially, the aggregate prefunding of future expenditure obligations. Specifically, it would require an immediate and sustained adjustment in the tax rate, for example, to yield fiscal sustainability over an infinite horizon. In principle such a rule would imply a buildup of surpluses in the immediate future and a drawdown thereafter. This would suggest the need

---

[38]Similarly, in the Netherlands, natural gas revenue goes into a special Economic Structure Enhancing Fund, to be used exclusively for investments in economic infrastructure such as high-speed rail links and highways.

[39]If the windfall is greater than 0.75 percent of GDP, three quarters goes to reducing the deficit and one quarter to tax cuts. If the windfall falls below 0.75 percent of GDP, half goes to tax cuts and the remainder to deficit reduction.

for the *operational* fiscal rule governing the medium-term fiscal balance to be *varied* over time, taking account periodically of new adjustments reflecting unforeseen circumstances. In effect this would constitute a broadening of the actuarial approach mentioned above for the U.S. Social Security system, but applied to the budget more broadly.

The rules discussed above have different implications for the target ratio of the debt (or assets) to GDP. The SGP approach implies a diminishing debt-to-GDP ratio over time. By definition, the U.K. approach requires a net debt-to-GDP ratio under 40 percent of GDP. The New Zealand approach nominally calls for net debt to be kept under 20 percent of GDP. However, if the assets of the Superannuation Fund (which is kept separate from the net debt measure) are included, the adjusted net debt ratio would decline over a long period, eventually turning negative, until the NZSF begins to be drawn down to help finance pension obligations. The U.S. approach has varied since the original Clinton administration initiative, which suggested that the gross debt target would decline gradually over time. Under the current Bush administration, with its anticipated deficits over the medium term, this debt trajectory appears more uncertain. For Norway, the rules associated with the GPF imply a growing net asset accumulation over time. The tax smoothing approach implicit in the "fiscal gap" hypothesized above would require an initial reduction in debt and a subsequent buildup of assets over time, until the time comes when aging populations or other factors would require a drawdown of assets.[40]

Institutional Mechanisms to Support Fiscal Rules

Governments that have explored the option of accumulating assets to finance higher expenditure over the long term have had to confront the twin problems of sustaining the needed fiscal discipline and protecting the accumulated assets. It was noted above that, if aggregative fiscal measures are introduced to reduce outstanding government debt and accumulate assets, pressure needs to be maintained on the electorate, on legislators, and on future governments to stay the course. Policymakers must consider how to prevent a future loosening in the fiscal regime—whether an increase in expenditure or a reduction in tax rates. This has led some countries to introduce institutional mechanisms to limit this type of political economy risk.

---

[40]In an interesting study, Scarth and Jackson (1998) examine the relative merits of alternative measures of the debt-to-GDP ratio in terms of efficiency, stability, and equity objectives.

Fiscal rules may be seen as an attempt to support fiscal discipline, particularly if the rules have an independent legal basis or can be enforced by some type of multilateral or peer-group surveillance mechanism. One institutional mechanism that can be used to support a fiscal rule is to set resources aside in an earmarked fund, with clear guidelines limiting their use. As noted earlier, New Zealand's NZSF and Norway's GPF are the clearest examples of such a lockbox approach. The NZSF is not expected to be drawn upon for at least 20 years.

Two points are of interest. First, the New Zealand authorities could have chosen simply to run surpluses, or at least a balanced budget, in order to limit or reduce the government's *gross* debt before developing a positive net asset position. Yet the approach taken effectively implies that there will be *both* new borrowing and an accumulation of financial assets. For example, assume that in a given year the government's fixed investment outlays, combined with its contribution to the NZSF, exceed the current operating surplus: the lockbox approach allows the government to keep the *gross* debt ratio roughly at the limit set out in the Fiscal Responsibility Act (namely, 30 percent of GDP), while still accumulating financial assets in a separate fund. The alternative would have been to finance the fixed investment out of the operating surplus and thus reduce the level of new borrowing.

Second, New Zealand has chosen not to combine the assets accumulated in the NZSF with its other financial asset holdings in stating its net debt. This is the benchmark measure that is targeted under the Fiscal Responsibility Act. (Presently, the net debt-to-GDP ratio is targeted to be kept at less than 20 percent.) Thus a mechanism was adopted that allowed resources to be set aside for future expenditure needs, while at the same time avoiding the temptations that might arise from having a lower level of gross or net debt or a larger operating surplus. As the New Zealand Treasury explained:

> Importantly, much of the debate has assumed that in the absence of [the NZSF], debt would be reduced. However, in the absence of [the NZSF], fiscal discipline may be reduced and the Government may find it difficult to maintain a surplus...[reflecting that,] there would be political pressure to increase spending on other government services; there may also be pressure to give tax cuts; paying down debt may be weaker politically as a justification for maintaining surpluses; [and] government debt would be reduced [in any case] to zero in around ten years. The issue of whether to accumulate assets would still need to be addressed. A general accumulation of assets may exert less fiscal discipline on the government than a specific or dedicated fund. (New Zealand Treasury, 2001a, p. 3)

If New Zealand is successful, the sustained implementation of the NZSF should, in association with continued limits on gross and net debt, result in the government's net debt position (inclusive of the NZSF) turning negative within a decade. Nevertheless, by continuing to have some gross debt outstanding, the government has sought to restrain public expenditure pressures while also allowing the market in government debt to continue to function, thus satisfying other macroeconomic policy objectives.

This approach, however, has raised interesting questions about how the NZSF should invest its resources. The New Zealand authorities have moved to expand the shares of the NZSF held in equities and external assets, thus exposing the NZSF to both foreign exchange and rate of return risks. Will the NZSF investment portfolio's earnings exceed the cost of government borrowing? And will the funds be insulated from political economy pressures?

Norway is instructive in this latter regard. In principle, the GPF's accumulation of resources has spent less political capital, because the prefunding has come from natural resource royalties rather than higher taxes or reduced expenditure. The value of the GPF rose from about 18 percent of GDP at the end of 1999 to 27 percent of GDP by the end of 2000; it was projected at about 45 percent of GDP by the end of 2001. Net of public debt, the government thus had positive assets in 2000. (Government gross public debt has hovered at about 22 percent of GDP during this period.) Yet, as the resources have accumulated, the government has found it difficult to prevent the emergence of larger-than-planned fiscal deficits, originating principally from larger outlays on health and education by lower levels of government, and to resist calls for tax reduction. The mounting political pressure to use some of the GPF resources to benefit current generations led, in 2001, to a revision of the earlier guidelines on the GPF. The new guidelines now allow for a gradual increase in the annual structural fiscal deficit, with a significant part of the expansion being used to reduce the tax burden. Expenditure growth is to be kept below the GDP growth rate.[41]

The 2002 IMF Article IV Staff Report for Norway provides an interesting characterization of the political economy issues involved:

---

[41]The guidelines call for the structural non-oil central government budget deficit to correspond approximately to the expected real return on the GPF at the beginning of the fiscal year. In the event of extraordinarily large changes in the GPF's capital or in factors underlying the structural, non-oil deficit from one year to the next, the change in the use of oil revenue will be spread out over several years.

> The authorities viewed the new fiscal guideline as a useful clarification and a reasonable political compromise in the face of the clamor to spend the oil wealth. Officials noted that the public pressure to use more oil resources in the near-term had proven politically difficult to resist, with the visible accumulation of wealth in the GPF blunting public awareness of Norway's large public pension liabilities.... [The authorities] cautioned that keeping non-oil structural deficits on a trend implied by the rule over the next ten years was by no means easy as assets continued to build up in the GPF. (IMF, 2002a, pp. 21–22)

The report also suggests that, under the new guidelines, assets in the GPF will peak around 2012 at about 120 percent of GDP (rather than at 150 percent under the previous guidelines) and will be depleted 10 years earlier, in about 2035.[42] Yet it is illuminating that the report also indicates that gross contingent obligations for old-age and disability pensions in Norway are presently estimated at over two and a half times GDP, and even this does not take into account the additional resources that will be needed for medical care and long-term services for the very elderly. Thus, even in the face of significant long-term financial pressures, it has proved difficult to rely wholly on an aggregative prefunding approach.[43]

Other examples can be given of such lockboxes and the political pressures to which they are subject. The U.S. Social Security trust fund is an autonomous budget entity financed from earmarked payroll taxes. In recent years its policy has been to run significant surpluses in order to achieve some level of prefunding. Trust fund resources must be invested in U.S. government securities. However, as a lockbox mechanism, the trust fund's effectiveness has been reduced by virtue of its inclusion within the unified U.S. government budget. In the absence of explicit limits to the U.S. government's on-budget balance, or any independent limit to federal government debt as a percentage of GDP, it is apparent that the surplus of the Social Security system has long financed the deficits of the rest of the federal government. In recent years these deficits have reemerged, so that a surplus in the overall unified federal budget has once again turned into a deficit. Moreover, given that the trust fund's assets are U.S. government securities, the issue of fiscal sustainability is ultimately a function of the size

---

[42]The IMF projects that net cash flow from petroleum activities will decline sharply to negligible levels over the next several decades (IMF, 2002a, p. 23).

[43]It is thus no surprise that both the IMF and the Norwegian authorities have emphasized the importance of policy reform to reduce the contingent liabilities of the public pension system.

of the U.S. government's outstanding debt (implicit and explicit) to the public at large, relative to GDP.

Finally, the lockbox approach is, at best, a financial vehicle that seeks to ensure that a government can meet its financial commitments. It is not sufficient as a means of raising the aggregate national saving rate. For example, in the New Zealand case, households might exhibit behavior consistent with Ricardian equivalence effects (see Chapter 5), offsetting the higher government saving rate by lowering their private saving rate (from its already low level—see Claus and Scobie, 2002). Households might perceive that, as a consequence of the NZSF being established, there is less risk of a potential default or backsliding in superannuation payments. Of course, such a reaction would vitiate the basic objective of trying to augment the national saving rate through the NZSF. However, even in the absence of such an offsetting "reaction function," the desired impact of the NZSF is only achieved under the assumption that it truly does raise the government's saving rate. If the same operating surplus had been realized in the absence of the NZSF (for example, if there were no increased expenditure or tax cutting as a consequence of running such surpluses), the NZSF would make no difference to the level of government saving.[44]

Specific Policy Reforms

Approaches based on fiscal rules rely on the aggregate fiscal policy stance to finance long-term expenditure policy commitments, reducing debt or building up assets to meet expenditure pressures in the future. For most governments, however, reforms of specific programs or policies—a scaling back on future commitments rather than fiscal adjustment in the present—is the approach taken to address financial sustainability concerns. Often the dynamic of the overall fiscal situation (that is, the size of the aggregate tax burden or the overall debt) is the factor motivating the reform of programs that contribute to a lack of long-term fiscal sustainability. In other cases the specifics of the individual scheme and its financing, rather than the aggregate fiscal picture, may be the principal motivating factor.

---

[44]There is one possible route by which the establishment of the NZSF, rather than a simple debt paydown, might yield greater government saving. This would occur if the strategy of investing in equities rather than bonds were to yield a higher risk-adjusted rate of return.

Typically, a policy reform is initiated on the basis of a long-term assessment of a program's financial viability. But reforms may also arise from the recognition that a change in policies may engender significant future savings. The incidence of policy reforms may be narrowly focused to affect only future beneficiaries, contributors, or taxpayers. But reforms may also entail some reneging on commitments to current beneficiaries, or higher taxes, or larger contributions from workers. It is beyond the scope of this book to enumerate all the actions taken by many different governments in recent years to improve the long-term financial sustainability of particular sectoral programs or policy frameworks, much less to characterize the adequacy or the timeliness of such actions.[45] Thus what follows is only an attempt to categorize the approaches that have been taken. Most relate to government benefit programs for which there is a well-specified system of commitments. However, some may relate to policies that specify the extent of a government's contingent responsibilities, or that adjust revenue policies to compensate for anticipated changes in the expected responsiveness of revenue to changes in the economic base, or that address structural barriers impeding gains in labor productivity.

Reforms of Financing Parameters

The aggregate *financing* parameters of a program may be adjusted without adjusting the program's specific benefit characteristics. For example, the contribution rate of existing participants in a public pension program may be increased, or a general tax increase (say, an increase in the value-added tax or the income tax) may be enacted, thus distributing the fiscal burden more widely among the population. Such an approach maintains the level of benefit commitments but does have implications for the intergenerational distribution of the burden of financing the program. Current and future workers may find their tax burden greater, and thus the implied rate of return, in terms of benefits (if any) from their taxes or contributions, lower. The motivation of such a reform may be simply to restore the financial budget balance of a specific program over some time period, or some prefunding may be sought as well. The periodic adjustments of the payroll tax rate for the U.S. Social Security system are one obvious example of this kind of reform (although, given its scale and magnitude, this is effectively analogous to adherence to an aggregate fiscal rule).

---

[45]Such surveys do, of course, exist. For example, in the sphere of pension reform see Lindbeck and Persson (2003) and Wallace (2002).

Reforms of Benefit Parameters

Discrete adjustments can also be made to particular parameters of a program's benefit structure. One way to do this is by adjusting the rate at which program benefits accrue (for example, by reducing the annual accrual rate, shifting from a final-salary to an average-salary basis for benefits, or ensuring greater actuarial fairness in accrual rates, particularly for those working past the normal state pension age). Another way is to change the age of eligibility for receiving a particular benefit (for example, by delaying the age at which a retirement pension may be received). A third is through a change in any so-called clawback provisions, such as the rate at which benefits (for example, pensions) are taxed; or a change in the minimum benefit level; or a change in co-payments required or in the initial deductible (for example, with respect to medical insurance systems). Reforms may affect existing beneficiaries or be limited to new beneficiaries. They may be phased in over time or formulated to take effect at some future date.

Parametric reforms may also be specified in terms of the *process* by which benefits are determined in the future, rather than the precise magnitude of a particular parameter. Analogous at the program level to aggregate fiscal rules, such reforms may allow for the benefit structure to "self-adjust" in response to the uncertainties to which a program may be exposed, whether directly from the financing side of the program or indirectly from market or demographic developments. Thus, under the recent Swedish and Italian pension reforms, pension benefit payouts, at the time a worker becomes eligible, will take account of the life expectancy of the retiring worker's cohort. For example, if a worker retires in 2030, his or her pension annuity will be influenced by the life expectancy of the cohort at that time, as well as by the recent experience of the government in terms of prevailing market interest rates on government debt. Thus the longer the life expectancy and the lower the prevailing expectations of interest rates, the smaller would be the annual pension annuity (see Palmer, 2001; Disney and Johnson, 2001). The intent is to ensure that neither an increased life expectancy nor a less favorable interest rate environment leads to a weakened long-run financial position for the program.

Adjustments to the indexation formula are a similar type of reform. The shift by the United Kingdom, in the early 1980s, from indexing state pension benefits to earnings to indexing them to the consumer price index is another example. Most projections suggest this will have a dramatic impact in reducing state pension outlays in coming decades, although at the time it was perceived as enhancing the benefits to then-current pensioners.[46]

The benefit parameters of a program may also be revised in order to encourage or discourage certain behavior on the part of affected groups. Sweden's pension reform sought to ensure neutrality with respect to the timing of the retirement decision. Similar examples include policies that adjust the effective tax on retirement benefits to encourage greater labor force participation of pensioners, that provide for higher pensions for older pensioners, that increase the co-payment required from medical insurance beneficiaries, or that establish tax or insurance penalties for those purchasing houses in coastal areas or flood plains.

Lastly, governments have introduced explicit legal requirements for program parameters to be periodically reviewed, to ensure both the continued long-term financial viability of a program and the appropriateness or adequacy of benefits.

Changes in the Quality or Quantity of Benefits or in the Extent of Coverage

Somewhat distinct from parametric reform (but with some obvious overlap) are approaches that narrow the coverage or eligibility of groups to receive benefits, or that reduce the number of services or the generosity of the benefits provided. These include, for example, a shift to means testing of benefits or a more restrictive definition of eligibility for disability benefits or long-term care. In this category might also fall the elimination or reduction of previously provided benefits, such as a cutback in pension benefits for certain groups of survivors in a pension scheme, or more restrictive insurance coverage of particular types of medical procedures or pharmaceuticals.

A number of potential reforms relate to the quality and quantity of services provided by a government-run medical care system. Tighter budgets may entail cutbacks in a wide range of services or in the quality or timeliness of care provided. Options include rationing of or longer queues for services, or more-restrictive eligibility criteria for particular medical procedures or for access to newly developed pharmaceuticals. However, other governments may opt for an expansion of services.

---

[46]Pursuit of such an approach must recognize its potential intergenerational impact. The United Kingdom's approach was much like a gradual switch to prefunding: current elderly and soon-to-retire generations were unaffected. Future generations of taxpayers gained, whereas transition and future generations of retirees bear the cost.

The United Kingdom recently announced a tax increase to finance a substantial strengthening of its National Health Service over the next 10 to 15 years. Many emerging market economies in Asia, faced with the aging of their populations, have introduced new social insurance benefits in the spheres of both medical insurance and retirement pensions.

Commitment Reform

Sometimes governments may view sustainability as achievable only through a total revamping of a program or substitution with a new one. Recent pension reforms that replace a PAYGO, defined-benefit system with a funded, defined-contribution scheme are the most obvious example.[47] In some cases reform may involve an effective reneging on existing commitments. In others it may entail limiting the losses that would be engendered by continuing an unsustainable scheme. In still others it might involve a revamping of the program that reduces the probable scale of future commitments. The pension reforms of the United Kingdom and Chile may be the most obvious examples, but by now many others have been implemented in Eastern Europe and Latin America, and there have been many reforms of medical insurance schemes as well.

Preemptive Action

Policy reform may also take the form of preemptive action to prevent the emergence of future costs or the loss of future revenue bases. This may involve budgetary outlays, but it may also include strengthening the regulatory regime or adjusting excise taxes (Energy Savings Trust, 2002). In the area of climate change, the Kyoto treaty can be seen as a regulatory restriction that would require governments that have approved the treaty to take steps to reduce greenhouse gas emissions. In essence, it is a form of down payment, which may have some effect on reducing the future adverse effects of global warming. Similarly, investments in research and development in the agricultural sector may be seen as critical to protecting the sector's productivity in the light of expected climate change. Tighter restrictions may be placed on buildings in coastal areas susceptible to rising sea levels or to storm surges

---

[47]See Burtless (2001) for a discussion of whether such a change should be contemplated in the United States and Germany.

in coming decades, or requirements for insurance coverage may be increased. Resettlement schemes or new infrastructure construction may also be seen as relatively low-cost preventive strategies to minimize losses associated with climate change. Governments may need to adapt their role as co-insurers, to the extent that private insurance markets fail to provide coverage of certain risks associated with extreme weather events or terrorist acts.

In the health sphere, prevention programs addressed to the principal groups at high risk of contracting HIV/AIDS may be necessary to limit the overall prevalence of the disease. Similarly, immunization programs for childhood diseases may attempt to limit future expenditure burdens associated with high morbidity. In the security sphere, although overseas development assistance is often tied to narrow political or commercial interests, another justification is to enhance the likelihood of political stability in a strategic region, to avoid the need for even more costly forms of engagement later.

Expenditure Policy Rationalization and Tax Reform

Efforts to rationalize policies may include periodic government reviews of expenditure or tax policies with a view to rationalizing ineffective or low-priority programs, compensating for diminished productivity of revenue from existing sources, or enhancing the responsiveness of revenue to movements in the tax base. All of these constitute additional approaches for creating fiscal leeway or mobilizing additional revenue to finance long-term expenditure.

Deferring Action on the Long Term

A final approach commonly taken by governments in response to the uncertainties associated with the long term has been simply to defer taking action. Sometimes a government may accompany this decision with efforts to narrow the range and sources of uncertainty. The argument is clear. The opportunity costs of policy change—be they economic or political—are perceived as too high to justify changing an existing policy regime when the benefits of change are uncertain. If any leeway is seen to defer a decision—if the costs of delay are not too significant relative to the costs of earlier action—deferral represents a sensible strategy. Where a policy change also requires the undertaking of irreversible investments, it may be sensible, in a cost-benefit sense, to delay the decision pending additional information on prices, costs, the nature of future technological change, or the underlying technological or scientific evidence for moving ahead (Pindyck, 1991; Goodson, 1995).

Recent economic analyses of the costs and benefits of efforts to mitigate climate change provide an obvious example. Research by Nordhaus (1998) suggests that the costs of any significant efforts at mitigation—that is, of policies to reduce the emission of greenhouse gases by enough to have any appreciable effect on the expected pace of climate change over the next century—are likely to be extremely high. Given the uncertainties involved, he argues, the expected benefit from such actions appears inadequate to justify the costs of an inevitable substantial scrapping of existing energy-related plant, equipment, and technologies.[48] However, Nordhaus also emphasizes the importance of a concerted international effort, within the window of time during which decisions can be deferred without significant cost, to narrow the band of uncertainty about the consequences of *not* pursuing a policy of significant emission reduction.[49]

In the social insurance sphere, a similar justification has been made for delaying action to reform what might be seen as a financially unsustainable system. Fiscal gap analyses often provide some measure of the cost of deferring action. For example, Janssen's (2002) recent analysis of the New Zealand long-term fiscal situation quantifies how much larger the fiscal adjustment would have to be were it delayed for a decade. Given an objective function for government that includes intergenerational fairness, some might argue that the opportunity cost of immediate tax smoothing is too high relative to the implied costs of delayed action.

The arguments just presented, of course, put the best face on the reasons governments offer to justify deferring action. Political opposition and current economic pain are likely to have been far more pressing factors in the eyes of most governments, given the uncertainties as to the benefits of immediate action.

---

[48] The irreversibility argument can also be used, however, as a reason for moving ahead with efforts at dealing with climate change. If delaying a policy change will itself give rise to an irreversible loss, the result may be to narrow the capacity to correct the situation or realize certain benefits. With climate change, delays involve a further accumulation in the stock of greenhouse gases, with long-term effects that may take decades if not centuries to overcome. In a similar vein, Mabey (1998) has argued that the "precautionary principle" would justify a different approach to handling such uncertainty.

[49] The Kyoto process, of course, does not imply pursuit of such an approach, although the analyses mentioned here partly underlie the opposition in some quarters to its ratification.

Relying on the Market

In principle, another important mechanism often forces governments to take long-term factors into account, namely, their reliance on financing from global capital markets. Many industrial governments borrow long term. Although the bulk of the securities they issue have maturities of 10 years or less, some sovereign debt instruments have maturities of as long as 30 years. If there is any depth to the markets for a country's debt, it might be expected that the risk premiums on market interest rates on that debt would reflect any concerns about the sustainability of the issuer's fiscal policy. Rising risk premiums are a signal to governments that such issues must be addressed or that the consequences of higher debt-servicing costs must be faced. Long-term concerns may also have a bearing on medium-term rates. When governments are forced to stay away from the longer end of the maturity range, the overall risk associated with a government's debt portfolio is increased.

In addition to the signals conveyed by market interest rates, private sector credit rating agencies (for example, Moody's, Standard & Poor's, and Fitch-IBCA) increasingly take account of fiscal sustainability issues in their assessment of sovereign risk.[50] To some extent, other capital market analysts also incorporate long-term risks into their assessments of a country's macroeconomic policy framework.

In the published analyses of the various credit rating agencies, some long-term fiscal issues, notably the aging of populations, have appeared as a source of concern. Recent studies by Fitch Ratings IBCA (2000, 2001a), Merrill Lynch (Mantel, 2000, 2001), Standard & Poor's (Kraemer, 2002), Credit Suisse-First Boston (2000), UBS Warburg (2002), and Goldman Sachs (Culhane, 2001) have all attempted to assess the impact of aging trends on both individual countries' fiscal positions and global capital market conditions more generally. These have relied upon and supplemented the work of multilateral agencies: the European Commission, the OECD, and the IMF. In contrast, other long-term risk factors (such as climate change, resource shortages, and global insecurities) do not appear to have had a major influence on ratings. In part this reflects the fact that most government debt instruments are in the short- to medium-maturity range (Missale, 1999).

Discussions with rating agencies suggest a dichotomization in focus, with the principal emphasis, not surprisingly, on those countries that

---

[50]For example, see recent reports of Fitch Ratings IBCA (2000, 2001a–e) or of Standard and Poor's (Kraemer, 2002).

are active participants in markets: the industrial countries and a few emerging market countries. (All other countries are much lower in most rating categories, if they are rated at all.) For these countries, long-term factors, particularly the impact of aging, are seen as a source of concern. However, they do not appear to be critical in determining current sovereign risk ratings unless debt is already extremely high relative to GDP and the maturing of public pension commitments is imminent (as is the case, for example, in Greece). A recent Standard & Poor's report (Kraemer, 2002, p. 2) illustrates the shorter-term focus:

> Age-related fiscal pressures will typically build up only after 2015, which exceeds a typical long-term rating horizon (3 to 5 years). As a result, although in the more distant future fiscal stress associated with demographic change will become a dominant factor in rating Western European sovereigns, rating revisions based on the aging challenge alone will remain the exception in the coming decade.

As a qualifying caveat, however, the same report also notes (p. 15) that if, in the future,

> [n]o resolute political leadership brings forward the pre-emptive correction of looming intergenerational imbalances, the dramatic fiscal turmoil laid out in the surplus ceiling scenario might materialize. If this were to happen, Standard and Poor's would certainly react with corresponding rating actions in a forward-looking fashion, however unimaginable these might appear from today's vantage point.

Some rating agencies appear more concerned about the effects of aging industrial country populations on government saving rates and, in particular, on the supply of government debt instruments. If many governments pursue fiscal rules that limit gross debt issuance, the supply of government bonds might dwindle. Indeed, one analyst suggested in late 2001 that, in a few years, 90 percent of government bonds issued globally could be Japanese. Such a scenario could have implications not only for interest rates in general but also for the challenges faced by public and private pension agencies in their efforts to balance risk and return objectives, especially as minimizing risk becomes increasingly important with a rising share of elderly in the population.[51]

---

[51]One would expect that both corporations liable to payouts under defined-benefit plans and insurance companies seeking to provide long-term annuities will increasingly wish to invest in low-risk financial instruments.

There does not appear to be much evidence that concern for long-run issues has had much of an impact on the risk premiums embedded in long-term interest rates. Again, this may principally reflect the fact that the maturities of most long-term debt instruments are of 10 years or less. It may also imply a narrowness in focus as to which long-term factors to consider.

Finally, there are other ways in which the market may exert pressure on governments to address long-term issues more effectively. If the nature of the risks confronting the private insurance industry—whether from climate change, terrorism, or technology—should create excessive losses, the industry may prove reluctant to provide such coverage thereafter. Already such issues are arising with respect to coverage in flood plains and for terrorist actions. Events since September 11 illustrate that some governments have been forced by a combination of such market actions and political pressures to play a greater role in providing reinsurance. In effect, the market may force a rebalancing of the roles of the government and the private sector in the management of risk. Another illustration is the extent to which governments have been obliged to respond to the competitive pressures stemming from globalization by investing in the public goods infrastructure necessary to maintain or achieve competitiveness.

Public Debt and Risk Management

In recent years a literature has developed arguing that public debt risk management practices should contribute to the overall minimization of budgetary risks, both on the revenue and on the expenditure side (see Missale, 1999; Marcet and Scott, 2001; Brixi and Mody, 2002). Missale (1999, p. 218) argues,

> No doubt, refinancing risk is relevant, but the uncertainty of public spending and tax bases is also important.... [T]his implies that unexpected changes in the tax-base, mainly due to output fluctuations, should be hedged by debt instruments as much as [by] interest-rate variations and exchange rate risk should be avoided.... [Conventional debt] instruments can be combined so as to provide the optimal hedge against budgetary uncertainty, that is, low debt returns at times when output and thus tax revenues are lower than expected.

Missale's focus derives from the earlier work of Robert Barro, who argued that tax smoothing can be a means of minimizing welfare distortions due to fluctuations in tax rates. Missale and others have argued that, in the context of a tax smoothing strategy, it would be desirable for unanticipated shocks to revenue or expenditure to be offset by corresponding reductions in debt-servicing costs. In principle this could be accomplished if governments could issue debt instruments that are *state-contingent,* with the interest rate prevailing in given states negatively correlated with such shocks. Specifically, if the mix of debt instruments could result in lower debt-servicing costs at times when unanticipated demand or supply shocks result in higher than expected expenditure or lower than expected revenue, the overall budget risks associated with these shocks could be minimized. Even in the absence of such instruments, if other, more available debt instruments are chosen whose returns correlate with such contingent "states," the same results could conceivably be achieved.[52]

For the purposes of this chapter, the relevant question is whether any governments have actively sought to behave in this way. Missale (1999) recently surveyed the public debt management practices of a number of OECD countries. The principal motive of debt managers appeared to be the minimization of long-term financing costs. Next in priority was avoiding the risk of refinancing, that is, of having to roll over large amounts of debt at unfavorable interest rates. The survey also suggests a strategy of issuing securities with a low risk premium. But Missale notes that practices vary substantially across countries with regard to what this means in terms of the length of debt maturities issued and the extent of diversification.

However, the notion of minimizing budget risks does not appear, as a matter of practice, to have been a significant concern (even in the United Kingdom). Leong (1999, p. 2) asserts flatly that "debt managers do not try to use debt management to insure against large macroeconomic risks to the government's finances." Moreover, given that, in most countries, the maturities of government debt instruments do not exceed 10 years, it would appear unlikely that the notion of budgetary risk minimization for long-term factors has yet become a common practice among government debt managers.[53]

---

[52]Leong (1999) notes that most governments do not issue state-contingent debt: "...making the return on debt contingent on government spending outcomes would create a strong incentive for the government to consistently overspend—it is unlikely that any government would be able to find a buyer for such bonds at a sensible price" (p. 21).

[53]The United Kingdom is unusual among OECD countries in having an average debt maturity of 9.7 years. Only Poland has a longer average maturity (Leong, 1999).

The concept of fiscal risk management broadens the concept of deal-ing with risk beyond that of the government's approach to its manage-ment of public debt instruments. Brixi and Schick (2002) emphasize that governments should be encouraged to examine the broad range of risks to which they may be exposed and to formulate a coherent ap-proach to taking account of such risks in the budget process. This would include identifying and classifying the fiscal risks faced by the government, the sources of those risks, and, if possible, their potential fiscal costs and the associated probabilities of their occurrence. Going beyond Missale, Brixi and Mody advocate an "extended assets and lia-bility management framework," in which a "Fiscal Hedge Matrix...com-plements the Fiscal Risk Matrix to illustrate the different sources of potential revenues that can serve to cover government obligations" (Brixi and Mody, 2002, p. 25). Few governments have adopted such an approach. Barnhill and Kopits (2003), in a study of Ecuador's short-term vulnerability to financial crises, discuss the possible relevance of value at risk (VaR) methodologies—presently used for assessing the short-term riskiness of bank portfolios—in assessing the riskiness of the bal-ance sheet of the public sector.[54] However, their study suggests the difficulties that would arise if the methodology were extended to ad-dress longer-term risk factors.

---

[54]The VaR summarizes "the worst possible loss over a target horizon with a given level of confidence" (Jorion, 2000, p. 22).

4

Some Conceptual Issues in Addressing Long-Term Fiscal Developments

Those future generations—what have they done for us?
—a senior government official

The next chapter of this book will discuss various ways in which governments can strengthen their approach to issues of the long term. First, however, it will be useful to discuss some key concepts and underlying trade-offs. A fundamental trade-off is that between short-term costs and long-term gains. The ironic comment by the senior government official quoted above raises some real questions. Why *should* a government focus on actions that may have a significant short-term cost, both economic and political, when the benefits will only be realized decades into the future? How should such trade-offs be considered? Might failure to address long-term fiscal issues actually impinge on a government's *current* capacity to act? And are there forces that might prevent a government from addressing long-term concerns even if it believes it should?

This chapter begins with a discussion of the social welfare function, a useful, if theoretical, conceptual framework for identifying and balancing the interests of multiple generations. The chapter then examines the various issues that a government and its citizens must consider in determining how to address issues of the long term. These include the legacy of past policies and the current state of their implementation; the sustainability of the country's fiscal position; the allocative efficiency of revenue and expenditure policies; fairness in the distribution of tax burdens and spending; the political obstacles to fiscal reform; the possible reactions of markets to such reform (or its absence); the proper approach to risk; and concern for the maintenance of the credibility of the state. Although the discussion may seem at times more philosophical

120

than practical, the issues raised lie at the core of any comprehensive discussion of how to address long-term fiscal concerns.

The Social Welfare Function

The social welfare function (SWF) is a concept used by economists to characterize how a government weighs the welfare of different groups in society in its decision making on public policy issues. Several aspects of the SWF are particularly relevant to the discussion of long-term fiscal policymaking.

First, among the factors that the SWF must take into account are the interests of future generations. How much weight to attach to the welfare, or utility, of each of a succession of generations is obviously a critical question, but the choice of those weights (as well as the process of choosing them) raises several complex issues.[1] A key issue is the choice of the rate used to discount future consumption to its present value. One approach would apply a low discount rate to consumption in the distant future, so that the interests of future generations are not shortchanged relative to those of current generations. This contrasts with the more conventional economic argument that the discount rate should be based on interest rates actually observed in the market (see, for example, U.S. OMB Circular No. A–94; U.S. Office of Management and Budget, 1992). However, because markets do not typically offer interest rates for terms exceeding 30 years, this approach does not provide a ready answer to the problem. As discussed in Chapter 2, Weitzman (1998) and Newell and Pizer (2002a, 2002b) have argued for a weighting of discount factors, which yields an expected discount factor. For purposes of long-term decision making, this would be the effective equivalent of using the lowest possible discount rate, weighted by the probability of it being the correct one.

But timing is not the only consideration in judging the relative importance to attach to the welfare of present and future generations. Several others also enter the picture. It would not be surprising, first of all, if today's citizens—and politicians seeking their favor—arbitrarily attached a higher social welfare valuation to their own interests than normal discounting procedures would indicate.[2] A more enlightened

---

[1]This is hardly a new issue. Ramsey (1928), for example, argued that it was ethically indefensible to discount the utility of future generations at all.

[2]See Beckerman and Pasek (2001) for a stimulating discussion on the "rights" of unborn generations.

perspective would regard such a bias as excessively myopic, even self-ish, taking inadequate account of the interests both of the young genera-tion living today and of generations yet unborn.

A second issue is how to measure utility. An individual's utility is a function of that individual's consumption, including consumption of leisure. A comprehensive definition of a generation's consumption, however, would go beyond consumption of ordinary goods, services, and leisure to encompass some measure of the quality of the environ-ment during that generation's lifetime. A polluted environment, or one characterized by exposure to hazardous disease vectors, should count as a negative in any such measure of consumption.[3] Beyond the mea-surement of consumption in the aggregate, political leaders may also be concerned about how consumption is distributed, not only across time but also within a given population at any point in time.

Third, the SWF should take account of risk. In theory, policymakers seek to maximize a given SWF, but they do so in a world of uncertainty. They, and the citizens they represent, should be expected to have strong preferences about how likely it will be to achieve different wel-fare outcomes. But, in fact, politicians and policymakers might act as if their objective were principally the *level* of welfare to be sought, disre-garding how likely it would be to realize that objective.[4] For example, consider a policy option that offers a high probability, with a limited variance, that elderly citizens in the future will receive at least a mini-mum basic pension. Would that policy be preferable to one that offers the possibility of a higher average pension, but that also has a high probability of falling short of providing even the minimum pension?[5]

Fourth, the SWF should take account of the role that government it-self, as an actor in the economy, will play in the achievement of a given level of social welfare. Government does play such a role even if it re-mains strictly an agent, such that social welfare is measured only in

---

[3]Such a welfare function would take account of the negative impact of current con-sumption that would deplete environmental assets.

[4]As argued by Lee and Edwards (2002), "How [do] different kinds of policies perform in the context of uncertainty[?] Do some reduce the uncertainty and others amplify it?" (p. 35).

[5]More generally, any given policy option is subject to a more general "state of the world" probability function, which recognizes that the desired or targeted probability distribution may *itself* be realized only with a discrete probability. Specifically, a set of probability distributions can be imagined, each tightly centered around a median, but each also subject to a given probability, depending on the state of the world (it may not even be possible to gauge the likelihood of these different probability functions). A risk-averse choice of policy in such a case would tend to be biased toward risk-averse options *within the set* of alternative states of the world.

terms of the utility of the citizenry, present and future, with no weight attached to any utility accruing to government itself. The decisions and behavior of government determine the quality of public goods and services consumed, the constraints imposed on citizens by laws and regulations, and the stability of expectations about the government's ability to deliver on its commitments and about the tax burden it will impose. Any comprehensive measure of social welfare must take these things into account. But because the government, as an institution, has a continuing interest in the welfare of the country that exceeds the time frame of any individual citizen, its own interests and capacity to act cannot be assumed away as irrelevant. This point is important, because it raises difficult and complex issues of political economy, including whether political leaders and government bureaucrats act only as agents for their citizens, or whether they are to some extent principals as well.[6]

The discussion thus far, although obviously abstract, highlights some key factors that bear on how government policies take account of long-term issues. These include

- the weight to place on the interests of unborn generations relative to the interests of those living today;
- the approach to use in choosing the discount rate;
- the weights to be placed on the distribution of income and consumption across generations;
- the limits to be set on the depletion of a country's environmental capital;
- the relative importance of the expected mean and variance of the components of the social welfare function;
- the sensitivity of outcomes to alternative uncertain states of the world; and
- the roles of government as both agent and principal in promoting social welfare.

Policymakers and politicians seldom fully articulate their views on the underlying welfare function of their society, particularly with respect to the distribution of that welfare across generations. A rare example of such a statement can be found in the recent Intergenerational Report of Australia (Australia, Commonwealth of, 2002). Referring to the Charter of Budget Honesty Act 1998, the report notes that maintenance of fiscal stability promotes fairness in distributing public

---

[6]Also ignored for the present is the equally complex relationship between political leaders and government bureaucrats, as well as the specific motivations of each group.

resources across generations, promotes greater stability and certainty of fiscal outcomes, ensures that governments will continue to provide essential goods and services that the private sector does not provide efficiently, reduces the risk that external shocks will cause a significant disturbance in living standards, and allows government debts to be sustained at low interest rates while also helping keep rates low for other borrowers. The report also notes that keeping government debt under control will improve the government's capacity to respond to unforeseen circumstances, such as natural disasters.

Expanding on an approach originally laid out by Musgrave (1959) in his seminal work on public finance, we can consider the long-term issues faced by policymakers in terms of six broad objectives. The first three—stabilization, efficiency, and redistribution—also matter in the short term.[7] When the focus is broadened to include the long term, three other objectives, subsidiary to the first three, become relevant: financial sustainability, the approach to risk and uncertainty, and the maintenance of a political capacity to implement policies.

Sustainability bears critically on whether a government's policies are perceived by its citizens, domestic creditors, and international capital markets as *financially* credible over a long period. A government's *approach to risk and uncertainty* will influence how policy issues are addressed, what specific targets are set, and how the balance of risk taking is struck between the government and its citizens, both today and across generations. *Capacity for implementation* emphasizes the question, which is largely one of political economy, of whether a government is able to implement its policy intentions on a sustainable basis, while preserving its credibility and the continuity of its role over time. In other words, can it be assured that a financially sustainable set of policies will not be overturned in the future, calling into question the political credibility of a state's actions?

The following discussion elaborates on how these various objectives should influence a government's choice of policies, both in the aggregate and at the program level, in addressing long-term issues. What emerges is a clearer picture of the complex balancing of considerations—political and economic—that necessarily influence such choices. Solutions that appear appropriate when viewed from one perspective may prove suboptimal or infeasible when others are considered. Even a government's leeway to affect outcomes may be limited, if constraints are imposed by market pressures and political imperatives.

---

[7]This should explicitly include an emphasis on the distribution of intergenerational burdens and fairness.

Assessing Financial Sustainability

Much of the literature on the longer-term dimensions of fiscal policy concerns fiscal sustainability. Can government assure its citizens and the financial markets that it can meet its financial and policy commitments over the long run? Put simply, is the government solvent over the long term? If the answer is no, it can have adverse ramifications for the management of government budgeting and for macroeconomic policy even in the short run.[8] Countries that mobilize funds on international capital markets are particularly sensitive to the risk of long-term insolvency. An increased risk premium on government debt can result in a vicious circle, whereby the higher costs of debt service further worsen the fiscal balance, making short-term adjustments in the overall balance still more difficult.[9]

A government's *current* policy targets are thus constrained by perceptions about whether it can meet its long-term policy commitments. Longer-term objectives for growth may also be imperiled by such concerns. Recent investment models emphasize that achieving stability and credibility in macroeconomic policy—in other words, reducing uncertainty—may be more important than any specific fiscal incentives aimed directly at stimulating investment (Pindyck, 1991).

Sustainability also has a political economy dimension: an adverse assessment of sustainability suggests that a government might renege on its commitments. The political consequences will depend on whether the politicians currently in power are perceived as responsible for the problem or as working effectively to remedy it.

Thus it is no surprise that the prospect of aging populations has prompted appraisals from many quarters of governments' ability to meet their policy commitments with respect to pensions, medical care, and long-term chronic care (Frederiksen, 2003; European Commission, Economic Policy Committee, 2001; OECD, 2001a; Australia, Commonwealth of, 2002; and Hewitt, 2002, are just a few examples). Nor is it surprising that governments, in their own analyses, tend to place a favorable gloss on whether their policies are sustainable, and to defer action to increase their sustainability pending further information.

---

[8]This has led the IMF to place increasing emphasis on assessments of sustainability (see IMF, 2002b).

[9]This is not just a theoretical issue. One can readily find recent analyses by rating agencies of the likelihood of specific countries remaining solvent in the face of the risks posed by an aging population (see Kraemer, 2002).

The following are some of the questions that policymakers should pose in judging the sustainability of their government's fiscal commitments:

- Looking out over many years (50, 75, or even longer), can the government finance its present policy commitments, including social insurance transfers, debt service, and the provision of public goods and services, without an increase in the tax burden? Answering this question forces an assessment of the nature of a government's policy commitments (in terms of the magnitude of transfers or the quality and quantity of public service provision),[10] of the feasibility of a higher tax burden, and of the possibilities for retrenchment on existing expenditure commitments.
- Is the analysis of sustainability sufficiently comprehensive that it covers all the principal risks and uncertainties to which the fiscal position is subject? How robust are the sustainability calculations to shocks or to the relaxing of key assumptions?
- Even if the government's fiscal position appears plausibly sustainable on the above terms, is the implied pattern of surpluses and deficits viable in all periods over the relevant time horizon? Even if the fiscal position appears sustainable over the long term, the deficits that might need to be financed during some period, or the assets that might need to be built up in another, may prove difficult to manage.[11]
- Even if sustainability appears plausible in the long run and in all periods in between, is the *current* tax burden itself sustainable, and are the government's current commitments to transfers and the provision of goods and services sustainable? Several European governments appear to be pursuing fiscally sustainable policies, but at the cost of supporting extremely large primary surpluses (exceeding 10 percent of GDP) through high tax rates or difficult cutbacks in public service provision. Other governments have

---

[10]For example, most analyses assume that expenditure on the provision of public goods (such as defense, the judiciary, and security) will be kept constant as a share of GDP and that spending on such services as education will be maintained at a constant real level per capita. Are these assumptions valid or appropriate? Also, is the government committed to maintaining a given standard of medical care provision? What level of indexation of pension benefits is presumed, and should it be assumed to be linked to prices or wages?

[11]For example, suppose that sustainability is predicated on running large fiscal surpluses for a long period. Are citizens likely to accept the burden of high taxes when the government is running surpluses? The potential for expenditure creep (Pinfield, 1998; Kraemer, 2002) is a risk to such a strategy.

sustainable fiscal positions principally because they have made very limited commitments to state-provided pensions. Political pressures to expand such commitments may challenge the robustness of the sustainability assessment.

- Are there institutional mechanisms in place that can help ensure that future policymakers and other political actors will continue the country's adherence to a fiscally sustainable position?

Preserving Scope for Stabilization Measures

Long-term issues influence whether a government can pursue its short- to medium-term stabilization objectives. Obviously, governments want to have fiscal policy available as an instrument with which to influence aggregate economic activity, even if they also recognize its limits on that score (Heller, 2003; Hemming and Petrie, 2002). If the long-term fiscal position appears unsustainable, however, use of the budget for macroeconomic stabilization may be precluded. Increasing the fiscal deficit and building up debt may then reinforce the perception of unsustainability, leading to a higher risk premium on the government's borrowing, which could further worsen the short-term situation. It may also lead to behavior that offsets the intended fiscal stimulus (for example, higher private saving, or capital flight) if it raises concern about the consequences of an unsustainable fiscal position.

Thus any government that would like to use fiscal policy as an effective macroeconomic policy instrument needs to ensure both that its fiscal position is perceived as sustainable and that the stimulative use of fiscal policy does not itself jeopardize that perception. Accomplishing the latter suggests the importance of a medium-term fiscal framework that provides sufficient leeway for countercyclical fiscal policy without jeopardizing sustainability.

Obviously, the reality of policymaking is more complex. Governments have considerable scope to pursue policies that raise questions about fiscal sustainability over the long term but that appear quite sustainable and financially credible at least within the current time horizon of the citizenry and of capital markets. Credit rating agencies may, for example, rate a government highly for its financial viability over the next 10 to 15 years, even while expressing serious concerns about its viability beyond that time frame. At the same time, there may be considerable uncertainty among analysts as to whether a government's position is sustainable or not.

The notion of building in a safety margin for fiscal policy within a medium-term fiscal framework is a sound one and has been adopted by a number of governments. It is, for example, embodied in the European Union's Stability and Growth Pact, discussed in Chapter 3, which allows an overall deficit of 3 percent of GDP in periods of recession, even though the overall fiscal objective is to be in balance or a slight surplus over the business cycle.[12]

Achieving Fairness Across Generations

Whenever a government relies on long-term borrowing to finance its outlays or makes policy commitments that will benefit or be financed by future generations, the issue arises of whether all generations affected thereby are being treated fairly.[13] The concept of an intertemporal budget constraint—the idea that existing public debt and any future deficits must eventually be offset by future surpluses—indirectly relates to this issue as well. There should be no Ponzi schemes. Ultimately, some taxpayers, present or future, must pay off the debts incurred today. As the following discussion will show, these intergenerational issues are quite complex.

First, one must identify which generations need to be considered, and what their interests are. The population alive today encompasses several generations and groups within generations, each with a different perspective. Today's elderly perceive themselves as having accumulated certain rights from their past relations with the public sector (whether from their contributions to a social insurance scheme or from legislated policy commitments). The working-age population includes

---

[12]See Hostland and Matier (2001), Robson and Scarth (1999), and Scarth and Jackson (1998) for interesting discussions of some of the trade-offs that arise in seeking to follow alternative rules for debt reduction while still providing flexibility for fiscal policy to be used for countercyclical objectives.

[13]Addressing the issue of intergenerational rights and obligations with respect to the quality of the environment that is left for future generations, Beckerman and Pasek (2001) argue persuasively that unborn future generations have no *absolute* rights in this regard. They do argue strongly, however, that current generations have a moral obligation to at least "take account of the interests of these future generations." There is, however, an interesting twist to their argument, which is that they also argue that "rights" and "obligations" are paired. There can be no rights without obligations. Yet if one switches to the field of social insurance, it is palpably clear that current generations have built a system of intergenerational relations that assumes that future generations are *obligated* to pay for the pensions of current generations, at least in any PAYGO-type insurance system. Sinn (2000) raises this point in assessing the argument for a shift to a funded rather than PAYGO system.

several cohorts with possibly divergent interests: those close to retirement, those in the prime of their working years, and those newly arrived in the labor market. These are the groups most strongly affected by government policies that involve the financing of current outlays and transfers. They have a primary interest in the government's commitments regarding the quality and quantity of the retirement or medical insurance benefits for which they will eventually be eligible; they also have a powerful interest in the quality of the environment—political and physical—in which they will live the rest of their lives.

The youngest generation living today, from the newly born to those presently in college, is likely to be tapped to finance much of the government's outlays over the next several decades. They and their children will also be the principal inheritors of what today's working and retired generations will have bequeathed in terms of capital endowments and overall productivity of the economy, the state of international relations, and the state of the environment.

In a political sense, the interests of the nearest *unborn* generations also need to be considered. Certainly, their prospective parents and grandparents see their welfare as important. Those interests are largely the same as those described for the youngest generation alive today. Beyond these generations, however, interests inevitably become less personal. But taking account of just the generations already mentioned is enough to force policymakers to consider a time frame that extends well beyond the end of this century.

Second, a country's present income per capita plays an important role in judging the weight to be attached to the welfare of present as opposed to future generations. A developing country with low income per capita is likely to have a very high social time preference rate. It may be hard put to defer consumption so as to devote additional resources to saving for any but the most productive investments. Schelling (1992) and Beckerman and Pasek (2001) have stressed this point eloquently as it relates to whether or not low-income countries should invest in technologies to control carbon emissions. Given that any reasonable assumptions about future economic growth should place their populations at a significantly higher level of real income per capita in 30 to 50 years, saving for the purpose of reducing the burden of climate change on future generations may not make much sense. It would mean further impoverishing those who are poor today to benefit others tomorrow who will likely be much better off.

This is not to imply that poor countries can simply ignore all long-term risks. Some potential developments may be sufficiently prejudicial to a country's long-term growth prospects or to its fiscal sustainability to warrant current policy action (or, in some cases, inaction). For example, Chapter 2 noted that global climate change is likely to have a significant impact on mean temperature or precipitation, or both, in many of the world's poorest countries, threatening the productivity of the agricultural resources on which they depend. There may thus be strong grounds for government programs in these countries to facilitate adaptation to climate change as an important element of their economic development strategy. Infrastructural investments, agricultural research and development, and resettlement schemes may need to be considered and phased in over time; it may also be appropriate for these countries to prepare for the possibility of adverse fiscal outcomes associated with extreme climatic events (Heller and Mani, 2002). Similarly, for countries where HIV/AIDS is widespread, the adverse implications for the human capital base are likely to impair growth prospects. Fiscal policy planning may need to take account of the potential cost of outlays on antiretroviral drugs or, at least, on the medical infrastructure necessary to complement any foreign assistance in the purchase of these drugs. In sum, for poorer countries, concern for long-term risks should at least focus on ensuring that structural factors that will adversely affect the productive base of the economy are taken into account in the current investment strategy.

Third, there is no single definition or universally accepted measure of fairness. Should fairness be determined simply by the magnitude of the positive or negative net transfers (taxes paid less transfers received) to each generation over its lifetime, as in the generational accounting framework (Kotlikoff and Raffelhuschen, 1999; see Chapter 3)?[14] Or should it be defined in terms of each generation having equal rights and bearing equal obligations? Or, more specifically, should future generations be expected to bear a higher tax burden than current generations would be willing to accept for themselves, because they will be richer?[15] What obligations should future generations have toward current working generations?

---

[14]Should a generation's contributions instead be evaluated in a broader sense, including not only its payment of taxes but also its contribution in terms of the production of human capital? Sinn (2000) argues that the current working-age population, having opted for fewer children than past generations, should be saving more to compensate for the smaller cohorts to whom they have bequeathed the task of providing for their own old-age support. Sinn uses this argument to justify a double financing burden on current generations in the transition from an unfunded to a funded pension system.

[15]This is the type of philosophical question that John Rawls would pose in laying out his theory of justice in terms of "fairness" (see Beckerman and Pasek, 2001).

In a world of increasing productivity, tomorrow's working generations will have higher incomes than the generations that have preceded them, and in that sense will be the beneficiaries of the investments made by those earlier generations. Is it therefore reasonable for those future generations to bear higher tax rates, if they are still left better off, in terms of net income per capita, than those previous generations? If so, then how should one value the "consumption" by current generations of society's environmental capital, which *reduces* the quality of the environmental endowment that they will bequeath to future generations? Should today's adult (working-age and elderly) generations bear more of the burden caused by the deterioration of the environment that their consumption decisions have caused?[16] Or does intergenerational fairness simply require that each generation honor the contract made with past generations, just as those generations honored their similar obligations to previous generations, no matter what the financial returns to each generation might turn out to be under that arrangement (a notion enshrined in PAYGO pension systems)? To put the matter more simply, what right does a current generation have to insist on the fulfillment of promises made by past governments, when the burden of that fulfillment will be borne by future generations?

For any generation, its expectations concerning the government's role and public policy promises are fundamental inputs to its decisions about the trade-offs between consumption and saving, or between income and leisure. It will clearly be seen as unfair if one generation reneges on its commitments to another in a way that leaves the latter little time to make offsetting adjustments in its work or saving decisions. This is no less true if the government's past commitments were excessive.

Fourth, issues of intergenerational fairness are intensely political, because the interests of different generations often diverge. Economics can shed light on, and provide measures to assess, the relative financial positions of different generations. But, as should be obvious by now, judging the fairness of those outcomes is not easy. Moreover, it is the *political* reconciliation of these divergent interests that ultimately matters. This reconciliation may have less to do with the relative merits of each generation's claim than with the weight of different generations in the political decision-making process. For example, a rising share of elderly in the electorate may tilt the outcome in their favor.

---

[16]In an international context this question becomes even more complicated, given that industrial countries have been responsible for much of the environmental damage that will be borne by future generations, in developing and industrial countries alike.

Thus, in practical terms, when confronting issues of intergenerational fairness, governments should seek to answer the following questions (in addition to, and independent of, the solvency and efficiency considerations discussed elsewhere in this chapter):

- *How should differences in the welfare of current and future generations be reconciled?* As already noted, a high social time preference rate should be expected in poor countries, even though this limits the social profitability of investments with long gestations. But the argument for a high social time preference rate has also been made for wealthier countries, where the presumption of higher incomes per capita in the future suggests that, even if future generations bear higher tax rates as a consequence, their absolute consumption will still be much higher than that of today's working generations (Guest and McDonald, 2001a).

- *How should countries facilitate an equitable sharing, across generations, of the burden of excessive past policy commitments?* Questions can always be raised about whether the benefits of past borrowing or past legislated promises were worth the cost. The debts must nonetheless be repaid and the promises kept. The question then becomes, how much of that burden should be shared with future generations more distant from the original obligation? The issue arises in stark terms when the welfare of future generations would argue for fiscal consolidation to reduce a large public debt, yet at the same time the expansionary use of fiscal policy is seen as a critical short-term need. (This is arguably the case of Japan today.) Public debt burdens will look much lighter, years or decades hence, in an economy that has seen healthy growth during that time than in one that has been stagnant. Many economists would therefore advocate accepting a larger public debt in the short term if it pays for fiscal stimulus that restores the economy to full employment and rapid growth.

- *Will capital investments generate sufficient returns to future taxpayers to justify shifting the burden of their financing into the future?*

- *What burden is "reasonable" to impose on future generations?* The answer may be framed in different ways: in terms of future tax rates, for example, or the quality of bequeathed environmental conditions. As a practical political matter, most governments would wish to avoid placing such a heavy burden on future generations as to create strong incentives for the commitments that these burdens support to be overturned.

- *How should countries respond if there are widespread perceptions that existing commitments will impose an excessive burden on future generations?* If future generations are likely to reject the financing of these burdens, governments would need to assess, now, whether and how these commitments can be scaled back. Since such a reduction would imply reduced benefits for some groups, it would be desirable for governments to provide adequate lead time to enable them to take steps to adjust and adapt to this lower level of benefit provision. What are the costs and who bears the burden of a wholesale or a partial reneging on long-standing commitments?

Improving Allocative Efficiency

All else equal, governments wish to achieve their objectives for social welfare in a way that maximizes total income and minimizes allocative inefficiency. Many see the latter as particularly important in evaluating alternative approaches to long-term issues, whether at an aggregate level or at the level of specific sectors or programs. Allocative efficiency has been invoked in a number of contexts bearing on long-term issues. It has been used to argue for prefunding of expenditure commitments for which spending is likely to rise sharply in the future, to avoid having to raise taxes when these commitments fall due. It has been used to argue against the high negative tax rates often associated with means-tested transfer programs. And it has been cited as a reason for governments to play a greater role in managing risk (see below). Thus allocative efficiency issues often influence what would otherwise be strictly macroeconomic policy considerations.

Because taxes are typically imposed as rates on income, spending, or some other economic variable rather than as a lump sum, they almost inevitably give rise to allocative inefficiencies, or deadweight losses. Because these losses, according to theory, rise quadratically with the tax rate, many economists argue on allocative efficiency grounds for limiting the overall tax burden as a fraction of GDP (Barro, 1979). This has led to arguments for tax smoothing in financing the growing prospective burden of PAYGO pension systems and medical care in countries with aging populations (Bohn, 1990; Davis and Fabling, 2002). If tax rates are raised modestly today, before the funds are needed, surpluses can be accumulated and invested (that is, prefunding can occur). The proceeds of those investments can then be used to limit the tax hikes that would otherwise be needed in the future. Tax smoothing is thus seen as a more efficient alternative to a pure balanced-budget or PAYGO approach, in which taxes are raised periodically to offset necessary increases in expenditure as they arise. But because tax smoothing shifts some of the burden from future taxpaying generations to those paying taxes today (Jensen and Nielsen, 1995; Davis and Fabling, 2002),[17] distributive considerations also enter into any comprehensive assessment of such a strategy.

Several issues should be flagged when considering the appropriateness of a tax smoothing strategy. First, how large are the deadweight losses that could emerge under the alternative, balanced-budget approach? This is empirically controversial. Cutler and others (1990) and Jensen and Nielsen (1995) suggest that these losses would be low, whereas Davis and Fabling (2002) find them to be much larger.[18] But to answer this question requires an assessment of how much tax smoothing is likely to be required. Should one take account only of the possibility of those adverse scenarios on key assumptions that are directly related to population aging (such as a potential improvement in life expectancy)? Or should one also take account of the potential additional expenditure burdens that might arise from other risk factors and uncertainties that are likely to influence the fiscal situation over the long term? A policy of tax smoothing based on a less than comprehensive consideration of fiscal risks may leave a government still facing an unsustainable fiscal position.

Second, even if the deadweight losses associated with a balanced-budget approach are large, are they large enough to offset what might be the negative growth effects from higher tax rates in the short term under a tax smoothing approach (as suggested in OECD, 1997)? And will citizens accept the amount of prefunding required as protection against multiple risks, even if they understand that doing so limits the

---

[17]One important consideration with achieving a tax smoothing policy is to ensure that the choice of time frame actually facilitates smoothing. Thus, in the context of an aging population, having an infinite time horizon rather than a discrete terminal period (even as far out as 75 years) may prevent the need for annual adjustments in the smoothed rate. For example, Lee and Yamagata (2003) note that the U.S. Social Security system's choice of a 75-year time horizon should, in principle, result in annual tax rate adjustments, taking account of the impact of increasing life expectancy beyond the terminal point (also see Auerbach, 1994).

[18]Part of the difference in results reflects Davis and Fabling's assumption that the assets accumulated under tax smoothing would earn an average return that exceeds the government's cost of borrowing. In this case the preference for tax smoothing is robust with respect to variations in discount rates, expenditure growth assumptions, labor supply elasticities, and the mix of asset allocation (but not to political economy considerations, in connection with expenditure creep).

likelihood of further tax increases or cutbacks in expenditure?[19] Will citizens accept the notion of higher taxes now to avoid an even higher tax burden tomorrow? Also, once decided upon, when should a policy of tax smoothing begin? Any delay is likely to entail much higher tax rates during the period over which taxes are smoothed.[20]

Third, the argument for prefunding presupposes that the government is able to insulate the accumulated resources from being diverted to other uses (in other words, that those resources will be protected from expenditure creep). It needs to be determined whether this is a plausible assumption.

Fourth, there may be allocative efficiency grounds for arguing *against* tax smoothing. A recent paper by Bohn (1990) argues why a defined-benefit pension system that essentially relies on PAYGO financing might be preferable to a defined-contribution system, which is essentially a prefunded system.[21]

Fifth, the information requirements of a tax smoothing approach are huge, requiring detailed calculations on the long-run fiscal position under alternative scenarios on various policy programs. Hence there may be an option value in waiting and not tax smoothing, because the cost of getting it wrong may be high. It can prove costly to have raised taxes to finance an expenditure profile that then does not materialize as expected (Davis and Fabling, 2002).

Sixth, if tax smoothing is justified by the reduced deadweight losses from lower future tax rates, similar considerations would presumably also argue for expenditure policy reforms that would lower the

---

[19]To the extent that policymakers and economists have a view as to the maximum tax rates that are acceptable in efficiency terms, the fiscal framework should be set so as to allow leeway for unanticipated fiscal outlays, within this revenue constraint, without excessive pressure for abrupt cutbacks in other policy commitments that would involve a serious reneging or default. In the New Zealand context, Bradbury, Brumby, and Skilling (1997) have argued for levying an additional, "precautionary" tax as a buffer against unanticipated shocks. Skilling (1997) has subsequently argued that this would be appropriate only when the balance sheet position is weak, with significant net debt.

[20]Where there are delays in adjusting the fiscal framework in response to presently anticipated fiscal burdens, the tax rates eventually required (whether for budget balancing or tax smoothing) could be significantly higher than the rate that would be required if tax smoothing were implemented immediately (Auerbach and Gale, 2000; U.S. Congressional Budget Office, 2000; Janssen, 2002). The deadweight efficiency losses will be consequently greater as well. An analogy can be drawn to the adaptation of agriculture to climate change: greater efficiency losses are likely to arise if these efforts are delayed.

[21]Essentially, models like Bohn's take account of the changes in the relative prices of capital and labor that are likely to emerge in the context of a significant demographic shift, and the resulting impact on the incomes of different generations derived from capital and labor.

smoothed tax rates still further. But this inevitably involves a trade-off between the adequacy of government expenditure programs and policy commitments and the growth and efficiency gains to be had from lower taxes. If lower tax rates do lead to faster growth and ultimately higher incomes, for both the current and future working generations, this may create capacity to pay for other needed expenditures. But initially it may involve a welfare loss for the older (current and future) generations in the form of lower future transfers (Sinn, 2000). Here intergenerational equity issues again come to the fore. The current working generations would pay the higher tax rates associated with a tax smoothing strategy, whereas future working generations would be spared the burden of much higher tax rates.[22]

Finally, concern for the allocative distortions of higher tax rates may lead policymakers to limit the generosity of public social insurance schemes or to institute individually funded pension approaches coupled with targeted or means-tested welfare schemes. But the latter approach can itself give rise to allocative distortions. For example, some governments guarantee at least a minimum pension annuity. Low-income households whose accumulated private savings are likely to be insufficient to generate income in retirement above the floor guarantees would then have little incentive to save during their working lives. This issue has arisen in the United Kingdom in the context of its minimum state pension and its minimum welfare guarantee. Similarly, it has long been recognized that means-tested benefits can imply high negative tax rates for the lowest income groups.

Managing Risk

Robert Samuelson (2002b) has observed that

> We have gone from a world of seemingly small and understandable risks to one of huge and imponderable hazards. Terrorism? Who knows? It may be an immense danger—or merely a periodic tragedy. The accuracy of corporate accounting? Another black hole.... Increasingly, economic psychology depends on hopes and fears that lie outside recent experience. We don't know what we don't know.... There's a rediscovery of risk.

---

[22]The trade-off is not zero-sum, however, because both generations would benefit to some degree from the higher efficiency gains from avoiding higher tax rates.

Central to issues of long-term fiscal planning by the government is the fact that the future holds considerable risks and uncertainties. These may be financial in nature (such as uncertainty about future interest yields and earnings possibilities), or demographic or health-related (both the cost to government pension programs of greater than expected longevity and the uncertainty about the costs associated with providing medical care to the elderly), or environmental (such as exposure to extreme weather events), or security related (such as the threat of terrorist attack). Households and businesses can insure against some of the risks in private markets, with government's role, if it has one, limited to regulation and the provision of social insurance or reinsurance. But the private insurance market may not cover other risks effectively, and governments may choose to correct for this failure, or for individuals' myopia or lack of information, or for their inability to afford insurance when it is available, by establishing social insurance systems, social safety nets, reinsurance programs, and emergency assistance programs.

As was noted in Chapter 3, governments also face risk management issues in the context of public debt management policies, where they must choose how to balance the trade-off between a higher return and greater risk. For example, governments often must decide whether to issue a succession of short-term debt instruments rather than borrow long term; they must also decide in which currency their debt instruments should be denominated, and whether debt is to be defined in real terms (that is, using inflation-indexed bonds) or in nominal terms (IMF and World Bank, 2001; Bohn, 1990; Missale, 1999; Skilling, 1997; New Zealand Debt Management Office, 1997). Such issues also arise in the government's management of its financial assets and its liabilities other than debt, and in its policy interventions that involve financial commitments of one kind or another.

Yet it is important to recognize that many other elements of a government's budget can also be regarded as risky assets or liabilities, with differing mean-variance properties that will influence the probability of alternative outcomes in the future. Each of a government's various revenue instruments and sources can be seen as subject to different types of risk, depending on its underlying determinants—aggregate economic activity within the country or its principal trading partners, demographic factors, or international commodity prices, for example. Spending on each element of a government's portfolio of legislated entitlement commitments—unemployment insurance, health insurance, pension benefits, and the like—can also be characterized in terms of its mean-variance properties. The further out in time one looks, the greater the uncertainty associated with each of the factors that determine these expenditures. Uncertainties likewise surround the level of future spending on public goods and on redistributive transfers. A probability distribution may also be assigned to the likelihood that a government will need to meet costly implicit reinsurance commitments in the event of extreme weather events or terrorist incidents.

How a government approaches risk can have substantial consequences. Failure to deal with risk appropriately can lead to a precipitous cutback in expenditure commitments, a sharp and abrupt increase in tax rates, or even to default on the government's debt (whether by explicit default or by inflating the debt away). It can influence the macroeconomic picture if excessive risks are taken in a government's approach to borrowing (witness the experience of Russia, Argentina, Korea, and Indonesia in recent years) or in the kind of assets purchased (witness the losses experienced by poor investment management by state-run pension systems in Latin America; Hausmann, 2002). As we have already seen, by accumulating unsustainable public debt, governments risk losing the capacity to use fiscal policy in an active countercyclical way or to ensure that the budget can respond appropriately to unanticipated shocks. This suggests that a government's appraisal of the risk and return characteristics of its balance sheet needs to be comprehensive, taking account of all forms of assets and liabilities.

Even if it were easy to present policymakers and the public with a clear picture of the future probability distribution of some key indicator of fiscal sustainability, a decision would still have to be made about how much risk to accept. With what degree of confidence should a government assume that its long-term position is sustainable? In formulating its policies, a government cannot avoid taking a position on its attitude to risk. The question is to what extent the government should be risk neutral or risk averse in framing its aggregate fiscal position.

Although they are seldom expressed formally, governments and the body politic are likely to have strong views about how much risk should be tolerated along each of the various dimensions of fiscal policy, including the level of tax rates, disbursements on benefit entitlements, and the amount of flexibility needed in the budget to respond to unanticipated crises without compromising macroeconomic stability. These views on risk are embodied not only in the design of particular policy instruments and commitments, but also in the choice of the overall fiscal policy stance. Particularly if there is considerable uncertainty about the long term, views on risk tolerance may influence the appropriate target for the government's net debt position.[23]

This attitude toward risk will also influence how political decision-makers weigh different policy objectives and the trade-offs among them. As Lee and Edwards (2002, p. 35) put it, "Should the probability of worse outcomes lead us to take additional precautionary measures today, or should the possibility of better outcomes lead us to postpone action until we are sure action will be necessary?"[24] This question bears on policy choices in many spheres, from population aging to climate change to threats to international peace. It becomes particularly acute when policy decisions entail substantial and irreversible capital outlays (for example, with respect to climate change mitigation). To what extent does the degree of risk associated with achieving a given objective influence the policy balance between objectives that is ultimately chosen?

For example, uncertainty about the future rate of technological progress related to climate change (both technologies that make carbon consumption more efficient and technologies that mitigate the effects of carbon emissions) may tempt governments to defer action. If technological progress is then slower than expected, however, such delay may prove inefficient and costly. One of the difficulties that policy advisers often face is that a number of objectives may all be deemed important, but decision makers are loath to clarify how they trade off the risk and return characteristics of alternative policy choices with respect to those different objectives. Also, as with tax smoothing, it is difficult

---

[23]Much of the literature relates to whether there are efficiency grounds for the government taking an active approach to risk management and whether, in doing so, it should seek to mirror the degree of risk aversion of its citizenry (perhaps of the median voter), or be more risk averse (reflecting a number of market failures that limit the ability of citizens to hedge against the government's risk position), or be risk neutral.

[24]An important consideration in the choice between the public and the private sector, as the agent responsible for managing a scheme that involves the investment of assets or the delivery of services, is the extent to which there is more or less risk to individuals. For industrial countries at least, one could argue that the assumption by the government of a commitment to provide a given level of benefits entails more risk to the government and less to the beneficiary than in the case of the private sector provider or agent. Although government default is certainly an option, it carries with it extremely serious consequences. For private sector agents, in contrast, there can be no ready "deep purse" to compensate for a failure of an investment strategy, and thus more of the risk is borne by the individual if a company fails or goes bankrupt. In contrast, when it relates to the issue of services, there may be less difference, as the quality of services can be varied depending on the financial position of the provider.

to evaluate the appropriateness of a policy choice wholly on efficiency grounds; equity considerations enter the picture as well.

Political economy considerations will play an important role in determining the degree of risk aversion that a government chooses. They will influence how risks will be spread across taxpayers as a group, and which individuals or groups will bear the brunt of those risks. In a recent study, Auerbach and Hassett (2001) present a model of government decision making under uncertainty and conclude that "with a risk averse population, the costs of future outcomes [that are] even worse than those expected outweigh the benefits of outcomes [that are] better than expected. Action thus should not only not be delayed but ...should be accelerated." But they also note that a government's approach to risk and uncertainty is likely to depend on whether it has the political capacity to make important policy adjustments as needed, or is constrained to make such adjustments only infrequently—say, once in a generation. If the latter, Auerbach and Hassett's model suggests that governments may indeed choose inaction even when fiscal tightening is called for.

Current electorates may be more disposed to accept a high degree of risk in the future if they believe that the consequences of an unfavorable outcome (in terms of, say, higher tax rates or greater climatic deterioration) will be borne principally by future generations. However, it cannot be assumed that a government's role is likely to remain constant over time, particularly as it is subjected to significant pressures consequent upon an aging society. Future electorates, in response to such adverse outcomes, may be willing to pursue time-inconsistent policies, for example cutting back on commitments made by today's government. The likelihood of this happening may also influence how today's voters appraise and deal with future risks. Some authors have noted that the prospect of aging populations may itself be leading governments, for reasons of political economy, to shrink their obligations today (Breyer and Stolte, 2000; Razin, Sadka, and Swagel, 2001).

Other, independent pressures may weigh on a government's approach to risk. The government, as an institutional entity, has an interest in ensuring a fiscally sustainable policy stance that minimizes the risk of its insolvency. However, the government is also an agent of the electorate, which may have broader welfare objectives that conflict with the government's narrow interest. Thus there can be a tension between the government's duty as an agent of its citizens and its own institutional interests.

Additionally, in an interconnected world, the risks of inconsistency in a country's policies over time are not a matter of concern for the citizens of that country alone. If a country is borrowing in international capital markets, concern among market participants about the country's fiscal sustainability may put pressure on the risk premium on the interest rate it pays, creating an independent incentive for a more conservative fiscal position. For countries that are of systemic global or regional importance, multilateral surveillance pressures may also be brought to bear when the country pursues potentially unsustainable fiscal policies or becomes overextended in its policy commitments.

Finally, governments also need to decide how to deal with genuine uncertainty, the real wild cards that cannot be measured in mean-variance terms, as discussed in Chapter 2. This is typically the rationale for the contingency accounts normally included in annual budget appropriations.[25] It may also be reflected in the approach taken in specific policy design and the overall fiscal stance to ensure that a particular policy can be implemented and financed sustainably with a high degree of certainty.

Dealing with Political Obstacles

Considerations of political economy cast a large shadow over any discussion of the fiscal impact of long-term issues. Government decisions are rarely made by independent "wise men," scrupulously calculating the parameters of an intertemporal social welfare function while minding constraints and taking due account of various risks and uncertainties. Nor are they made by social philosophers or economists, capable of striking an unambiguously fair balance between the conflicting interests of multiple generations in a world of increasing uncertainty while also giving efficiency considerations their due.

Rather, policy decisions affecting the long-term fiscal position are normally made by politicians and political parties, and they share that stage with other agents who are seldom shy about asserting their role in setting policies and whose incentives may diverge from those of the party in power. These agents include the government bureaucracy and, increasingly, a set of external players that includes international bureaucracies, both at a regional and at the global level, and even nongovernmental organizations (NGOs). Their involvement limits the

---

[25]Schick (2002b) speculates that, in the future, surveillance of countries within the European Economic and Monetary Union might entail assessments of those countries' budgets that focus more on issues of sustainability or risk than on annual or medium-term outlooks.

range of decisions that elected officials are free to make. Those officials must also contend with political, international, and economic constraints (not to mention a historical legacy of past policy commitments that are not easily undone, as discussed below).

The motives of these multiple agents are likely to differ. Ignoring the interests of external agents and abstracting from more venal or personal interests, one can cite, among others, a concern for the broad social welfare, the need to deliver on promises made to constituents in the most recent election campaign, the desire to be reelected, the preservation and protection of the continuity and credibility of the state and its bureaucracies (even in the context of new, politically motivated reforms), and the achievement of sustainable and durable results from recently instituted policy measures.

It is in this swirling political economy mix that the various considerations that influence how issues of the long term—the financial and welfare consequences, the approach to risk taking and uncertainty—are identified, weighed, and ultimately resolved. The political economy of any country is a vast and complex topic, but a few key generalizations can be made.

First, it is difficult to be optimistic, on political economy grounds at least, that governments will address long-term fiscal issues adequately, unless strong pressure is brought to bear on them to do so. Taking the long term into account requires that political decision makers be willing to ask generations living today, whether working or retired, to sacrifice a portion of their own interests for those of later generations, including those yet unborn. Those sacrifices may involve higher taxes, or cutbacks in government benefits, present or future. Even if the merits of such action appear sensible in strict economic benefit-cost terms, the political costs may seem to today's politicians to be better spent addressing current needs. Yet inaction on long-term issues is itself a policy act, and one that may force more drastic action in the future, either because time has been lost during which productive investments in the future could have been made, or because the losses due to today's inaction—for example, the failure to limit greenhouse gas emissions—are by their nature irreversible.

Second, actions that involve the long term may have different impacts on the narrow personal interests of different groups within the electorate. As Schick (2002b, p. 21) notes, "Whether by sector or class, the budget battles of the future will be over how much should be allocated to each set of claimants." It is not just that politicians find it difficult to turn issues of long-term significance into a basis for political support. It may indeed be in the interest of a majority *not* to confront such issues and not to seek change.[26]

Third, one should never underestimate the complexity of the political economy forces acting on any given issue. Policies that are adopted for the sake of short-term expediency may have dynamic political economy consequences that are not easily anticipated. For example, commitments to social insurance, once established, may create vested interests in maintaining and perhaps even increasing those commitments. Expectations about what is an appropriate level of public service provision (for example, in the area of medical care) may become inflated and be difficult to change. Similarly, the policy response to a crisis, such as a devastating flood or a terrorist attack, may lead the public to expect similar treatment in the future.

On the other hand, it is always possible that the electorate will at some point realize its critical role in determining its own and its children's future, and choose to address long-term issues in a way that balances short- and long-term interests. Sometimes that role involves a measure of gamesmanship. For example, in assessing recent pension reform legislation in Western Europe, some economic and political theorists have noted that gaming considerations might have motivated current generations to reduce their own future benefits in order to reduce the likelihood that future generations would make decisions even more detrimental to their interests (Breyer and Stolte, 2000; Leers, Meijdam, and Verbon, 2001; Razin, Sadka, and Swagel, 2001).

Fourth, it may be far easier to motivate voters to take action when they are faced with an immediate and imperative need. A frank budget crisis can prove far more compelling than any number of technical policy analyses warning of deficits far in the future and threatening dire consequences that are hard for laypersons to comprehend or assess (Auerbach and Hassett, 2001). Even when the general public recognizes that delays in policy reform will eventually result in higher taxes or cuts in benefits, "these adjustments [are] easier to do in the face of actual circumstances than in the face of forecasts" (Weil, 2001, p. 247). A crisis may thus prove more effective than rational analyses in forcing a political consensus on the need for action.

---

[26]Sinn and Uebelmesser (2002) cite results from a model they have constructed that shows that, in Germany, a potential political majority for switching from a PAYGO to a fully funded pension system exists only until 2020. By 2027 more than 55 percent of German voters can be expected to oppose reform. By 2030 Germany would effectively be a gerontocracy that would strongly oppose reform.

Fifth, political economy factors may also make it difficult to *sustain* past policy decisions that were taken with a long-term focus. For example, many current fiscal regimes are predicated on policies that require continued budget surpluses in order to keep the fiscal situation sufficiently sound to confront future challenges. Such a regime faces both the difficulty of maintaining political support for continued fiscal adjustment and discipline, and the political temptations that a strong fiscal position offers (even if it is recognized to be strong only over the short to the medium term).[27] Such policies need to hold firm in the face of various potential challenges: shifts in political regime, changes in the weight of different age cohorts in the population and in the interests of each cohort over time, and changes in the fiscal situation itself, both anticipated and unanticipated.[28] Chapter 5 expands on this issue.

Sixth, political economy arguments underscore the importance of the institutional approaches and mechanisms that some governments have recently adopted in the hope of securing a basis for addressing certain long-term issues in a sustainable way. As discussed in Chapter 3, these include, among other approaches, the use of lockboxes, that is, the establishment of separate trust accounts for the buildup of a positive gross asset position (concurrent with the maintenance of a significant level of gross debt). But lockboxes can be politically hazardous, precisely because of the arbitrary nature of government accounting labels. The constraints they impose on actual fiscal policy can thus be open to interpretation (and manipulation).

Finally, greater transparency in policymaking can support a more informed consideration of long-term issues, which may result in sounder long-term policies (see Chapter 3). Discipline in fiscal decision making is promoted when information on the state of public finances, on the nature of the existing policy regime, on the nature of the principal risks on the horizon, and on the nature of any policy changes being considered is both widely available and broadly comprehensible. This discipline derives from forces both in the political arena and in markets,

---

[27]Pinfield (1998), in a discussion of the consequences of "expenditure creep," develops a model to illustrate this point. Kraemer (2002) presents persuasive evidence about what would happen if some of the EU countries with strong fiscal positions (primary surpluses of up to 5 percent of GDP) were to be constrained to run overall budget surpluses of no more than 1 percent of GDP. The sustainability of their current positions would be dramatically eroded.

[28]Davis and Fabling (2002), who argue for tax smoothing rather than a balanced-budget strategy, suggest that political economy considerations would tilt the argument in favor of the latter approach: "Hence, strong fiscal institutions are a prerequisite for achieving the welfare gains of tax smoothing" (p. 2).

because both voters and markets seek transparency in order to form a judgment on the capacity of a government to meet its commitments. Transparency ensures that any potential policy changes are subject to full public scrutiny and debate. It enables people outside of government to form expectations about government actions—from future tax rates to transfer entitlements to pricing policies—while recognizing that moral hazard considerations may inevitably leave some possible government responses uncertain. It also allows for an assessment of the potential risks to the long-run fiscal situation.

Anticipating Market Reactions

In an apolitical world, a country's leaders, once seized with the urgency of addressing a fiscally unsustainable position, allocative inefficiencies, or intergenerational inequities, would surely take action to implement policy adjustments. The previous section suggested, however, that political economy constraints might limit those leaders' willingness or capacity to implement politically difficult measures. International agreements may also narrow their scope to modify certain tax regimes and may require minimum levels of expenditure in particular areas. The pressures of tax competition—competition with other countries to lower taxes to attract foreign investment—may place limits on or even force reductions in the amount of revenue that can be extracted from some tax bases. And governments may find their fiscal leeway squeezed by the pincer effect of limits on the feasible tax burden, the need for adequate spending on traditional public goods and services, constitutionally imposed transfers to regional and local governments, and policy commitments on entitlement spending.

Markets are yet another force that can limit the effectiveness and scope of government policy actions. Chapter 3 has already alluded to the possibility of Ricardian equivalence effects: households may offset fiscal policy actions by reducing or increasing their saving (see Chapter 5 for a more detailed discussion). This highlights the fact that the success of a prefunding initiative might depend on how it is implemented. Cutbacks in future expenditure commitments may have a twofold effect: they may prompt an increase in offsetting private consumption (as households anticipate that smaller future deficits will mean lower future tax rates); however, they may raise saving rates if the cuts in future expenditure commitments mean reduced future benefit payments to households.

Other examples of market "resistance" can be cited. A government's efforts to raise tax rates to strengthen its financial viability may induce a negative supply response from either labor or capital that undercuts the revenue base. The experience of Western and Central Europe suggests that the share of the economy operating in the informal sector is sensitive to tax rates (although not to the extreme degree postulated by some Laffer curve apologists). In some cases workers appear to opt for more leisure when tax rates become very high.[29] Similarly, businesses may seek, at the margin, to transfer some of their operations to jurisdictions with lower taxes.

General-equilibrium effects might also prove confounding. Governments may seek to prefund future expenditure commitments through larger public surpluses, but whether this is a viable approach depends on future interest rates. Rates might decline as a consequence of increased saving by government and by the private sector (in an economy with a large and efficient capital market), or as a consequence of a softening in global capital markets (perhaps as a result of comparable saving efforts by other industrial countries with aging populations). Thus prefunding may fail to accumulate the full amount of resources that it was intended to.[30]

The possibility of vicious and virtuous circles in market responses also needs to be considered. It is not difficult to imagine circumstances in which a government's fiscal policy stance would produce such a response. For example, a government's ability to borrow may be limited to the extent that the private sector exacts a higher risk premium in response to a perceived increase in the government's debt exposure. By increasing the cost of government borrowing, the higher risk premium can then raise the government's overall budget deficit, which can then further exacerbate market solvency concerns, leading to further pressure on the fiscal stance.

Three final qualifications should be noted. First, in examining the behavioral response of markets to a policy action, it is important to distinguish among possibly offsetting effects of various specific types. Market forces may simply undercut the effectiveness of macroeconomic policy in stimulating or inhibiting economic activity. Or they may vitiate the government's efforts to achieve a stronger fiscal position. Or they may

---

[29] In Denmark and some other European countries where the tax share is already high, a decline in the number of hours worked may be evidence of an increasing demand for leisure.

[30] Attanasio and Violante (2000) have developed a multicountry general-equilibrium model that illustrates this point quite forcefully. See also Bohn (1999).

weaken the impact of the government's efforts at achieving specific microeconomic policy objectives (such as the adequacy of pension coverage, private or public, for the elderly population). In the Ricardian equivalence case cited above, although some of the induced market response may limit the macroeconomic impact of a government's policies, it may not reduce the impact on the government's own fiscal position. In other words, the same tax increase may have limited macroeconomic effects yet still contribute to fiscal sustainability.

Second, determining the plausible range of market responses may not be straightforward. Indeed, those responses may go in either direction—or in both directions, offsetting each other. For example, policy actions that restore credibility to a public pension scheme (such as a gradual increase in the age at which beneficiaries are entitled to pensions) may have both positive *and* negative effects on saving. Some individuals may increase their saving to offset the effective reduction in the pension benefits they will receive, while others may reduce their saving, anticipating that their future tax rates will fall as a consequence of the improved fiscal outlook.

Third, policy actions can have side effects, which might dampen their desirability. Policies that entail the buildup of financial assets or the elimination of government debt might prove detrimental to the operation of a country's capital markets or to the country's capacity to pursue monetary policy through open market operations. Also, corporate governance issues inevitably arise when the government is the owner of a significant portion of a country's equity.

Legacy Effects and Dynamic Nonlinearities

Two final considerations weigh heavily on any country seeking to address long-term issues. The first might be termed the "legacy factor." The above discussion laid out the political economy constraints that may make policy reforms difficult to realize. But every country also has a legacy of past policy commitments, in the form of debt obligations, the inherited fiscal policy stance, and the present structure of expenditure (for example, the balance among subsidies, income transfers, and provision of public goods). Also part of the legacy is any legislation that specifies how different categories of expenditure shall respond to changes in external factors—demographic, economic, or otherwise.

It should be obvious, but is worth emphasizing nevertheless, that a country with little debt and a strong fiscal position—that is, one with more fiscal slack—is much better positioned to address future potential fiscal risks. This is true even if the country's social insurance policy obligations are relatively generous given prospective demographic trends. In a recent study by Kraemer (2002), what differentiated the fiscal positions projected for 2050 of what the study termed the "pioneer" EU countries (Denmark, Finland, Ireland, Luxembourg, Sweden, and the United Kingdom) from those of the "laggards" (including, among others, France, Germany, the Netherlands, and Spain) was "the level of already achieved fiscal consolidation" rather than the differences in the groundwork laid for containing future age-related spending.

A country that starts with an adverse fiscal legacy will find it far more difficult to cope with the fiscal risks that it will face in coming decades. For example, countries such as Belgium and Italy, although included in the "pioneer" category because of their strong primary surplus position, also inherit an adverse legacy in the form of their large national debts (a point often stressed by the European Commission; see European Commission, 2002a). Although all projections of age-related spending suggest that these countries are in a strong fiscal position, the caveat is always made that this presumes that their extremely large primary surplus positions can be sustained for the whole period. These countries will need to have a very resilient political economy if they are to sustain such positions.[31]

Unbalanced expenditure structures can also constitute an adverse legacy. As an example, to achieve the budgetary guidelines in the 1992 Maastricht Treaty, Italy pursued a policy of fiscal consolidation, largely accomplished through adjustments in tax revenue, reductions in capital expenditure, and limits on transfers to local governments. Balassone, Momigliano, and Monacelli (2002) note that if further expenditure consolidation in coming years is to avoid any cutbacks in pension, health, or capital outlays, it will be necessary to reduce other expenditures by about a quarter (or from 16 percent to 12 percent of GDP), implying annual real cutbacks of 3 percent. (To note the presence of these adverse legacies is not to suggest that actions to reduce projected growth in age-related outlays are unimportant. The point is rather that the urgency of doing so is compounded by the lack of sufficient budgetary consolidation to date.)

---

[31] Indeed, for countries in Latin America, high starting debt positions, with the additional legacy of vulnerability to foreign exchange or inflation pressures, are even more risky, because they are often unaccompanied by as strong an initial primary surplus position (see Hausmann, 2002).

A second factor that can constrain policy is that some structural developments may suddenly intensify in their impact. Just as a bunching of the maturities of government debt instruments can complicate debt refinancing, so, too, there may be nonlinearities in the pressures that particular structural issues engender. For example, demographic pressures in many countries will not increase smoothly, but rather will rise sharply after a certain point. Recent analyses by the OECD, Standard & Poor's, and Deutsche Bank illustrate well the dynamics of age-related burdens.[32] Kraemer's (2002) analysis for Standard & Poor's notes that the burden of age-related adjustment appears fairly small over the next 10 to 20 years, but that then the picture changes dramatically:

> the necessary adjustment burden quickly piles up [thereafter]. The NPV [net present value] of the adjustment during the 2030s exceeds 100% of the respective GDP in more than one half of the EU-15 member states. Missing the window of opportunity to react early could lead to a severe crisis as early as the 2020s. (p. 20)
>
> If surpluses are not sustained and no substantial assets are accumulated during the next 10–15 years, the eventual required adjustment will become formidable once health and pension spending begins its rapid and relentless rise. We call this the "mañana trap," because incentives to maintain an austere fiscal course are largely absent in the run-up to the 2020s, when fiscal flexibility starts to evaporate. The temptation will always be to postpone necessary adjustment until the political environment is more conducive to change. (p. 11)

This was also the conclusion of the OECD (2001a), which noted that "there is a narrow window of opportunity before dependency ratios begin to rise rapidly.... Clearly, if policies are implemented with a considerable delay, stronger measures will be required to achieve the same fiscal outcomes by mid-century" (p. 165). A less obvious example of nonlinearities was mentioned in Chapter 2, namely, the possibility of abrupt changes in climate conditions; such possibilities should at least be recognized, even if they have a low probability of occurring.

Such nonlinearities can create nontrivial problems for assessments of fiscal sustainability that focus only on the medium term. Thus, fiscal forecasts carried out today and looking ahead 10 to 15 years may imply that a government's fiscal position is sustainable. But similar exercises carried out 5 years hence may begin to include periods in which the fiscal situation starts to deteriorate sharply, leading to the opposite conclusion.

---

[32]The Deutsche Bank study (Bräuninger and others, 2002) notes that the problem of absolute population decline in Germany will become particularly serious after 2015. The population decline, which will be only about 90,000 a year until that year, will increase to 180,000 a year in the next decade and rise to 325,000 a year during 2025–50.

Summing Up

This chapter has laid out some normative arguments why policy-makers, and the public generally, should pay significant attention to the possible fiscal impact of structural developments and risks that may take several decades to materialize. The welfare impact on many of those alive today, to say nothing of that on the next generation, may be significant. But the discussion has also advanced arguments why a rational citizenry might choose to be less responsive to these concerns. It has also noted the incentives and biases of political leaders toward discounting the need to act now to put the public sector on a more sound footing to deal with these potential risks and uncertainties.

As the next chapter will show, the implications of this discussion are twofold. First, there is much to be gained from further research to clarify the characteristics of potential long-term risks and their consequences for governments and for public welfare. Second, there is a strong argument to be made on political economy grounds that countries should put institutional mechanisms in place that can establish an independent perspective on their fiscal position. Such mechanisms, which may include independent budget assessment agencies, could be created internally, perhaps through changes in countries' constitutions, as elements of the domestic budget process. Or they could grow out of the surveillance processes of independent external agencies such as the IMF and the OECD. The next chapter discusses both types of mechanism. But however it is achieved, the public welfare will be well served by having an independent voice that has less of an incentive than most conventional political institutions to heavily discount the future.

5

The Way Forward: Embedding Long-Term Issues in the Fiscal Policy Framework

The preceding chapters have made two principal arguments. First, in the decades to come, countries will confront structural change—in their demographics, in their economies, and elsewhere—that will pose serious fiscal challenges, particularly for governments that have already made significant social insurance commitments. Although these challenges are fraught with uncertainty, policymakers cannot be absolved from addressing the risks that they pose. Second, the ways in which governments, in their fiscal policy framework, presently take account of these long-run developments are inadequate. Weaknesses exist at all levels: in the analytical framework, in established budgetary procedures, in accounting methodologies, and in the specifics of fiscal policy both in the aggregate and at the program level. As a result, few governments are now well positioned to address these fiscal challenges.

This chapter will examine how governments can begin to place their aggregate fiscal policies and their individual revenue and expenditure programs on a more sustainable course in an uncertain world with many long-term risks. The overarching challenge is to ensure that a long-term perspective is made integral to the way in which fiscal policy is considered, designed, and implemented. This challenge has several dimensions. The first, which the first section of this chapter discusses, is how to embed a longer-term perspective both in the way a government analyzes the sustainability of its policies, at the program level and in the aggregate, and in the way it presents its findings to the public. Considerations of risk and uncertainty must necessarily enter into such assessments for them to be valid.

A second but equally critical dimension relates to the institutional processes by which policy decisions are made. The second section of the chapter therefore examines ways in which the budget process can be strengthened to ensure that long-term issues are adequately considered when policies are being formulated. Such institutional processes can be a valuable counterweight to the inevitable tendencies of political decision makers to focus only on the short term.

An obvious third dimension relates to the *substance* of a government's policies in the face of these long-term challenges and the associated uncertainties. How should public pension or medical insurance systems be reformed in the face of adverse demographic pressures? How should the potential fiscal consequences of global warming be addressed, or the constraints that globalization may impose on the fiscal framework? This chapter does not attempt to answer these or other specific questions of the substance of policy reform. Rather, it suggests, in the third section, a broad strategy for governments confronted with the likelihood of a fiscally unsustainable position over the longer term. It argues that aggregative approaches are important but insufficient, whether they seek to adjust the overall fiscal balance through higher taxes or lower expenditure, or attempt to prefund long-term obligations through a stronger sustained fiscal position. Relying on tightening the aggregate fiscal policy stance *alone* as a means of creating sufficient leeway to address long-term risk factors is unlikely to be a successful strategy. Fiscal rules, although potentially useful, have their limits as well. The chapter argues that although some of the specific rules that have been suggested would, if observed to the letter, result in a viable long-run fiscal position (almost by definition), some of the corollary implications of pursuing such rules on a long-term basis do not appear to have been adequately considered.

Nor can a government simply count on its capacity to raise tax rates to finance burgeoning future expenditure, even with the help of higher real incomes. Adjustments to the *specific* policies that give rise to an unsustainable expenditure or revenue trajectory will be necessary. Governments will have no option but to reform their policies and programs in a way that reduces and restructures their policy commitments; to exhibit caution in taking on new policy obligations; to undertake regulatory reforms that affect how the private sector responds to risk; to prune unproductive or inappropriately targeted public expenditure; and to adopt a broader approach to asset and liability management by the public sector.

A fourth dimension to reform recognizes that many of the long-term risks faced by one country give rise to external, or spillover, effects on other countries. The approach to long-term issues taken by one country may indeed affect the welfare of others. Policy coordination among countries may therefore produce mutually beneficial outcomes. The fourth section of this chapter thus examines whether there is any scope for enhanced international policy coordination in confronting common challenges.

What should be underscored about the thrust of the reforms that this chapter will discuss is that there are no magic bullets. No single policy reform will suffice; a multipronged, comprehensive approach is required. Indeed, there is a necessary symbiosis among the various policies and strategies just outlined. If decision makers and the public lack the data they need to assess whether the current fiscal policy framework is sustainable, they will not be able to act in an informed way. If the fiscal accounting framework does not adequately disclose the potential liabilities arising from given risks, there will not be a sufficient basis for confronting politically difficult reforms. A revision of budget procedures, enhanced transparency, and independent assessments of budgetary risks may also be required, to foster the public debate necessary for such reforms to move forward. Greater transparency, together with changes in procedures and analytical approaches, is intrinsic to the successful undertaking of meaningful policy reforms.

Strengthening the Analysis of Long-Term Fiscal Sustainability

Ensuring a Long-Term Focus

Most assessments of fiscal sustainability, particularly those concerned with the vulnerability of macroeconomic policy, focus on the medium term. Within the IMF, experience suggests that the average medium-term framework used in country work extends about 6 years out. A recent IMF proposal for strengthening assessments of fiscal sustainability calls for projections and stress tests that extend 10 years into the future (IMF, 2002b). For detailed macroeconomic scenarios, such a time frame would appear appropriate. A longer horizon would require increasingly conjectural assumptions about many variables. Yet even a 10-year horizon exposes assessments of fiscal sustainability to significant risks.

For example, in most industrial countries, the impact of aging populations on the fiscal position will not begin to be felt for at least 10 years, and even then the consequences for the expanding burden of social expenditure will become apparent only gradually.

Thus, if countries fail to take account of potential risks that mainly arise well into the future, they may not be compromising their assessment of the sustainability of the *current* fiscal position, or even that of assessments made in a few years' time. But this failure may prove much more prejudicial to an assessment of the macroeconomic policy environment within a time frame that extends not very many more years further. And because the absence of an adverse assessment may result in needed policy action being deferred, such action may prove more difficult when finally the need for it is recognized and addressed.

Several arguments may be advanced for bringing longer-term developments far more into the picture. First, missing from a more limited medium-term approach is recognition of the potential nonlinearities in the time path of future commitments or potential expenditure shocks. As discussed in Chapter 4, some of these nonlinearities are well known, in particular the fiscal consequences of aging populations in many industrial countries (Kraemer, 2002). Fiscal sustainability analyses looking 10 years ahead may not envisage significant problems. Indeed, the same 10-year analysis carried out 5 years from now (that is, looking out from $t + 5$ out to $t + 15$) may still fail to detect a significant fiscal threat. However, when the analysis at $t + 10$ looks out to $t + 20$, a far larger fiscal burden may suddenly have appeared on the horizon, which will be far more burdensome to address if action has been delayed until that time. An assessment of the net present value of that added burden, at plausible discount rates, might seem to diminish the threat. Yet even so, it should be a source of concern if a country's fiscal position is likely to be viewed as unsustainable not too many years in the future. In effect, any medium-term assessment of fiscal sustainability should take account not only of sustainability as perceived in the present, but also of whether the position will appear sustainable looking ahead from *each year* of that medium-term framework. This approach is particularly to be recommended for countries that loom large in the global economy or in a regional economy.

Second, a policy that aims at addressing long-term imbalances in the present may involve a much smaller sustained increase in the fiscal burden than would later be necessary if the adjustment were deferred. Most recent assessments of the fiscal gap associated with an aging industrial country population underscore the significant difference between the adjustment required to close the fiscal gap if taken today, and that required if such action were to be delayed by 5 or 10 years or more. Thus, although certain fiscal policy adjustments may appear difficult in the present, they become far more costly when postponed. Similar considerations may apply to global warming: many policies currently being proposed to address climate change would prove more costly if taken years in the future rather than today, either because they would involve scrapping inappropriate plants and equipment or because more adaptation-related investments may be required. To ignore such long-term risks and policy issues because they do not fall within the relevant medium-term time frame is to seriously constrain the options available to future policymakers.

Third, limiting the time horizon implicitly attaches a lower weight to the welfare of those who will be living and working during the decades beyond that horizon. Yet even a time frame of 20 to 30 years is not particularly long—certainly it is well within the horizon of most people alive today. They will undoubtedly face heavier tax burdens or sharper cutbacks in government services and transfers to pay for solving the problems that today's policymakers neglected to address.

Strengthening Sustainability Assessments

If one accepts the proposition that issues of the long term should not be ignored in the current fiscal policy framework, some important and difficult issues then arise. Schick (2002b) notes that extending the time frame of a budget involves more than simply adding years to the projections. It also changes the perspective of a government, "transforming the central fiscal issue from the current balance to future sustainability and to the vulnerability of the budget to surprises and shocks" (p. 11). Schick's observation implicitly highlights that the focus of assessments of sustainability needs to be broadened so that policymakers and the public are in a position to gauge the *size* of the fiscal gap to which a government is exposed.

Broadening the Scope of the Assessment

Presently, most assessments of sustainability start with a projection of the government's debt-service obligations. The assessment may also assume that some contingent government liabilities will be realized or that some guarantees of local government or public enterprise debt will have to be made good. The assessment may go on to examine some of the implicit debt arising from the government's social insurance commitments. In most industrial countries, the assessment covers the government's likely obligations under public pension schemes and possibly its obligations associated with the provision or insurance of medical care and long-term residential care.

One way in which such assessments may need to be broadened is to take account of the possible variance in the scope of obligations arising under some types of implicit commitments. In some areas, such as medical care, welfare, or long-term care, governments may, in principle, have significant latitude in determining the nature of their commitments and thus in managing the fiscal consequences of their involvement. In practice, however, defining the scope of these commitments is likely to be difficult, both technically and politically.

Account also needs to be taken of several *additional* areas of possible government involvement. A government may be exposed to other fiscal risks that are less immediately apparent than those just mentioned but that may prove relevant in future decades. Identifying these risks and gauging the government's vulnerability to them requires some assessment of the government's role in society. Obviously, the more expansive the role that government is expected to play, the broader must be the assessment of what those risks might be, how likely they are to be realized, and the potential fiscal consequences. Thus a government that limits its old age pension commitments to a flat real benefit is likely to be far less concerned about adverse demographic developments than a government committed to a PAYGO pension system with high earnings replacement rates. Likewise, a government that has only limited commitments in the area of health care, or that relies on the private sector to absorb most risks associated with natural disasters, will be far less concerned about aging or extreme weather events than one that is more active and involved.

For most industrial countries, expectations of the government's role are likely to be embodied not only in legislation but also in the context of prevailing practices and of history. Current practice and past experience strongly influence how policymakers and the public view the government's obligations and how it should respond in different situations. For example, the degree to which a government-provided medical insurance plan accommodates medical cost inflation constitutes an implicit framework for understanding the role of government in this sphere. The same could be said with respect to how a government responds to natural disasters with relief or reconstruction assistance (witness the response of Germany to the floods of the summer of

2002, or of the United States to the Midwest floods of the early 1990s). In contrast, in many developing countries the government's role may be less well defined or is still being elaborated. It may involve only certain general commitments, for example to extend primary or secondary school education to a larger share of the population, or to develop a broader scheme for public pensions or medical insurance.

In any country, however, full clarity about the government's role and appropriate commitments can never be achieved, if only because of the moral hazard that could arise. If a government explicitly announced its willingness to absorb the full costs of extreme weather events, for example, it would weaken the incentives for households or businesses to make an effort to adapt to such disasters or avoid their consequences. Similarly, if medical care providers were given to assume that governments would fully absorb all medical cost increases, they would have little incentive to restrain those costs.

Also, in assessing fiscal sustainability, some attention may need to be paid to the *durability* of the government's existing policy framework. Chapter 4 noted that, for some industrial countries, it seems quite implausible that the prospective increase in formal social insurance obligations will actually be met, and the sustainability assessments undertaken by these countries are likely to make this clear. But the converse may also be true. The results of the assessment may suggest that government policies *are* sustainable in aggregate fiscal terms when, in fact, a more disaggregated analysis would likely find the contrary. For example, in the United Kingdom, it is likely that existing pensions policies will need to be reformed not because the government cannot afford the promised benefits, but because, at the current implied replacement rate, those benefits will not be enough for recipients to live on. In this case, an analyst of fiscal sustainability would be forced to judge whether the hard commitment on pensions is likely to be overridden by the softer commitment implicit in recent policy practices on the minimum income guarantee.

Beyond a broadening of the risks included in sustainability assessments, Schick's observations highlight that policymakers and the public also deserve greater clarity from budget analysts about the risks associated with the government's current policy framework and commitments. This is necessary in order to minimize the likelihood of a significant inconsistency in policies over time. Chapter 3 argued that *deterministic* assessments of sustainability can prove misleading to policymakers because they do not reveal the probability of a given scenario occurring. Thus, for example, the recent fiscal gap indicators estimated by the European Union do not quantify the likelihood that these gaps will occur, or the probability that the gap will be significantly larger or smaller than the baseline projection. Although scenario analyses can provide a useful perspective that supplements the baseline projections by highlighting the consequences of best- or worst-case outcomes, what should be important for policymakers is clarity about the *probabilities* of such scenarios coming to pass. Presumably, if government policymakers were informed that the probability of the government's fiscal position being sustained was only 30 percent, their response would be very different than if that probability were estimated at 80 percent.

Thus the challenge in considering long-term sustainability goes beyond simply extending the time period or broadening the range of long-term issues to be examined. It is also critical to understand the *likelihood* that the present fiscal policy framework can be sustained over a sufficiently long time frame. Achieving such an understanding requires the use of analytical techniques that gauge the probabilities of alternative policy outcomes.

However, the limits to the value of these more sophisticated sustainability assessments should also be recognized. Even with this information in hand, the harder challenge is to get policymakers to articulate what level of confidence will satisfy them that a given policy stance is sufficiently robust that no further adjustments are required. As discussed in Chapter 4, this becomes a question of whether the government considers itself risk averse, risk neutral, or risk seeking in pitching its policies. The degree of risk aversion on the government's part is thus relevant to whether and how much it needs to respond to an assessment that its position may not be sustainable over the long term.

Ideally, the political process should facilitate an open and transparent dialogue, both on the types of structural risks likely to confront an economy and on the degree of risk aversion that characterizes the government with respect to various risks. To be effective, this dialogue requires improved forms of analysis and a strengthened budgetary process.

Recognizing External Vulnerabilities

Particularly for emerging market economies and other developing countries, sustainability assessments cannot be undertaken in isolation from some consideration of how long-term developments may affect the global economic environment. In addition to the long-term risk factors at work within each of these countries, the shifts in the global economic environment associated with globalization and the aging of populations in the industrial economies may need to be considered. The range of potential effects is large, and the consequences are uncertain. Many developing countries are already heavily financed by remittances sent home by expatriate workers; in many cases these remittances far exceed what the country receives in foreign assistance and private foreign investment. With globalization exerting pressures that will likely increase migration in coming years, it will be important for the authorities of labor-exporting countries to manage their macroeconomic policies with an emphasis on limiting volatility in transfers and short-term capital flows. This will put a heavy premium on ensuring a conservative fiscal stance (see Heller, 1997; Kopits, 2002) and on avoiding the prospect of a government finding itself implicitly guaranteeing the domestic commercial banking system or public enterprises.

Global capital markets will be heavily influenced by the demographic passage of the baby-boom generation in the industrial countries. In principle, life cycle theory suggests that there should be a significant expansion of capital flows from the industrial economies during the next decade or so, when the baby-boom generation is in its later working years and accumulating savings for retirement. But the recent spate of capital market crises in emerging market economies has already dampened the volume of such flows, and it is uncertain whether they will soon return to levels seen in the recent past. Chapter 3 noted the uncertainty surrounding global interest rates in the next decade and beyond, as industrial country populations face growing fiscal burdens and potentially negative pressures on asset prices.

Labor market developments are equally likely to be a source of concern, in a number of respects. Will the industrial countries, more receptive to attracting both skilled and unskilled workers in the face of shrinking labor forces, intensify the brain drain from the developing world? Will globalization put further upward pressure on wages for skilled public sector workers in these economies? Will declining real growth rates in the industrial economies dampen the prospects for rapid growth in the rest of the world economy, or will emerging market economies provide a counterbalancing impetus to growth? How are commodity prices likely to be affected by population aging in the industrial economies?

The key point is that long-term risk factors, although potentially very different from those that are currently the focus of industrial country economists, may still be important considerations in fiscal sustainability assessments for low- and middle-income countries. The challenges, however, in assessing the fiscal implications of likely structural developments, and determining the appropriate policy stance, may indeed be more difficult for these countries. Issues of social time preference are also likely to be much more complex to reconcile in cases where there is an argument for a conservative fiscal stance in the short term. Uncertainty in the external environment, although relevant for the industrial economies as well, may be even more significant for the generally more open economies of the developing world. The kinds of uncertainty that would need to be built into any stochastic modeling of the fiscal sector in these countries are also likely to be more difficult to pin down in quantitative estimates.

Extending the Scope of Analytical Approaches

Budget forecasting is a treacherous occupation. Studies of the accuracy of past forecasts by even the best budget analysts, and even when looking as little as four to five years into the future, are not encouraging. And the longer the projection period, the greater the error tends to be. Yet pessimism about the accuracy of forecasts needs to be balanced by the important recognition that long-term forecasts and analyses do nonetheless contain important information. Penner (2001), in particular, emphasizes the information value of long-term forecasts. He notes that it is less important to know in which precise year the U.S. Social Security trust fund will be exhausted—whether it is 2032 or 2034 or 2041—than it is to know that these long-run forecasts suggest an extremely high probability that the trust fund *will* be exhausted sometime within that interval. It is the *fact* of unsustainability, not the precision in predicting the date when the threshold of unsustainability will be crossed, that is the key. Penner also notes the value of having a rough quantitative sense of the costs or savings associated with a policy change over time, recognizing that the margin of error may still be wide.

Chapter 3 reviewed the strengths and weaknesses of the various analytical approaches that have been used to judge the fiscal implications of potential long-run developments. Such long-term forecasts and the calculation of fiscal gap or sustainability indicators do indeed have value and should be pursued with even greater emphasis.

Governments need to start with a clear picture of what the long-term fiscal profile looks like under alternative scenarios. It is particularly important to estimate *time path analyses,* which provide a sense of the trajectory of government expenditure and revenue over time and of the fiscal imbalances that may arise at different points in time. Fiscal gap indicators can then provide some sense of the aggregate fiscal adjustment that would need to be implemented and maintained in order to achieve fiscal sustainability. By examining the *revised* time path implied by such an adjustment, an assessment can be made as to the potential implied decumulation of net public debt (or accumulation of assets). If the analysis suggests that the implied accumulation of assets is unlikely to be achieved in reality, alternative scenarios may need to be constructed that entail specific policy reforms to realize the needed level of aggregate financial savings in specific periods. Such projections also need to indicate to policymakers the amount of resources available for public investment as well as the implied fiscal leeway or margin for new policy initiatives or to respond to contingencies.

Six additional areas should receive greater attention. First, *stochastic approaches* are particularly valuable, because they provide policymakers with at least a rough quantitative sense of the likelihood of alternative scenarios occurring. Indeed, the stochastic estimation of primary or fiscal gap indicators is the most obviously desirable extension to the types of fiscal sustainability analyses currently being undertaken. It would provide useful information on the probability of the estimated fiscal gap being within a given range. It would also provide some sense of how much confidence can be attached to projections of the impact on the fiscal gap of particular policy reforms under consideration.

The stochastic approach itself, however, could be strengthened if it were to take into account the *multiplicity* of fiscal risks faced by government. To date, such analyses have focused principally on demographic uncertainties and how different demographic assumptions might influence the pace of population aging and its associated fiscal consequences. Yet other risks are clearly important as well. Policy reforms that significantly reduce the risks to the budget associated with an aging population may still prove inadequate in the context of other potential risks, as discussed earlier. Some potential developments other than population aging may be subject to greater uncertainty or less amenable to quantitative assessment, yet may ultimately prove to have far more important fiscal effects. Failure to consider the sustainability of the fiscal burden in the event these various developments occur concurrently may subject future generations to excessive risks.

This suggests several possible areas where future work on stochastic fiscal forecasts might be focused. *Historical analyses* could be undertaken to judge the size of possible shocks or the variance estimates to be used in stochastic simulations. For example, this could involve estimating a measure of the variability of revenue and expenditure not anticipated in past budgets (see Buckle, Kim, and Tam, 2001). This type of information may be gleaned from past forecasts, taking care to separate out the fiscal effects of unanticipated discretionary policy changes that were not a response to exogenous shocks. Additionally, a review could be undertaken of the assumptions underlying forecasts of key expenditure categories. Analyses could also be undertaken of the variability of specific categories of expenditure or the degree to which the elasticity of spending with respect to GDP in an area has significantly diverged from unity. Stocktaking of the adequacy of any contingency funds set aside in past budgets may also be useful.

However, the obvious problem with historical analyses is that past experience may fail to capture new structural developments that bear on future fiscal forecasts and whose effects may be nonlinear. Aging populations and climate change may both fall in this category. Creedy and Alvarado (1998) have illustrated how stochastic analyses can be adapted to make assessments based on judgmental guesses about key parameters.[1] It might also be useful to build in a stochastic term that captures the small probability of large, nonlinear shocks to the budget.

Second, there is considerable value to the *multiregional general-equilibrium approach* that some researchers have pursued. One important area of risk stems from the fact that a number of significant structural developments are likely to be experienced in various large industrial countries at the same time. The *combined* effects might put pressure on certain global macroeconomic variables, particularly interest rates, which would not appear as an obvious source of variability in single-country simulations. Multilateral organizations and academic institutions remain the obvious places where such work could usefully be undertaken. However, national budget agencies could use the results in both scenario and stochastic analyses.

Third, assessments are needed of the *scope for change in the structure of the budget*. To the extent that long-term forecasts are carried out, they tend to emphasize certain key areas of the budget likely to be affected. The results suggest the potential magnitude of the fiscal impact, in

---

[1]They note that "the approach used to translate informed judgments into distributional parameters can be used in other contexts where projections need to be based on variables whose distributional characteristics cannot be obtained from a time series of data, either because there are few data or because there are good reasons for believing that past variations give little insight into potential future variations." They also cite work by Peter Pflaumer, who used subjective specifications of demographic distributions on the grounds that past variations are unlikely to be a good guide to future variations.

terms of increased expenditure or reduced revenue. Although policy reforms to mute such an impact are one obvious approach to reducing fiscal risk, it is also important to have some sense of how much "give" there may be in other areas of the budget or of the extent to which an increase in the tax burden might be considered feasible (see below).

Fourth, there is considerable value in undertaking *actuarial calculations* of the net present value of the net benefits of alternative social transfer schemes. Such an approach highlights the differences across generations in the relative benefits and taxes or payments, looking forward over each generation's lifetime, from a given scheme at any point in time (taking account of their chances of death; see Steuerle and Bakija, 1994). Thus, such calculations in the United States would highlight the significant difference in net benefits received by older rather than younger contemporary or future generations from Social Security and Medicare. They also can highlight the differential impact across generations of policy commitment reforms.

Fifth, the *uncertainties surrounding the appropriate long-term discount rate* need to be explicitly reflected in analyses of the costs and benefits of policies or investments with very long-term implications. The analyses of Newell and Pizer (2002a, 2002b) as well as those of Weitzman (1998), both discussed in Chapter 2, underscore the biases that can occur with an inappropriate analytical treatment of such uncertainty.

Finally, whatever analytical tools are used in accounting for long-term risks (see Box 5.1), it is important to develop *indicators that clearly illuminate the key fiscal imbalances*. The various fiscal gap measures are appealing in this regard and would be particularly useful if provided on a stochastic basis, giving some sense of the confidence interval surrounding the estimate of the size of the gap.

Building the Long Term Into the Budget Process

The annual budget process is the critical point at which decisions are made that influence the long-term sustainability of a government's fiscal framework. Today's government policy commitments influence the likely magnitude of expenditures that will take place in the future. They dictate the factors that will influence the growth of entitlement spending, the amount of public infrastructure that will need to be maintained, and the size of government programs whose inertial influence on future budgets will be strong. They shape the government's future response to presently uncertain events that will call for public

---

**Box 5.1. Some Useful Indicators for Clarifying
Long-Term Fiscal Issues**

- Inclusion of accrued liabilities in the balance sheet
- Gap measures: the tax or primary balance gap, preferably on a stochastic basis (also a measure of the gap assuming a maximum feasible tax rate)
- Risk-weighted assessments of the government's assets and liabilities
- Net debt measures
- Fiscal and generational imbalance measures
- Alternative simulation or stress tests, including stochastic simulations
- Actuarial measures of the underfunding of pension systems
- Calculation of the lifetime value of benefits promised

---

spending. But current budget decisions do not relate only to the budgetary "space" that will be absorbed in current and future budgets. They also delimit the budget margins that are left unencumbered (and thus free for future spending or reduced taxation), and in doing so determine how much flexibility the government will have to respond to new challenges in the future.

Taking better account of long-term issues in the deliberations on the annual budget requires building four central elements into the process:
- Transparency and comprehensiveness of information that not only highlights issues of aggregate fiscal sustainability, but also characterizes the longer-term distributional and welfare implications of current public programs;
- A mechanism that ensures that an informed view, *independent* of government, is provided on the data and on the issues that emerge from greater transparency and a longer-run analytical focus;
- A mechanism that ensures public debate on the central questions involved in the government's approach to issues that have a long-term character; and
- Most difficult of all, a solution to the political economy problem of how to ensure that the interests of future generations are adequately considered in today's fiscal policy decisions.

Strengthening the Budget Document to Take Account of the Long Term

It is increasingly customary for annual budgets to be presented in a medium-term context of 3 to 5 years. But budgets that focus only on the medium term, even those whose time horizon is as long as 10 years, may miss important issues of the longer term that ought to be considered in the short to medium term. They may also accommodate short-term expenditure decisions that appear reasonable within the framework of the medium term but have more serious longer-term consequences. However, strengthening the budget document to take account of the long term does not necessarily mean that the detailed budget itself needs to be extended beyond a 3- to 5-year horizon. As Schick (2002b) notes, a simple extension in years may only undercut the budget's realism and lend a false accuracy to projections.

Rather, the key objective should be the transparent provision of both more information and a perspective that highlights the key ways in which current policy decisions on the budget relate to the long term and, conversely, how issues of the long term may bear on current policy decisions. Such assessments can also add value in that governments can use them to frame the public debate on long-term issues. For example, Posner and Gordon (2001) have argued that the success of recent initiatives by governments to enhance public saving rates has hinged on how effectively the need for higher saving has been framed and defined at the outset of the debate.

In considering how to proceed, a useful starting point is the approach now followed by the United Kingdom, New Zealand, and Australia. Although the detailed programmatic estimates in their budgets continue to be provided only on a medium-term basis, an annex paper or separate report is also prepared that considers long-term sustainability issues.[2] This approach is consistent with the recent recommendation by the OECD (in its Best Practices Code on Fiscal Transparency) that countries carry out periodic fiscal assessments of long-term issues in the budget. But the important question is what types of information and assessments are provided.

Estimating the Long-Term Fiscal Consequences of New Budget Initiatives

Whether in the main body of the budget or in an annex, the long-term fiscal implications of any new budget initiative—be it a tax reform, a spending program, a transfer scheme, an investment plan, a guarantee, or a contingent liability—should be quantified and the likely time path indicated, both in real terms and as a share of projected

---

[2]Whereas in Australia and the United Kingdom this approach is required by law, in New Zealand it has been established more on the basis of precedent.

GDP. This is an issue that relates as much to failure to project the expenditure needed to operate and maintain new public investments as it does to neglecting the need to quantify the implications of a new social insurance guarantee.

Providing an Analytical Perspective on Sustainability

The annex to the budget should seek to characterize whether fiscal policy under the proposed policy regime is sustainable over a horizon of at least 25 years. It should consider alternative assumptions about what might be the political economy constraints influencing the magnitude of both feasible tax burden adjustment and net asset accumulation. Chapter 3 has already highlighted the challenges involved in doing this. The uncertainties that bear on any such projections and the multitude of assumptions required inevitably render the exercise highly conjectural. But this does not vitiate either the importance of the questions to be asked or the need for transparent answers. For example, under current policies and under alternative scenarios, what are the likely implications for the buildup of debt or net assets, and what surpluses or deficits would emerge in different periods? A stochastic approach could shed light on the likelihood of alternative outcomes, given uncertainty about key economic and demographic assumptions.

Fiscal gap measures should be provided (again, ideally on a stochastic basis), highlighting the immediate change in revenue or the primary balance necessary to achieve a sustainable position over the long term. Complementing such measures should be estimates of the tax or primary surplus adjustment that would be required if such fiscal adjustment decisions were deferred for 5 or 10 years. The aggregate consequences of such decisions should also be analyzed. For example, what would such an adjustment imply for the tax burden and for net asset accumulation (or net debt decumulation)? If constraints have been imposed on the aggregate tax burden as a percentage of GDP, or on the range of allowable ratios of net assets or net debt to GDP, how much fiscal leeway or margin would exist after the indicated adjustment, either for new initiatives or to respond to other challenges? If further budget adjustments are needed as a consequence of constraints placed on the aggregate tax burden, the net asset or debt position, or the amount of the desired fiscal margin, what do these imply for the ratio of government expenditure to GDP? If, furthermore, certain parts of the budget (say, social insurance transfers) are to be regarded as off-limits for further adjustment, by how much would the rest of the budget have to be cut, and when would these adjustments have to take place? Estimates of net assets or net debt should also clarify the assumptions being made about the treatment of government investments, in order to avoid any biases against government investment that might arise by focusing only on the overall fiscal balance.

Strengthening Accounting Concepts Relating to Government Debt

Chapter 3 discussed the various initiatives of multilateral agencies to harmonize and strengthen the presentation of government accounts and to enhance the transparency of a government's commitments— whether explicit or implicit, and whether in the form of guarantees or contingent liabilities. Most notable are the transparency codes of the IMF and the OECD and, in the government accounting sphere, the new 2001 *Government Finance Statistics Manual* (IMF, 2001d). Two developments are of particular importance for long-term fiscal concerns.

First, the movement toward accrual accounting (side by side with a cash presentation of the budget) represents an important step toward ensuring that some account is taken of future consequences of government policy decisions that have only long-term effects on the budget. Second, the emphasis in these initiatives on the presentation of the government's balance sheet forces some consideration of the full measure of a government's accrued liabilities, discounted to the present, as well as the potential liabilities that would arise in the future from new policy commitments.

More controversial are questions relating to *how* certain specific liabilities should be presented on the balance sheet. In particular, how should governments treat or value the liability stemming from various kinds of implicit commitments (such as those described in Box 2.3 in Chapter 2) or from contingent liabilities or guarantees? For example, should the balance sheet formally recognize all liabilities accrued to date to existing pensioners or to workers in recognition of their past payroll tax contributions to a PAYGO public pension scheme? Or should such liabilities be merely disclosed as a memorandum item *off* the balance sheet? How should governments account for their exposure to contingent liabilities or for guarantees of public enterprise or local government debt (a topic discussed further below)?

It is generally agreed that liabilities to those who are already receiving pensions should be recognized. But for workers who have not yet retired, the issues are debatable and indeed are still being debated within the accounting profession. How, for example, should such liabilities be valued? What should a government do when fully honoring its pension promises would raise serious questions about fiscal sustainability? Such questions become important when a government considers formally recognizing debts associated with past commitments that may prove not to be financeable, given realistic assessments of long-term fiscal sustainability.

In the last year or so, there have been increasing calls for greater disclosure of accrued liabilities. For example, in the area of social insurance, Jackson (2002, p. 1) argues for accrual accounting procedures comparable to those that govern private pension plans (that is, generally accepted principles of accrual accounting) and other long-term liabilities of the federal government. He estimates that such an approach would reveal an accumulated deficit for the U.S. Social Security system of $12.2 trillion as of December 31, 2002, or more than triple the amount of federal debt outstanding to the public. At a minimum, he argues, this would facilitate a more "responsible and intelligible debate" among citizens and their leaders. In a similar vein, Shoven (2003) argues for capital accounting for the U.S. Social Security Trust Fund.

The U.S. General Accounting Office (2003, pp. 21–22) highlights the various accrued costs that are not reflected in the present U.S. budget, despite their potentially large cost implications for future budgets. These include much of the accruing pension costs of civilian and military employees and virtually none of the accruing costs of retiree health benefits for civilian or military retirees under the age of 65; environmental cleanup and disposal costs resulting from federal operations; a significant element of likely federal insurance benefit payments against a wide variety of risks (for example, natural disasters under flood and crop insurance programs, as well as bank and employer bankruptcies under the deposit and pension insurance programs); and the expected future operations and maintenance costs of capital assets.

The GAO (2003, pp. 4–5) notes that

> The complexity and uncertainty surrounding some [fiscal] exposures creates significant cost estimation challenges, which in turn raises concerns about using these estimates as the sole basis of budget and other policy decisions. These issues need to be considered carefully to avoid subjecting the primary budget data to large and volatile estimates. Nevertheless, information on the existence and estimated cost of fiscal exposures needs to be considered along with other factors when making policy decisions. Not considering the long-term costs of current decisions limits Congress's ability to control the government's exposure at the time decisions are made.

As an example, the agency notes that "the decision to purchase a building or another fixed asset implicitly commits the government to the life-cycle costs associated with its future operation and maintenance.... Even an activity that appears to decrease government involvement such as privatization, may carry with it an implicit assumption that the government will step in if necessary to provide the service or good" (p. 17).

In sum, the reality is that many types of government commitments are, at best, only contingent on the maintenance of current law or program rules. Yet it is absolutely critical that the fiscal consequences of existing commitments be explicitly disclosed, whether formally, on the balance sheet, or in an annex disclosure, so that the public at large can understand the costs associated with such commitments under alternative economic and demographic assumptions, assuming they will in fact be honored.

Clarifying Key Sources of Expenditure Pressure

Long-term fiscal assessments should be sufficiently disaggregated to clarify how much each major expenditure program contributes to the projected growth of aggregate expenditure. Such analyses should be undertaken using alternative assumptions about the growth of such programs. Clarity about the welfare implications of current policies, particularly with respect to key transfer programs, is desirable. The objective would be to provide a picture of what can be expected in the future, under current policy commitments, in terms of the level and distribution of social insurance transfers.

Such clarification might include an estimate of the expected replacement rate of a state-provided pension (that is, the ratio of the pension benefit to the average salary that will then prevail), or of the percentage of the population eligible for a given benefit transfer, or of projected average spending per recipient on specific goods (such as pharmaceuticals) and services (such as medical care) relative to expected average spending for the population at large. It should specify what assumptions are being made, relative to past experience, about the sensitivity of forecasts of government medical outlays to medical cost inflation. Generational account balances could be presented to provide a measure of how different generations will fare in terms of the degree of redistribution entailed. Alternatively, estimates could be made of the lifetime value of promised benefits (Steuerle, 1998).

A more difficult challenge would arise if doubts emerge either about the adequacy of the projected benefits or about the sustainability of the aggregate fiscal position. In the former case, policy changes might be expected that would raise benefits, and these would have implications for the aggregate sustainability assessment. In the latter, the policy changes needed to achieve sustainability might reduce benefits from what they would be under the current policy regime. Simple answers to conjectural situations such as these are not likely to be possible. Rather, the objective would be to *inform the public* as to the long-term consequences of the current fiscal policy regime—in the aggregate and for particular programs—thus clarifying what can and cannot be expected from the government, and to provoke discussion of the policy issues thereby raised. A large part of the challenge faced by analysts will be to encapsulate more detailed analyses into a narrow set of simplified indicators that accurately characterize the key policy choices and challenges being faced.

Assessing Key Risks to Which the Government Might Be Exposed

Governments should be required to identify the key uncertainties underlying the budget projections and the principal risk factors that might impinge on aggregate fiscal sustainability, both in the short and in the long term. The public should also be able to ascertain the government's position with respect to the principal risks to the budget (in effect, whether it is risk neutral or risk averse), as well as the concrete consequences should adverse outcomes prevail.The U.S. General Accounting Office, in its recent report, advocates that the government be required, on an annual basis, to provide a concise list and description of fiscal exposures as well as "cost estimates, where possible, and an assessment of methodologies and data used to produce cost estimates of such exposures" (U.S. GAO, 2003, p. 6). Supplemental reporting of the cost of the risk assumed by federal insurance programs allows time to assess the reliability of cost estimates, refine estimation methodologies, and assess the reliability of cost estimates. Alternatively, the future estimated costs of certain exposures—termed the "exposure level"—should be included as a notational item in the budget.

In characterizing the aggregate fiscal position, the government should highlight the extent to which its fiscal position is vulnerable to particular risks. It should describe whether current policies embody any efforts to attenuate those risks, as well as any strategies for maintaining sustainability in the event of adverse shocks. It should indicate whether the government believes that its net debt or asset position provides sufficient flexibility to cope with unexpected risks, without the need for a dramatic scaling up of taxes or printing of money.[3]

Where governments are, in effect, self-insuring or acting as a reinsurer for the private sector, the budget annex should indicate whether contingency provisions or reserves sufficient to cope with this insurance role are being established. The fiscal costs associated with the realization of contingent liabilities and guarantees—and the likelihood of such a realization—also need to be recognized in assessing whether the existing contingency budget is sufficient.[4]

Beyond that, the exposure of governments to risks for which there are not hard policy commitments needs to be clearly confronted and the potential fiscal consequences assessed. The occurrence of such adverse shocks as a September 11 or a major environmental disaster may create a claim on a government's resources that is difficult to dismiss. Governments may need to conduct analyses similar to those done by private insurance and reinsurance companies, which are increasingly developing "risk maps" to assess their financial vulnerability to potential catastrophe.[5]

Conceptually, a further type of financial risk presentation might be considered. The private insurance industry has recently raised the

---

[3]The question could be raised as to whether a government always has the option of massively expanding its issuance of debt or currency in response to a crisis (such as a war or a natural disaster) that forces a large increase in public expenditure. The answer, of course, is yes. The success of such a strategy would depend, however, on whether its citizens accept the importance of making a sacrifice, and reduce their consumption or their investment accordingly. In the absence of such support, the government would either engender a major inflationary impulse (effectively reneging on past debt by inflating it away), run into balance of payments difficulties, or find that in the future it could only borrow at a cost (that is, at a higher interest rate) that would trigger financial collapse at some point.

[4]Schick (2002b) notes, "the failure to properly budget for contingent liabilities induces government to substitute guarantees for conventional expenditures and to take risks that may imbalance future budgets" (p. 13).

[5]Munich Re Group (2001) emphasizes the importance of knowing, in any given sphere in which an insurer operates, the locally significant catastrophe hazards and the insurer's degree of exposure to them, its liability situation in all relevant lines of business, and the vulnerability of the insured portfolio. Governments, however, face a more difficult challenge in that their exposure is potentially far more open ended, and not limited by the specifics of coverage provisions or liability limits. The challenges of assessing financial vulnerability are not to be minimized. As Chapter 2 demonstrated, the range and scope of risks are large, and the degree of uncertainty is high in many respects. Simply defining the relevant risks is a challenge. Although the probability of any individual risk being realized may be small, the probability of at least one among many such risks being realized is considerably larger. Understanding the factors that contribute to the probability of a given risk may also be difficult.

issue of whether its own extant risks (such as those related to terrorism) are adequately priced (Munich Re Group, 2002). To the extent that governments effectively provide self-insurance, through the budget, against various risks, some calculation of the pricing of such risks might appropriately be disclosed on their balance sheets. This would provide a clearer valuation of the risks to which a government is exposed, by imputing a shadow price to the value of its liabilities. Some level of provisioning might also be contemplated. Schick (2002b, p. 14), for example, argues that, with respect to guarantees and contingent liabilities,

> The most sensible option would be to provision for estimated losses from guarantees on the government's balance sheet. If actual losses diverge from the estimate, the amount provisioned would be adjusted to reflect this experience. Corresponding entries would be made on the government's budget, which would show estimated or actual losses as expenditures.

At a minimum, governments may need to appraise more realistically the provision made for contingencies in their annual budgets.

Finally, where governments indicate that long-term uncertainties are such as to warrant deferring action until more information is available, they should be required to report on any efforts being undertaken (such as research) to reduce the degree of uncertainty. Any information gathering or other research required should be adequately funded and a time frame specified for revisiting the issue.

Ensuring an Independent Perspective

It may be reasonable to envisage governments becoming more transparent about their current fiscal position and about the assumptions underlying their fiscal forecasts. However, it is probably unrealistic to expect that they will be self-critical with respect to the issues suggested above for the proposed budget annex. To do so might require either admitting that an unsustainable fiscal stance is being proposed or highlighting the weaknesses of the budget commitments. The challenge then is to ensure that a credible alternative view is presented, independent of the government in power, both on the data in the budget and its annex and on the issues that emerge therefrom. This is vital to ensure a thorough and resilient public process for addressing issues of the long term.

An Independent Budget Scorekeeper

The IMF's transparency code (IMF, 2001c) calls for an independent audit of the budget, with "independent experts [to] be invited to assess fiscal forecasts, the macroeconomic forecasts on which they are built, and all underlying assumptions," although the extent to which this relates to forecasts beyond the medium term is not clear. In the United States, an independent, nonpartisan public agency—the U.S. Congressional Budget Office (CBO)—plays the role of scorekeeper. Other countries may wish to consider this model. In principle, the CBO carries out long-term budget forecasts independent of the executive branch, as a check on any excessive optimism on the part of the latter. In practice, although the CBO may be able to play this role effectively when the Congress and the White House are controlled by different parties, its independence is less clear when the two branches are controlled by the same party.

Such an independent agency, however, needs to do more than simply vouch for the accuracy of government forecasts. It must force policymakers and the public to confront, in the budget debate, the larger risks to which public policies are exposed and their implications. In effect, it should seek not only to provide an independent perspective on the issues, but also to provoke debate on the key choices facing the government. Thus the agency could raise questions about whether a given fiscal policy is sustainable over a given time frame. It could spell out the possible implications, in terms of benefit cutbacks or tax increases, if a fiscal gap should have to be closed precipitously. The result would be the type of "what if" debate that may ultimately be necessary to resolve underlying questions about the sustainability of the budget or its exposure to risk. In their recent work on fiscal risk management, Brixi and Mody (2002) call for an independent agency to assess and report on both direct and contingent fiscal risks.

Establishment of such an agency inevitably raises some difficult issues. How to guarantee that it has adequate funding? How to establish a governance structure that ensures its political neutrality? How to ensure that its staff are sufficiently qualified to ensure credibility? The agency might need to be financed from an earmarked revenue source or be made financially responsible to the legislative branch.

Multilateral Surveillance

When a country neglects the potential fiscal consequences of its long-term risks, the consequences are not borne by its citizens alone. They may also affect the country's neighbors, and in some cases the global economy, and may do so even in the short to medium term. The potential for negative spillovers is a matter of concern both for individual countries and for the global community. The challenges posed by such spillovers are difficult, because the international system lacks mechanisms to compel countries to pursue appropriately farsighted policies. This highlights the importance of multilateral surveillance in helping countries consider their long-term risks. Indeed, in some cases countries may find it useful to rely on multilateral processes to take the initiative in promoting policy actions that would be difficult to initiate at the national level.

The annual surveillance process of the European Union has begun to have an element of this type of pressure, as member governments have been asked to prepare an assessment of long-term issues. The European Commission has also begun to request government participation in studies addressing the fiscal implications of aging. The "handle" for making this request has been the Stability and Growth Pact (SGP) and its associated fiscal rule, which could be breached if long-term risk factors are not addressed.

But even in the absence of an explicit fiscal rule, multilateral surveillance can play an important role. Chapter 3 noted that the IMF, in its Article IV surveillance of member countries, has occasionally undertaken assessments of long-term issues that are seen to have macroeconomic consequences for the country in question. In principle, the IMF's annual surveillance process could be broadened to encompass a more routine analysis of long-term risk factors. Fiscal sustainability indicators could be calculated. Even in the absence of specific fiscal rules, comparative analyses would provide some sense of the adequacy of the fiscal position in the face of long-term risks. Analyses of the sources of fiscal disequilibria should be undertaken.

One advantage of the IMF's surveillance process is its transparency: a significant proportion of consultation assessments are now published on the Internet, where they are available to the citizens of the country under assessment as well as to participants in global markets. The consultation process also allows for some exercise of peer group pressure. A limiting factor on the IMF playing this role is that it lacks the staff resources necessary to undertake in-depth long-term fiscal analyses on a routine basis. This underscores the fact that such work should be a regular part of the domestic budget process itself, with multilateral surveillance serving an independent review role.

Stimulating Public Debate and Raising Awareness of Long-Term Issues

It is now accepted that transparency is an important prerequisite to sound policymaking. But for transparency to have the desired effect, it is essential to foster public awareness and debate on the key long-term issues confronting public decision makers. How this is engineered institutionally will depend on a country's political and legislative framework. In some countries the legislative branch may prove the most obvious forum for ventilating the key long-term issues raised by the government in its budget document or by an independent budget review agency. A mechanism could be introduced into the budget process to force such a debate.

For example, if an independent forecasting agency's projections suggest, to a significant probability, that the long-term position is fiscally unsustainable, the legislature might require the government to address explicitly the issues raised in the forecast, outlining the areas of disagreement. If the government shares the assessment, it would be expected to outline the policy approach it intends to pursue to enhance sustainability. Obviously, the strategy chosen would need to take account of the role of fiscal policy in terms of short-term fiscal stabilization needs, but at least the government would be required to explain how it intends to reconcile short- and long-term considerations.

An alternative approach has been recently proposed by the U.S. General Accounting Office (2003). This would require that the annual budget resolution set limits on the creation of new (or the expansion of existing) fiscal exposures, "with points of order permitted against legislation violating such limits."[6] Indeed, triggers could be established to "signal when the costs of existing exposures exceed some predetermined amount" (p. 5). As with a point of order, such a trigger would necessitate "explicit consideration of exposures facing the government without adding uncertainty to primary budget data." If it were felt necessary to change budgetary incentives, inclusion of estimates of the future cost of budgetary commitments in the budget itself might be

---

[6]The agency suggests that a "different point of order method would be to permit a point of order that could block legislation lacking appropriate cost information about an exposure....This alternative would provide a greater incentive to improve cost information...because it presents congressional members with an opportunity to challenge the creation of programs without sufficient information on long-term costs" (p. 34).

required (see U.S. GAO, 2003), in effect in the context of an accrual-based measurement of the budget.[7]

Finally, it might be appropriate in some countries to consider establishing an independent fiscal commission, charged with highlighting key fiscal issues for the electorate before each national election. Regardless of the institutional approach taken, what is fundamental is that there be a mechanism that ensures that the electorate is made aware of the principal long-term risks that confront the country and that their potential consequences are spelled out, including the costs of their not being addressed.

Safeguarding the Interests of Future Generations

There remains one large and possibly insuperable problem in addressing issues of the long term. Transparency of information, an independent perspective from the government, and adequate public debate may all be possible. But political leaders inevitably have an incentive to underestimate—and often the ability to circumvent—any fiscal sustainability concerns, even when ostensibly limited by formal rules. (For example, most observers argue that the Gramm-Rudman limits and later spending caps in the United States did not work well.) "Short-termism" on the part of politicians is a common problem. Electorates, too, may prefer to ignore the problems that their own and subsequent generations will confront in several decades' time. The electorate may have an unspoken preference for a risk-favoring or a risk-neutral posture over one of risk aversion. These are obvious and long-standing concerns, although usually the focus is on governments not pursuing responsible macroeconomic policies in the short to medium term.

One proposal that has occasionally surfaced involves the establishment of an independent fiscal agency with constitutional authority to force pro rata adjustments on aggregate expenditure or on the overall tax bill. An alternative might involve constitutional ceilings on or targets for the allowable tax burden or the net debt-to-GDP ratio.

---

[7]The report also notes the limitations of an accrual-based measurement: it would delay cost recognition of capital assets, it might result in large and volatile estimates of primary budget data, and, under current federal accounting standards, it would still not recognize social insurance benefits. The report also recognizes that, for many programs, the future costs of some exposures are "dependent upon many economic and technical variables that cannot be known in advance, making accrual based measurement directly in the budget more difficult" (p. 40).

Other institutional mechanisms to force discipline might also be considered. Fiscal rules constitute one obvious solution. Rule-based approaches that focus on maintaining a target for the overall or the current balance may need to be supplemented by independent expenditure ceilings.[8] Otherwise, the emergence of larger asset holdings (or revenue windfalls) may be used to justify expenditure creep. Expenditure ceilings exert independent downward pressure on the forces for budgetary expansion. Alternatively, overall balance rules may need to be replaced by net asset or debt rules: these target a path for the overall net debt or asset position, although with a more comprehensive definition of outstanding debts to include implicit debt liabilities and provisions for contingent liabilities and state-guaranteed debt. However, rule-based approaches have their limitations, as discussed later in this chapter.

Another approach has involved the creation of independent public funds to manage public assets for the prefunding of pension schemes; the New Zealand Superannuation Fund and the somewhat abortive efforts to create a lockbox for the U.S. Social Security system are examples. Despite the well-recognized problems associated with earmarking, such institutional funds may serve the political purpose of fostering and enhancing concern for addressing long-term risks.

Why Isn't an Aggregate Approach Sufficient?

Important though they are, the proposals just described can only bring the policymaker to recognize the fact of an unsustainable fiscal position. Thus, in the European Union, for example, a fiscal gap analysis may reveal that sustainability can be achieved by a sustained tightening of the fiscal stance, that is, an immediate and permanent increase in the tax burden or reduction in expenditure. Operationally, this would suggest the need for an increase in the aggregate medium-term budget target under the SGP. In the context of a social insurance scheme such as the U.S. Social Security system, there would need to be a permanent increase in the payroll tax or a cutback in aggregate benefit payments. A fiscal gap approach to measuring what is needed to achieve sustainability lends itself, in effect, to an aggregate fiscal policy perspective on how to restore sustainability.

---

[8]Norms are applied in a few countries, for example in Belgium, Denmark, France, and the Netherlands, to guide the evolution of expenditure over the short to the medium term. Other countries, such as Sweden and Finland, apply multiyear expenditure ceilings (European Commission, 2002a).

Two types of aggregative approach can be contemplated. One, which can be described as the "fiscal gap filling" approach, derives from a fiscal gap analysis and relies on an immediate but sustained (over the long term) aggregate fiscal adjustment—through either an increase in taxes (that is, tax smoothing) or a reduction in expenditure—to raise the targeted budget balance to be maintained over the long term. This can be conceived of as akin to a prefunding approach. The other—a "balanced budget" approach—relies on annual or otherwise periodic increases in the tax burden or cutbacks in expenditure, as needed, in order to finance the burden of higher expenditure that arises in the future from prior policy commitments (say, from social insurance) or in response to exogenous shocks. It is thus more of a pay-as-you-go approach to meeting budgetary needs.

A fiscal gap filling approach would imply a policy of bringing down the aggregate net public debt-to-GDP ratio. It may also entail a sustained period during which aggregate debt is eliminated and prefunding occurs, with the government accumulating net financial assets, followed by a period of asset decumulation and perhaps even new borrowing. In principle, such an approach would entail a reduction in debt service or, ultimately, the earning of interest income. The objective would be to provide a sufficient fiscal margin to cover the higher expected expenditure, whether it arises from existing policy commitments or in response to plausible future shocks.[9]

This section will argue that although, in principle, reliance on an aggregative approach might be a plausible strategy, governments can and should rely on it only within certain limits. The following section will then draw out the implications of this argument, contending that, to achieve fiscal sustainability, governments must also rely on more immediate adjustments at the level of specific policies and programs. Such adjustments would have the effect of scaling back on the government's prior policy commitments and reducing the government's role in responding to the readily predictable range of structural shocks described in Chapter 2.

---

[9]In 2001 the EcoFin Council of the European Union revised its code of conduct relating to the content and presentation of stability and convergence programs by member countries. The revised code clarifies the interpretation of what constitutes an appropriate medium-term target of near-balance or surplus. The revised code notes that a "more ambitious budgetary target going beyond the *strictu sensu* obligations of the [Stability and Growth] Pact could be justified on several grounds, for example, to reduce high levels of public debt at a faster pace, to prepare for the budgetary costs of aging populations, or to create room for appropriate discretionary policies" (European Commission, 2002a, p. 43).

The argument for limiting reliance on an aggregative approach starts with essentially macroeconomic concerns about the limited feasibility of such a strategy in the presence of Ricardian equivalence effects. Political economy concerns may also be important: these relate to doubts as to whether it is politically feasible for the government to accumulate the stock of assets that would be needed under a tax smoothing approach, to raise the overall tax burden to the extent that is likely to be required, or to find adequate sources of expenditure cutbacks that do not touch many prior policy commitments. The argument also makes the normative point that other important objectives of government policy may be compromised by such a strategy. And although a more limited reliance on an aggregative approach does remain desirable, particularly through the use of fiscal rules, some modifications of existing rules may be necessary to avoid some of the biases to which they presently give rise.

Ricardian Equivalence and Other Macroeconomic Effects

Market forces may limit the effectiveness of an aggregate, rules-based fiscal policy approach. The clearest, perhaps extreme, model of such limitations emerges from the literature on Ricardian equivalence, which says that it is irrelevant, in terms of macroeconomic effects, whether the government raises taxes or takes on debt to finance current outlays. Private sector agents, endowed with rational expectations, would respond in a way that offsets the direct macroeconomic effects of the fiscal instrument chosen. An increase in government deficit financing would induce an increase in private saving, as taxpayers strive to ensure their capacity to pay the higher future taxes that they foresee will at some point be needed to service the increased government debt. By the same token, an increase in taxes or a cut in expenditure, undertaken to address a concern for fiscal sustainability, would prompt a reduction in private sector saving. Although the conditions necessary for Ricardian equivalence to hold are quite restrictive, the model importantly signals the need to recognize that the macroeconomic implications of public policy actions, taken to achieve a given policy objective, may be significantly offset by countervailing private actions.

Recent empirical literature on Ricardian equivalence suggests that households do act to some extent as the theory predicts (Hemming, Kell, and Mahfouz, 2002). However, their reaction to fiscal policy measures taken to reduce the deficit is affected by how this objective is accomplished. Cuts in expenditure are far more likely (by a factor of five) to lower national saving than an increase in taxes. This suggests that efforts by a government to prefund would require increasing resources by more than the nominal amount of the gap. In addition, the amount of overcompensation required would be greater, the more that prefunding is attempted through increased taxation rather than through expenditure cutbacks.

Another possible effect on private behavior can arise from an aggregative approach; this effect is perhaps more subtle than the Ricardian effect, yet it may have an important bearing on the prospects for maintaining rapid productivity growth in the coming years. This is the effect that a significant shift in the balance of saving toward the government may have on the propensity of businesses to undertake risky investments. Federal Reserve Board Chairman Alan Greenspan recently articulated this view:

> The answer to whether government or private saving does more to foster productivity growth arguably thus comes down to the propensity to take risks by U.S. savers. The less the willingness on the part of the nation's savers to hold risky securities, the more that business enterprises must be induced to undertake less risky endeavors. That inducement will occur as relative preferences shift toward debt instruments and away from equity, thereby driving interest rates lower and earnings price ratios higher. Government saving is largely reflected in a retirement of debt. Having chosen to hold at least a portion of their savings in riskless securities, government debt holders when confronted with debt retirement presumably would choose less risky debt securities over common stocks to rebalance their portfolios. Thus an increased share of savings from the government is a markedly more conservative financial strategy than if the saving were undertaken in the private sector. Obviously, the federal government could invest in higher-risk assets, such as equities. But...I do not believe that, other than in defined contribution plans, such investment can be accomplished free of political pressures that would distort the efficient use of capital. (Greenspan, 2002, p. 3.)

Political Economy Difficulties in Sustaining a Tight Fiscal Policy Stance

Most analyses of the time profile of aggregate deficits and surpluses associated with an aggregative fiscal gap filling approach imply the accumulation of significant assets followed by decumulation of those assets. A serious political economy question is whether it is plausible for governments to maintain surpluses year after year so as to achieve a low debt or high net asset position. One obstacle is the likelihood of falling prey to political pressures to relax the fiscal stance through expenditure creep or tax cuts.[10] Once a fiscal position is seen as sufficiently strong, it becomes difficult politically to prevent its relaxation.[11] Future political leaders of a government that has successfully reduced or eliminated the public debt (or even raised public asset levels) must be able to resist the temptation to relax the budgetary stance by reducing taxes or increasing expenditure commitments (Buti and Costello, 2001; Pinfield, 1998). The sustainability of such policies is especially open to question when it has been achieved through tax rates that are high by international standards or that distort allocative efficiency. Fiscal policy as a source of macroeconomic stimulus can readily take precedence over long-term needs; the same applies to fiscal resources as a source of tax relief or public spending.

Although a fiscal rule can prove a powerful mechanism for holding a disciplined fiscal policy stance for a time, particularly if associated with some larger policy objective (for example, meeting the requirements of the Maastricht Treaty), the evidence is already emerging that sustaining such a stance may prove difficult. The recent experience in the European Union (France, Germany, and Portugal) with slippages in fiscal policy provides an obvious case in point. But the budgetary resolve of the United States to maintain surpluses likewise evaporated quickly in 2002, for a number of reasons. One can also note in retrospect how soft the commitment was not to draw on Social Security surpluses, and the failure of the U.S. Congress to adjust the payroll tax rate regularly so as to maintain a 75-year actuarial balance in Social Security. Each of these cases illustrates the difficulty of creating institutional constraints that will dictate, in any precise way, the actions of future policymakers. For obvious constitutional reasons, future majorities cannot be forced to adhere to past promises.

Moreover, fiscal rules that take account of the need for countercyclical fiscal policy may prove asymmetric in their bias, leading them to err on the side of insufficient debt reduction. Specifically, in the down phase of the economic cycle, a rule such as the SGP rule allows for a larger deficit (within the 3 percent of GDP constraint). In principle, if

---

[10]Schick (2002a) recently speculated, "perhaps a tight budget policy applied over an extended period begets a counter reaction to spend more, or perhaps a change in party control of government triggers a reaction."

[11]For example, Pinfield (1998) notes that tax smoothing may minimize the economic costs of raising taxes to finance a varying profile of expenditure. However, in the presence of expenditure creep, tax smoothing may no longer be the optimal tax policy.

the medium-run target is a balanced budget or a small surplus, higher surpluses in boom years should countervail the deficits in lean years to ensure that the medium-run target is indeed achieved over the cycle. Yet political economy pressures in boom years might be such that higher surpluses are not realized, but rather simply the medium-run target itself; this would lead to a bias toward a medium-run average balance below the target. Kilpatrick (2001, p. 28) notes that "a windfall, if fully spent, will have to be clawed back before long." Quinet and Mills (2001) have similarly argued that the SGP provides no reward for virtuous behavior in good years.[12]

Another political economy issue arises when a government pursues a tight fiscal policy stance to prefund long-term obligations. As the government does so, its movement to a stronger net financial balance position may further weaken its capacity to implement the policy reforms necessary in the event of adverse outcomes. The implied fiscal discipline associated with the sustained pursuit of the aggregative fiscal gap filling approach in effect reinforces perceptions about the depth of the government's obligation to stand by its policy commitments. Reliance on aggregative fiscal rules may reduce the urgency faced by governments and political decision makers in addressing the sources of fiscal pressure that derive from the underlying policy framework. If there is a presumption that adequate aggregate fiscal room is being created, governments may be reluctant to undertake the reforms of specific policies necessary to reduce the risk that an aggregate solution may prove insufficient. Reneging would thus become increasingly difficult as such perceptions become hardened. In effect, a government would then bear all the risks associated with the uncertainty as to whether its targeted level of funding is sufficient to cover the expected cost of given policy commitments in the future.

This is particularly the case when there is prefunding of future expenditure commitments of a defined-benefit nature. When there is significant risk associated with such commitments, stemming from uncertainties about the future state of the world, a rule hardens the extent to which the government is exposed to that risk. This can be illustrated with respect to the rate-of-return risk that arises in prefunding pension obligations. To the extent that a country relies on a private sector–funded, defined-contribution system, private individuals bear this risk, since they manage their own portfolios.

---

[12]This suggests that there might be an argument for building an adequate margin into the target for the rule. It might also be the case that the institutional lockbox approach described in Chapter 3 arises principally from such concerns.

In contrast, if the government is the intermediary that builds up the fund, it will be much more difficult politically, if the rate of return on the fund is disappointing, for the government then to shift the burden of the shortfall back onto the pension beneficiaries.[13] An adverse outcome for the fund could happen for any of several reasons: interest rates may turn out lower than anticipated, demographic outcomes may prove more adverse, and other risks may impose associated expenditure burdens. When all these are taken together, the government may find that the accumulated funds are not sufficient, and that either a reduction in benefits or an increase in taxes is still called for but politically far more difficult to accomplish. Fiscal rules thus may reduce a government's degree of freedom in responding to adverse shocks or to unfavorable outcomes on key economic variables. For the governments of large economies in particular, it may be difficult to rely on financial market instruments to insure against such adverse aggregate risks.

The volume of asset holdings that a government can build up is also a matter of uncertainty. Few governments have ever accumulated appreciable net asset holdings relative to their country's GDP, and the same is true of most industrial country governments today (Table 5.1). The Norwegian case is instructive, principally because it illustrates how quickly pressures build to relax fiscal constraints. New Zealand is attempting to insulate its Superannuation Fund by keeping its net asset accumulation separate from the overall budget—this is another effort that will be well worth monitoring. But certainly the weight of analytical studies suggests that a fiscal gap filling approach can require dramatic changes in the aggregate ratio of debt (or assets) to GDP. Davis and Fabling's (2002) study suggests that the median financial asset holdings of New Zealand would exceed the country's GDP by 2051–52. Frederiksen (2003) points to long-term debt reduction arising from such a strategy of sustainable fiscal consolidation of about 62 percent of GDP for the OECD countries on a GDP-weighted basis (84 percent on an unweighted basis). Australia, Canada, Denmark, Greece, Ireland, the Netherlands, and Spain would accumulate assets equal to about 30 to 50 percent of GDP.

This suggests that one significant factor that might facilitate reliance on an aggregative fiscal gap filling approach would be greater clarity about the extent of a government's overall potential liabilities.

---

[13] Another illustration can be drawn from Norway's experience with its Government Petroleum Fund. One reason that the authorities have proven reluctant to switch to a funded pension system, using the GPF balances, is their concern that "any incomplete reform involving partial funding could be misread to mean that the system had been fixed, and thereby lead to even higher pressure to spend any residual oil wealth" (IMF, 2002a, p. 24).

Table 5.1. General Government Net Financial Liabilities in OECD Countries

(In percent of GDP)

Country	1997	1999	2001
Australia	21	15	10
Austria	48	49	47
Belgium	118	107	99
Canada	74	67	53
Denmark	38	31	23
Finland	−16	−62	−48
France	41	43	42
Germany	43	44	44
Greece[1]	108	104	100
Iceland	38	24	26
Ireland[1]	65	50	37
Italy	107	104	97
Japan	28	45	59
Korea, Rep. of	−23	−26	−34
Luxembourg[1]	6	6	6
Netherlands	55	51	42
New Zealand	29	24	20
Norway	−44	−54	−75
Portugal[1]	59	54	56
Slovak Republic[1]	30	30	37
Spain	52	46	40
Sweden	18	13	1
United Kingdom	40	37	31
United States	57	49	42

Source: IMF (2002c); OECD (2002).

[1]Data are gross rather than net financial liabilities; data on gross assets are unavailable.

When both implicit liabilities and potential contingent liabilities are included in measuring a government's net worth, indicators of net assets are lowered (or net debt increased), adding further weight to the argument for fiscal discipline. For example, Norway might find it easier to argue for fiscal discipline if all its implicit debts were added to its explicit debt, thus converting its present net asset position to one of net liabilities.

One further complexity associated with reliance on an aggregative approach relates to the management and governance of any net assets accumulated under such a strategy. As just noted, for some countries, estimates suggest that the total assets accumulated under an aggregative prefunding approach would equal or exceed the country's GDP. The government would bear the full burden of risk in the investment of these assets. The issue of how to diversify the portfolio, both between domestic and foreign currency assets and between different types of equities and fixed-income instruments, would arise. To the extent the portfolio is invested in the domestic economy, important governance issues would also arise should the government become a principal shareholder in many of a country's enterprises. These are not new issues: many governments, central, local, and in between, have invested in assets in connection with civil service pension schemes. But the potential for conflicts of interest and interference in corporate governance could grow as the government's share of total equities in the economy rises. For governments that are small in relation to international capital markets, foreign investments represent an alternative option (see the discussion below on public debt and asset management), but this would present other important policy issues, including how to manage and hedge foreign exchange risk.

Another issue often raised in the context of an aggregative prefunding approach is the constraints it can impose on the conduct of monetary policy and on the operation of financial markets in a country by eliminating government debt. Open-market operations, for example, are predicated on the capacity of central banks to buy and sell government securities in a reasonably liquid securities market. To influence the money supply in the absence of government debt, central banks would need to take a position in corporate equities or bonds, exposing them to market risk. In a small economy, the government might skirt this problem by maintaining both a stock of public debt and significant asset holdings. As noted in Chapter 3, New Zealand is moving in this direction. Also, conflicts of interest might arise if governments took financial positions in companies whose policies are subject to government regulation (see Schinasi, Kramer, and Smith, 2001; Jackson, 2001).

In short, several political economy considerations make it difficult for governments to rely on prefunding as an aggregative approach to long-term fiscal problems. But it is important to underscore that these difficulties do not constitute an argument for relaxing the fiscal stance, say, relative to the requirements of the SGP or any other fiscal rule that might be in place. Getting government debt, both explicit and implicit, down to more manageable levels is certainly key to any fiscal policy strategy for addressing the consequences of prospective long-term developments. The argument, rather, is that reliance on prefunding *alone* may prove unrealistic and unsustainable as a policy option.

Table 5.2. Tax Ratios in OECD Countries
(In percent except where stated otherwise)

Country	Tax-to-GDP Ratio		Real Annual Growth Rate[1]	Absolute Change in Tax-to-GDP Ratio (in percentage points)			Shadow Economy as Fraction of Official GDP[2]			Tax-to-GDP Ratio Adjusted for Shadow Economy[3]
	1965	1999		1965–79	1980–89	1990–99	1970	1980	1996–97	1996–97
Australia	22	31	3.5	4	1.9	1.2	..	..	14	26
Austria	34	44	2.8	5.9	0.6	3.4	2	3	9	40
Belgium	31	46	2.9	13.3	0.3	2.5	10	16	22	37
Canada	26	38	3.3	5.2	3.4	1.6	..	10	15	33
Denmark	30	50	2.1	14.6	5.3	3.3	6	9	18	42
Finland	30	46	3.0	6.4	6.4	1.6	..	..	..	..
France	35	46	2.6	5.7	2.3	2.9	4	7	15	39
Germany	32	38	2.3	6.2	0.2	5.1	3	11	15	32
Greece	18	37	3.1	6.7	2.5	7.8	..	..	30	25
Iceland	26	36	4.2	..	3.2	5.3	..	..	..	..
Ireland	25	32	4.6	4.9	2.5	-1.2	4	8	16	28
Italy	26	43	2.6	1.3	7.4	4.4	11	17	27	34
Japan	18	26	3.7	6.1	4.5	-4.5	..	..	11	25
Luxembourg	28	42	4.9	13.6	-0.1	1.3	..	..	..	..
Netherlands	33	42	2.7	11.7	-0.3	-0.7	5	9	14	37
New Zealand	25	36	2.4	8	6.1	-2.4	7	9	..	..
Norway	30	42	3.1	11.6	-1.4	-0.2	..	..	19	35
Portugal	16	34	3.7	6.6	4.8	4.9	7	11	23	26
Spain	15	35	3.1	8.6	10.2	2.1	10	17	23	27
Sweden	35	52	2.2	14	5.8	-1.4	7	12	20	42
Switzerland	20	34	1.6	9.6	1.9	3.8	4	7	8	31
United Kingdom	30	36	2.3	1.8	1.2	0.4	2	8	13	26
United States	25	29	3.1	2	0	2.2	4	5	9	..

Source: *OECD Revenue Statistics* (2001d) and Schneider and Enste (2000).
[1]Average of annual growth rates of GDP over the period 1970–2001.
[2]Estimates from Schneider and Enste (2000).
[3]Official tax-to-GDP ratio in percent divided by (1 + s), where s equals the ratio of the shadow economy to official GDP.

Limits on Increasing the Tax Burden

Arguably, a second difficulty with an aggregative approach may arise to the extent that it requires significant increases in the tax burden or reductions in other (not previously committed) expenditure. This would certainly be the case under a balanced-budget approach. Indeed, the tax smoothing argument is predicated on the premise that deferring adjustment would mean a sizable increase in the tax burden in the future, which would cause significant allocative distortions in the economy. If tax smoothing were implemented over a long period as part of a fiscal gap filling approach, the necessary tax increase would be smaller, but still significant. Yet for many countries it is difficult to argue on a priori grounds that a ratcheting up of the aggregate tax burden is simply not possible. Table 5.2 presents data on tax ratios in the OECD region over the last four decades. The data for 1999 suggest that tax burdens in some countries are still far below those in many others. Moreover, it is not obvious that the real economic growth rates of many countries with high tax rates are significantly lower than those in countries with lower tax rates.

Even so, a number of arguments suggest that countries seeking to finance the higher expenditures in prospect in future decades may find it difficult to increase the average tax burden appreciably. Box 5.2 presents these arguments in some detail, but their essence can be distilled as follows. First, there does seem to be a limit to the aggregate feasible tax burden sustainable in practice by a market economy that is not at war: the Scandinavian countries appear to be at that limit (roughly 50 percent). Second, the data on the size of the shadow economy suggest that the pressures on businesses to go outside the formal sector to avoid taxes, or on consumers to shift consumption to nontaxed goods, increase with higher average tax burdens in a country. This suggests that there may be diminishing returns to increasing tax rates, and that the true tax take, as a percentage of total output *inclusive* of the shadow economy, is subject to a ceiling. Third, the average tax burden in any given country seems to vary within a fairly narrow range over time, whether because of political economy factors, historical resistance, or shared values or ideologies. Finally, globalization, which may bring with it pressures for tax competition among countries, may also play a role in restraining tax rates.

Box 5.2. Is There Scope for Higher Tax Burdens?

In principle, one option available to industrial countries in the face of growing expenditure commitments is to increase the overall tax burden. But how much scope do they have for such an increase? Basic data on trends in general government tax burdens among OECD countries since 1965 (Table 5.2) suggest that there may be limits. The data reveal a considerable range across these countries in the ratio of taxes to GDP, from highs of around 50 percent in Denmark and Sweden down to around 30 percent in the United States and Japan. It is interesting to note that real economic growth rates do not appear significantly lower in the countries with higher tax burdens. The data also suggest that, although there were significant increases in the tax burden in most OECD countries through the 1970s, the amount of increase has been far smaller in the last decade or so. Indeed, one could argue that there appears to be an effective ceiling to increases much beyond 50 percent. Is there then scope for an increase in the tax share for countries below these ceilings?

Several considerations enter in. First, such simple comparisons across countries do not take account of differences in what services are financed publicly rather than privately. For example, in the United States a substantial share of health outlays is financed privately, whereas in some of the high-tax-share countries the government-run health care sector is largely financed from taxes. If the cost of health care financing were added to the present tax burden of the lower-tax-share countries, the differences in tax ratios would be considerably reduced. Similarly, retirement saving in the United States and the United Kingdom is presently carried out mostly through the private sector, unlike in most continental Western European countries. (In fact, the simple comparison overlooks the fact that the United States already provides a significant tax subsidy to private health care spending and retirement saving.) Absent a wholesale change in the mix of public-private financing of health care and retirement in the lower-tax-burden countries, the scope for higher tax rates in countries like the United States and the United Kingdom may be limited.

Second, the apparent differences in tax burdens may be overstated, if the higher-tax-rate countries have larger shadow economies than the lower-tax-rate countries. Table 5.2 provides some rough data on the share of the shadow economy in the OECD countries over time and adjusts the tax ratio for the higher level of GDP that results when the shadow economy is included. This suggests that the ceiling for the tax burden as a percentage of GDP may be closer to the low 40s. Coupled with the evidence that the underground economy seems to have grown in recent decades (particularly in the higher-tax-rate countries), this finding also suggests that the scope for further increases in the "true" tax ratio may be limited.

Third, there are additional ways in which higher tax rates may both give rise to a less buoyant tax response and prove a source of inefficiency as many countries seek to improve the functioning of their labor markets. Estimates of the shadow economy do not take account of the extent to which higher tax rates increase legal tax avoidance or illegal tax evasion. Moreover, impressionistic evidence suggests that one response of labor in high-tax-rate countries is an increased demand for leisure—a nontaxed "good"—both in the form of demands for reduced hours and more vacation and in the form of voluntary early retirement. Highly skilled workers may also choose to migrate when tax rates at home reach excessive levels. Many have also conjectured that tax rates on mobile capital are likewise constrained, because countries wish to avoid discouraging foreign investment with high taxes (Grubert, 2002). The increasing international convergence of corporate income tax rates and of other taxes on capital may limit governments' ability to tap this revenue source.

Fourth, even with the increase in the tax burden that has taken place over the last several decades, the implicit ceiling on a country's tax burden seems to differ from country to country. For Australia, Japan, and the United States, that ceiling seems to be somewhere close to 30 percent of GDP. For Ireland, Switzerland, and the United Kingdom, it appears to be in the high 30s. This does not mean that higher tax rates are impossible: these same countries have certainly borne higher burdens during exceptional periods, such as World War II. But the political economy forces maintaining these thresholds must be nontrivial.

One can conjecture that these ceilings are in part a function of a country's population. It is striking that the highest tax burdens are observed mainly in the smaller OECD countries. These countries also tend to be relatively homogeneous in their ethnicity, which may facilitate a consensus linking higher tax rates with higher benefits. A perception of fairness—that there is a direct link for a given individual or household between taxes paid and benefits received during the lifetime of the household's members—may support acceptance of such high tax rates. In contrast, when households perceive that a large percentage of government spending largely benefits "others" (including those who pay little or no taxes), resistance to a higher tax burden may be greater.

Population size and homogeneity do not wholly explain differences in tax burdens, however. Some of the larger OECD countries, notably France and Italy, have high tax ratios. But these factors might partly explain the lower tax ratios observed among some of the other large OECD countries, including the United States (which is also more ethnically diverse). Other factors of a political, economic, and historical nature—not to mention differences in the scope of the public sector (as noted above)—might also contribute to explaining why tax burden thresholds are where they are and why they are so difficult to cross.

In sum, there may be scope, at the margin, for some of the lower-taxed industrial countries to raise tax rates further to address higher future fiscal obligations. Future generations might even be willing to accept that higher tax burden if their after-tax incomes are still considerably higher than those of today (as they will be, under conservative assumptions about real growth in coming decades). But even for these countries, differences in the public-private mix of financing of key social insurance functions may overstate whatever margin may exist. For most Western European countries, the scope for a further increase in tax shares would appear limited, not only because of efficiency arguments, but because of the likelihood that it would induce further movement into the underground economy, emigration, and increased consumption of leisure.

Limits on Further Sustained Cutbacks in Expenditure

Without significant policy reforms that affect the time path of expenditure arising from existing policy commitments—say, for pensions or medical care—a reduction in expenditure to implement either an aggregate fiscal gap filling approach or a balanced-budget approach would have to rely on cutbacks in other areas of government spending.[14] Under a fiscal gap filling approach, such cutbacks would be needed immediately and would have to be sustained for the long term. Under a balanced-budget approach, the need for such cutbacks would be deferred to the future, as the impact of present policy commitments becomes greater; however, the magnitude of these cutbacks would be far larger if deferred than if made today (in a manner analogous to the tax smoothing case).

It is not easy, from published data sources, to judge how much room OECD countries have within their current budgets for a further significant rationalization of government expenditure (Table 5.3). In considering this option, it is useful to note that most OECD governments have, in the last decade or so, already made significant efforts at rationalizing their expenditure profiles. Certainly the EU governments were confronted with this task as part of their efforts to qualify for participation in the euro zone (European Commission, 2002a).

---

[14]This is somewhat of a simplification in that some of the policy reforms discussed in the next section may also have consequences for short-term spending on social insurance or other types of policy commitments. The key difference is whether the expenditure cutbacks effectively facilitate a significantly higher fiscal balance in the short term, create fiscal room in the future, or reduce expenditure pressures that would eventually emerge.

Table 5.3. Composition of General Government Expenditure in OECD Countries[1]

Country	Defense (in percent of GDP)	Public Goods Other Than Defense[2]		Subsidies		Economic Services Other Than Subsidies[3]	
		Percent of GDP	Difference from industrial country mean[4]	Percent of GDP	Difference from industrial country mean[4]	Percent of GDP	Difference from industrial country mean[4]
Australia	1.9	6.3	1.8	1.2	-0.1	4.4	1.5
Austria	0.9	3.6	-0.9	2.5	1.3	0.6	-2.3
Canada	1.4	1.5	-3.0	1.1	-0.2	1.3	-1.6
Denmark	1.7	4.3	-0.2	2.3	1.1	3.3	0.4
Finland	1.6	1.7	-2.8	1.5	0.3	-0.4	-3.3
France	2.9	6.3	1.8	1.3	0.1	1.8	-1.1
Germany	1.4	3.8	-0.7	1.2	0.5	2.8	-0.1
Italy	1.7	4.8	0.3	0.6	-0.1	3.4	0.5
Japan	0.9	3.6	-0.9	0.3	-0.7	4.7	1.8
Korea, Rep. of	2.9	2.8	-1.7	—	-1.0	3.4	0.5
Netherlands	1.8	10.0	5.5	1.6	0.4	4.8	1.9
New Zealand	1.1	4.2	-0.3	0	-1.3	—	-2.9
Norway	2.6	3.7	-0.8	2.5	1.3	4.7	1.8
Portugal	2.2	6.1	1.6	1.2	-0.1	5.1	2.2
Spain	1.4	8.5	4.0	1	-0.3	4.9	2.0
Sweden	2.3	3.1	-1.4	1.8	0.6	1.6	-1.3
United Kingdom	3.2	2.2	-2.3	0.5	-0.8	2.8	-0.1
United States	5.2	4.0	-0.5	0.2	-1.1	2.6	-0.3
Mean	2.1	4.5	—	1.3	—	2.9	—
Standard deviation	1.0	2.2	—	0.8	—	1.7	—

Source: Atkinson and van den Noord (2001).
[1]Data are the latest available of either 1993, 1994, or 1995.
[2]Public goods are defined in the source (p. 9) as "the provision of essential 'pure' public goods and services that cannot be rationed by the price mechanism." Examples include national defense and general public services such as public administration, legislation, and regulation.
[3]Economic services are defined in the source (p. 9) as the "provision or co-funding of private goods or services by the government." This includes "public utilities...and financial support for service activities such as research and development, small and medium-sized enterprises and agriculture."
[4]In percentage points of GDP.

Atkinson and van den Noord (2001) present a functional classification of expenditure that allows some assessment of whether a country's spending on functions other than social insurance significantly deviates from the OECD average. In principle, the data suggest that governments have little room for significant cutbacks in their outlays on public goods outside of defense. Some savings may be realized in spending on educational outlays, but a number of analyses suggest that even those savings will not be substantial (Heller and others, 1986; OECD, 2001a; European Commission, 2001b). Further cutbacks in defense and security outlays from their post–Cold War lows would also seem unlikely, although it is perhaps pessimistic to draw such a conclusion in the immediate aftermath of September 11 and in the heat of crises in Iraq and North Korea. If cutbacks on social insurance and defense are ruled out, the principal candidates for further rationalization would appear to be economic services and subsidies.

As discussed below, cutbacks in economic services may be undesirable because they would worsen existing biases against physical investment on the part of many governments facing pressures to balance their budgets. (However, many OECD countries are currently below the OECD mean in spending on economic services, the key exceptions being Australia, Japan, the Netherlands, Norway, Portugal, and Spain.) The most likely candidate for further expenditure rationalization, therefore, is subsidies. However, it does not appear that any OECD country (with the possible exceptions of Denmark and Norway) has a particularly excessive level of subsidies, and the average expenditure on subsidies by these countries is only about 1.3 percent of GDP. It would also be a source of concern if governments were to allow redistributional transfers and social insurance payments either to crowd out the essential functions of government or to restrict substantially the government's capacity to respond to evolving needs and challenges.

Maintaining the State's Capacity for Action

The arguments to this point have suggested that feasibility is the principal difficulty in relying on an aggregative fiscal policy approach. But other arguments speak to the consequences of relying on such an approach to address long-term concerns.

An important normative argument against a purely aggregative approach is the significant risk that a government's fiscal leeway may become marginalized by the combined pressures for tax reduction and entitlement spending. Governments may then find that they are little more than vehicles for the redistribution of income, with scant remaining capacity to use fiscal policy as an instrument of macroeconomic policy, to provide key public goods, to address the challenges of globalization, or to formulate new initiatives in response to a variety of external shocks and risks (Aninat, Heller, and Cuevas, 2001).

Reliance on an aggregative fiscal strategy may indeed significantly curtail a government's flexibility, including its flexibility in the countercyclical use of fiscal policy. As Schick (2002a) has observed, governments are finding that aggregate fiscal rules, high tax rates, and substantial entitlement spending leave them less and less room for maneuver. Denmark may be an extreme case, but its position is instructive. Because of its extremely high tax burden, it has little room to raise taxes further. Yet because so much of its present expenditure burden is devoted to entitlements, it also has very little room for cutbacks in discretionary expenditure. Thus, if faced with an asymmetric shock such as a tightening of the labor market that boosts inflationary pressures, Denmark would find its ability to use fiscal policy as a countercyclical instrument has largely vanished.[15] A country facing constraints on the realistic level of the tax burden, with expenditures pared to the bone of essential public goods and intractable social insurance commitments, and with an aggregative approach to sustainability limiting the budget deficit, may have little scope to pursue countercyclical fiscal policy or to make adequate provision against shocks.

Addressing Weaknesses in Existing Fiscal Rules

Tailoring the Rule to a Country's Situation

One obvious issue in setting a fiscal rule is whether the rule is appropriate for the country in question. Most rules are designed with the virtue of institutional simplicity—balanced-budget rules and the United Kingdom's Golden Rule are obvious examples. The SGP rule has some flexibility in the sense that it does not specify whether a country should aim for budget balance or a surplus over the economic cycle. Operationally, this raises the issue of what a country's specific target should be. To date,

---

[15]Denmark's present macroeconomic policy stance also allows little latitude for action via the exchange rate or monetary policy: although Denmark is not in the euro bloc, it maintains tight links to the countries in the euro zone by what is effectively an informal peg to the euro.

most of the discussion on the application of the SGP rule has focused on ensuring that the rule leaves a sufficient margin to allow fiscal policy to play an appropriate countercyclical role. This has led to assessments of the sensitivity of revenues or outlays to the "output gap," or the difference between actual and potential output. Countries whose automatic budgetary stabilizers have been found to be highly sensitive to the output gap are thus advised to aim for a larger surplus over the medium term. In the event of a recession, there would then be ample room for the larger deficit to be accommodated within the 3 percent ceiling (Brunila, Buti, and Franco, 2001; Beetsma and Jensen, 2001; Buti, Franco, and Ongena, 1998; Dalsgaard and de Serres, 1999; and Barrell and Dury, 2001).

However, setting the target for the rule on the basis of short-term stabilization considerations may not be optimal in terms of the country's long-term objectives. For example, assume that a country anticipates significant expenditure pressures emerging from the aging of its population or other structural factors. A prefunding approach would set the fiscal balance so that, over time, debt-service obligations are sufficiently reduced to provide room in the budget to finance those anticipated expenditures. Yet there is no reason to assume that the target implied by the SGP rule (that is, a small surplus or near balance) meets this objective. With the baby boomers' retirement looming for many EU countries, spending might mount faster than any fiscal savings generated from observance of the rule.[16]

For some countries this is almost the equivalent of recognizing that there is still a fiscal gap, and that even if a very long-term intertemporal perspective is assumed, an aggregative approach would require a more ambitious fiscal target. This point, that the EU countries are still faced with a fiscal gap over and above what is implied by the SGP rule, has been made in one way or another in several recent publications (Buti and Costello, 2001; European Commission, 2001a; Frederiksen, 2003). Indeed, Frederiksen suggests that a primary surplus gap of about 2.9 percent of GDP remains for the (GDP-weighted) average EU country. He also concludes that several countries may need to run surpluses so that net government assets are acquired.

---

[16]Thus Robson and Scarth (1999) argue that, over time, the choice of rule may influence the long-term outcome far more than the short-term outcome. Their research suggests that an SGP approach, which allows for countercyclical variability around a targeted surplus, is preferable to one that aims simply at balance in good times and deficits in recession: "In short, the stakes involved in the choices rise over time: Canadians will care a good deal more in 20 years' time which choices were made than they will in 10 years' time." This underscores the importance of relying on other instruments besides fiscal rules to address the various objectives of public decision makers.

But even if a country's current fiscal stance appears consistent with the absence of a fiscal gap, the operational fiscal rule for that country may still need to specify surpluses in the initial years and deficit targets thereafter. In effect, the "band" of the fiscal margin, rather than ranging from balance to a 3-percent-of-GDP deficit (as in the SGP rule) over all periods, might need to start with a target surplus of, say, 3 to 6 percent of GDP (with the lower figure applying in a recession) for a number of years, and then gradually shift to a target deficit of, say, 3 to 6 percent in later years. In effect, the rule would need to take account of the need to accumulate assets in the initial years and later draw them down. This also highlights the important point that there is no reason for the rule to be the same for all countries. Nor should the appropriate target remain invariant across time, even for countries within a monetary union. Long-run expenditure pressures differ across countries as a function of the different magnitude and time path of the demographic pressures to which they are exposed and as a function of their chosen policy frameworks.

The Practicalities of Adhering to a Fiscal Rule

Assume that a country with an aging population has chosen a target fiscal balance under its fiscal rule and that it is estimated that there is no corresponding tax or primary gap. In principle, then, if the rule is observed, debt-service reduction may create adequate fiscal room over time to be used for meeting future expenditure pressures. But the important issue of ensuring that the rule is actually observed over time would still remain. This provides an additional perspective on the previous point. It could simply be argued that a fiscal rule, such as the SGP rule, is at all times sufficient, by definition. Specifically, if a fiscal imbalance arises in any given year relative to the target, the rule would call for policies to cut expenditure or raise revenue. But success in meeting the rule then rests on how readily such fiscal adjustments can be made.

In other words, the existence of the rule begs the question of *how* it is to be observed.[17] This raises important issues about the scope for a further increase in the tax burden (whether on equity or allocative efficiency grounds), the nature of competing claims for public expenditure,

---

[17]The recent EC report on aging populations notes, "the Council cannot simply assume that Member States will always be capable of complying with the SGP provisions in the future in the face of large increases in age-related expenditures" (European Commission, 2001b, p. 84).

and the welfare implications of adjusting social insurance benefits, all of which were discussed above.

In effect, the observance of the SGP rule or the Golden Rule is akin to a PAYGO approach to fiscal policy in a world where there are long-term structural pressures. Taxes or expenditure would need to be adjusted over time in order to comply with the rule, without any tax or expenditure smoothing. In contrast, a differentiation of the rule across countries and time, as suggested above, is equivalent to a tax smoothing approach to long-term fiscal policy.

This point has added resonance in the context of a point noted by Buti and others about the challenges faced by countries with high public debt-to-GDP ratios (Buti and Costello, 2001; Buti, 2000). They note the misleading character of analyses that suggest that these countries have more fiscal room to address issues of population aging, owing to the large reduction in debt service arising from their observance of the balanced-budget rule. Buti emphasizes that, for these countries, meeting the balanced-budget criterion requires, on a sustained basis, a far larger primary surplus than countries with low debt have to achieve, and that realizing such surpluses necessitates a much higher tax burden, or far more severe expenditure constraints, or both. In the context of a balanced-budget rule, these countries are thus far closer to the edge in terms of their capacity either to sustain such high primary surpluses or to tighten further in the face of additional expenditure pressure.

Biases Arising From the Absence of Accrual Accounting

A further problem with aggregate rules may arise from the way in which they are formulated and applied. The issue is whether the rule is written so as to ensure that a government has an incentive to pursue a policy reform even when doing so yields benefits in the long run but not in the short run. This is even more of an issue when such reforms are costly in the short term. Thus, for example, an increase in the retirement age, scheduled to take effect in 10 years, may significantly strengthen long-run fiscal sustainability but do nothing for today's fiscal cash balance. If the focus of the fiscal rule is on the cash balance rather than on an accrual measure of the fiscal balance, policymakers will have no incentive to introduce the policy change. Similarly, policies that imply costly buyouts, in the short term, of a government's long-term pension obligations may make adherence to a cash-based fiscal rule difficult, yet improve long-term fiscal sustainability (a point also emphasized by Buti and Giudice, 2002). In effect, in the absence of an accrual accounting approach, particularly one that takes account of a change in the net present value of future expenditure obligations, the incentives under a fiscal rule are biased against long-run policy reform.

This problem can be illustrated in the context of the European Union. There are two obvious reasons why a fiscal gap problem has emerged in some EU countries in the context of aging populations. First, observance of the SGP rule has not been defined on an accrual basis. Second, the Maastricht criteria, from which the SGP rule evolved, took no account of implicit debt liabilities, either the formal kind, such as government pension liabilities, or the informal kind, such as those related to medical or long-term care. In principle, even to begin to achieve fiscal sustainability through observance of the rule would require the application of an accrual approach in measuring the fiscal balance and the government's net debt. It would thus need to recognize the creation of new implicit liabilities as well as the elimination of existing ones.

This would not be an easy step, because the level of implicit debt would be affected not only by policy changes, but also by changes in the economic environment. For example, changing the assumption regarding long-term interest rates would significantly influence the net present value of the implicit debt. Changes in expected tax or contribution revenue would also influence the estimates. Moreover, as discussed earlier, even countries such as New Zealand that have moved to accrual accounting have not yet taken account of accruing obligations that relate to future contingent events (such as the retirement of current workers).[18] But it does argue that, in monitoring and assessing adherence to a fiscal rule, account needs to be taken, at least qualitatively, of the impact on the government's implicit debt of policy reforms that have important long-term fiscal implications.

Biases Against Pro-Growth Investments

Fiscal rules that focus on the overall budget balance rather than net worth may imply a bias against government infrastructure investment and in favor of the government holding financial assets. In its 2002 review of public finances, the European Commission noted this tendency within the European Union, particularly for those countries that have

---

[18]New Zealand has extended its accrual approach to take account of the swing in asset values associated with movements in foreign exchange rates or prices of other assets (such as timber). As a result, the observed volatility in asset prices has led to specific policy reforms (for example, in the composition of foreign exchange-denominated assets or in the amount of government-owned forests).

not yet reached the near-balance requirement of the SGP or that have a large interest burden (European Commission, 2002a). Such biases may give rise to distortions: they can lead governments to limit capital outlays (on physical and human capital as well as on research and development) that can facilitate growth, they can discourage governments from efforts to contain the prospective financial damages from extreme weather events, and they can deter efforts to mitigate climate change.[19] If investments are well chosen, there is little economic reason not to use debt to finance them (see Pisani-Ferry, 2002). Not only would net worth be unaffected, but it would also be reasonable to spread the costs of that financing across different generations of beneficiaries. (The definition of "well chosen," however, remains difficult but critical.)

In this context it is useful to distinguish between the treatment of capital expenditure under the SGP and, in the United Kingdom, under the Golden Rule and the Sustainable Investment Rule. Under the SGP, capital expenditure is treated like any other expenditure and is subject to the overall balance constraint. The effect is that new debt incurred for the purchase of capital goods may not exceed the overall deficit target. If the target is a surplus over the economic cycle, this can be an extremely limiting constraint. In contrast, there is no limitation on capital expenditure under the Golden Rule itself (other than to the extent that capital consumption must be included in current spending). Rather, the limit on capital spending arises from the Sustainable Investment Rule (or, in New Zealand, the gross debt ratio), which limits capital expenditure to the sum of the operating surplus and the amount of new debt that may be incurred consistent with the debt limit. Because the debt limit is defined as a ratio to GDP, this would be equivalent, for a country that is already at its debt limit, to the operating surplus plus the amount of additional debt allowed by growth in GDP.

From the perspective of the long term, several considerations are relevant. First, rules like the SGP are likely to be more restrictive of capital outlays, because they force investment to be funded essentially out of surpluses on current operations, at least over the medium term. Over time this might cause investment in capital infrastructure to fall below what is necessary, for example, to adapt to climate change or to respond to competitive pressures. This would especially be the case if

---

[19]The Italian government has recently sought to counter this anti-investment bias, in part out of concern that globalization will intensify the need for government to provide for a more economically competitive environment (Balassone, Momigliano, and Monacelli, 2002).

there are other expenditure pressures stemming from increasing transfers to the elderly or social services needs. Some alternative approaches have been already introduced to avoid this limitation. Private-public partnerships and other kinds of lease arrangements allow the leasing of capital infrastructure from the private sector, so that the constraint then only applies to the cost of leasing within the framework of the overall budget target.

In contrast, the Golden Rule explicitly allows for investment to be treated separately, recognizing that it is an outlay that produces value across generations. Because it more readily allows the government to borrow for investment, it is less constraining, at least in the current period.[20] Leasing arrangements allow further flexibility for capital purchases, over and above any ceiling implied by the debt limit and the operating surplus. However, the Golden Rule may impart a bias toward investments in physical rather than human capital, because the latter principally take the form of current outlays.

This is not to ignore the important problems that arise in ensuring that government investments are in fact well appraised and profitable. To the extent that public investment decisions are far less subject to a market test than private investments, it is more difficult to ensure that an investment will be genuinely profitable in a benefit-cost sense. There is always a concern that pressures for capital spending may weaken the government's ability to limit its overall net debt position.[21] Japan's recent experience with unproductive infrastructure investment argues for caution, and a number of writers in the European Union have emphasized the principal-agent biases that can lead to overinvestment (Buti and Guidice, 2002; Fottinger, 2001). Again, obtaining adequate measures of a government's net worth position becomes critical in considering approaches to address issues of the long term.

---

[20]In fact, the Golden Rule is not that much less constraining than the SGP approach. Instead of treating investment as an outlay in the current period (much like expensing for income tax purposes), it imputes a flow of depreciation expenses in the future. It is thus less constraining in the current period, but more constraining in the future.

[21]In principle, capital outlays should not be incurred if the net present value of the project does not exceed its cost. Put another way, the value in use of the infra-marginal investment should exceed its market cost. But given the limited nature of markets for many types of public infrastructure and capital goods, and the fact that it may be hard or undesirable to charge for the flow of services from public capital goods, it may be difficult to judge whether the market value of the services produced by a capital good recoups the cost of the investment. Certainly in many countries there is a concern that many public investments have been unproductive.

Uncertainty Issues

It was noted earlier that most prevailing fiscal rules allow some flexibility, in the short term, for fiscal policy to play a countercyclical role. However, issues of long-term uncertainty are not addressed other than to the extent that, in the choice of target, authorities may in principle include an additional margin against contingency risks. Whether that margin is adequate and accounts for all possible contingencies is an important issue. Should there be any allowance for the probability that the government will not be able to meet its promises? Thus, in appraising the adequacy of a rule or aggregative fiscal policy stance, the probability that a given rule can actually be adhered to over time must be considered, as well as the costs associated with doing so. Economic shocks can certainly bear on this probability. Some recent papers (Hostland and Matier, 2001; Buckle, Kim, and Tam, 2001) suggest that the choice of target—the budget balance versus the debt-to-GDP ratio—can determine the confidence interval over which the target can be met and the likely cost of realizing that target over the long term.[22]

Other kinds of uncertainty bear on the effectiveness of fiscal rules. A conceptual analogue to this issue is the recent work by the U.S. CBO (2001b) and by Lee and Edwards (2002), which uses a stochastic approach to appraise the adequacy of the reserves of the U.S. Social Security system. In principle, the setting of the payroll tax rate is equivalent to setting a rule that is meant to provide actuarial balance over a 75-year period. Yet these studies suggest that the probability of the rule achieving its objective over this time frame is barely above zero.

Applying stochastic approaches to prevailing aggregative fiscal rules may expose the sensitivity of these rules to outstanding demographic or other risks. This could help clarify the scope of the task facing governments seeking a reasonable assurance that the rules can be observed. Kilpatrick (2001, p. 33) observes that "in trying to meet a set of

---

[22]Hostland and Matier conclude that, to achieve the targeted debt-to-GDP ratio within a 10-year planning horizon with a high degree of confidence, a surplus needs to be pursued rather than budget balance, although there is still a 90 percent confidence interval of 7 to 12 percentage points of GDP. Targeting the debt-to-GDP ratio too rigidly can result in a narrower range of the debt-to-GDP ratio for the same confidence interval, but at the cost of large and frequent discretionary changes in program spending and taxes and with the possibility of fiscal policy becoming pro-cyclical. A more flexible debt rule could be an alternative, allowing countercyclical responses to unanticipated fiscal developments, but making discretionary changes to bring the debt-to-GDP ratio gradually back to its desired level.

fiscal rules, some assessment needs to be made of how likely it is that they will be achieved and whether additional action is required to improve the chances of doing so." Such an assessment would need to focus not only on the risk attributes of particular policy approaches, but also on the broader issue of the other fiscal risks that a government may need to address in the future.

Concluding Thoughts on Aggregative Fiscal Approaches and Fiscal Rules

The preceding discussion has explored a number of concerns about the difficulties of relying on an aggregative prefunding approach to long-term fiscal issues, and about the capacity of a government to adhere to fiscal rules in a sustainable fashion. In many respects the size of the obligations involved in adhering to a given rule or aggregate fiscal policy target would appear to be a critical factor in determining whether it is likely to be feasible. If adherence to a fiscal rule entails maintenance of tax rates that are significantly higher than has historically been the norm for the country, or that are significantly higher than those in comparable countries, the political feasibility of such an approach comes into question. Likewise, if the primary fiscal balance required entails a sustained reduction in expenditure on essential public goods, services, and transfers, this will inevitably raise intergenerational concerns: are current generations being squeezed to benefit future generations? Similarly, a fiscal strategy that implies the steady and significant accumulation of net assets relative to GDP could become a lightning rod for those opposed to what they perceive as high taxes or inadequate expenditure (apart from the governance and financial management issues raised above).[23]

---

[23] An additional concern relates to how a rational expectations perspective would be linked to an aggregative prefunding approach. If households believe that their government is indeed saving and investing adequately on their behalf through a public pension scheme, would household saving rates fall accordingly? If so, this would have macroeconomic implications and would bear on the overall welfare of generations dependent on government pension schemes. But if households have doubts about the credibility of the government's commitment to its public pension obligations—in effect, questioning the credibility of the government's adherence to the fiscal rule—this may well be reflected in *higher* private sector saving in anticipation of a possible partial reneging. In that case a more realistic positioning of a government's policy commitments might have little effect on private sector saving, to the extent that it has already been anticipated, and might, in the long run, enhance the government's overall credibility.

Fiscal rules may be an effective political device for managing short- to medium-term fiscal policy. They provide an important mechanism to continuously remind governments of their obligations and constrain their fiscal behavior. However, if the rules are also tailored to support an aggregative fiscal strategy aimed at the long term, some clear pre-requisites are entailed. As the above discussion implies, the rules must be realistic in terms of what they require with regard to tax burdens and expenditure provision over the long term in a given country context. They must be comprehensive, so that surpluses in the central government are not offset by deficits by other elements of the government or the public sector. And they must be based on an accrual concept that takes full account of the implications of policy reforms with longer-term financial implications.

Restructuring a Government's Policy Commitments

The previous section argued that there are important limits to relying on an aggregative approach to achieve long-term fiscal sustainability in the face of pressures from demographic, climatic, globalization-related, and geopolitical developments. The argument rested principally on the premise that political economy forces would make it difficult to create or carve out the fiscal leeway necessary in the future to respond to growing fiscal pressures. To the extent that international tax competition further constrains a government's ability to raise tax rates, it could constitute another, independent factor. The previous section also emphasized the importance of not allowing past policy commitments to compromise the capacity of the state to respond to new challenges and risks. Such responses are likely to require governments to begin formulating new approaches to the management of risks, and this will inevitably require that room be made both for new fiscal initiatives and for a capacity to respond to unforeseen challenges.

In essence, a restructuring of government policy commitments should not be seen as a vehicle by which to reduce or weaken the role of the state or its public welfare function. Rather, it is a means to ensure that the state remains relevant—in providing public goods, in achieving fundamental redistributional objectives, and in standing ready to respond to new challenges. A restructuring of government policy commitments entails more than simply scaling back current commitments. It also involves the creation of new policy structures to reduce and manage risks and a reconsideration of the role that government can and should play. For countries that have yet to introduce significant policy commitments, particularly in the social insurance sphere, the issues raised in this section underscore the importance of caution in evaluating costly fiscal commitments and assessing the risks to longer-term fiscal sustainability.

For such countries it may also be relevant to consider whether the specifics of the policies adopted in an area might have broader macroeconomic effects. For example, some writers on pension reform in emerging market economies and other developing countries argue that, with prefunded retirement systems in place, population aging can become an engine for capital accumulation. For countries that stay with either familial support systems or PAYGO public pensions, population aging simply raises the dependency burden. Lee and others (forthcoming) calculate that population aging alone would roughly double the capital-labor ratio under life cycle saving, which is closely related to prefunded retirement, even though aggregate saving rates decline under life cycle saving during the last stage of the demographic transition, when population aging is occurring, because labor force growth has also substantially slowed at that point.

Scaling Back

Chapter 3 has already summarized the various approaches that governments have adopted to limit the fiscal impact of past policy commitments in the face of demographic pressures, particularly in the social insurance sphere. From an aggregate sustainability perspective, the objective is to reduce the net present value of a government's implicit and explicit liabilities. But it is equally important to ensure that the *time path* of a government's expenditure obligations is consistent with its expected stream of revenue and the constraints imposed by net asset or debt limits.[24] These issues pertain equally to decisions that might entail the creation of new fiscal commitments.

Yet the political and economic challenges and complexities involved in reducing a government's potential exposure to commitments in the social insurance sphere should not be minimized. Fundamental distributional issues, both within and across generations, must be confronted,

---

[24] In effect, if there are limits to how large a net asset buildup is feasible, then there are also limits to the extent to which expenditure can be financed from enhanced investment revenue or a drawdown of assets. This implies the need for a limit on the deficits that can be financed in the future as a consequence of pressures related to population aging.

and past policy commitments and expectations cannot be casually dismissed.[25] This underscores the importance of approaches that rely on a gradual phasing in of reduced benefit expectations, whether for existing or for prospective beneficiaries. Governments need to be transparent, both about the increased risks that households will have to assume in the future and about the underlying redistribution of risk and income. Governments must also be clear about the basic underlying welfare support that they will continue to provide.

A shift toward a more narrow targeting of benefits or more reliance on means testing is an obvious approach, implying a more focused role for government in the social insurance sphere. But moral hazard and allocative efficiency concerns are always in the background. If a government seeks to provide a minimum of social safety net benefits as an alternative to more extensive involvement, it must anticipate the risk of a reduced incentive for some individuals to save for their own future needs (primarily those lower-income individuals most likely to be the focus of a targeted approach, since their efforts at saving would not bring them above the minimum income guarantee). The high negative marginal tax rates associated with targeting may also create allocative distortions (as noted in Chapter 4).

Among industrial countries, there is now a wide difference between the minimalist position on pensions, represented by the United Kingdom with its low basic state pension and Australia with its "demogrant" approach, on the one hand, and the more extensive commitments of some Western European countries on the other. The viability of either extreme over time, whether from the vantage point of political economy or in terms of fiscal sustainability, may be doubted. Certainly, it is likely that current long-run fiscal forecasts, taken at face value, would suggest greater optimism than is warranted. The political pressures to scale up social benefit regimes that are likely to be too meager will be intense.

But it is important to emphasize that both the United Kingdom's and Australia's strategies do put them in a far stronger position to

---

[25]The recent debate within the United States over the President's Commission on Social Security is instructive. That the report received scathing criticism from a number of noted economists does not imply that there was not a shared recognition of the need for reform. In their critique, Diamond and Orszag (2002) note that "some combination of a reduction in benefits, an increase in revenues, and an increase in the rate of return earned on the reserves of the Social Security Trust Fund is required to bring the system back into balance. A fundamental issue is whether the balance among the possible elements of a reform plan is appropriate."

maintain a realistically sustainable fiscal position, over time, than other countries that will have to *reduce* existing benefits. In effect, the greater flexibility that they have acquired in their social insurance options is a considerable asset.

One approach that some countries with extensive social commitments have pursued is worthy of note. The recent reforms adopted by Italy and Sweden are important for their effort to shift some of the risks faced by government—notably relating to longevity and rate of return—back onto individuals (what Aaron, 2000, has called "built-in flexibility with uncertain outcomes"). But equally important for the viability of such reforms is that households be made fully aware, and well in advance, of the likely financial consequences of such risk transfers, so that they are in a stronger position to plan ahead.

The complexities of a downscaling of commitments are perhaps even more difficult in the area of social service provision. Most industrial country governments are still grappling with the challenge of how to limit the pace of expansion of government-financed medical care outlays, while still ensuring that all members of society have access to basic medical care.[26] This may involve requiring co-payments and deductibles, setting limits on the guarantees to medical care, rationing access to specific services, and limiting coverage for specific health problems. Governments may find themselves in the unpleasant position of having to deny patients access to high-quality medical care technologies or pharmaceuticals that could significantly prolong their lives but that are extremely expensive, invasive, or still unproven. In their 2002 Intergenerational Report, the Australian authorities note the challenge of reconciling the rising expectations of individuals (in part fueled by the Internet) as to what medical science can accomplish with what may be financially feasible. In the area of long-term care, governments may seek to limit new commitments on the amount of residential services to be provided, while still providing some minimum benefit to assist the indigent. Commitment reform (whether in pensions, medical care, or long-term residential care) may thus need to be linked to regulatory reform that encourages the private sector to underwrite some of the risks heretofore covered by the government.

---

[26]The importance of assumptions about the medical care expenditure growth rate can be illustrated in the Gokhale and Smetters study (2003), where the differential between the growth rate of GDP and that of medical care costs is enormously influential in determining the size of their fiscal imbalance measure. Of their $44.2 trillion estimate of the U.S. federal fiscal imbalance, Medicare accounts for $36.6 trillion.

A downscaling of commitments is clearly difficult. Yet, despite these difficulties, an important counterfactual assumption must be recognized in considering such policy reforms: if nothing is done, severe fiscal constraints may at some point force the government to abandon its policy commitments in a far more abrupt and damaging way. There have been enough recent, painful cases of governments reneging on their debt or pension commitments to make it clear that this outcome is as plausible as it is undesirable. Thus the objective of reform must be to place a government's policy commitments on a more secure track, in the light of known demographic risks and other risks less known, to ensure that those commitments are genuinely sustainable and can be relied upon.

Reducing and Managing Risk

Another, equally critical, aspect of governments' efforts to restructure their policy commitments relates to how they will respond to the various risks they may confront in coming decades.[27] The very nature of government involvement is likely to change, both in relation to providing or facilitating insurance coverage and with respect to the actions governments take, through spending on infrastructure and through regulation, to limit the extent and the consequences of countries' (and individuals') exposure to risk.

Whether from natural phenomena (such as disease or climate change or earthquake), the threat of terrorist attack, the dangers that accompany new technologies (such as oil spills or nuclear plant breakdowns), or the effects of globalization or market contagion, private households and industry will continue to confront new or aggravated risks, which they will seek to insure themselves against. September 11 illustrated the costs that can arise from major terrorist incidents. The consequences of extreme weather events can be illustrated by multiple examples: the floods in England in the fall of 2000 and in Western and Central Europe in the summer of 2002 are among the most recent. These and other acute weather events may or may not be related to climate change. But even the gradual effects of climate change may impose significant costs on certain industries, as heretofore abnormal weather conditions become the norm (Swiss Re, 2002).

---

[27]As noted earlier, Brixi and Mody (2002) discuss many of the conceptual issues associated with fiscal risk management.

The risks of globalization are of many types. Biological and genetic accidents are more readily spread in a more tigl,tly interconnected world: the HIV/AIDS epidemic and the outbreaks of foot-and-mouth disease and bovine spongiform encephalitis (mad cow disease) in England are just a few examples. Computer viruses and cyberterrorism in the financial sector are examples of the risks posed by new technologies (Hundley and others, 2000).

The private insurance industry may respond to these emerging risks by offering coverage against them, perhaps at higher premiums than in the past. Expanded coverage is particularly likely as insurers continue to develop more forward-looking approaches to valuing the costs of adverse outcomes.[28] New insurance products may also be developed. But the industry may instead choose to reduce its coverage of such risks, either by excluding coverage or by setting tighter limits on the amounts it will insure.[29] Or its coverage may be made contingent on the government taking specific actions to foster an environment that limits the economic consequences of adverse events.[30]

---

[28]It is interesting that most of the losses from the floods in Austria, the Czech Republic, Germany, and the Slovak Republic in the summer of 2002 appear not to have been privately insured. Kapner (2002) reports that, after the 1997 floods in the Czech Republic, insurers were liable for only about 20 percent of the total economic loss and that the coverage ratio was likely to have been even lower in Austria and Germany, "where fewer people and businesses tend to be insured against flood damage." In Austria the expectation was that no more than 3 percent of the preliminary damage estimate was likely to be covered by private insurance. Kapner (2002) also suggests that governments "will wind up bearing much of the uninsured cost of flood relief and repair" (Section W, p. 1). Munich Re Group (2002, p. 43) notes that "in view of the loss trends that are observable, their past practice of retrospective underwriting...inevitably leads to premiums lagging behind and hence results in losses.... The insurance industry...must at long last adopt a policy of adequate prospective underwriting."

[29]In its 2002 annual report, Munich Re Group (2002) noted that "after September 11, the insurance industry needs to reconsider its future strategy with regard to covering terrorism risks. What is insurable and what is not? Is 'protection against terrorism'...primarily the task of the State[?]" (p. 65). It notes that France, Spain, and the United Kingdom have created pool solutions with government participation to cover terrorism risks. It then asserts that, in the interest of shareholders, "we have a duty to pursue a very restrictive underwriting policy here. Where we do reinsure the terrorism risk, we have narrowly limited the coverage in property and aviation third party business...in property reinsurance we have also stipulated a right of termination with a period of notice of 14 days. This right is absolutely essential, given that assumptions about occurrence probability—like those made for natural hazards—are not possible with regard to terrorist attacks" (p. 71).

[30]Crichton (2002) notes that, since 1961, British insurers have formed an effective partnership with the government: insurers would offer flood insurance to all at a reasonable price as long as the government maintained adequate flood defenses and planning controls. In recent years the insurance industry has expressed concern that, particularly in England and Wales, the government has failed to keep its side of the bargain, resulting

Governments may thus find themselves increasingly asking what their posture should be regarding such risks. To what extent should they provide insurance when the private sector is unwilling to do so? This may entail creating a financial backstop for the private insurance industry in the form of reinsurance. Or it may effectively take the form of the government budgeting for contingencies and then spending on emergency relief and reconstruction or providing guarantees for borrowing by industries affected by extreme events or unanticipated shocks. Thus, following September 11, the German government decided to pay the state airline $70 million to defray the costs incurred when the United States closed its airspace. This obligation was neither an implicit nor even a contingent liability. In 2002, the European Union was considering the establishment of a virtual fund through which member governments would make payouts for the "biggest disasters—perhaps those with a bill in excess of £2 billion," arguing that neither airlines nor insurers should bear the brunt of terrorist attacks aimed at nation-states rather than individual companies (Dombey, 2002). In November 2002 the United States passed legislation requiring private insurers to provide terrorism insurance, at rates to be set by the insurers but with the federal government covering 90 percent of the cost of all damages that exceed $10 billion.

Here, again, moral hazard considerations come into play. If the perception becomes widespread that the government will step in to cover the economic consequences of adverse events, it might weaken the private sector's own efforts to obtain insurance coverage, or induce risky behavior that would aggravate those economic consequences.[31] The private insurance industry may see the government's intervention as an opportunity to shift the burden of a costly area of coverage. Heading off such moral hazard effects may require that governments limit their role as reinsurers through enlightened regulation that forces the private sector to internalize the cost of insurance against such risks. Governments should support rather than supplant the private sector in this regard.

Another issue, which the OECD has raised, is "the way governments communicate with and involve the public when managing risk.... How, when, and what governments communicate to the public, as well as

---

in a large accumulation of exposure in flood hazard areas. He argues that the recent issuance in England of draft planning guidelines allowing flood plain development signals a breakdown in the partnership, leading insurers to advise that they would give notice of their withdrawal from their guarantee by the end of 2002.

[31]Crichton (2002, p. 8) notes that the government in England has stated that "it would be foolish for any government to provide compensation in such circumstances."

how they involve the public in decisions and actions, is often crucial to public confidence in decision-makers" (OECD, 2001c, p. 8). The evidence is clear that, in the past, governments have stepped in, at least to a limited extent, to provide some but by no means all of the financing for relief and reconstruction in the event of a disaster or adverse shock.[32] What remains to be seen is whether the nature of the risks and uncertainties that arise in coming decades will shift the balance in terms of what private insurers will cover, and the extent to which the government's role will change.

A government may thus be forced to consider more actively whether it can affect its exposure to risk by modifying its regulatory policies and its infrastructure investment decisions. Analytically, decision makers need to be able to determine "where and when a simple possibility may evolve into a high probability that a given risk may occur" (OECD, 2001c, p. 8). Risk reduction may need to become a more central consideration in the formulation of a government's investment program. For example, investments in infrastructure can play a critical role in reducing the likelihood that extreme weather events will have significant economic (and fiscal) consequences.[33] Andersen (2003, p. 2) notes that "Governments can mitigate the impact of disasters—for example, by enforcing urban planning standards, building codes, and land-use regulations more stringently than they do now, and by establishing alternative risk-transfer arrangements to ensure that funds are available for reconstruction before events occur."

Similarly, scientists recognize the high degree of uncertainty about whether climate change will be gradual or abrupt, reflecting the "difficulty of identifying and quantifying all possible causes of abrupt climate change, and the lack of predictability near thresholds.... Given the deep uncertainty about the nature and speed of future climate changes,

---

[32]A recent U.S. General Accounting Office (2002) review of studies of the impact of the September 11 terrorist attacks indicates that the U.S. federal government made payments of about $14 billion in the New York area alone. This did not include payments made to cover losses to airlines or, obviously, the cost of the military effort in Afghanistan and Iraq.

[33]Recent media reports in the United States have highlighted the increasing probability that a Category Five hurricane will strike New Orleans in the coming decades, the large losses that would be suffered, and the high price tag presently placed on restoring the Louisiana wetlands and building walls to protect the city (National Public Radio, 2002). In the United Kingdom, recent reports indicate the significant cost of addressing the consequences of sea level rise, storm surges, and flooding due to climate change (United Kingdom, Department of Environment, Food, and Rural Affairs, 2002). The value of the assets at risk is estimated to be £222 billion; 5 million people are estimated to be potentially at risk.

policy-making thus might focus on reducing vulnerability of systems to impacts by enhancing ecological and societal resiliency and adaptability" (Alley and others, 2003, p. 2009).

The recent U.S. *Climate Action Report* noted that

> Existing or new infrastructure can also be used to dampen the impacts of climate-induced influences on flow regimes and aquatic ecosystems of many of our nation's rivers. While significant adaptation is possible, its cost could be reduced if the probable effects of climate change are factored in before making major long-term investments in repairing, maintaining, expanding, and operating existing water supply and management infrastructure. (U.S. Environmental Protection Agency, 2002, p. 102.)

Similarly, the Canadian government, in its *Third National Report on Climate Change*, notes that

> Adaptation measures [in coastal zones] include construction of physical protection structures; natural shore stabilization measures; land use regulations that restrict development along coastal areas.... Community and infrastructure [planning should] incorporate climate change into land use, community and transportation planning; revise building codes and regulation; revise design parameters for flood protection infrastructure. (Canada, Minister of Public Works and Government Services, 2001, p. 101.)

Government regulatory policy may also be critical in forestalling or modifying proposed private sector investments that would accentuate the country's exposure to adverse economic shocks.[34] Governments may need to take measures that either encourage modification of the technologies embedded in new investments or raise their costs sufficiently to take their negative spillovers into account.

Governments may also need to undertake an active program of preventive infrastructure investment as a means of addressing climate change, either facilitating adaptation or reducing the fiscal risks associated with the occurrence of extreme weather events. These issues are as

---

[34] In its recent *World Disasters Report*, the International Federation of Red Cross and Red Crescent Societies (2002) notes that "decentralization can undermine risk reduction efforts. Cash-strapped central governments essentially abdicate their responsibilities, leaving local governments and NGOs to take on the task of managing disasters." In effect, risk reduction is essentially fragmented into a series of small-scale initiatives, focusing on particular hazard events and artificially separated from the broader conditions of vulnerability and ongoing development programs (p. 28; see also Inter-American Development ment Bank, 2002).

relevant in developing countries as they are in industrial countries (see, for example, Vordzorgbe, 2002a, 2002b, on the role of risk management and disaster preparedness in Africa).[35] Governments may also need to respond to the competitive pressure exerted by globalization by improving their transportation or telecommunications infrastructure.

As noted in Chapter 3, additional outlays on research may be necessary to support policy responses to the more uncertain risks. For example, regarding abrupt climate change, a recent study by prominent U.S. scientists and economists suggests that "improved understanding of the processes of abrupt climate change may increase the lead time for mitigation and adaptation…. More-precise estimates of impacts of abrupt climate change could make response strategies more effective. The persistence of some uncertainty regarding future abrupt climate changes argues in favor of [no-regrets policies] …to improve resiliency and adaptability in economies and ecosystems…. Slowing the rate of human forcing of the climate system may delay or even avoid crossing of thresholds" (Alley and others, p. 2009).

Finally, Giddens (2000) notes that a key characteristic of globalization is the extent to which some risks are now "manufactured." Certainly, climate change might be perceived as such a risk. Similarly, the risk of terrorism may be seen as a consequence of the policy actions of some countries, whether positive or negative. In a similar vein, and along the same lines as the argument for greater risk management, governments might seek to reduce their exposure to risk by revising their current policies. For example, policies to dramatically augment overseas development assistance have been argued as critical for reducing global poverty and thereby reducing potential global threats and tensions.

Broadening Policy Approaches

In the face of significant risks, governments might explore policy options that raise fundamental issues concerning the role and character of the state. For example, to mitigate the effects of population aging, some in Europe have advocated policies to encourage increased fertility,

---

[35]This is not new. The U.S. Army Corps of Engineers has for years engaged in such actions to limit the risks of Mississippi River floods (although some would argue that this has ultimately only accentuated these risks over time). See also Dialogue on Water and Climate (2003) for a valuable discussion of ways in which climatologists and water managers can interact to find adaptive solutions to reduce the risks of climate change.

by influencing either the timing of births or family size (Lutz and others, 2003). Recognizing that one of the principal sources of lower fertility rates is the number of childless women, some have proposed child benefits that are highest for the first child (Bräuninger and others, 2002).

Others see immigration as a way of addressing the economic consequences of demographic change. Yet demographic projections suggest that, in many European countries, the number of immigrants that would be required to offset the effects of aging would be so large as to swamp the national culture. For example, a recent United Nations study suggests that just to hold the working-age population (the population aged 15–64) in the European Union constant between now and 2050 would require net migration of about 1.5 million people a year (about double the levels experienced in 1993–98; United Nations Population Division, 2000). Holding the elderly dependency ratio (the ratio of those over 64 to the population 15–64) constant would require an even more dramatic scaling up in the number of net immigrants a year—by a multiple of 15 over current rates—resulting in a tripling of the EU population. At least three-quarters of the population would then have immigrated sometime between today and 2050.

Such statistics make it apparent why the alternative policy approach of raising the retirement age might appear more desirable. For example, in the European Union, the same United Nations study suggests that increasing the retirement age to 76 would keep the implied population support ratio (in this case the ratio of the number in the population over age 76 to those aged 15–76) the same as the present ratio based on a retirement age of 65 (see Coleman, 2001).

Other Ramifications of Policy Reforms

The kinds of policy reforms described above are intended to realize budgetary savings in either the short or the medium term, but are presumed to increase long-term savings as well. Obviously critical to any assessment of a particular reform are its implications for a government's broader welfare objectives. This will influence whether realizing such savings is worth the other costs that may be entailed and whether alternative, more cost-effective approaches should be explored. Chapter 4 has already alluded to the need to consider both the distributional and the allocative efficiency implications of any given reform.

The distributional question is, which income groups or generations are the net gainers or losers from reform? The efficiency questions include the following: What allocative distortions might a given reform (for example, a shift to means testing) engender, and by how much do they counterbalance any potential gains in equity or budgetary savings?[36] How do tighter regulatory restrictions or insurance coverage requirements influence private investment decisions? How does any scaling back in citizens' expectations associated with more restrictive government benefit programs influence private saving behavior, and with what macroeconomic effects? What effect do policy reforms have on households' expectations about the likelihood of further changes taking place during their lifetime? And, from a rational expectations perspective, does the fact of present policy reform, seen in the light of past reforms, influence perceptions about the likelihood that the present policy framework can be sustained?

Additionally, government actions to scale back some of its benefit and service commitments will importantly influence the distribution of exposure to risk and uncertainty between the public and the private sector. Households and enterprises may thus find themselves exposed to greater risk and uncertainty, including the possibility of higher than anticipated costs of medical care, lower rates of return on retirement savings, greater longevity risks, and, for some households, a variety of losses (including lost income, adverse health consequences, and property damage) due to climate change.

The prospect of having to unravel such a tangled web of worries easily explains why governments are slow to introduce policy reforms that are likely to entail a significant scaling back of commitments. Certainly, recent OECD and EU reports indicate both the extent of the policy reforms that have been implemented and the concerns that remain as to whether they have been sufficient or timely enough. Auerbach and Hassett (2001) strike a cautionary note, arguing that, in the face of uncertainty, governments tend both to delay the undertaking of serious reforms until a crisis emerges and to overcompensate, when the crisis comes, by adopting reforms that go beyond what is really needed. The complex ramifications of reform may

---

[36]The cost of means testing is the distortions in private sector behavior (in labor supply, private saving, or both) that it may induce. These costs can be significant. Thus, there is, as always, a trade-off between efficiency and equity. Also, whenever means testing is introduced, it is equivalent to a one-time wealth tax.

also explain why some reforms in some programs do no more than retard the growth of outlays, rather than truly reduce them.

Public Debt and Asset Management

Chapter 3 discussed the various ways in which governments are increasingly adopting a risk management approach in considering the
asset and liability structure of their financial reserves. It can be expected that these approaches will increasingly be extended to the management of public assets and debt. Certainly for the industrial
countries, the prospect that fiscal rules will sharply reduce public debt,
and even lead to an increase in publicly held assets, will require a
broader consideration of the risk attributes of countries' portfolios. It is
plausible that the future will see a further extension of risk management to the overall risk characteristics, over time, of a government's expenditure commitments and revenue base. Recent works by Bohn
(1990, 1995), Missale (1999), Davis (2001), Davis and Fabling (2002),
IMF (2002b), Leong (1999), and Brixi and Mody (2002) suggest that consideration of these issues can be an important factor in both the management of risk and the realization of public sector savings. Barnhill
and Kopits' (2003) effort at constructing a value-at-risk assessment of
Ecuador's fiscal balance sheet is one such attempt, although one with
a very short-term focus.

Chapter 3 noted Missale's suggestion that, in managing public debt,
governments should seek to offset unanticipated shocks to revenue or
expenditure with corresponding reductions in debt-servicing costs.
Such an approach would require the issuance of state-contingent debt
instruments, with an interest rate that is indexed so as to fall with the
occurrence of such shocks. If a country's debt consisted of a mix of such
instruments, it could achieve lower debt-servicing costs at precisely
those times when unanticipated demand or supply shocks result in
higher than expected expenditure or lower than expected revenue. The
result would be to minimize the overall budget risks associated with
such shocks. Given that such instruments are unlikely to be available,
existing debt instruments whose interest rates are correlated with such
contingent "states" should be sought.

Is it realistic to seek to apply such a strategy to the kinds of long-term
structural factors to which budgets are at risk? It is not clear whether the
approach can be readily broadened in this way. Some of the long-run issues that were discussed in Chapter 2 are clearly predictable, despite the

uncertainty surrounding their precise characteristics and effects. For these issues, countries would need to deal with the budget impact directly, either through policy reform or through a budget smoothing approach at an aggregate level. Because these expenditure shocks are so readily predictable, it is questionable whether countries could issue debt instruments at low interest rates during these high-expenditure periods. On the other hand, certain other potential long-run developments, although identifiable, are subject to considerable uncertainty, and their occurrence would effectively be manifested as a demand or a supply shock. For these the Missale argument appears relevant.[37]

The effectiveness of such a debt management strategy also remains open to debate. The existing literature suggests a number of theoretical and practical difficulties. Leong's recent survey for the U.K. Debt Management Office notes that the empirical literature "does not make a convincing argument for restructuring the portfolio with a focus on risk management" (Leong, 1999, p. 2). She notes that a government's optimal portfolio will "vary for different countries and different periods, depending on what sort of shock is likely to dominate" as well as with the nature of the correlation between specific supply and demand shocks and the types of debt instruments available to country authorities. Leong also cites Missale (1997), who, in a study on Italy and the United Kingdom, concluded that "choosing debt instruments to minimize budget risk appears to be quite a difficult task" (p. 26).

Despite these arguments, some innovative recent approaches offer the prospect of some degree of risk management through such instruments. Freeman, Keen, and Mani (2002) as well as the Inter-American Development Bank (2002) suggest the possibility of tailoring financial instruments to the shocks a country is likely to face. One approach is the idea of a GDP-indexed bond, where "interest payments vary as GDP growth is above or below some reference value—[to] provide some financial relief in times of natural disaster" (Freeman, Keen, and Mani, 2002, p. 17; Borensztein and Mauro, 2002). The Inter-American Development Bank (2002) has also broached the concept of various catastrophe-related instruments (catastrophe bonds, contingent surplus notes, exchange-traded catastrophe options, catastrophe equity puts, catastrophe swaps, and weather derivatives). The basic concept of a catastrophe bond is the waiving of interest and principal in the event

---

[37]Missale's thesis also assumes that it can be applied in the context of a tax smoothing strategy. It is not clear whether the optimality of the approach carries over to situations where tax smoothing has not been adopted.

that a specified catastrophe occurs, thus providing a mechanism to securitize catastrophe risks within the wider capital market. However, these approaches must be regarded as still very much in their infancy.

Leong (1999, p. 34) concludes her survey by suggesting that further work is needed before the approach of minimizing budgetary risks can provide a practical basis for debt management: "In particular, given uncertainty over the nature of future shocks, and also practical constraints on the size of government financial asset holdings, there does not yet appear to be a consensus on the optimal risk-minimizing portfolio." Similarly, Barnhill and Kopits (2003) argue that calculation of risk-weighted public sector balance sheets (analogous to the risk weighting of bank capital under the Basle Committee's approach) is unrealistic, particularly within a long-term perspective.

It seems, therefore, that further exploration of how governments might approach the management of both their assets and their liabilities in anticipation of long-term budgetary risks and income needs (IMF and World Bank, 2001) would be worthwhile. The focus needs to be on the determination of a portfolio balance that takes account of the covariance relationship between government revenue and government expenditure commitments and interest costs. Historical patterns may prove to be not wholly accurate indicators of the future. An aging population in the industrial world may result in both the shrinkage of government bond markets in industrial countries and greater volatility in equity markets.

Governments may also need to consider further to what extent an active government bond market may need to be maintained (which would require not repaying some government debt), even if side by side with the government's own accumulation of assets. Consideration of the risks and benefits associated with diversification, both in terms of the equity-bond mix and in terms of the balance between domestic and foreign currency-denominated assets, would also be important.

The Role for Policy Coordination

Coordination by countries of their policy efforts in a number of spheres could enhance the prospects that many of the fiscal burdens arising from long-term structural developments will someday be addressed. Population aging is a phenomenon that will be witnessed initially in the industrial countries, and later in some of the larger emerging market economies such as China and Korea. But the major structural economic changes that will be associated with an aging population will occur not in isolation, but in the context of a global economy that will see the world's population significantly increase in the next century, although most of that growth will occur in countries whose incomes will still lag far behind those in the industrial countries. Global climate change will be occurring at the same time, and its adverse effects will be felt principally by the developing countries. The economic and political security of aging industrial country populations will be inextricably linked with what happens in the rest of the world. Political instability, weak growth, or tensions associated with natural resource shortages will inevitably have consequences for all countries, not just those affected directly.

Aging Populations

Many of the long-term uncertainties related to population aging that countries have to consider are outside the control of their decision makers. For example, interest rate and equity market developments over time will be strongly affected by the buoyancy of growth among non-OECD countries and their capacity to absorb capital flows from the OECD. The capacity of the governments of industrial countries with aging populations to find further budgetary room to finance social insurance transfers will be affected by the degree to which their security outlays can be reduced. This in turn will be strongly affected by whether there is political stability in many presently volatile regions of the world. The revenue base in industrial countries could be significantly influenced by how much immigration they allow. Certainly, pressures to allow immigration can readily be expected, given the rapid population growth of many very low income countries. These various interdependencies suggest that, in some spheres, it may be in the interest of the industrial countries to agree on coordinated policies that can foster stable political regimes and rapid economic growth in the developing world.

For example, industrial countries would appear to have a common interest in strengthening the capacity of low- and middle-income countries to absorb capital inflows productively. Attanasio and Violante's (2000) model, although narrowly focused on two regions—the United States and the European Union on the one hand, Latin America on the other—clearly illustrate the important impact of capital flows (in the absence of labor mobility). By broadening the size of the capital market to include other sources of demand outside the industrial countries, such flows could partially limit the decline in the real return to capital in the industrial countries that would arise if industrial country investors invested only in their own equity markets. Without a broadening to emerging market and developing country capital markets, the return in industrial markets would reflect a rising capital stock (due to increased saving for retirement) and a shrinking labor force (if these industrial aging economies remain relatively closed to immigration). Conversely, for the developing countries, the greater infusion of capital would allow an increase in aggregate investment and higher real wages. Turner and others (1998) note that a significant strengthening in non-OECD regions' demand for capital would "boost OECD net foreign investment income by a larger amount than a similar increase in OECD savings because it also raises the rate of return" (p. 30).[38] Enabling industrial country capital to be used productively to foster growth outside the OECD could thus be mutually advantageous for all concerned.[39]

Both studies, however, underscore the fact that full capital mobility between the OECD and the non-OECD countries cannot be readily assumed. It would imply much larger capital flows than were observed even in the late 1990s, raising issues of absorptive capacity unless the flows are spread more or less evenly throughout the developing world. Most important, it would be critical to reduce the risk presently associated with such investments. The Asian crisis of the late 1990s and the more recent bankruptcies of some large corporations and accounting firms in the United States and Europe suggest that much work will be needed to strengthen the capital market regulatory structure of potential recipient economies. Governance reforms, strengthened accounting practices, and greater transparency will all be necessary if a significant expansion of capital flows, particularly in the form of direct investment, is to be forthcoming.

---

[38]"A major uncertainty concerns the future growth potential of the non-OECD region over the coming decades. Given a considerably more optimistic outlook for the non-OECD, based, for example on the assumption of major supply-side reforms, there would be greater scope for OECD investment in those regions. In such a 'high performance' scenario, the rate of return earned on accumulated assets might also be substantially increased, so that investment income flows would provide a more substantial offset to the adverse effects of aging on OECD living standards. However, for the OECD to reap such benefits there would have to be a major structural change in the non-OECD economies, not only in product and factor markets, but also in capital markets, to facilitate the massive resource transfers involved" (Turner and others, 1998, p. 30).

[39]One cautionary note relates to the uncertainty that might arise from exchange rate movements. If the prediction by Turner and others of an appreciation of industrial country currencies proves correct, the return to industrial countries might be smaller as they seek to repatriate earnings from non-OECD regions with depreciated currencies (also see Heller and Symansky, 1998).

Conversely, and most important, if industrial countries *do not* facilitate the capacity of developing countries to absorb more capital, the result observed for closed-economy models (with the OECD countries, in effect, acting as one large closed economy) becomes more likely, namely, a decline in interest rates. This would reduce the rates of return on capital earned by those in retirement and would increase the amount of accumulated capital necessary to purchase annuities yielding adequate replacement rates. Governments, meanwhile, would discover that their prefunding schemes yield a smaller return than anticipated, forcing them to resort to higher payroll taxes to finance their social insurance obligations.

Climate Change

The Kyoto Treaty is a first step toward the coordinated implementation of policies to limit global greenhouse gas emissions and to reduce the pace at which climate change is likely to occur. There is much controversy over whether and when full implementation of the treaty will have an impact on the forces influencing the world's climate system.[40] Many argue that, to have any successful impact, these mitigation efforts need to be extended to those developing countries that will be an important source of growth in greenhouse gas emissions as their economies develop during the coming decades. Such countries are likely to need significant financial assistance from the industrial countries if they are to implement such programs.

Similarly, there is a strong consensus on the current weaknesses in our knowledge base concerning both the dynamics of climatological systems and the economic consequences that may be felt in different regions of the world. Many argue that there is still a window of time to accumulate greater understanding of how greenhouse gas concentrations are affecting the dynamics of climate systems before a decision must be made whether or not to undertake a significant increase in mitigation efforts (Nordhaus and Boyer, 2000). But this will require an intensification of research efforts.

In terms of adaptation strategies, much of the detailed research on the specific ways in which climate change will be manifested in different regions, and the possible economic effects, has been heavily focused on some of the large industrial countries. Yet many of the adverse effects will be felt by developing countries that lack the financial or academic

---

[40]For example, see the more skeptical perspective of Lomborg (2001).

capacity to undertake this research. The adaptation efforts of developing countries would be enhanced significantly if the industrial countries were to assist in financing an intensified research program.

Geopolitical Tensions

Finally, many contend that September 11 constituted a wake-up call to the industrial world. Significant disparities in income and power across countries, especially when access to the Internet makes those disparities obvious to all, are not easily accepted by those at the bottom. Tensions arising from scarcity of natural resources in some regions may spill over to others, affecting product markets, at least, outside the regions directly affected, and possibly creating political and security risks as well. In the last year or so, various international conferences— in Johannesburg, Monterrey, and Doha—have underscored how much more needs to be done to address the smoldering tensions arising from global poverty, global income inequality, and environmental concerns, not to mention religion-based tensions of the sort hypothesized by Samuel Huntington (1998).

This has led many to advocate a number of initiatives that would have the effect of transferring resources to the developing world. These include an expansion of direct foreign assistance, the elimination of industrial country agricultural subsidies and tariff barriers, and the promotion of trade among developing countries. The possibilities for policy coordination in other areas are many. For example, the recent work of the United Nations Development Programme (Kaul and others, 2003) highlights the scope for expanded provision of global public goods.

Each of these topics deserves far more discussion and analysis than can be offered here. For purposes of this volume, the principal and obvious message is that what these initiatives could accomplish could greatly affect the nature of the uncertainties that weigh on any assessment of the long-term fiscal position of any country. Implementation of many of these initiatives would, of course, also have costs. These would need to be factored into the long-run fiscal assessment of any country that accepts to share in the burden of those costs.

6

Summary and Conclusions

One of the questions raised in Chapter 1 was the following: Given so much uncertainty about what might or might not happen several decades into the future, is it not fruitless for policymakers to worry about the long term in considering the stance of fiscal policy? This study argues against such fatalism. Uncertainty about the future is real and considerable. But four points appear reasonably clear.

First, few would dispute that certain important structural changes *will* occur, with a high degree of probability, in the coming decades, both in human societies and in the natural environment. They will include shifts in the age structure of populations, changes in climatic conditions, continued globalization, and ongoing dramatic technological progress. Regrettably, the prospect of increased geopolitical tension is also very real, whether arising from global economic disparities, competition for scarce natural resources, nonstate-sponsored terrorism, or cultural or religious conflicts.

Second, these structural developments are likely to have significant fiscal consequences, whether as a result of market pressures, explicit public policy commitments, or states acting on what are perceived to be their implicit responsibilities. Certainly, explicit policy commitments already made by governments of the world's industrial countries have predetermined, to a historically unprecedented degree, much of the fiscal priorities of future generations. These commitments largely serve the needs of middle classes in retirement, and consumption rather than investment. But expectations about the role of government also have implications for tomorrow's fiscal priorities: as this study has shown, they give rise to implicit policy commitments that are no less real than those set out in laws and budget documents. Were it not for this heavy overhang of government commitments, both explicit and implicit, concern for the fiscal consequences of future structural developments would be much less.

Third, what may seem today like far-distant concerns may begin soon enough to affect both the current economic environment and short- to medium-term policy decisions. Forecasts made today that peer only a decade into the future may suggest that a government's fiscal position is sustainable, but in just 5 or 10 years' time that judgment may well be reversed. That is because the forces driving some of these key structural changes on the horizon do not proceed in straight, predictable lines, but rather evolve dynamically, and can therefore emerge explosively. Even if they do not, a policy framework that delays addressing these long-term fiscal challenges will almost certainly prove far more costly than one that recognizes and responds to them expeditiously.

Finally, failure to address the implications of these long-term developments will affect the future welfare of many living today, as well as many yet to be born. For many to whom the state has made explicit promises, postponing solutions to looming fiscal imbalances may result, when the problem can no longer be put off, in an unnecessarily abrupt change in financial circumstances. Delay also exposes societies to far greater risk than if the inevitable adjustment had been anticipated and implemented much earlier, allowing them to adapt. A more general risk is that a haphazard portfolio of fiscal commitments collected over decades will leave the state with diminished capacity, scarcely able to carry out its essential functions, to practice countercyclical fiscal policy, or to respond to genuinely unforeseen challenges.

It follows from these four points that governments—and the societies they represent—need to take much more explicit account *in the near term* of the potential fiscal consequences of long-term developments, despite the uncertainty that surrounds them. Doing so poses practical as well as political problems. Despite continuing advances in analytical techniques, economists, demographers, political scientists, and meteorologists must all still contend with considerable uncertainty in the forecasts they supply for public policy analysis. There are problems of prediction error (what will tax rates need to be in the future?), scientific uncertainty (by how much is the climate warming, and with what effects?), and policy uncertainty (what policy actions will suffice? and will international cooperation be necessary?).

Even if one could attach specific probabilities to different possible future events (and their fiscal consequences), the public debate would still need to focus on *how* governments and society should respond to such assessments. Should policies be based on a worst-case scenario, or only on evidence of future calamity proved beyond a reasonable doubt? Or should they be based simply on the mean or the median forecast outcome, in effect splitting the difference? The choice will have important implications. Different generations will be affected by the degree to which governments choose to inoculate themselves against future risks.

Moreover, stimulating real debate, let alone action, on such issues is not easy, whether inside or outside the budget process. The political economy of fiscal decision making in most countries makes it difficult to focus the attention of either policymakers or the public on far-off future risks, even if those who will bear the consequences are already alive today. Even when the risks are fully recognized, solutions that address the danger of an unsustainable fiscal burden may be difficult to find, given not only the uncertainties but also the politically complex challenge of apportioning the burden of adjustment across and within generations. Some types of risk can be readily addressed, by known but politically painful policy solutions. Others, however, are more difficult even to know how to address, other than by ensuring that the government has sufficient fiscal leeway to respond if and when needed.

One other thing that is certain is that there are no magic bullets. No single policy reform will suffice in addressing the long-term challenges facing countries today. Rather, a multipronged approach is required. Indeed, there is a necessary symbiosis to the various policies. If decision makers and the public lack the data needed to assess whether the current fiscal policy framework is sustainable, debate will be hindered, and they will not be able to act (or choose not to act) in a sufficiently informed way. If the fiscal accounting framework does not adequately disclose the size of a government's potential liabilities arising from known risks, there will not be sufficient political support for confronting difficult reforms, whether in terms of aggregate policy adjustments or in terms of specific program modifications. A revision of budget procedures may be necessary to foster and inform, if not explicitly catalyze, the public debate necessary for determining the desirability of policy reforms.

Chapters 3 through 5 distinguished between two broad sets of issues in approaching problems of the long term. The first set relates to the way in which governments and societies think and act on such problems—the types of analyses that can clarify potential fiscal consequences and the adaptations needed to deal with them. Chapter 3 suggested that the approaches now used to take account of the long term in fiscal policy formulation—the analytical techniques, budget procedures, and accounting methodologies—are deficient. Analytical processes are only beginning to grapple with the size of the imbalances that may lie ahead. Moreover, these processes tend to focus on particular issues, in a country-specific setting, rather than on the possibility of multiple structural forces operating simultaneously, in a global context. Budget processes in almost all countries today do not go beyond medium-term frameworks. The need to insure against future risks is neither adequately considered by policymakers nor publicly debated, particularly in terms of the need to create sufficient fiscal room for the less easily identifiable potential pressures on the budget. Institutional approaches to better ensure the time consistency of budget decisions are a work still in progress.

Chapter 5 started by advocating a long-term perspective as an integral part of the way in which fiscal policy is thought about, designed, and implemented. It argued for strengthening the analytical techniques used to assess the impact of long-term risks, including far greater reliance on approaches that clarify and, where possible, quantify the probabilities of different possible outcomes. The chapter also called for a broader macroeconomic vision that takes account of aging populations, climate change, and other developments as *coincident* processes, while recognizing the nature of existing policy commitments.

Assessments of the sustainability of fiscal policy must address the long term. Although it is reasonable for such assessments to focus primarily on the medium term, it is nevertheless critical to take account of looming longer-term fiscal pressures, both certain and uncertain. Market perceptions of the consequences and difficulties posed by potential long-term imbalances and fiscal risks may begin, at some point *within* that medium-term time frame, to exert important pressures on the macroeconomic and fiscal situation. Rising risk premiums on government debt instruments are typically the most concrete evidence of this.

Also needed is more explicit consideration of the fiscal consequences of long-term risks in the budget document itself and in the give and take of the budget deliberation process. This may require that budget documents include an annex that takes a longer-term perspective, particularly if the detailed formal budget focuses only on the medium term. But equally, greater transparency and more detailed analyses of the magnitude of the principal risks, their sensitivity to key assumptions, and the implications of adverse scenarios need to be presented in order to better inform the public debate. Most important, the budget process should require independent assessments of long-term risks and of the implications of current government policies. The goal is to counteract the tendency of many governments to downplay, for political reasons, the long-term risks they face.

There is also an important role to be played by peer pressure from multilateral or regional institutions. Chapters 3 and 5 described the work being done by multilateral agencies in this regard, but an increased role for regional peer surveillance would also be desirable. Here the surveillance mechanisms within the European Union provide a useful model. Strengthening the sustainability analyses that underpin such surveillance is critical—particularly with respect to ensuring that the fiscal position is sustainable in *each* year of the medium-term framework, which means looking ahead 10 to 15 years from each year's vantage point.

The second set of issues transcends analysis and procedures to confront the more difficult problem of how countries should address long-term issues substantively, in their actual policies. This study does not provide answers to specific questions of the substance of policy reform. Rather, it outlines a broad strategy for how governments should respond when confronted with the likelihood of a fiscally unsustainable position over the longer term. Many countries in the industrial world could use this strategy to redress the long-term fiscal imbalances in their current fiscal policy frameworks. The strategy is also applicable in most transition and some emerging market economies.

Many empirical analyses have now demonstrated the significant likelihood that existing policy commitments will require further fiscal adjustment (either because they are excessively generous or because they are too minimalist) in the face of current demographic trends. The potential challenges from other likely structural developments will only exacerbate the problem of fiscal unsustainability and the need for significant policy change. Although some may argue that there is room for an increase in tax burdens over time, the political obstacles to raising taxes cannot be easily dismissed. Nor is there much scope for significant cutbacks in other areas of spending to make room for the anticipated growth of precommitted expenditures. This casts doubt on the hope that a balanced-budget approach—gradually increasing taxes or cutting expenditures in the future as needed—would be successful.

This study has also underscored the difficulties associated with relying solely on the alternative approach of prefunding, that is, seeking a sustained and immediate strengthening in the aggregate fiscal stance. It has argued that there are limits to relying on this type of aggregate approach (whether or not explicitly based on fiscal rules), for several important reasons. First, there are important political obstacles. As countries begin to develop strong fiscal positions, reducing their debt or even accumulating positive net asset positions, fiscal discipline becomes harder to maintain when there are political benefits to be derived by cutting taxes or increasing spending. Governance issues as well as macroeconomic management concerns may also intrude on a government's ability to pursue a policy that involves a substantial buildup of net assets. It will be interesting to see whether, in the few cases where such a buildup might actually occur in the next few years (for example, in Norway and New Zealand), such a policy can be sustained. Ricardian equivalence theory poses another important obstacle. Households do respond to government efforts to increase national saving in ways that may offset those efforts, at least in part. Equity is also an issue: it is not clear that current generations should have to pay for generous benefits for later generations who may be better off in any case. In the face of significant uncertainties in the fiscal situation, the potential for moral hazard is also important. Governments that choose an aggregate approach may find it difficult to back down on their commitments if that approach still proves insufficient to meet fiscal needs.

Programmatic reforms—changes in the nature of the commitments underlying the various elements of the budget—are therefore a critical complement to an aggregate approach. Although some governments have recognized the need to free themselves from commitments that are clearly unsustainable, it is remarkable how narrowly attention remains focused on the bottom line of the total required fiscal adjustment. The *signaling* role of commitment reform is nonetheless crucial, because shifting some of the risk now borne by national governments back to individual households and local communities represents an important, though politically difficult, aspect of the needed change in approach. The nature of the uncertainties faced and the difficulties confronted by individuals in addressing them need to be met early on. And the fact of commitment reform itself, as well as the changes in private sector behavior it provokes (including but not limited to increased private saving), may generate new policy issues that governments will have to address in their short- to medium-term fiscal policy frameworks.

Thus governments should carefully calculate the long-run implications of their existing programs. Where possible, these programs should be scaled back and restructured in a manner that focuses more narrowly on core public goals—among others, the provision of public goods, the regulation of markets, and the redistribution of resources to alleviate poverty and foster equality of opportunity. Existing programs, particularly in the areas of pensions and medical care, must adapt to changing circumstances. By seeking to change the time path of future program expenditures, governments have a better chance of being time-consistent in their policies and can focus on those commitments they can reasonably honor, and thus create sufficient fiscal leeway to adapt and respond to uncertain challenges. The efforts of Sweden and Italy to incorporate self-activating adjustments in the parameters of their pension programs to respond to increases in life expectancy are an important example.

Governments should also be very cautious about taking on new obligations, especially when to do so would threaten long-run fiscal sustainability. A lesson learned in recent decades is that governments find it very difficult to abrogate or pull back from policy commitments once made. This is particularly important because governments *will* from time to time have to make some new commitments or undertake new initiatives, either in the context of preventive actions that forestall larger, more serious future fiscal contingencies, or in response to unanticipated events or developments. Limiting the extent to which future budgets are excessively precommitted should thus be a key and enduring guidepost as governments formulate their fiscal policy frameworks. On the expenditure side, this is of particular importance for developing countries that have not gone too far down the road already traveled by the industrial countries. But even the latter should heed this advice, particularly with regard to policies that reduce taxes in the short term at the expense of longer-term fiscal viability, constraining the future capacity of governments to mobilize additional resources.

There are, however, some areas where an activist approach may be necessary. Although all governments must recognize and respond to many developments over which they have little control, in many other areas government policies can either influence private behavior or reduce the likelihood of future problems emerging. In a number of areas, preventive and adaptive measures may help forestall the need for large new expenditures in the future. This applies especially to the need to mitigate and adapt to climate change. Investments in global public goods as well as efforts to defuse geopolitical tensions, prevent conflict over scarce natural resources, reduce global income disparities, and overcome absolute poverty are other areas where forward-looking actions could yield high returns.

Governments must also do more to narrow uncertainty. This will require a far greater commitment to research, for example to identify possible efficiency gains in health care delivery, or to improve our understanding of the natural phenomena that will determine the impact of increased greenhouse gas concentrations on global and regional climates.

Beyond analysis, changes in procedures, and domestic policy actions, there is also scope for enhanced policy coordination among countries in confronting many challenges. The *interdependence* of countries in facing the multiple risks and pressures that will emerge in coming decades needs far more attention. Although some of the world's smaller economies may be able to redress their long-term fiscal imbalances without concern for spillover or general-equilibrium effects, the same is not true for larger economies, much less the industrial countries as a group. What quickly becomes clear is that countries have many long-term problems in common—from aging populations to climate change to globalization—and that this requires a consideration of the global macroeconomic imbalances that could arise if many countries pursue similar strategies toward them. Certainly, treating the aging industrial economies as if they were one large closed economy is unlikely to be a viable strategy, or even an appropriate analytical device. How the industrial countries address their demographic problems, in particular, will have important consequences for the global economy.

For example, assume that each of the industrial countries decided independently to undertake sustained action to consolidate its fiscal position and raise national saving in response to the prospect of population aging. What would be the implications for the global economy of such a simultaneous shift in the macroeconomic policy stance of a group of countries that account for three-quarters of world GDP? Would it give rise to global deflationary pressures, or would it be offset by higher investment or exports by these economies? Reliance by the industrial countries on export-led growth to raise saving would require shifts in exchange rates to support larger current account surpluses; it would also require a stronger impulse for growth in the rest of the world, bolstered and financed by a greater capacity for the latter to absorb capital inflows. Identifying the potential sources of expanded demand in the rest of the world would go far beyond the scope of this book, raising important issues about how to foster growth and development in those countries where a large share of the world's population already resides.

Increasing the flow of capital from the industrial countries to the rest of the world not only would intensify competitive pressures on emerging market economies that have historically relied on export-led growth, but would also require that these countries address weaknesses in their financial and regulatory structures. Expanded development assistance would be needed to foster growth among the poorest developing countries. For some of these, faster growth would require a transformation of their economies, shifting their output away from reliance on primary commodities. Yet such a shift would be unlikely to happen unless those countries first achieved growth in incomes *within* the primary sector, and that would require giving those countries far greater access to industrial country markets.

Other scenarios for achieving global macroeconomic balance might depend on a significant expansion of labor flows from poor, high-population countries to industrial and emerging market economies with aging populations. Increased migration could lessen pressure for higher saving in the latter group of countries in a number of ways, while also accelerating the flow of resources to developing countries, in the form of remittances.

For all countries, the future poses enormous uncertainties, as it always has. Making policy for the long term in the face of those uncertainties is a dauntingly complex undertaking. But the fact of those uncertainties and complexities does not absolve policymakers from addressing issues of the long term, because what they do or fail to do will critically influence both the welfare of current and future generations and the role and capacity of the state. Amid the many uncertainties, some things about the future are known with sufficient certainty to raise doubts about the capacity of governments to finance the explicit and implied commitments they have already made to their citizens, present and future.

This is not a problem that can simply be passed along to some unknown wealthier future generation. Doing so would impose a dramatically larger burden on generations of future taxpayers, and there is scant evidence to suggest that they will be more willing than current generations to tolerate such a burden. In any case, if governments of the future were to abandon or suddenly scale back on their commitments, the burden would be borne in part by many still alive today. In an era of increasing longevity, many of tomorrow's recipients of government transfers are today's workers and their children and grandchildren. If tomorrow's governments find that these inherited commitments have drained their fiscal capacity to respond to adverse shocks, economic crisis and political upheaval could be the result. And, in a democratic system, the political will to address these issues, already weak today, will be feebler still in the gerontocratic world of tomorrow.

Finally, as is by now clear, the issues raised in this study are not of concern just to the aging industrial countries. They will be very much on the policy agenda of emerging markets, transition economies, and developing countries in every region of the world. Certainly the issues to be faced, the strategic approaches that will work, and the weight to attach to policies affecting different generations will differ across regions and countries as their incomes differ. But the gathering force of these long-term developments is worldwide in its scope, and it is a force that the world community cannot any longer ignore.

Appendix Tables

Table A.1. Sources of Long-Term Fiscal Pressure: United States and Canada

Sources of Pressure	Possible Fiscal Consequences	Sources of Uncertainty
Demographic and epidemiological factors		
Aging population, with increased share of population over age 65, reduced youth population, increased elderly dependency ratio	Increasing share of budget required for social security and health insurance outlays	Direction of fertility rates Pace of improvement in life expectancy made possible by biomedical innovations Morbidity and disability rates associated with increased longevity Future acute and chronic care needs of very elderly Political scope for rationing of high-cost medical technologies Scope for further pushing back retirement age and adjusting pension system parameters Cost effects of biomedical innovations
Sharp increase in share of population that is very elderly	Increasing demand for financial support for long-term care facilities and services; increasing demand for support of high-quality medical care, including high-technology procedures, pharmaceuticals, and diagnostic tests	
Continuing substantial immigration	In short to medium run, more rapid growth in labor force, hence faster economic growth and partial deferral of age-related social welfare costs; possible pressure for higher social services costs in short run; possible social frictions due to changing ethnic mix. In long run, offsetting fiscal pressures from pension costs associated with retiring immigrant labor force	

Increase in life expectancy	Possibly improved quality of health, possibly reduced growth of medical care spending, but possibly higher costs of long-term care	Shifts in exchange rates, with effects on capital repatriation
Growth in population by 16-60 percent between 2000 and 2050 (depending on fertility outcome)	Faster economic growth and increased capacity to finance some long-term costs	Future rate of productivity growth
Economic growth and development and globalization		Response of interest rates to population aging
Emergence of new potential risks with increasing globalization, including increased terrorism	Pressure for increased government outlays for reinsurance against emerging risks	Future labor force participation rate of elderly
Need for new R&D to maintain productivity growth and compensate for shifting composition of output toward low-productivity sectors	Pressure to increase public R&D spending	Scope for policy reform to shift balance of roles of government and private sector
Persistence of large numbers of poor in developing countries	Pressure to maintain or increase spending on foreign aid	Political limits on increasing tax burdens
Sectoral adjustments in some industries due to globalization, potentially resulting in bankruptcy of some industries	In United States, potential costs associated with underfunding of federal pension insurance agency	Extent to which insurance burdens can be shifted to private sector

Table A.1. Sources of Long-Term Fiscal Pressure: United States and Canada *(continued)*

Sources of Pressure	Possible Fiscal Consequences	Sources of Uncertainty
Competition from rising economic powers in Asia	In United States, increased vulnerability of current account position, with possible rise in interest rates	
Globalization-induced exposure to new diseases transmitted from other regions	Pressure to increase health spending	
Environmental developments		
Strong regional effects from climate change, positive and negative, with some areas suffering significant loss of comparative advantage; potential for drought in U.S. Great Plains and Canadian prairies; worsening of water shortages in U.S. Southwest and California; potential for reduced summer water availability for irrigation	Costs (only partly borne by public sector) of adaptation, particularly in agriculture, through improved technologies, improved management practices, and shifts in crop choices to reduce demand for water; costs of facilitating regional production shifts in agriculture, especially for adversely affected regions; continued controversy over farm subsidies	Overall pace of global climate change and nature of regional effects Potential for abrupt climate change Nature and level of irreversibility thresholds Future probability of extreme weather events Political capacity to institute major changes in land use planning and energy consumption
Possible increase in extreme weather events, including increased frequency, duration, and intensity of heavy precipitation events, leading to higher risk of flooding, landslides, sewerage overflows, and water pollution	Vulnerability of current settlement and water control infrastructure policies to more extreme weather events; increased costs of financing new infrastructure needs; need for new or reformed regulatory policies to deal with land use management, particularly in coastal areas and areas prone to flooding, to avoid even higher cost of climate change and increased moral hazard associated with long-lived infrastructure investment	

Risk of breaching critical biological thresholds, undermining resilience of natural biological (including aquatic) systems and agriculture	Region-specific economic losses due to loss of economic base, leading to loss of revenue; forced sectoral adjustments
Risk of large environmental disasters (such as hurricane striking large city)	Potentially high costs of emergency assistance and rebuilding
Increased risk of illness due to severe heat waves and, potentially, from spread of tropical illnesses	Increased emergency medical care outlays
Greater vulnerability of private insurance systems if actuarial estimates do not recognize effects of climate change; tensions in allocation of risk between private insurance and public disaster relief; potential for moral hazard arising from government insurance of crops, floodplains, and coastal settlements	Increased fiscal costs if government must act as reinsurer of last resort
Pressure for intensified efforts to mitigate climate change	Costs of subsidies for restructuring of energy plants and for energy-related innovation; to extent energy taxes are used to encourage mitigation, possibly stronger revenue performance
Tensions between countries over sharing of common water resources (Great Lakes, river systems)	Regional costs from loss of economic base as a consequence of reduced water resources
Increased risk of extreme forest fire damage	Adverse impact on revenue from losses to affected sectors; increased costs of emergency assistance
Risk of abrupt climate change due to changes in El Niño-Southern Oscillation or in Gulf Stream	Potentially enormous costs if significant change in regional climate affects economic base and appropriateness of infrastructure

Table A.1. Sources of Long-Term Fiscal Pressure: United States and Canada (*concluded*)

Sources of Pressure	Possible Fiscal Consequences	Sources of Uncertainty
Political and cultural issues		
Differences in social insurance philosophies between Canada and United States	Pressure for harmonization of social insurance systems, particularly in medical care, given porous borders	Future role of United States in international security
		Shifting geopolitical balances
		Evolution of Middle East politics
		Evolution of European role in security matters
		Resolution of intergenerational tensions over sharing of burden of spending for elderly
In United States, growing African-American and Hispanic shares of population, possibly accompanied by widening income disparities	Possible pressure for increased welfare outlays for poorest groups	
Potential for future overseas military involvement; increased internal security risks due to increased threat of terrorism	Potential costs of repairing damage caused by terrorist attack; increased costs of prevention and provision of greater security	
Intergenerational conflict associated with burden of support for elderly	Possible scaling back on social insurance commitments	
Continued large share of U.S. population uncovered by health insurance	Increasing fiscal burden of absorbing costs of medical care for uncovered population	

Scientific and technological developments

Innovations in biogenetics and medical care	Effects on cost of medical technologies and government health insurance outlays	Potential for cyberterrorism and bioterrorism
		Potential for inadvertent release of imported toxins, climate change–induced illnesses, or biogenetics-induced problems
		Pace and direction of advances in medical technology
		Prospects for integrating technical advances to yield significant gains in productivity
		Effects of innovation on life expectancy, productivity, energy use, and in other areas
Innovations in miniaturization, new materials, computer technologies	Expansion of revenue base due to increased productivity	
Increased vulnerability to biological warfare and bioterrorism	Increased costs of maintaining security of food supplies, early warning systems, and flexible response provision	
Increased vulnerability of financial networks and communications systems to cyberterrorism	Increased outlays for preventive and counterterrorist efforts	

Table A.2. Sources of Long-Term Fiscal Pressure: Latin America and the Caribbean

Sources of Pressure	Possible Fiscal Consequences	Sources of Uncertainty
Demographic and epidemiological factors		
Dramatic increase in elderly population (tripling by 2050 in Brazil, Colombia, and Venezuela, almost quadrupling in Mexico)	Pressure on social security and government pension system from aging of formal sector workers participating in defined-benefit pension plans	Direction and magnitude of any change in fertility rates Potential for gains in life expectancy Intensity of future migration pressure Trend in HIV/AIDS prevalence rates
Bulge in youth share of population, raising potential for political instability, high unemployment, high crime rates, domestic security risks; gradual subsequent diminution of youth bulge, particularly in Brazil, Colombia, Jamaica, Mexico, and Venezuela	Increased government security outlays; pressure for social welfare and education spending; but also opportunity provided by growth in working-age population to achieve faster economic growth, to take advantage of human capital formation needs and reduce unemployment	
Growth of megacities in several countries (including Mexico and Brazil)	Pressure for increased social services (health and education) and increased demand for urban infrastructure (clean water and sanitary services, energy, roads)	
Emigration of skilled labor ("brain drain") from some countries, leading to weakened economic growth potential, but also acting as safety valve for growing population	Higher labor costs associated with provision of some social services (particularly health); higher costs of training; adverse effects on growth potential, and thus revenue, but also increased remittances from workers abroad	
Spread of HIV/AIDS, in part due to possibility of increased resistance to current treatment regimen	Pressure for increased health spending, particularly if governments opt to treat at industrial country standards (for example, in Brazil)	

Economic growth and development and globalization

Continued widespread tax evasion and poor governance, including widespread corruption	In some countries, reduced capacity of government to mobilize resources because of narrowing of revenue base; inadequate spending on social services for human capital formation in education and health due to inadequate fiscal resources, possibly leading to weaker long-term growth	Likelihood that political elites will address sources of poor governance and extreme inequality Ability to maintain competitive market environment Future long-run energy prices Future global interest rates
Persistence of marked inequality of assets and incomes	Revenue increases will flow principally from sales taxes, rather than corporate and personal income tax, limiting opportunity to narrow income inequalities	
Pressure stemming from globalization (heightened awareness of industrial country consumption standards) for middle- and upper-income groups to overconsume and undersave	Rising expectations for provision of social services; reduced growth prospects due to low public and private saving	
Absence of long-term perspective by policymakers; tendency toward procyclical policies abetted by open capital markets, which allow countries to borrow without immediate economic or political costs being felt	Increased public debt; greater volatility in economic and fiscal performance; outcomes of poor investment choices imposed on future governments and generations	
Limited efforts at risk avoidance; inadequate preventive measures to contain potential fiscal costs of natural disasters	Potentially high costs of responding to future natural disasters (including emergency assistance and rebuilding of infrastructure)	

Table A.2. Sources of Long-Term Fiscal Pressure: Latin America and the Caribbean (*concluded*)

Sources of Pressure	Possible Fiscal Consequences	Sources of Uncertainty
High domestic and external debt, both explicit and implicit (the latter including pension-related debt plus contingent liabilities of government), largely dollar-linked or at variable interest rates	Weakened fiscal capacity to provide vital economic services or transfers; potential for reneging on budgetary commitments	
For some Caribbean countries, potential threat to economic viability from loss of preferential financing and access to industrial country markets	Weakened growth potential leading to erosion of revenue base	
Environmental developments		
Degradation of rural environment (including degradation of land, desertification) due to pressures for expansion of cropland	Weakened growth potential and erosion of economic base leading to loss of revenue	Pace and regional effects of global climate change Extent of sea level rise Frequency and intensity of future extreme weather events
Rapid urbanization (in part stemming from rural environmental degradation) creating problems of water quality, waste management, air pollution, and urban sprawl	Pressure for increased spending on urban infrastructure and social services	
Growth-induced deforestation	Loss of economic base, land degradation, costs of environmental restoration	
Caribbean states at particular risk of more frequent and intense hurricanes and surges in sea level	Pressures for increased spending on disaster preparedness and adaptation	

Effects of glacial melt, including increased prospect of flooding and reduced potential for hydroelectric power generation	Cost of providing alternative sources of electric power generation; costs associated with emergency relief and reconstruction of infrastructure	
Potential sharp increase in populations living in areas exposed to water stress	Pressures for internal security measures; increased cost of providing vital urban services	
Seismic and volcanic activity (especially in Central America), as well as hurricanes, forest fires, and droughts	Increasing pressure for disaster preparedness; high costs of responding to disasters	

Political and cultural issues

Political backlash against globalization (for example, attempts at capital controls), possibly resulting in policies exacerbating open capital market pressures, resulting in capital flight and limits on foreign capital inflows; weak governmental authority and institutions (for example, corrupt judiciary) as well as weaknesses in legal framework; lack of respect for property rights; high incidence of crime	In some countries, weak facilitating environment for investment; potential for political and economic instability requiring increased internal security expenditure; deterrence of foreign investment and increased foreign capital outflow; risk of increased state intervention in economy and more restricted external posture	Pace of democratic reform Likelihood that political elites will address sources of poor governance and extreme inequality Pace and direction of advances in medical technology Prospects for integrating technological advances to yield significant gains in productivity Effects of innovations on life expectancy, productivity, energy use, and in other areas

Scientific and technological change

Through Internet and access to high-quality universities, full awareness of scientific innovations at the frontier	Increased demand for sophisticated products and high-quality services, for example in medical care, putting pressure on government health care spending

Table A.3. **Sources of Long-Term Fiscal Pressure: Europe**

Sources of Pressure	Possible Fiscal Consequences	Sources of Uncertainty
Demographic and epidemiological factors		
Fertility rates below replacement rates, resulting in population decline in some important countries, notably Germany and Italy; gradually improving life expectancy; decline in population of working age	Reduced output growth, and thus reduced revenue capacity, absent rising productivity growth or increased labor force participation among elderly and women	Direction and magnitude of change in fertility rates Pace of improvement in life expectancy Cost effects of biomedical innovations and approaches to provision Impact of increased longevity on morbidity and disability rates Future acute and chronic care needs of very elderly Political scope for rationing of high-cost medical technologies Scope for pushing back retirement age, adjusting pension system parameters, and increasing emphasis on defined-contribution pension systems
Increased population share of elderly; doubling of elderly dependency rate from 25 percent to about 50 percent (but varying across countries)	Increased social insurance outlays as share of GDP	
Reduced share of young people in population	Strains in maintaining military preparedness; weakened supply of labor contributing to reduced economic growth rate, hence reduced revenue potential	
Dramatic increase in population share of very elderly	Pressure to increase outlays on long-term care	

Pressure to allow rising immigration to supplement labor force, both in low-skill jobs and in critical occupational niches (for example, in medical and long-term care)	Some support for economic growth and thus for revenue; possible pressure for higher spending on social services and internal security	Scope for reducing unemployment and increasing labor force participation among elderly and women
In some countries (particularly in central Europe), relatively high HIV/AIDS burden	Increased spending by publicly financed medical care system	Scope for increased immigration to limit decline in labor force
Economic growth and development and globalization		Productivity change associated with aging of labor force
Rising incomes per capita together with high marginal tax rates resulting in further increase in demand for leisure, possibly offset by increased labor supply from immigration and working elderly	Given limits on capacity to raise existing high tax rates or increase tax on mobile capital, increased difficulty in maintaining fiscal sustainability	Effect of evolving global balances of saving and investment on interest rates
		Ability of countries to continue to achieve EU-mandated budgetary targets so as to reduce debt-service costs despite increase in age-related expenditure
High public debt-to-GDP ratios in some countries	Reduced capacity in these countries to maintain large primary fiscal surpluses	
Rising incomes per capita concurrent with persistence of large numbers of poor in many developing countries	Pressures to increase foreign aid and to maintain military and internal security expenditure	
Continued economic and financial volatility in global capital and product markets	Sensitivity to changes in global interest rates given increased reliance on private financial assets for funding of some retirement costs	

Table A.3. Sources of Long-Term Fiscal Pressure: Europe (*continued*)

Sources of Pressure	Possible Fiscal Consequences	Sources of Uncertainty
Environmental developments		
Increased temperatures (particularly in summer months) due to climate change, with impact depending on global climate change outcome and varying across subregions	Risks to tourism industry; potential need to restructure tax regimes (increasing road and carbon taxes); costs of restructuring and reforming publicly owned energy systems; costs of possibly needed investment in public transport in connection with mitigation efforts	Impact of global climate change on region and subregions Future probability of extreme weather events Probability of low-frequency, high-consequence climatic events, such as change in Gulf Stream Presence of irreversibility thresholds Possible Common Agricultural Policy reforms and their effects on importance of agricultural sector
Reduced precipitation, particularly in Mediterranean area; reduced soil quality in southern Europe under certain scenarios; potential increase in areas subject to extreme water stress, depending on land use policies, water pricing, technological developments	Costs of adaptation, particularly in agriculture (improved technologies, management practices, and shifts in crop choices to reduce water demand), possibly involving some public sector subsidization; region-specific economic losses depending on extent of loss of economic base; forced sectoral adjustments	
Increased flooding (especially in northern Europe); rise in sea level; greater frequency and severity of extreme weather events	Costs of building up or relocating infrastructure in coastal areas; new regulatory policies required to deal with land use management, particularly in coastal and flood-prone areas; possible need for government to act as reinsurer of last resort; possible moral hazard leading to increased public contingent liabilities	

Failure to set regulatory and land use restrictions or to adapt land use management, particularly in coastal and flood-prone areas	Increased cost of adverse climate change scenarios and accentuated moral hazard problems associated with long-lived infrastructure investments in coastal areas at risk; possibly higher cost from delayed mitigation and adaptation
Risk of critical thresholds in natural systems being breached	Loss of economic base and forced sectoral adjustments in affected regions, resulting in loss of revenue
In some areas, increased incidence of tropical diseases (such as malaria)	Increased public health spending

Political and cultural issues

Conflicts over tolerable scope, magnitude, and character of immigration; possible increase in political tensions if immigrants are not effectively integrated into domestic cultures	Increased security and related expenditures; continued pressure for social welfare outlays for new immigrants
Tensions arising from length of time needed to bring living standards in EU accession countries up to existing EU level	Pressure for higher equalization-related outlays from existing EU members
Economic disparities with bordering countries in former Soviet Union; tensions associated with narcotrafficking, smuggling, and weapons proliferation	Pressures for higher security outlays
	Political will to foster cultural integration
	Effects of widening military gap with United States

Table A.3. Sources of Long-Term Fiscal Pressure: Europe *(concluded)*

Sources of Pressure	Possible Fiscal Consequences	Sources of Uncertainty
Scientific and technological developments		
Innovations in biogenetics and medical care	Cost pressures in medical care, partly technologically induced, partly related to pressures of unmet expectations for care	Extent of vulnerability to cyber threats Extent of vulnerability to risks to food supplies Pace and direction of advances in medical technology Prospects for integrating technical advances to yield significant gains in productivity Effects of innovation on life expectancy, productivity, energy use, and in other areas
Innovations in miniaturization, new materials, computer technologies	More rapid productivity growth leading to faster growth in revenue base	
Increased vulnerability to food supplies from imported toxins, climate change–induced illnesses, or biogenetics-induced problems	Higher potential costs of maintaining security of food supplies; increased importance of early warning systems and flexible response	

Table A.4. Sources of Long-Term Fiscal Pressure: Former Soviet Union

Sources of Pressure	Possible Fiscal Consequences	Sources of Uncertainty
Demographic and epidemiological factors		
In most countries, including Russia, absolute decline in population by about 30 percent by 2050, reflecting declining life expectancy and reduced fertility rates; significant reduction in size and share of working-age population	Potential shrinkage in GDP as consequence of declining labor force and aging of population, leading to absolute decline in tax base; strains in maintaining military forces; for countries with large oil reserves, increasing relative importance of oil sector; need to maintain necessary infrastructure for public goods despite declining tax base	Future trends in fertility rates Prospects for reversing decline in life expectancy Long-term care requirements of very elderly Scope for rationing of high-cost medical technologies Scope for pushing back retirement age, adjusting pension system parameters, and increasing emphasis on defined-contribution pension systems In Russia, extent of future governmental efforts to address and contain HIV/AIDS and tuberculosis
Gradual decline in both size and share of under-15 population	Fiscal adjustment associated with decline in absolute size of under-15 population (for example, in education); issues of downscaling of services	
Doubling (in some countries tripling) of population share of elderly by 2050, with significant increase in elderly dependency ratio	Increased social insurance outlays arising out of government commitments for old age pensions, disability, and medical care; increased social welfare benefits; increased cost of providing long-term care	
High prevalence of tuberculosis and HIV/AIDS, with significant risk of explosion in cases	Pressure for government provision of medical care to address these and other major disease problems; possibly significant adverse effects on labor force growth, productivity, and output growth, and hence on revenue	

Table A.4. Sources of Long-Term Fiscal Pressure: Former Soviet Union *(continued)*

Sources of Pressure	Possible Fiscal Consequences	Sources of Uncertainty
Economic growth and development and globalization		
Significant differences between oil-exporting and oil-importing countries in region and between relatively well-off and relatively poor countries in exposure to specific economic risks and uncertainties	In oil-exporting countries, problems of fiscal mismanagement, corruption, inefficient investment, and "Dutch disease" posed by abundant oil revenue; danger of decline in oil price requiring sharp increase in non-oil tax base; in lower-income countries, tension between very low tax revenue and inherited expectations of high social services provision	Unpredictability of tax revenue Uncertainty about long-run price of oil Magnitude of growth impetus from Western Europe Global economic growth rates
Greater sensitivity to volatility in global capital markets as countries become more open; large underground economy; governance weaknesses	Decline in tax compliance, capital flight, dollarization, increased tendency toward underground accounts; fragile balance of agents working in formal v. informal economy; adjustments associated with decline in tax base; potential volatility of tax revenue	
Emigration of young and skilled workers	Loss in human capital as consequence of emigration incentives	
Environmental developments		
Potential water shortages, for example in Aral Sea basin in Central Asia	Costs of adaptation of agriculture, other forced sectoral adjustments; in some areas, loss of economic base and hence of revenue	Pace of global climate change and nature of its impact on region
Past environmental damages associated with policies of former Soviet Union	Continuing high cost of cleanup	

Increasing temperature in region, with warming greater than global average in most scenarios (and most dramatic in Siberia and along Arctic coast); variable precipitation patterns—in some areas (western Russia, Arctic region) an increase in precipitation, in others a decline	Adverse effects on real GDP, with decline in production capacity in agriculture and livestock in most countries, reduction in forestry production due to reduced boreal forest area in Russia; reduced hydropower production in some countries; decline in permafrost; roughly ¼ reduction in river flows in some countries, putting pressure on water supply; fiscal costs associated with increasing R&D outlays in agriculture; higher disaster management expenses; need for risk management to counter adverse weather-related shocks	
Rising sea level	Destruction of infrastructure in coastal areas (especially Black Sea coast)	

Political and cultural issues

In Baltic countries especially, strong exposure to developments in Europe	Major pressures in these countries for social expenditure increases to match European levels	Pace of political reforms and democratization
Potential for political instability, including from rising ethnic tensions; possible emigration from China into Russia	Pressure for increased outlays on internal security	Success of policies to defuse ethnic and cultural tensions
Instabilities potentially arising from failure to control or eliminate nuclear stockpiles and safeguard nuclear energy facilities	Possible need for international assistance to address problems of nuclear stockpiles	
Varying pace of political reform across countries	Nontransparency of budget support for political reasons	

Table A.4. Sources of Long-Term Fiscal Pressure: Former Soviet Union *(concluded)*

Sources of Pressure	Possible Fiscal Consequences	Sources of Uncertainty
Concentrated wealth holding and capture of state by large businesses and oligarchic interests	Pressure for tax privileges; reduced prospects for economic growth and thus for revenue	
Scientific and technological developments		
Biomedical innovations in West	Rising cost pressures in medical care, partly technologically induced, partly related to unmet expectations for care	Capacity of medical systems to introduce and absorb new technologies
Innovations in nanotechnology, information technologies, and cognitive sciences	Potential cost savings, but also cost-increasing effects on outlays for medical care	Impact of innovation on rate of productivity growth

Table A.5. Sources of Long-Term Fiscal Pressure: Middle East and North Africa

Sources of Pressure	Possible Fiscal Consequences	Sources of Uncertainty
Demographic and epidemiological factors		
Significant population increases in many countries; high fertility rates	Increased demand for spending on education and health	Pace of decline in fertility rates Life expectancy trends Contribution of growing population to political instability
Substantial increase (in some cases tripling) in elderly share of population	Pressure to provide social insurance and welfare to rising share of elderly	
Increase in labor force, weighted toward younger workers, but with high unemployment and large share of population still below working age	Opportunity for more rapid economic growth with youth bulge, but also potential source of tension; pressure for increased outlays on internal security, as unemployed younger workers create potential for political instability; pressure for increased antipoverty spending; pressure for social services for still-growing numbers of children	
Increased urbanization, rural–urban migration, and growth in refugees, with lack of clean water and sanitation creating potential for spread of infectious disease	Heavy demand for strengthened urban planning, improved urban infrastructure, and government services to meet basic needs	
Economic growth and development and globalization		
For oil exporters, potential for fluctuation in oil prices	Pressure on revenue to the extent it depends on oil market developments	Future prices of oil and petroleum products Foreign growth rates, especially in Western Europe

Table A.5. Sources of Long-Term Fiscal Pressure: Middle East and North Africa (*continued*)

Sources of Pressure	Possible Fiscal Consequences	Sources of Uncertainty
Continued large inequalities in income	Pressure for job creation, employment subsidies, and other state intervention in labor market; pressure for increased spending on internal security	
Continued interregional divergence in pace of economic growth; shrinking of labor forces in Western Europe and elsewhere	Increased pressure for emigration in response to faster growth and shrinking labor force abroad, reducing domestic unemployment while providing source of remittances, but also creating brain drain; potential for slowdown in economic growth abroad weakening demand for region's exports	
Growing income gaps with industrial and emerging market economies leading to pressure for emigration	Pressure to raise wage rates in public sector to counter emigration; opportunity to increase revenue by taxing inward remittances	
Environmental developments		
Potential for rising temperatures and declining summer precipitation in some areas due to global warming (intensifying as century proceeds), resulting in depletion of soil moisture, increased desertification	Increased need for R&D to facilitate agricultural adaptation, for example by introducing low-water-use crops, more intensive greenhouse cultivation, and aquaculture	Scale and regional impact of global climate change Effects of increasing temperature on agricultural productivity Future probability of extreme weather events Existence of environmental irreversibility thresholds
Potential rise in sea level	Need for infrastructure to prevent coastal flooding and limit saltwater intrusion	

Increased potential for damaging floods, dust storms, and other extreme weather events	Increased potential outlays for relief and reconstruction; need for regulatory and land use restrictions or adaptation of land use management to limit cost of adverse climate change scenarios and avoid accentuating moral hazard problems associated with long-lived infrastructure investments in areas at risk	
Pressure on water supply from economic growth and climate change, creating competition from neighboring countries over scarce water resources	Pressure for outlays to strengthen water management and conservation (including desalinization); potential need for increased defense spending in context of competitive pressure	
Land degradation and soil erosion due to economic and population growth and climate change, leading to food supply shortfalls and increased food imports	Need for better land use planning and effective policies to protect arable land; pressure for government outlays to address food shortages	
Danger of breaching critical ecological thresholds, undermining resilience of natural systems.	Loss of economic base; forced sectoral adjustments	

Political and cultural issues

Risk of political instability; difficulty of maintaining autocratic regimes linked to West; cultural and religious tensions and potential clash between Islamic traditions and modern Western values; potential for political radicalization	Pressure for increased internal security outlays; increased difficulty in attracting foreign direct investment, weakening economic growth prospects and growth of fiscal base	Adaptability of political regimes to growth in population and in youth share of population
Likelihood of resolving existing political tensions
Risk of flare-up of regional conflicts	Need to maintain adequate defense capability	

Table A.5. **Sources of Long-Term Fiscal Pressure: Middle East and North Africa** *(concluded)*

Sources of Pressure	Possible Fiscal Consequences	Sources of Uncertainty
Scientific and technological developments		
Potential for new water-saving technologies, including more efficient irrigation methods and wastewater recycling systems; potential for biotechnology to boost crop production through increased drought resistance and higher yields	Technological progress could yield economic growth effects to moderate adverse effects on agriculture from water shortages	Pace and character of biogenetic engineering developments in agriculture
Heightened awareness of and internal disparities in income	Increased political instability leading to pressure for increased internal security spending	

Table A.6. Sources of Long-Term Fiscal Pressure: Sub-Saharan Africa

Sources of Pressure	Possible Fiscal Consequences	Sources of Uncertainty
Demographic and epidemiological factors		
High fertility rates declining slowly, with continued growth in under-15 population and sharp growth in working-age population as share of total	Continued heavy and increasing demand for social spending and for medical and public health spending for under-15 population	Pace of fertility rate decline Life expectancy trends Effects of biomedical innovations on prevalence of HIV/AIDS, tuberculosis, malaria, maternal mortality, gastrointestinal illnesses
Emergence of several megacities due to population growth and rural-urban migration	Heavy demand for improved urban infrastructure to meet basic needs for clean water and sanitation	
In a few countries, modest increase in elderly share of population	In these countries, possible pressure from excessively generous civil service pension schemes, particularly if overseas development assistance (ODA) has fueled expansion of government sector	
High-risk behavior contributing to spread of HIV/AIDS; continued high prevalence of other infectious diseases due to lack of clean water, poor sanitation, and abundant habitat for disease vectors	Weaker economic growth; loss of human capital through multiple channels; diminished saving; pressures for increased health care spending likely to keep countries dependent on ODA	
Economic growth and development and globalization		
Weak economic growth; increasing likelihood of high unemployment	Weak growth of revenue base	Pace and consequences of climate change and its characteristics Pace of resource depletion

Table A.6. Sources of Long-Term Fiscal Pressure: Sub-Saharan Africa *(continued)*

Sources of Pressure	Possible Fiscal Consequences	Sources of Uncertainty
		Magnitude and effectiveness of ODA Whether there is potential for decline in terms of trade Extent of Dutch disease effects from significant expansion of foreign aid Extent to which exporters will be able to shift exports to regions with more dynamic growth
High rate of rural-urban migration	Weakened agricultural productivity; increased need for urban infrastructure and services	
Increasing ODA stimulating poverty reduction efforts and eventually leading to faster economic growth	Significant expansion of government sector, fueled by increased ODA; pressure for increased expenditure on operations and maintenance of aid-funded projects; debt sustainability pressure (if ODA has heavy loan component); risk of Dutch disease; risk of continued dependence on aid	
Widening income disparities between region and industrial countries, leading to emigration of skilled workers and continued governance problems; potential for increased productivity possibly limited by shortage of skills	Difficulty in strengthening revenue base, despite opportunity to tax inward remittances; upward pressures on wages in public and private sectors to retain skilled workers; wasteful, low-productivity public expenditure	
Pressure for tariff liberalization combined with competitive pressure from expanded world supply of labor-intensive goods	Increased demand from business sector for higher-quality government services and infrastructure	

Introduction of social insurance systems for workers in modern sector	Increased spending for unemployment benefits and other social insurance benefits	
Possibly slower growth in Western Europe	Weakened impetus for growth of regional exports	

Environmental developments

Increasing temperatures and declining precipitation in some areas due to global warming, resulting in reduction of soil moisture and reduced runoff, more frequent periods of low water reserves, and increasing desertification and deforestation	Pressure for increased outlays on adaptation, risk management, and disaster preparedness; need for increased R&D outlays to facilitate agricultural adaptation	Effects of increasing temperature on agricultural productivity Regional effects of climate change Future probability of extreme weather events
Increased potential for damaging floods, dust storms, and other extreme weather events	Potentially high outlays for associated damages	
Potential intensification of health hazards due to climate change	Further increased demand for health services	
Rise in sea level threatening coastal areas and low-lying island states	Increased outlays for infrastructure required to prevent coastal flooding and saltwater intrusion	
Intensifying pressure on aquifers, combined with growing pressure on land, leading to land degradation, soil erosion, and further desertification and deforestation; competition between adjoining countries for access to water sources	Need for outlays to address potential food shortages and maintain food security (may require food imports), improve soil management, and strengthen water management and conservation	

Political and cultural issues

Continued political instability and guerrilla activity; continued fragility of borders	Pressure for increased internal security outlays	Likelihood that ethnic and religious conflicts can be successfully mediated

Table A.6. Sources of Long-Term Fiscal Pressure: Sub-Saharan Africa *(concluded)*

Sources of Pressure	Possible Fiscal Consequences	Sources of Uncertainty
Continued cultural, ethnic, and religious tensions between countries	Need to maintain adequate defense capability	
Scientific and technological developments		
Transfer of technological advances of various kinds from outside region	Opportunities for increased productivity, increasing economic growth and thus revenue	Capacity for innovation and spread of R&D to address risks to agricultural productivity
Possible development of technologies to combat infectious diseases and other major medical problems	Reduced pressures on medical care spending; opportunities for resumption of growth of human capital	Outlook for possible development of vaccines or other more effective treatments for HIV/AIDS
Risk that use of genetic use restriction technologies (requiring annual imports of seeds) may aggravate disparity in available agricultural technologies	Potential for serious erosion of incomes and of agricultural growth potential, and hence of revenue	
Risk of technology substitution in industrial countries resulting in weak demand for primary commodity exports	Further weakening of terms of trade resulting in slower economic growth, and hence loss of revenue	
Risk that widening of technology differential with rest of world may increase difficulties in escaping low-equilibrium growth trap	Further loss of competitive capacity and hence of revenue	
Risk of heightened awareness of disparities in income with rest of world	Increased political instability and emigration of skilled labor (brain drain)	

Table A.7. Sources of Long-Term Fiscal Pressure: South Asia

Sources of Pressure	Possible Fiscal Consequences	Sources of Uncertainty
Demographic and epidemiological factors		
Substantial increase in regional population, with fastest growth in Pakistan and Bangladesh but largest absolute increase in India (despite declining fertility rates); near halving of share of under-15 population by 2050; corresponding sharp increase in potential labor force, heavily weighted toward younger workers; tripling in population share of elderly in India and Bangladesh, doubling in Pakistan	Pressure for increased provision of public services, especially health and education; increased need for food subsidies or food distribution programs; pressure for increased spending on labor force training programs	In India, rate of spread of HIV/AIDS and extent of governmental efforts to address and contain disease Future rate of economic growth and of urbanization Within Indian states, ability to reconcile fiscal pressures between rural and urban populations
Internal population movements in response to rising sea level, particularly in Bangladesh; further dramatic growth of megacities, further stressing already overstretched urban infrastructure and services	Rising demand for public infrastructure, especially in urban areas, creating demand for new sources of financing (property taxes, user fees)	
Especially in India, high risk of explosion in incidence of HIV/AIDS	Significant effects on labor force growth, productivity, and output growth, leading to loss of revenue and high medical costs	
Economic growth and development and globalization		
Buoyant economic growth and rising incomes per capita	Pressure for rising public expenditure share in GDP to provide public goods, social spending, and entitlements	Magnitude of growth impetus from major industrial countries Ability of regional financial markets to absorb increased capital inflows

Table A.7. Sources of Long-Term Fiscal Pressure: South Asia *(continued)*

Sources of Pressure	Possible Fiscal Consequences	Sources of Uncertainty
Continued large fiscal deficits threatening fiscal sustainability; inability of some Indian states to divest money-losing public enterprises; potential weaknesses in financial sector due to nonperforming assets	Risk of default if fiscal sustainability cannot be restored, possibly leading to inflationary pressure and leakages through capital account; risk of government crowding out private sector and weakening impetus for growth, in turn limiting possibilities for rising revenue	
Pressure for emigration of skilled labor (brain drain)	Positive effects on inward remittances, but loss of human capital undermining capacity of social service sector to deliver services	
Slower growth in consumption demand in industrial countries due to population aging	Potential weakening in demand for region's exports	
Prospect of expanded capital flows from industrial countries through about 2015	Higher growth rates and increased employment, and hence increased revenue	
Prospect of continued trade liberalization (tariff and nontariff, including removal of agricultural subsidies) by industrial and emerging market economies	Increased production, exports, and employment in tradable goods sector, leading to increased revenue	
Environmental developments		
Climate change leading to changes in temperature and precipitation (increased precipitation in summer but decreased precipitation in winter), affecting productivity	Need for R&D and agricultural extension to develop new high-yielding, low-water-use crops and promote adjusted calendar and crop rotation; need for R&D to develop	Changes in seasonal precipitation Future probability of extreme weather events Nature and level of environmental irreversibility thresholds

Timing of effects of climate change (sea level rise and extreme weather events) on coastal areas

of existing crops and requiring changes in planting seasons; in India, productivity of wheat and (especially) rice cultivation adversely affected despite positive effects of elevated carbon dioxide concentrations	pollutant-eating bacteria; radical changes in water management strategies required; development of flood and drought control management systems also needed
Extreme pressure on water supply in Indus and Ganges-Brahmaputra river basins	Potential for extreme intraregional tensions arising from water shortages; high cost of inaction if problems can only be remedied later at much greater expense
Likelihood of sea level rise causing large-scale inundation; increased intensity of tropical cyclones	Significant losses and high adaptation costs associated with failure to prevent development of infrastructure in coastal areas; more rapid growth of urban areas due to internal migration, requiring investment in infrastructure; costs of disaster relief following extreme weather events and coastal surges
Increased risk of vector-borne diseases	Increased pressure for spending on medical care; economic losses associated with illness
Losses in forest area causing pollution, flooding, and land degradation, especially in Bangladesh	Potential for major economic losses in some areas, leading to pressure for rural-urban migration, pressure on urban infrastructure and services, and pressure for emigration to neighboring countries (with attendant risk of political instability)
Significant pressure on urban areas, including land use pressure, air and water pollution, and solid waste overload, partly a function of climate change but also of increased population, economic growth, and urbanization	Additional pressure for spending on urban infrastructure and services

Table A.7. Sources of Long-Term Fiscal Pressure: South Asia (*concluded*)

Sources of Pressure	Possible Fiscal Consequences	Sources of Uncertainty
Political and cultural issues		
Continuing political and religious tensions between India and Pakistan and, potentially, within Sri Lanka; widening gap in income between India and Pakistan adding to tensions over Kashmir; internal political and security tensions from relative youth of populations and significant unemployment	Continued pressure to maintain spending on internal security and defense, including nuclear weapons programs	Prospects for resolving political tensions on the subcontinent Prospects for reduced religious polarization
Tensions within Indian states arising from disparities in income distribution and caste and tribal divisions	Pressures on financing by Indian states in allocation of resources	
Scientific and technological developments		
Prospect of technology transfer with globalization and continued technological change in industrial countries	Increased employment and higher productivity leading to increased revenue	Pace of technological progress in industrial countries Capacity of some countries and Indian states to absorb and utilize new technologies
Progress in biogenetic engineering for agriculture and medical care (particularly HIV/AIDS)	Potential for reduced losses from HIV/AIDS and other diseases; possibly significant effects on cost of medical care, even with reliance on generic medicines	

Table A.8. Sources of Long-Term Fiscal Pressure: Southeast Asia

Sources of Pressure	Possible Fiscal Consequences	Sources of Uncertainty
Demographic and epidemiological factors		
Aging populations in some countries, with sharp increase in elderly dependency rate; breakdown of traditional family structures; tight labor markets emerging in Singapore and Thailand by 2025	Increasing expenditure obligations for countries with developed public pension schemes; increased outlays on medical care and possibly long-term care; absence of generalized social insurance schemes leading to pressure for increasing outlays on social safety nets	Prevalence of HIV/AIDS and other infectious diseases Pace and ultimate extent of reform of currently underfunded civil service pension schemes Potential for higher fertility rates with increasing nationalism and religious orientation (particularly among orthodox Muslims in Indonesia and Malaysia) Whether attitudinal shifts toward more individualized lifestyles will require shift to formal social security systems at faster pace than anticipated
Growth of megacities	Pressure on urban infrastructure to provide clean water, sewerage, and transport; greater vulnerability of large coastal cities to extreme weather events	
Continued spread of HIV/AIDS	Increased pressure for medical outlays, especially in Thailand	
Progressive decline of under-15 population in most countries	Some decline in share of government outlays on lower levels of education, possibly offset by higher quality of services	

Table A.8. Sources of Long-Term Fiscal Pressure: Southeast Asia *(continued)*

Sources of Pressure	Possible Fiscal Consequences	Sources of Uncertainty
Increasingly high returns to human capital	Increased demand for education services, with possible consequences for government outlays on higher education; pressure for expanded outlays on medical services	
Net migration into region, with some countries possibly seeing their overseas workers returning in large numbers	Net immigration will increase fiscal costs in a variety of ways (higher outlays for education, social services, and infrastructure); some relief from increasing pension costs, at least temporarily	
Economic growth and development and globalization		
Potential for resumption of rapid economic growth	Pressure for rising expenditure share in GDP for public goods, social spending, and entitlements; opportunities created if countries maintain their flexible exchange rate policies	Stimulus to growth provided in future by Japan
Ability of Philippines and Indonesia to develop their financial systems without major crisis
Speed at which newer ways of raising resources through auctions, green taxes, and user charges will proceed (except in Singapore)
In Indonesia and Philippines, capacity to address weaknesses in fiscal resource mobilization
Danger of reduced growth prospects from aftermath of late-1990s financial crisis and increased competition from China	Large fiscal costs inherited from 1990s crisis, particularly in financial sector in Indonesia and Thailand; many contingent liabilities remaining as result of directed lending, various types of implicit and explicit guarantees, and in pension system	

Particularly in Indonesia and Philippines, weak management and poor governance in financial systems	High potential costs of recapitalizing financial system if weaknesses are not overcome
Effects of globalization and international trade agreements on trade regimes	Opportunities created for some producers presently shut out of Chinese rice market; losses for some countries from global trade agreements in textiles and agriculture; potentially significant consequences from loss in competitiveness to China for revenue base and social safety net–related outlays; temptations for tax breaks and direct subsidies to affected industries
Effects of globalization on resource mobilization	Tax competition possibly forcing reductions in income tax rates; declining revenue from import duties under global and regional agreements; loss of pricing power of state monopolies
Globalization as source of increased competitive pressure, especially from China	Loss of revenue base but also increased social safety net outlays and pressure for tax breaks and direct subsidies to affected industries; increased need for government expenditure, particularly in telecommunications and transport infrastructure and social sectors in order to remain competitive
Globalization spreading Western technologies	Raised expectations of medical care, leading to pressure for increased government outlays
Weaknesses in corporate governance, particularly in Indonesia, Korea, and Philippines	Potential fiscal costs from pressure for recapitalization and absorption of social welfare costs, if weaknesses are not addressed

Table A.8. Sources of Long-Term Fiscal Pressure: Southeast Asia *(concluded)*

Sources of Pressure	Possible Fiscal Consequences	Sources of Uncertainty
Environmental developments		
Climate change leading to changes in temperature and some increase in summer precipitation but possibly increased precipitation in winter; productivity of existing crop varieties and planting seasons affected	Need for R&D and agricultural extension to develop new high-yielding, low-water-use crop varieties and promote adjusted calendar and crop rotation; need for R&D to develop pollutant-eating bacteria; potential for dramatic decline in availability of water for agriculture, industry, and domestic use, requiring radical changes in water management; need for development of flood and drought control management systems	Future behavior and variability of monsoons Regional effects and timing of global climate change Future probability of extreme weather events Nature and level of environmental irreversibility thresholds
Significant pressure on urban areas, including land use pressures, air and water pollution, and solid waste overload, partly as function of climate change, but also of increased population, economic growth, and urbanization	Pressure for increased spending on both urban infrastructure and services	
Likelihood of sea level rise causing large-scale inundation along coastline; increased intensity of tropical cyclones	Increased internal migration as consequence of sea level rise, intensifying urbanization and requiring outlays for new infrastructure; higher costs of disaster relief relating to extreme weather events and coastal surges	
Higher risk of vector-borne diseases	Pressure for increased medical spending	
Significant deforestation	Economic losses in affected sectors, requiring outlays for their adjustment	

Political and cultural issues

Shift from monocentric power structures and unitary fiscal systems to polycentric power structures and decentralization	Political transition creating vertical and horizontal imbalances in fiscal system, but with potential for mobilization of greater resources to make fiscal system more efficient and equitable	Outcome of current crisis involving Iraq, North Korea, and Jehadi Islam
Intercountry rivalries, particularly between Malaysia and Singapore and between wealthier and poorer countries	Increased security spending; higher costs of domestic and international trade	
Potential for ethnic tensions associated with Chinese ethnic community in some countries	Pressure for increased internal security expenditure	
Potential for fallout from rivalries between China and India, Japan, and United States; potential competition with China over petroleum resources in South China Sea as well as over forest resources	Pressure for increased external security expenditure	

Scientific and technological developments

Risk of failure to develop sufficient scientific capacity to catch up with industrial countries; uncertain ability to tap talent of nationals living overseas; increased possibilities for business process outsourcing; opportunities for linkages with universities in industrial countries	Impact (positive or negative) on economic growth, and hence on revenue	Willingness of industrial countries to outsource some of their internal business processes Pace of technological progress
Prospects for biogenetic engineering concerning HIV/AIDS and in agriculture	Potential to reduce cost of medical care and prevent adverse economic effects of HIV/AIDS; potential to strengthen productivity in agriculture	
Innovations in medical care technologies more generally	Potential for increasing cost pressure if demand for latest technologies is high	

Table A.9. Sources of Long-Term Fiscal Pressure: China, Japan, Korea, and the Pacific

Sources of Pressure	Possible Fiscal Consequences	Sources of Uncertainty
Demographic and epidemiological factors		
Aging populations, initially in Japan but followed in later decades by other countries	In Japan, and later in other countries, pressures on outlays associated with existing public pension schemes	In China, extent of governmental efforts to address and contain HIV/AIDS In China, fertility rates In Japan, openness to immigration
In Japan, decline in absolute population and in workforce; sharp rise in elderly dependency rate; rising dependency rate among very elderly; near-doubling of elderly share of population by 2050	Possible slowing of rate of productivity growth, which would slow economic growth, and thus reduce revenue	
In China and Korea, tripling in elderly share of population by 2050, accompanied by slow (in China) or negligible (in Korea) total population growth	In China, given absence of generalized social insurance schemes, pressure for increased outlays on social safety net and on medical services, the latter driven by Internet-fueled demand expectations	
In Japan and Korea, significant pressure on labor markets from sharp decrease in working-age share of population	Increased demand for educational services driven by increasing returns to human capital, possibly raising pressure for increased government outlays on higher education	
Particularly in China, risk of explosion in incidence of HIV/AIDS	Possibly significant effects on labor force growth, productivity, and real output growth, with negative implications for revenue	
Growth of megacities	Increased pressures for urban infrastructure spending	

Economic growth and development and globalization

In China, significant income disparities in general and between urban and rural populations, leading to economic and political tensions; pervasive structural problems in agriculture and rural manufacturing	In China, pressure for absorption of rural and state enterprise labor force into modern economy and for transition of agriculture to higher productivity; pressure for rising share of public expenditure in GDP, for public goods, social spending, urban infrastructure, and entitlements	In China, whether rapid recent pace of economic growth can be maintained In China, approach taken to address breakdown of existing social insurance system, particularly as it affects rural and state enterprise workers
In China, possible widening differences in income per capita across regions	In China, increased need for spending on internal security if political tensions arise from interregional differences	In China, capacity of financial system to evolve, gain investor confidence, and avoid government bailout in event of banking system failures
In China, weaknesses in fiscal resource mobilization, and already emergent competitive pressures from market economy on viability of state enterprise sector	In China, fiscal sustainability concerns arising from cost of absorbing debts of state-owned enterprises, and as infrastructural spending swells government debt burden	In China, whether pace of rural-urban migration can be controlled Approach taken by industrial countries in response to their own aging populations Magnitude of potential foreign direct investment inflows
In some countries (particularly Japan and Korea), high existing public debt ratios, particularly when implicit pension liabilities are taken into account	In Japan and Korea, tensions between growing fiscal needs and limited resource availability due to sharp decrease in potential economic growth rate In Japan (and possibly China), fiscal sustainability constraints on ability to adopt fiscal stimulus measures	
Possibly increased capital flows to China and Korea from industrial countries due to population aging (until about 2015)	Possible opportunity (for China particularly) to import capital, facilitating sustained economic growth	

Table A.9. Sources of Long-Term Fiscal Pressure: China, Japan, Korea, and the Pacific *(continued)*

Sources of Pressure	Possible Fiscal Consequences	Sources of Uncertainty
Continued global trade liberalization, with industrial countries possibly curtailing agricultural subsidies, opening their agricultural markets, and reducing other nontariff barriers	Expansion of export markets, particularly for China; faster growth in agriculture, thus sustaining growth and employment and limiting burden on state to provide social safety net outlays	
Continued fragility of financial systems encumbered by weak asset portfolios, especially (in China) those holding state enterprise debt	Possible pressure for government recapitalization of financial sector (as happened in late-1990s Asian crisis)	
Environmental developments		
In East Asia, large northward shift of subtropical crop areas due to climate change; large increases in surface runoff leading to soil erosion and degradation, frequent water logging in south and spring droughts in north, with possibly adverse effects on agricultural productivity; possible enhancement of wheat productivity in north, reflecting increased carbon dioxide concentrations and longer growing seasons, but possible decline in rice yields; potential for extreme tension arising from water shortages; increased risk of vector-borne disease	Danger of inaction today leading to higher cost of adaptation later; significant risks associated with capital-intensive development of infrastructure for water management, if rate of return proves lower than anticipated; need for radical changes in water management strategies	Uncertainty about future behavior of monsoons Regional outcomes of global climate change Future probability of extreme weather events Nature and level of environmental irreversibility thresholds Timing of climate change as it will affect coastal zones In China, pace of development of insurance industry and its ability to help address climate change risks

In China, possibly severe problems in major river deltas from sea level rise and greater exposure to extreme weather events; high risks to megacities in coastal areas, with possibly extensive damage to infrastructure and loss of life	Need for R&D and agricultural extension to develop new high-yielding rice varieties that are water efficient and resistant to heat, pests, and disease; need to promote use of adjusted calendar and crop rotation; need for major rethinking of coastal development plans, evaluation of coastal subsidence rates in sensitive coastal regions, improved emergency preparedness for extreme weather events, contingency plans for migration; need to develop flood and drought management systems and improve flood warning and forecasting systems, including disaster management systems; likelihood of greater costs for disaster relief for extreme weather events and coastal surges, especially in China and Japan In China, increasing role of government (and increasing importance of policy issues) in disaster relief in absence of significant private insurance industry
In Australia, New Zealand, and Pacific islands (areas less threatened by climate change than East Asia), varying regional effects from changes in precipitation patterns	Need for major rethinking of coastal development plans, evaluation of coastal subsidence rates in sensitive regions, improved emergency preparedness for extreme weather events, contingency plans for migration; likelihood of higher costs for disaster relief relating to extreme weather events and coastal surges; need for outlays for adaptation to reflect change in precipitation patterns

Table A.9. Sources of Long-Term Fiscal Pressure: China, Japan, Korea, and the Pacific (*concluded*)

Sources of Pressure	Possible Fiscal Consequences	Sources of Uncertainty
In smaller Pacific islands, threat of inundation of coastal areas (and some entire islands) from rising sea level	Major threat to viability of these countries, possibly requiring resettlement and even forced emigration	
Political and cultural issues		
In China and Democratic People's Republic of Korea (DPRK), continued evolution of political system	In China, possible need for increased internal security expenditure and for interregional transfers to minimize income divergences; major fiscal pressures on Republic of Korea to absorb population of DPRK in event of its economic collapse	In China, resilience of Communist Party and prospects for gradual democratization In DPRK, prospects for survival of regime and choice of strategy by Republic of Korea to absorb DPRK population into its economy
Scientific and technological developments		
Continued rapid technological progress and productivity gains in industry; expansion of possibilities for business process outsourcing; opportunities for linkages with universities in industrial countries	Possible rise in economic growth rate, with positive impact on revenue	Willingness of industrial countries to engage in business process outsourcing
Increased prospects for biogenetic engineering in health care (especially HIV/AIDS) and agriculture	Possible reduction in cost of medical care and in economic effects of HIV/AIDS, but also potential for increasing cost pressure if demand for latest health care technologies is strong	

References

Aaron, Henry, 2000, "Seeing through the Fog: Policy Making with Uncertain Forecasts," *Journal of Policy Analysis and Management,* Vol. 19, No. 2, pp. 193–206.

Alley, R., and others, 2003, "Abrupt Climate Change," *Science,* Vol. 229 (March), pp. 2005–10.

Andersen, Torben Juul, 2003, "Natural Disasters and External Shocks" (unpublished; Washington: International Monetary Fund).

Aninat, Eduardo, Peter S. Heller, and Alfredo Cuevas, 2001, "Globalization: Toward a Definition and an Insight on Its Overarching Impact" (unpublished; Washington: International Monetary Fund).

Antón, Philip S., Richard Silberglitt, and James Schneider, 2001, *The Global Technology Revolution: Bio/Nano/Materials Trends and their Synergies with Information Technology by 2015* (Langley, Virginia: National Intelligence Council).

Asher, Mukul G., 2002, "Long-Term Fiscal Policy Challenges Facing the Singapore Economy" (unpublished; Singapore: National University of Singapore).

Atkinson, Paul, and Paul van den Noord, 2001, "Managing Public Expenditure: Some Emerging Policy Issues and a Framework for Analysis," OECD Economic Department Working Paper No. 285 (Paris: Organization for Economic Cooperation and Development).

Attanasio, Orazio P., and Giovanni L. Violante, 2000, "The Demographic Transition in Closed and Open Economies: A Tale of Two Regions," Inter-American Development Bank Working Paper Series No. 412 (Washington: Inter-American Development Bank).

Auerbach, Alan J., 1994, "The US Fiscal Problem: Where We Are, How We Got There, and Where We're Going," in *NBER Macroeconomics Annual,* ed. by S. Fischer and J. Rotemberg (Cambridge, Massachusetts: National Bureau of Economic Research).

———, and William Gale, 2000, "Perspectives on the Budget Surplus," *National Tax Journal,* Vol. 53, No. 3, Part 1 (September), pp. 459–72.

Auerbach, Alan J., and Kevin A. Hassett, 2001, "Uncertainty and the Design of Long-Run Fiscal Policy," in *Demographic Change and Fiscal Policy,* ed. by Alan Auerbach and Ronald Lee (Cambridge, United Kingdom: Cambridge University Press).

273

Auerbach, Alan J., and L.J. Kotlikoff, 1999, "The Methodology of Generational Accounting," in *Generational Accounting Around the World*, ed. by A.J. Auerbach, L.J. Kotlikoff, and W. Leibfritz (Cambridge, Massachusetts; Chicago: National Bureau of Economic Research; University of Chicago Press).

Australia, Commonwealth of, The Treasury, 2002, "Intergenerational Report 2002–2003," 2002–2003 Budget Paper No. 5 (Canberra).

Balassone, Fabrizio, and Daniele Franco, 2000a, "Public Investment, the Stability Pact and the 'Golden Rule,'" *Fiscal Studies*, Vol. 21, No. 2 (June), pp. 207–29.

———, 2000b, "Assessing Fiscal Sustainability: A Review of Methods with a View to EMU," in *Fiscal Sustainability* (Rome: Banca d'Italia).

Balassone, Fabrizio, Sandro Momigliano, and Daniela Monacelli, 2002, "Italy: Fiscal Consolidation and Its Legacy" (unpublished; Rome: Banca d'Italia).

Banks, James, Richard Disney, and Zoe Smith, 2000, "What Can We Learn from Generational Accounts for the United Kingdom?" *The Economic Journal*, Vol. 110 (November), pp. F575–97.

Barnhill, Theodore, and George Kopits, 2003, "Assessing Fiscal Sustainability under Uncertainty: Application of the VAR Approach" (unpublished; Washington: International Monetary Fund).

Barrell, Ray, and Karen Dury, 2001, "Will the SGP Ever Be Breached?" in *The Stability and Growth Pact: The Architecture of Fiscal Policy in EMU*, ed. by Anne Brunila, Marco Buti, and Daniele Franco (London: Palgrave Macmillan).

Barro, Robert, 1979, "On the Determination of Public Debt," *Journal of Political Economy*, Vol. 87 (October), pp. 940–71.

Beckerman, Wilfred, and Joanna Pasek, 2001, *Justice, Posterity and the Environment* (Oxford, United Kingdom: Oxford University Press).

Beetsma, Roel, and Henrik Jensen, 2001, "Contingent Deficit Sanctions and Moral Hazard with a Stability Pact" (unpublished; Rome: Banca d'Italia).

Blanchard, Olivier J., 1984, "Current and Anticipated Deficits, Interest Rates, and Economic Activity," *European Economic Review*, Vol. 25, No. 1–2, pp. 7–27.

———, 1985, "Debt, Deficits, and Finite Horizons," *Journal of Political Economy*, Vol. 93 (April), pp. 223–47.

Blejer, Mario, and Adrienne Cheasty, eds., 1993, *How to Measure the Fiscal Deficit: Analytical and Methodological Issues* (Washington: International Monetary Fund).

Blöndal, Jon R., 2001a, "Budgeting in Sweden," *OECD Journal on Budgeting*, Vol. 1, No. 1 (March), pp. 27–57.

———, 2001b, "Budgeting in Canada," *OECD Journal on Budgeting*, Vol. 1, No. 2 (August), pp. 39–72.

———, 2001c, "Budget and Management in the Netherlands" (unpublished; Paris: Organization for Economic Cooperation and Development).

Bohn, Henning, 1990, "Tax Smoothing with Financial Instruments," *American Economic Review*, Vol. 80 (December), pp. 1217–30.

———, 1995, "Optimal Crown Debt" (unpublished; London: Credit Suisse-First Boston).

———, 1999, "Social Security and Demographic Uncertainty: The Risk Sharing Properties of Alternative Policies," NBER Working Paper No. 7030 (Cambridge, Massachusetts: National Bureau of Economic Research).

———, 2001, "Retirement Savings in an Aging Society: A Case for Innovative Government Debt Management," CESifo Working Paper No. 494 (Munich: CESifo).

Borensztein, Eduardo, and Paolo Mauro, 2002, "Reviving the Case for GDP-Indexed Bonds," IMF Policy Discussion Paper 02/10 (Washington: International Monetary Fund).

Börsch-Supan, Axel, and Joachim Winter, 2001, "Population Aging, Savings Behavior and Capital Markets," NBER Working Paper No. 8561 (Cambridge, Massachusetts: National Bureau of Economic Research).

Bradbury, Simon, Jim Brumby, and David Skilling, 1997, "Sovereign Net Worth: An Analytical Framework" (unpublished; Wellington: The Treasury, New Zealand).

Bräuninger, Dieter, Bernhard Gräf, Karin Gruber, Marco Neuhaus, and Stefan Schneider, 2002, *The Demographic Challenge* (Frankfurt am Main: Deutsche Bank Research).

Breyer, Friedrich, and Klaus Stolte, 2000, "Demographic Change, Endogenous Labor Supply, and the Political Feasibility of Pension Reform," Deutsches Institut fur Wirtschaftsforschung Diskussionspapiere No. 22 (Berlin: Deutsches Institut fur Wirtschaftsforschung).

Brixi, Hana Polackova, and Ashoka Mody, 2002, "Dealing with Government Fiscal Risk: An Overview" in *Government at Risk: Contingent Liabilities and Fiscal Risk*, ed. by Hana Polackova Brixi and Allen Schick (Washington: Oxford University Press and the World Bank).

Brixi, Hana Polackova, and Allen Schick, eds., 2002, *Government at Risk: Contingent Liabilities and Fiscal Risk* (Washington: Oxford University Press and the World Bank).

Brooks, Rodney, 2002, "The Merger of Flesh and Machines," in *The Next Fifty Years: Science in the First Half of the Twenty-First Century*, ed. by John Brockman (New York: Vintage Books).

Brown, Patricia Leigh, 2002, "Blinded by Science," *New York Times*, July 14.

Brunila, Anne, Marco Buti, and Daniele Franco, 2001, *The Stability and Growth Pact: The Architecture of Fiscal Policy in EMU* (London: Palgrave Macmillan).

Bryant, Ralph, and Warwick J. McKibbin, 2001, "Incorporating Demographic Change in Multi-Country Macroeconomic Models: Some Preliminary Results" (unpublished; Washington: Brookings Institution).

Buckle, Robert A., Kunhong Kim, and Julie Tam, 2001, " A Structural VAR Approach to Estimating Budget Balance Targets," New Zealand Treasury Working Paper 01/11 (Wellington: The Treasury, New Zealand).

Buiter, Willem, 1985, "A Guide to Public Sector Debt and Deficits," *Economic Policy*, No. 1 (November), pp. 13–79.

———, 1997, "Generational Accounts, Aggregate Savings, and Intergenerational Distribution," *Economica*, Vol. 64 (November), pp. 605–26.

———, 2001, "Globalisation and Regional Integration: A View from Eastern Europe and the FSU," written evidence to the Economic Affairs Committee of the U.K. House of Lords (November 6).

Burtless, Gary, 2001, "The Rationale for Fundamental Pension Reform in Germany and the United States: An Assessment," CESifo Working Paper No. 510 (Munich: CESifo).

Buti, Marco, 2000, "Comments," in *Fiscal Sustainability* (Rome: Banca D'Italia).

———, and Declan Costello, 2001, "Population Aging and the Sustainability of Public Finances in EMU" (unpublished; Brussels: European Commission).

Buti, Marco, Daniele Franco, and Hedwig Ongena, 1998, "Fiscal Discipline and Flexibility in EMU: The Implementation of the Stability and Growth Pact," *Oxford Review of Economic Policy*, Vol. 14, No. 3, pp. 81–97.

Buti, Marco, and Gabriele Giudice, 2002, "EMU's Fiscal Rules: What Can and Cannot Be Exported" (unpublished; Washington: International Monetary Fund).

Canada, Minister of Public Works and Government Services, 2001, *Canada's Third National Report on Climate Change* (Ottawa).

Chalk, Nigel, and Richard Hemming, 2000, "Assessing Fiscal Sustainability in Theory and Practice," in *Fiscal Sustainability* (Rome: Banca D'Italia).

Chand, Sheetal, and Albert Jaeger, 1996, *Aging Populations and Public Pension Schemes*, IMF Occasional Paper No. 147 (Washington: International Monetary Fund).

Cheasty, Adrienne, James Daniel, and Max Alier, 2002, "Note on Fiscal Sustainability" (unpublished; Washington: International Monetary Fund).

Claus, Iris, and Grant Scobie, 2002, "Saving in New Zealand: Measurements and Trends" (unpublished; Wellington: The Treasury, New Zealand).

Coleman, D.A., 2001, "Replacement Migration, or Why Everyone Is Going to Have to Live in Korea: A Fable for Our Time from the United Nations," *Philosophical Transactions of the Royal Society, London*, Vol. 357, pp. 583–98.

Committee on Abrupt Climate Change, 2002, *Abrupt Climate Change: Inevitable Surprises* (Washington: National Academy Press).

Credit Suisse-First Boston, 2000, *Global Demographics Project—The Demographic Manifesto: New People, New Jobs* (London).

Creedy, John, 1999, "Population Aging and the Growth of Social Expenditure" (unpublished; Melbourne: University of Melbourne).

———, and Jose Alvarado, 1998, "Social Expenditure Projections: A Stochastic Approach," *Australian Economic Papers*, Vol. 37, No. 3, pp. 203–12.

Creedy, John, and Grant H. Scobie, 2002, "Projecting the Impact of Population Aging on Social Expenditures in New Zealand" (unpublished; Wellington: The Treasury, New Zealand).

Crichton, David, 2002, "The Implications of Climate Change for the Insurance Industry," paper presented at a Wilton Park Conference on "Climate Change, What Can Be Done?" Steyning, West Sussex, United Kingdom, May 13–17.

Culhane, Maureen M., 2001, *Global Aging—Capital Market Implications* (London: Goldman Sachs Strategic Relationship Management Group).

Cutler, David M., 2002, "Equality, Efficiency and Market Fundamentals: The Dynamics of International Medical-Care Reform," *Journal of Economic Literature*, Vol. 40 (September), pp. 881–906.

———, James M. Poterba, Louise M. Sheiner, and Lawrence H. Summers, 1990, "Aging Society: Opportunity or Challenge," *Brookings Papers on Economic Activity: 1*, Brookings Institution.

Dalsgaard, Thomas, and Alain de Serres, 1999, "Estimating Prudent Budgetary Margins for 11 EU Countries: A Simulated VAR Model Approach," OECD Economics Department Working Paper No. 216 (Paris: Organization for Economic Cooperation and Development).

Dang, Thai Than, Pablo Antolin, and Howard Oxley, 2001, "Fiscal Implications of Aging: Projections of Age-Related Spending," OECD Economics Working Paper No. 31 (Paris: Organization for Economic Cooperation and Development).

Davis, Nick, 2001, "Developing a Stochastic Long Term Fiscal Model to Analyze the Impact of Portfolio Composition of the Crown's Fiscal Aggregates" (unpublished; Wellington: The Treasury, New Zealand).

———, and Richard Fabling, 2002, "Population Aging and Fiscal Policy in New Zealand" (unpublished; Wellington: The Treasury, New Zealand).

Dawkins, Richard, 2002, "Son of Moore's Law," in *The Next Fifty Years: Science in the First Half of the Twenty-First Century*, ed. by John Brockman (New York: Vintage Books).

Delbecque, B., and Henri Bogaert, 1994, "L'Incidence de la dette publique et du vieillissement démographique sur la conduite de la politique budgétaire: une étude théorique appliquée au cas de la Belgique," Bureau Fédéral du Plan Planning Paper No. 70 (Brussels: Bureau Fédéral du Plan).

Denmark, Energy Agency, 2000, *Climate 2012: State and Perspectives for Denmark's Climate Policy* (Copenhagen).

Devereux, Michael P., Rachel Griffith, and Alexander Klemm, 2001, "Have Taxes on Mobile Capital Declined?" (unpublished; London: Institute of Fiscal Studies).

Devereux, Michael P., Ben Lockwood, and Michela Redoano, 2001, "Do Countries Compete Over Corporate Tax Rates?" (unpublished; London: Institute of Fiscal Studies).

Dialogue on Water and Climate, 2003, *Climate Changes the Water Rules: How Water Managers Can Cope with Today's Climate Variability and Tomorrow's Climate Change* (Delft, The Netherlands).

Diamond, Peter A., and Peter R. Orszag, 2002, *Reducing Benefits and Subsidizing Individual Accounts: An Analysis of the Plans Proposed by the President's Commission to Strengthen Social Security* (Washington: Center on Budget and Policy Priorities and The Century Foundation).

Disney, Richard, and Paul Johnson, eds., 2001, *Pension Systems and Retirement Incomes Across OECD Countries* (Cheltenham, United Kingdom: Edward Elgar).

Dombey, David, 2002, "State Top-Ups for Airline Insurance to Be Extended: Brussels Decision Expected," *Financial Times* (London), July 1, p. 8.

Eberstadt, Nicholas, 2001, "The Population Implosion," *Foreign Policy*, Vol. 123 (March/April), pp. 42–53.

———, 2002, "The Future of AIDS," *Foreign Affairs*, Vol. 81, No. 6 (November/December), pp. 22–45.

Energy Savings Trust, 2002, *Putting Climate Change at the Heart of Energy Policy* (London).

England, Robert Stowe, and Sylvester Schieber, 2001, *The Fiscal Challenge of an Aging Industrial World* (Washington: Center for Strategic and International Studies).

Eskesen, Leif Lybecker, 2002, "The Danish Fiscal Framework—Looking Back and Ahead," in *Denmark: Selected Issues* (Washington: International Monetary Fund).

European Commission, 2001a, *Presidency Conclusions: Goteborg European Council* (Brussels), June.

———, 2001b, *European Economy: Public Finances in EMU–2001* (Brussels: Directorate-General for Economic and Financial Affairs).

———, 2002a, *Public Finances in EMU 2002*, European Economy Reports and Studies No. 3 (March).

————, 2002b, *The European Economy: 2002 Review* (Brussels).

European Commission, Economic Policy Committee, 2000, *Progress Report to the EcoFin Council on the Impact of Ageing Populations on Public Pension Systems* (Brussels).

————, 2001, *Budgetary Challenges Posed by Ageing Populations: The Impact on Public Spending on Pensions, Health and Long-Term Care for the Elderly and Possible Indicators of the Long-Term Sustainability of Public Finances* (Brussels).

Ewald, Paul, 2002a, "Mastering Disease," in *The Next Fifty Years: Science in the First Half of the Twenty-First Century*, ed. by John Brockman (New York: Vintage Books).

————, 2002b, "Editorial on Pensions Policy," *Financial Times* (London), December 14.

Fitch Ratings IBCA, 2000, *One Foot in the Grave: The Pensions Time Bomb* (New York).

————, 2001a, *A Long Way to Go—German Pension Reform* (New York).

————, 2001b, *Will $100 Billion Be Enough?* (New York).

————, 2001c, *The Stability and Growth Pact—Will It Be Discredited by Germany?* (New York).

————, 2001d, *Between a Rock and a Hard Place; Japan's Financial Challenge* (New York).

————, 2001e, *Brazil's Challenging Debt Dynamics* (New York).

Fottinger, Wolfgang, 2001, "Balanced Budget versus Golden Rule: On the Remediability of Fiscal Restrictions," in *Fiscal Rules* (unpublished; Rome: Banca d'Italia).

Frederiksen, Niels Kleis, 2000, "Pension Funding, Fiscal Sustainability, and Government Debt" (unpublished; Copenhagen: Ministry of Finance).

————, 2002, "The Consumption Tax Treatment of Pension Assets: Conceptual Issues" (unpublished; Copenhagen: Ministry of Finance).

————, 2003, "Fiscal Sustainability in the OECD, December 2001" (unpublished; Copenhagen: Ministry of Finance).

Freeman, Paul K., Michael Keen, and Muthukumara Mani, 2002, "Dealing with Increased Risk of Natural Disasters: Challenges and Options" (unpublished; Washington: International Monetary Fund).

Giddens, Anthony, 2000, *Runaway World: How Globalization Is Reshaping Our Lives* (London: Routledge).

Glied, Sherry, 2003, "Health Care Costs: On the Rise Again," *Journal of Economic Perspectives*, Vol. 17 (Spring), pp. 125–48.

Global Reach, 2003, "Worldwide eCommerce Growth." Available via the Internet: glreach.com/eng/ed/art/2004.ecommerce.php3.

Gokhale, Jagadeesh, and Kent Smetters, 2003, "Fiscal and Generational Imbalances: New Budget Measures for New Budget Priorities," AEI Pamphlet (Washington: American Enterprise Institute).

Goodson, Matthew C., 1995, "Irreversible Investment, Uncertainty and Hysteresis: A New Zealand Investigation," *New Zealand Economic Papers*, Vol. 29, No. 2, pp. 119–41.

Greenspan, Alan, 2002, "Remarks at 2002 National Summit on Retirement Savings" (Washington: Department of Labor).

Group of Ten, 1998, *The Macroeconomics and Financial Implications of Ageing Populations* (Paris, Washington, Basle: OECD, IMF, and Bank for International Settlements).

Grubert, Harry, 2002, "Intangible Income, Intercompany Transactions, Income Shifting, and the Choice of Location" (unpublished; Washington: Department of the Treasury).

Guest, Ross S., and Ian M. McDonald, 2000, "Population Ageing and Projections of Government Social Outlays in Australia," *Australian Economic Review*, Vol. 33, No. 1 (March), pp. 49–64.

———, 2001a, "Ageing, Optimal National Saving and Future Living Standards in Australia," *Economic Record*, Vol. 77, No. 237 (June), pp. 117–34.

———, 2001b, "National Saving and Population Ageing," *Agenda*, Vol. 8, No. 3, pp. 235–46.

Hausmann, Ricardo, 2002, "Unrewarded Good Fiscal Behavior: The Role of Debt Structure" (unpublished; Cambridge, Massachusetts: Kennedy School of Government, Harvard University).

Heller, Peter S., 1997, "Fiscal Policy Management in an Open Capital Regime," IMF Working Paper 97/20 (Washington: International Monetary Fund).

———, 1999, "Aging in Asia: Challenges for Fiscal Policy," *Journal of Asian Economies*, Vol. 10, No. 1, pp. 37–63.

———, 2003, "Considering the IMF's Perspective on a 'Sound Fiscal Policy,'" *FinanzArchiv*, Vol. 59 (February), pp. 141–61.

———, Richard Hemming, Peter W. Kohnert, and a staff team from the Fiscal Affairs Department, 1986, *Aging and Social Expenditure in the Major Industrial Countries, 1980–2025*, IMF Occasional Paper No. 47 (Washington: International Monetary Fund).

Heller, Peter S., and Muthukumara Mani, 2002, "Adapting to Climate Change," *Finance and Development*, Vol. 39 (March), pp. 29–31.

Heller, Peter S., and Steven Symansky, 1998, "Implications for Savings of Aging in the 'Asian Tigers,'" *Asian Economic Journal*, Vol. 12, No. 3 (September), pp. 219–52.

Hemming, Richard, and Murray Petrie, 2002, "A Framework for Assessing Fiscal Vulnerability," in *Government at Risk*, ed. by Hana Polackova Brixi and Allen Schick (Washington: Oxford University Press and World Bank).

Hemming, Richard, R.M. Kell, and S. Mahfouz, 2002, "The Effectiveness of Fiscal Policy in Stimulating Economic Activity—A Review of the Literature,"

IMF Working Paper WP/02/08 (Washington: International Monetary Fund).

Henriques, Diana B., and David Barstow, 2002, "Change in Rules Barred Many from September 11 Disaster Relief," *New York Times*, April 26.

Hewitt, Paul, 2002, *Meeting the Challenge of Global Aging* (Washington: Center for Strategic and International Studies).

Holland, John, 2002, "What Is to Come and How to Predict It," in *The Next Fifty Years: Science in the First Half of the Twenty-First Century*, ed. by John Brockman (New York: Vintage Books).

Holzmann, Robert, Robert Palacios, and A. Zviniene, 2001, "Implicit Pension Debt: Issues, Measurement and Scope in International Perspective" (unpublished; Washington: World Bank).

Horgan, John, 1997, *End of Science: Facing the Limits of Knowledge in the Twilight of the Scientific Age* (New York: Little, Brown).

Hostland, Doug, and Chris Matier, 2001, "An Examination of Alternative Strategies for Reducing Public Debt in the Presence of Uncertainty," Department of Finance Working Paper No. 2001–12 (Ottawa: Department of Finance).

Hundley, Richard O., Robert H. Anderson, James A. Dewar, Tora K. Bikson, C. Richard Neu, Jerrold Green, and Martin Libicki, 2000, *The Global Course of the Information Revolution: Political, Economic, and Social Consequences* (Washington: National Intelligence Council).

Huntington, Samuel P., 1996, *The Clash of Civilizations and the Remaking of World Order* (New York: Simon and Schuster).

Inter-American Development Bank, 2002, "Phase II Background Study for the Inter-American Development Bank Regional Policy Dialogue on National Systems for Comprehensive Disaster Management: Financing Reconstruction" (unpublished; Washington).

Intergovernmental Panel on Climate Change, 2001a, *Summary for Policymakers: Climate Change 2001: The Scientific Basis* (Cambridge, United Kingdom: Cambridge University Press).

———, 2001b, *Summary for Policymakers: Climate Change 2001: Impacts, Adaptations, and Vulnerability* (Cambridge, United Kingdom: Cambridge University Press).

———, 2001c, *Summary for Policymakers and Technical Summary: Climate Change 2001: Mitigation* (Cambridge, United Kingdom: Cambridge University Press).

———, 2001d, *Summary for Policymakers to Climate Change 2001: Synthesis Report of the IPCC Third Assessment Report* (Cambridge, United Kingdom: Cambridge University Press).

International Federation of Accountants (IFAC), Public Sector Committee, 2001, *Provisions, Contingent Liabilities and Contingent Assets: Proposed International Public Sector Accounting Standard* (New York).

International Federation of Red Cross and Red Crescent Societies, 2002, *World Disasters Report: Focus on Reducing Risk* (Geneva).

International Monetary Fund, 2001a, *World Economic Outlook: Fiscal Policy and Macroeconomic Stability* (Washington).

———, 2001b, *Code of Good Practices on Fiscal Transparency* (Washington).

———, 2001c, *Manual on Fiscal Transparency* (Washington).

———, 2001d, *Government Finance Statistics Manual* (Washington).

———, 2002a, *Norway: 2001 Article IV Consultation—Staff Report, Staff Statement, Public Information Notice on the Executive Board Discussion, and Statement by the Executive Director for Norway,* IMF Staff Country Report No. 02/44 (Washington).

———, 2002b, *Assessing Sustainability* (Washington).

———, 2002c, *Economic Data Sharing System, Fiscal and Financial Indicators* (Washington).

———, and World Bank, 2001, *Guidelines on Public Debt Management* (Washington).

Internet Software Consortium, 2003, *Internet Domain Survey, January 2003.* Available via the Internet: www.isc.org/ds.

Jackson, Howell E., 2001, "Could We Invest the Surplus?" *Tax Notes,* February 26, pp. 1245–46.

———, 2002, "Accounting for Social Security and Its Reform" (unpublished; Cambridge: Harvard University Law School).

Jackson, Richard, and Neil Howe, 2002, "Preliminary Results from the CSIS Aging Vulnerability Index" (unpublished; Washington: Center for Strategic and International Studies).

Janssen, John, 2001, "New Zealand's Fiscal Policy Framework: Evolution and Experience," New Zealand Treasury Working Paper 01/25 (Wellington: The Treasury).

———, 2002, "The Fiscal Gap: An Application to New Zealand," New Zealand Treasury Working Paper (unpublished; Wellington: The Treasury, New Zealand).

Japan, Ministry of Finance, 2001, "Medium-Term Fiscal Projection and Medium-Term Fiscal Estimate, Based on Simple Assumption on General Expenditures," in *Budget Brief for 2001* (Tokyo).

Jensen, Svend E.H., and Søren B. Nielsen, 1995, "Population Aging, Public Debt, and Sustainable Fiscal Policy, *Fiscal Studies,* Vol. 16, No. 2 (May), pp. 1–20.

Jorion, Philippe, 2000, *Value At Risk: The New Benchmark for Managing Financial Risk* (New York: McGraw-Hill).

Kapner, Suzanne, 2002, "Economic Havoc from European Floods," *New York Times*, August 16, p. W1.

Kaul, Inge, Pedro Conceição, Katell Le Goulven, and Ronald U. Mendoza, 2003, *Managing Globalization* (New York and Oxford, England: Oxford University Press).

Kilpatrick, Andrew, 2001, "Transparent Frameworks and Fiscal Rules: Policy-Making Under Uncertainty," in *Fiscal Rules* (unpublished; Rome: Banca d'Italia).

Klare, Michael, 2001, *Resource Wars: The New Landscape of Global Conflict* (New York: Metropolitan Books).

Kopits, George, 2002, "Fiscal Policy and Capital Flows" (unpublished; Washington: International Monetary Fund).

———, and Steven Symansky, 1998, *Fiscal Policy Rules*, IMF Occasional Paper No. 162 (Washington: International Monetary Fund).

Kotlikoff, Laurence J., and Bernd Raffelhuschen, 1999, "Generational Accounting Around the Globe," *American Economics Review, Papers and Proceedings*, Vol. 89 (May), pp. 161–66.

Kraemer, Moritz, 2002, *Western Europe Past Its Prime—Sovereign Rating Perspectives in the Context of Aging Populations* (London: Standard & Poor's).

Lake, Anthony, 2000, *Six Nightmares: Real Threats in a Dangerous World and How America Can Meet Them* (New York: Little, Brown).

Lee, Ronald, 2001, "Report for Roundtable Discussion of Demographic Assumptions for the Social Security Trustees: Mortality and Fertility" (unpublished; Berkeley, California: University of California).

———, and Ryan Edwards, 2002, "The Fiscal Impact of Population Aging in the U.S.: Assessing the Uncertainties," in *Tax Policy and Economy*, ed. by James H. Poterba, Vol. 16 (Cambridge, Massachusetts: MIT Press).

Lee, Ronald, and Joshua Goldstein, 2003, "Rescaling the Life Cycle: Longevity and Proportionality," in *Life Span: Evolutionary, Ecological, and Demographic Perspectives*, a supplement to *Population and Development Review*, Vol. 29, pp. 183–207.

Lee, Ronald, Andrew Mason, and Timothy Miller, 2003, "Saving, Wealth, and the Transition from Transfers to Individual Responsibility: The Cases of Taiwan and the United States," *Swedish Journal of Economics* (forthcoming)

Lee, Ronald, and Timothy Miller, 2002, "An Approach to Forecasting Health Expenditures with Application to the U.S. Medicare System," *Health Services Research*, Vol. 37, No. 5 (October), pp. 1365–86.

Lee, Ronald, and Shripad Tuljapurkar, 2000, "Population Forecasting for Fiscal Planning: Issues and Innovations," in *Demography and Fiscal Policy*, ed. by Alan Auerbach and Ronald Lee (Cambridge, United Kingdom: Cambridge University Press).

Lee, Ronald, and Hisashi Yamagata, 2003, "Sustainable Social Security: What Would It Cost?" *National Tax Journal*, Vol. 56, No. 1, part 1, pp. 27–43.

Leers, Theo, Lex Meijdam, and Harrie A.A. Verbon, 2001, "The Politics of Pension Reform Under Ageing," CESifo Working Papers No. 521 (Munich: CESifo).

Leong, Donna, 1999, "Debt Management—Theory and Practice," H.M. Treasury Occasional Paper (London: H.M. Treasury).

Lindbeck, Assar, and Mats Persson, 2003, "The Gains from Pension Reform," *Journal of Economic Literature*, Vol. 41 (March), pp. 74–112.

Lomborg, Bjørn, 2001, *The Skeptical Environmentalist: Measuring the Real State of the World* (Cambridge, United Kingdom: Cambridge University Press).

Lutz, Wolfgang, Brian C. O'Neill, and Sergei Scherbov, 2003, "Europe's Population at a Turning Point," *Science*, Vol. 299 (March), pp. 1991–2.

Mabey, Nick, 1998, "The Economics of Precaution: Strengths and Limitations of an Economic Interpretation of the Precautionary Principle" (unpublished; London: World Wildlife Fund-United Kingdom. Available via the Internet: www.consumerscouncil.org/gmo/wwf98.htm.

Mantel, Jan, 2000, "Demographics and the Funded Pension System" (unpublished; London: Merrill Lynch).

———, 2001, "The Impact of Aging Populations on the Economy" (London: Merrill Lynch).

Manton, Kenneth, and XiLiang Gu, 2001, "Changes in the Prevalence of Chronic Disability in the United States Black and Non-Black Population Above Age 65 from 1982 to 1999," *Proceedings of the National Academy of Sciences of the United States of America*, Vol. 98, No. 11, pp. 6354–59.

Manton, Kenneth G., and Timothy A. Waidmann, 1998, International Evidence on Disability Trends Among the Elderly (Washington: U.S. Department of Health and Human Services). Available via the Internet at: http://aspe.os.dhhs.gov/daltcp/reports/trends.htm

Marcet, Albert, and Andrew Scott, 2001, "Debt and Deficit Fluctuations and the Structure of Bond Markets," in *The Changing European Financial Landscape*, ed. by Sylvester Effjinger (London: Centre for Economic Policy Research).

Mason, John, 2002, "Focus Falls on Science to Solve Farming Issues," *Financial Times* (London), November 11, p. 8.

Masson, Paul, and R. Tryon, 1990, "Macroeconomic Effects of Projected Population Ageing in Industrial Countries," *Staff Papers*, International Monetary Fund, Vol. 37, No. 3 (September), pp. 453–85.

McCulloch, Brian, and Jane Frances, 2001, "Financing New Zealand Superannuation," New Zealand Treasury Working Paper 01/20 (Wellington: The Treasury, New Zealand).

McFadden, Daniel, 2001, "Comments on Lee and Tuljapurkar," in *Demography and Fiscal Policy*, ed. by Alan Auerbach and Ronald Lee (Cambridge, United Kingdom: Cambridge University Press).

McMorrow, Kiernan, and Werner Röger, 1999, "The Economic Consequences of Ageing Populations: A Comparison of the EU, US, and Japan," Economic Papers No. 138 (Brussels: European Commission).

Miles, David, 1999, "Modeling the Impact of Demographic Change Upon the Economy," *The Economic Journal*, Vol. 109, No. 452 (January), pp. 1–35.

———, and Ales Cerny, 2001a, "Risk Return and Portfolio Allocation Under Alternative Pension Systems with Imperfect Financial Markets," CEPR Discussion Paper No. 2779 (London: Centre for Economic Policy Research).

———, 2001b, "Alternative Pension Reform Strategies for Japan" (unpublished; London: Imperial College).

Missale, Alessandro, 1997, "Managing the Public Debt: The Optimal Taxation Approach," *Journal of Economic Surveys*, Vol. 11, No. 3 (September), pp. 235–65.

———, 1999, *Public Debt Management* (Oxford, United Kingdom: Oxford University Press).

Moss, David A., 2002, *When All Else Fails: Government As the Ultimate Risk Manager* (Cambridge: Harvard University Press).

Munich Re Group, 2001, *Annual Review: Natural Catastrophes 2001* (Munich).

———, 2002, *Annual Report, 2002* (Munich).

Musgrave, Richard, 1959, *The Theory of Public Finance: A Study in Public Economy* (New York: McGraw-Hill).

National Public Radio, 2002, "New Orleans' Hurricane Risk" (Washington), September 20.

Netherlands, Ministry of Housing, Spatial Planning and the Environment, 2001, *Third Netherlands' National Communication on Climate Change Policies* (The Hague).

Newell, Richard, and William Pizer, 2002a, "Discounting the Benefits of Climate Change Mitigation: How Much Do Uncertain Rates Increase Valuations?" Pew Center on Global Climate Change Economics Technical Series (Arlington, Virginia: Pew Center on Global Climate Change).

———, 2002b, "Discounting the Benefits of Climate Change Policies Using Uncertain Rates," *Resources*, Vol. 146 (Winter), pp. 15–20.

New York Times, 2002, "Tentative Deal Is Reported in $100 Billion in Aid to Insurers Facing Terror Claims," *New York Times*, October 18.

New Zealand, Climate Change Programme, 2002, *National Communication 2001: New Zealand's Third National Communication under the Framework Convention on Climate Change* (Wellington).

New Zealand, Debt Management Office, 1997, "The Efficient Management of the Government's Risk" (unpublished; Wellington: New Zealand Treasury).

New Zealand, The Treasury, 1995, *Fiscal Responsibility Act of 1994: An Explanation* (Wellington).

———, 2001a, *Note on NZ Super Fund* (Wellington).

———, 2001b, *Budget 2001* (Wellington).

Nordhaus, William D., 1998, "New Estimates of the Economic Impacts of Climate Change" (unpublished; New Haven, Connecticut: Yale University).

———, and Joseph Boyer, 2000, *Roll the DICE Again: Economic Models of Global Warming* (Cambridge, Massachusetts: MIT Press).

Nozick, Robert, 1989, *The Examined Life* (New York: Simon and Schuster).

Oeppen, Jim, and James W. Vaupel, 2002, "Broken Limits to Life Expectancy," *Science Magazine*, Vol. 296 (May 10), pp. 1029–31.

Organization for Economic Cooperation and Development, 1997, *Taxation and Economic Performance* (Paris: Working Party No. 1 on Macroeconomic and Structural Policy Analysis).

———, 2001a, "Fiscal Implications of Aging: Projections of Age-Related Spending," *Economic Outlook 2001/1*, Vol. 69 (June), pp. 145–67.

———, 2001b, *Best Practices in Budget Transparency* (Paris).

———, 2001c, "Public Management Service," *Public Management Newsletter*, Vol. 21 (September), p. 8.

———, 2001d, *Revenue Statistics 1965–2000* (Paris).

———, 2002, *Analytical Database* (Paris).

Palmer, Edward, 2001, "Sweden's New Pension System," testimony before the Subcommittee on Social Security of the U.S. House Committee on Ways and Means, July 31.

Penner, Rudolph G., 2001, *Errors in Budget Forecasting* (Washington: Urban Institute).

Pindyck, Robert S., 1991, "Irreversibility, Uncertainty, and Investment," *Journal of Economic Literature*, Vol. 29 (September), pp. 1100–48.

Pinfield, Chris, 1998, "Tax Smoothing and Expenditure Creep," New Zealand Treasury Working Paper 98/9 (Wellington: The Treasury, New Zealand).

Pisani-Ferry, Jean, 2002, "Balancing the Stability Pact," *Financial Times* (London), June 28.

Posner, Paul L., and Bryon S. Gordon, 2001, "Can Democratic Governments Save? Experiences of Countries with Budget Surpluses," *Public Budgeting and Finance*, Vol. 21 (Summer), pp. 1–28.

Quinet, Alain, and Philippe Mills, 2001, "How to Allow Automatic Stabilizers to Operate Fully?: A Policymaker's Guide for EMU Countries," paper presented at the Third Workshop on Public Finance, Fiscal Rules 1–3 (unpublished; Rome: Banca d'Italia).

Ramsey, Frank, 1928, "A Mathematical Theory of Savings," *The Economic Journal*, Vol. 38, No. 152 (December), pp. 543–59.

Razin, Assaf, Efraim Sadka, and Phillip Swagel, 2001, "The Aging Population and the Size of the Welfare State," NBER Working Paper No. 8405 (Cambridge, Massachusetts: National Bureau of Economic Research).

Rees, Martin, 2003, *Our Final Hour* (New York: Basic Books).

Reuters World Service, 2002, "South Korea Drafts Extra Budget of Typhoon Relief," Reuters World Service, September 9.

Riley, Barry, 2002, "Victims of the Slide," *Financial Times*, August 5, p. 20.

Robson, William B.P., and William M. Scarth, 1999, "Accident-Proof Budgeting: Debt Reduction Payoffs, Fiscal Credibility, and Economic Stabilization," *C.D. Howe Institute Commentary*, No. 129 (September).

Samuelson, Robert, 2002a, "Ominous Signs from Japan," *International Herald Tribune* (Paris), June 17.

———, 2002b, "Corrosion of Confidence," *Washington Post*, June 12, p. 31.

Sandler, Todd, 1998, "Global and Regional Public Goods: A Prognosis for Collective Action," *Fiscal Studies*, Vol. 19, No. 3, pp. 221–47.

Scarth, William, and Harriet Jackson, 1998, "The Target Debt-to-GDP Ratio: How Big Should It Be? And How Quickly Should We Approach It?" in *Fiscal Policy and Economic Growth*, ed. by Thomas Courchene and Thomas Wilson (Kingston, Ontario: John Deutsch Institute and Institute for Policy Analysis).

Schelling, Thomas C., 1992, "Some Economics of Global Warming," *American Economic Review*, Vol. 82 (March), pp. 1–14.

Schick, Allen, 2002a, "Budget Rules versus Political Will" (unpublished; Washington: International Monetary Fund).

———, 2002b, *Does Budgeting Have a Future?* (Paris: OECD PUMA).

———, 2002c, "Budgeting for Fiscal Risk," in *Government at Risk: Contingent Liabilities and Fiscal Risk*, ed. by Hana Polackova Brixi and Allen Schick (Washington: Oxford University Press and World Bank).

Schinasi, Gary, Charles F. Kramer, and R. Todd Smith, 2001, "Financial Implications of the Shrinking Supply of U.S. Treasury Securities," IMF Working Paper 01/61 (Washington: International Monetary Fund).

Schneider, Friedrich, and Dominik Enste, 2000, "Shadow Economies Around the World: Size, Causes, and Consequences," IMF Working Paper 00/26 (Washington: International Monetary Fund).

Schwartz, Peter, 2003, *Inevitable Surprises* (New York: Gotham Books).

Shoven, John, 2003, "If the Trust Funds Are Real, the Surplus Numbers Are Wrong," (unpublished; Palo Alto: Stanford University).

Sinn, Hans-Werner, 2000, "Why a Funded Pension System Is Useful and Why It Is Not Useful," *International Tax and Public Finance*, Vol. 7, pp. 389–410.

———, and Silke Uebelmesser, 2001, "When Will the Germans Get Trapped in Their Pension System?" CESifo Working Paper No. 561 (Munich: CESifo).

————, 2002, "Pensions and the Path to Gerontocracy in Germany," *European Journal of Political Economy,* Vol. 19 (March), pp. 153–58.

Skilling, David, 1997, "A Framework for Crown Risk Management" (unpublished; Wellington: The Treasury, New Zealand).

Smith, James P., 2001, "Comments on Lee and Tuljapurkar," in *Demography and Fiscal Policy,* ed. by Alan Auerbach and Ronald Lee (Cambridge, United Kingdom: Cambridge University Press).

Steuerle, C. Eugene, ed., 1998, *The Government We Deserve: Responsive Democracy and Changing Expectations* (Washington: Urban Institute).

————, and John Bakija, 1994, *Retooling Social Security* (Washington: Urban Institute).

Stockholm European Council, 2001, *Presidency Conclusions,* NR: 100/1/01, March 24 (Stockholm).

Swiss Re, 2002, *Opportunities and Risks of Climate Change* (Zurich).

Tanzi, Vito, 1995, *Taxation in an Integrating World (Integrating National Economies)* (Washington: Brookings Institution).

Treverton, George, and Lee Mizell, 2001, *The Future of the Information Revolution in Latin America* (Washington: National Intelligence Council).

Turner, Dave, Claude Giorno, Alain De Serres, Ann Vourc'h, and Peter Richardson, 1998, "The Macroeconomic Implications of Aging in a Global Context," OECD Economic Department Working Paper No. 193 (Paris: Organization for Economic Cooperation and Development).

UBS Warburg, 2002, "Euro Area Demographics—Delivering a "Win-Win" Economy?" *European Area Structural Issues Monitor,* No. 1. Available via the Internet: www.ubswarburg.com/economics.

United Kingdom, Department for Environment, Food, and Rural Affairs, 2002, *Climate Change Scenarios for the United Kingdom* (London).

United Kingdom, Financial Services Authority, 2002, *Financing the Future: Mind the Gap! The Implications of an Ageing Population—Key Findings and Proposed Actions* (London). Available via the Internet: www.fsa.gv.uk.

United Kingdom, Government Actuary's Department, 2001, "National Population Projections: Review on Methodology for Projecting Mortality," National Statistics Quarterly Review Series No. 8 (London).

United Kingdom, H.M. Treasury, 2000, "Long-Term Fiscal Projections," in *The Budget 2000* (London).

————, 2001a, *Macroeconomic Frameworks for the Twenty-First Century* (London).

————, 2001b, "Illustrative Long-Term Fiscal Projections," in *The Budget 2001* (London).

————, 2002, *Long Term Public Finance Report: An Analysis of Fiscal Sustainability* (London: Controller of Her Majesty's Stationery).

United Nations Environment Programme, 2002, *Global Environment Outlook 3* (Nairobi).

United Nations, Population Division, 2000, *Replacement Migration: Is It a Solution to Declining and Ageing Populations?* (New York). Available via the Internet: www.un.org/esa/population/publications/migration/migration.htm.

———, 2003, *World Population Prospects: The 2002 Revision* (New York).

United States, Central Intelligence Agency, 2001a, *Global Trends 2015: A Dialogue about the Future with Nongovernment Experts* (Washington: National Intelligence Council).

———, 2001b, *Long-Term Global Demographic Trends: Reshaping the Geopolitical Landscape* (Washington).

United States, Congressional Budget Office, 1999, *Estimating the Costs of One-Sided Bets: How CBO Analyzes Proposals with Asymmetric Uncertainties* (Washington).

———, 2000, *The Long-Term Budget Outlook* (Washington).

———, 2001a, "The Uncertainty of Budget Projections," in *The Budget and Economic Outlook: Fiscal Years 2002–2011* (Washington).

———, 2001b, *Uncertainty in Social Security's Long-Term Finances: A Stochastic Analysis* (Washington).

United States, Environmental Protection Agency, 2002, *U.S. Climate Action Report—2002: Third National Communication of the United States of America Under the United Nations Framework Convention on Climate Change* (Washington).

United States, General Accounting Office, 2002, *Review of Studies of the Economic Impact of the September 11, 2001, Terrorist Attacks on the World Trade Center* (Washington).

———, 2003, *Fiscal Exposures: Improving the Budgetary Focus on Long-Term Costs and Uncertainties* (Washington).

United States, Office of Management and Budget, 1992, *Circular No. A–94* (Washington).

United States Senate, Committee on the Budget, 1998, *The Congressional Budget Process—An Explanation* (Washington).

Vordzorgbe, Seth D., 2002a, "Risk Management and Adaptation: Reflections with Implications for Africa," paper presented at the UNDP Expert Group Meeting on Integrating Disaster Reduction in Adaptation to Climate Change, Havana.

———, 2002b, "Review of Disaster Reduction in West Africa," report prepared for UN/International Strategies for Disaster Reduction, Africa Outreach Programme (Nairobi: UN Centre).

Wallace, Paul, 2002, "Pensions: Time to Grow Up," *The Economist*, February 16, Survey, pp. 3–22.

Walsh, Mary Williams, 2003, "$8 Billion Surplus Withers at Agency Insuring Pensions," *New York Times,* January 25, p. 1.

Weil, David N., 2001, "Comments on Raffelhuschen," in *Demography and Fiscal Policy,* ed. by Alan Auerbach and Ronald Lee (Cambridge, United Kingdom: Cambridge University Press).

Weitzman, Martin L., 1998, "Why the Far-Distant Future Should Be Discounted at Its Lowest Possible Rate," *Journal of Environmental Economics and Management,* Vol. 36 (November), pp. 201–08.

World Bank, 2002, *World Development Report 2003: Sustainable Development in a Dynamic Economy* (Washington).

World Panel on Financing Water Infrastructure, 2003, *Financing Water for All* (Marseilles).

Zhou, Jiannping, 2003, "Fiscal Strategies for Population Aging," in *Belgium: Selected Issues,* Country Report No. 03/49 (Washington: International Monetary Fund).

Index

Aaron, Henry, perspectives on long-term forecasting, 93, 95–97
Africa, climate change and, 39; young component of the population, 13. *See also specific regions and countries.*
Aggregate approach to fiscal policy planning
addressing long-term concerns through fiscal policy, 100–108
balanced budget approach, 178, 186, 190
conflicts of interest and, 185
fiscal gap filling approach, 178, 183–184, 186, 190
government debt and, 185
governments' flexibility and, 193
limits on further sustained cutbacks in expenditure, 190, 192, 225
limits on increasing the tax burden, 186
maintaining the state's capacity for action, 192–193
political economy difficulties sustaining tight fiscal policy, 180–185
prefunding long-term obligations and, 182–183, 225–226
programmatic reforms as a complement to, 226
Ricardian equivalence effects, 179–180
scope for higher tax burdens, 188–190
signaling role of commitment reform, 226
size of obligations and, 201
sufficiency of, 177–202

weaknesses in existing fiscal rules, 193–201
Aging of the population. *See* Population aging
Agriculture
economic pressure source, 39
global climate change and, 20, 21
shares of world population in 2025 in countries with water scarcity (figure), 31
shrinking agricultural land, 30
Algeria, elderly population increase, 13
Allocative efficiency of revenue and expenditure policies
citizens' acceptance of prefunding as protection against multiple risks and, 134–135
deadweight losses, 133, 134, 135–136
distortions of higher tax rates, 136
information requirements of a tax smoothing approach, 135
maximum acceptable tax rates, 135n
tax smoothing, 133–136
trade-offs, 136
Alvarado, Jose, stochastic forecasting, 77, 162
Analytical approaches to fiscal policy planning
accuracy of budget forecasting, 160
actuarial calculations of the NPV of net benefits of social transfer schemes and, 163
balance sheet approaches, 61–64
development of indicators of key fiscal imbalances, 163
extending the scope of, 160–163
fiscal gap indicators and, 161

291

Analytical approaches to fiscal policy
　　planning *(continued)*
　　futures studies, 83
　　general-equilibrium models and,
　　　　162
　　generational accounting, 73, 74–76
　　historical analyses, 161–162
　　limitations, 60, 223–224
　　long-term discount rate and, 163
　　medium- to long-run projections,
　　　　64–68
　　need for assessments of the scope
　　　　for change in budget struc-
　　　　tures, 162–163
　　overlapping-generation, multicoun-
　　　　try general-equilibrium mod-
　　　　els, 73, 80–83
　　stochastic forecasting, 73, 76–80,
　　　　161–162
　　strengthening analytical techniques,
　　　　224
　　synthetic indicators of sustainabil-
　　　　ity, 68–73
　　time-path analyses, 160–161, 203
Andersen, Torben Juul, government
　　mitigation of disasters, 209
Asia, demographic transition, 40. *See
　　also specific regions and countries.*
Atkinson, Paul, functional classifica-
　　tion of expenditure, 192
Attanasio, Orazio P.,
　　capital flow impact, 217–218
　　overlapping-generation, multicoun-
　　　　try general-equilibrium mod-
　　　　els, 81, 82
Auerbach, Alan J.
　　country-specific studies of genera-
　　　　tional accounting, 73–74
　　government deferral of reform until
　　　　a crisis emerges, 213
　　model of government decision
　　　　making under uncertainty, 140
Australia
　　asset accumulation as a percent of
　　　　GDP, 183
　　Charter of Budget Honesty, 86,
　　　　123–124

　　fiscal impact of aging industrial
　　　　country populations, 16
　　Intergenerational Report, 123–124
　　long-term budget planning, 84, 86,
　　　　165
　　medium-term fiscal framework
　　　　within the formal budget
　　　　process, 84
　　pension benefits, 204–205
　　tax burden limit, 189
　　technological change and health
　　　　treatments, 32n
Austria, insurance coverage for flood
　　losses, 207n; medium-term fiscal
　　framework within the formal
　　budget process, 84

Balance sheet approaches to fiscal pol-
　　icy planning
　　explicit or contingent liabilities and,
　　　　62–63
　　hazards and complexities, 63–64
　　principal focus, 61
Balassone, Fabrizio, Italy's expenditure
　　consolidation, 148
Bangladesh, population increase pro-
　　jection, 13
Banks, James, analytical differences
　　with the generational accounting
　　approach to fiscal planning,
　　75–76
Barnhill, Theodore, study of Ecuador's
　　short-term vulnerability to finan-
　　cial crises, 119, 214, 216
Barro, Robert, public debt risk man-
　　agement practices, 117–118
Beckerman, Wilfred
　　costs of global climate change to
　　　　future generations, 7n
　　low-income countries' investment
　　　　in technologies to control car-
　　　　bon emissions, 129
　　rights of unborn generations, 121n,
　　　　128n
Belgium, adverse legacy of national
　　debt, 148

Berz, Gerhard, climate change projections, 20

Blanchard, Olivier J., "tax gap" indicator, 69, 70

Bogaert, Henri, "recommended primary surplus" definition, 69–70

Bohn, Henning, public debt and asset management, 214; tax smoothing, 135

Bovine spongiform encephalitis, globalization and, 207

Bradbury, Simon, "precautionary" tax in New Zealand, 135n

Brazil, HIV/AIDS and, 35

Brixi, Hana Polackova
government debt management practices, 119
independent agency for budget oversight, 173
public debt and asset management, 214

Brooks, Rodney, technological change in medicine in the next half century, 33

Brumby, Jim, "precautionary" tax in New Zealand, 135n

Bryant, Ralph, extension of general-equilibrium models to include climate change considerations, 83

Budget process. See also Analytical approaches to fiscal policy planning; Domestic budget processes for fiscal policy planning; Government role in fiscal policy planning
accrual accounting and, 167–169
analytical perspective on sustainability and, 166–167
building long-term planning into, 163–177, 224
clarifying key sources of expenditure pressure, 169–170
establishing an independent fiscal agency, 176
estimating the long-term fiscal consequences of new budget initiatives, 165–166

fiscal gap indicators and, 166–167
fiscal rule-based approaches, 177
governments' contingency provisions for coping with self-insurance or reinsurance role, 171–172
governments' liabilities to those already receiving pensions, 167–168
independent assessment of, 173, 224–225
limiting precommitments, 227
multilateral surveillance for, 173–174
public debate and, 175–176, 223
risks to which the government might be exposed and, 170–172
safeguarding the interests of future generations and, 176–177
strengthening accounting concepts relating to government debt, 167–169
strengthening the budget document to take account of the long term, 164–172
time horizon for, 164–165
transparency and, 165, 167, 224

Buiter, Willem, "primary gap" indicator, 69

Buti, Marco, challenges faced by countries with high public debt-to-GDP ratios, 196

Canada
asset accumulation as a percent of GDP, 183
long-term budget planning, 87
medium-term fiscal framework within the formal budget process, 84
sources of long-term fiscal pressure (table), 232–237

Caribbean region, sources of long-term fiscal pressure (table), 238–241

Catastrophic events. *See* Extreme
    weather events; Terrorist attacks
    and other catastrophic events
CBO. *See* U.S. Congressional Budget
    Office
Center for Strategic and International
    Studies, fiscal impact of aging
    industrial country populations,
    18; studies on the fiscal implica-
    tions of aging populations, 13n
Chand, Sheetal, unfunded pension lia-
    bilities in industrial countries, 70
China
    climate change and, 39
    HIV/AIDS and, 35
    increase in the elderly population, 12
    sources of long-term fiscal pressure
        (table), 268–272
CIA. *See* U.S. Central Intelligence
    Agency
Climate change. *See* Global climate
    change
Club of Rome, limited availability of
    resources, 46
Computer viruses, 34, 207
Conceptual issues
    dealing with political obstacles,
        141–145
    dynamic nonlinearities, 149, 155
    financial sustainability assessment,
        125–127
    improving allocative efficiency,
        133–136
    intergenerational fairness, 128–133
    legacy effects of past policies,
        147–148
    market reactions to fiscal reform,
        145–147
    risk management, 136–141
    short- to medium-term stabilization
        objectives, 127–128
    social welfare function, 121–124
Congo, Dem. Rep. of, population
    increase projection, 13
Credit rating agencies, global capital
    markets and, 115–116; stabiliza-
    tion objectives and, 127–128

Credit Suisse-First Boston, assessment
    of the impact of aging trends on
    the global capital market, 115
Creedy, John, stochastic forecasting, 77,
    162
CSIS. *See* Center for Strategic and
    International Studies
Cutler, David M., deadweight losses,
    134
Czech Republic, insurance coverage
    for flood losses, 207n

Davis, Nick
    deadweight losses, 134
    estimate of New Zealand's financial
        asset holdings, 183
    fiscal impact of aging industrial
        country populations, 18
    public debt and asset management,
        214
    stochastic forecasting, 77
    tax smoothing, 144n
Dawkins, Richard, technological
    change in medicine in the next
    half century, 33
Delbecque, B., "recommended primary
    surplus" definition, 69–70
Demographic changes
    divergent treatment by the U.S.
        Social Security Administration
        and the U.S. Census Bureau in
        their construction of demo-
        graphic scenarios, 68n
    fertility rates, 11, 12–13, 39, 48, 79,
        211–212
    immigration and, 212
    increase in world population, 12–13
    life expectancy, 1, 11, 39, 49, 52
    population aging, 11–19
    social insurance commitments,
        14–19
    stochastic forecasting and, 77–78
    uncertainty about interactions
        between policy variables and
        economic and demographic
        variables, 53

Demographic changes *(continued)*
    uncertainty within existing eco-
        nomic and demographic mod-
        els, 48–50
    youth bulge, 1, 13, 39
Denmark
    asset accumulation as a percent of
        GDP, 183
    increasing demand for leisure
        among workers, 146n
    long-term budget planning, 87
    medium-term fiscal framework
        within the formal budget
        process, 84
    tax burden, 193
Deutsche Bank, analysis of the dynam-
        ics of age-related burdens, 149
Developing countries. *See* Economies
        in transition; Emerging market
        economies; *specific countries*
    capital flow impact, 218–219,
        228–229
    economic impact of climate change,
        21, 39, 219–220
    financing by expatriate workers,
        159
    implicit commitments, 157
    increase in elderly population, 19
    labor market developments and
        "brain drain" from, 159
    limiting budget precommitments,
        227
    population growth, 36
    population pressures for migration
        from, 29, 159, 229
    pressure on governments to absorb
        unemployed youth into the
        military, 37
    social insurance commitments, 40
    social time preference rate and, 129,
        132, 160
    sustainability assessments, 158–159
    urbanization and, 30, 39–40
Discount rate, implications of uncer-
        tainty about, 50, 51, 163; social
        welfare function and, 121

Disney, Richard, analytical differences
        with the generational accounting
        approach to fiscal planning,
        75–76
Domestic budget processes for fiscal
        policy planning, 92–94
    adaptations to government
        accounting systems, 88–92
    difficulty of providing financially
        for events that have a small
        probability of occurring, 93
    prevailing practices, 84–88
    problematic nature of forecasting
        results, 92–93
    public debate and fiscal policy, 92
    weak link between long-term pro-
        jections and balance sheet
        assessments of a government's
        liabilities, 93

Economies in transition, demographic
        shifts, 12, 39; social insurance
        systems, 39. *See also specific coun-
        tries.*
Ecuador, study of short-term vulnera-
        bility to financial crises, 119, 214,
        216
Edwards, Ryan, public's views on risk
        and political decision making,
        139; stochastic forecasting, 200
Egypt
    elderly population increase, 13
    pensions for public employees, 40
    population increase projection, 13
Elderly population. *See also* Population
        aging; Young persons
    dependency ratio, 212
    increase in, 1, 11–19
    medical and long-term care for, 49,
        156, 205
    perception of themselves as having
        accrued certain rights, 128
    projected shares of elderly in total
        population by world region
        (figure), 12

Emerging market economies. *See also*
specific countries
capital market crises, 159
demographic shifts, 12, 40
growth of financial burden comparable with industrial countries, 40
increase in elderly population, 1, 19
social insurance, 40, 112
sustainability assessments, 158–159
England, Robert, fiscal impact of
aging industrial country populations, 17
EPA. *See* U.S. Environmental Protection Agency
Ethiopia, population increase projection, 13
Europe, sources of long-term fiscal
pressure (table), 242–246. *See also*
specific regions and countries.
European Commission
assessment of the impact of aging
trends on the global capital
market, 115
biases against pro-growth investments, 197–198
Economic Policy Committee's
study on the long-run challenges facing countries with
aging populations, 70
fiscal impact of aging industrial
country populations, 16
studies on the fiscal implications of
aging populations, 13n
European Union. *See also* Stability and
Growth Pact
annual submission of Stability and
Convergence Programmes to
the Economic and Financial
Council, 94, 97
budget surveillance, 174
concern that fiscal policies might
jeopardize the prospect for
maintaining a common cur-
rency, 101–102
difficulties in sustaining a tight fiscal policy stance, 181

fiscal consolidation of "pioneer"
and "laggard" countries, 148
fiscal gap indicator estimates,
157–158
fiscal gap problems, 197, 199
forecasts of country outlays on age-
related social expenditure programs, 66
GDP-weighted surplus gap, 194
member countries' obligation to
submit to annual surveillance
assessments of their
economies, 94
migration and the working-age
population in, 212
standardization and, 28
virtual fund for payouts for the
"biggest disasters," 208
Ewald, Paul W., technological change
in medicine in the next half century, 34
Explicit fiscal commitments
definition, 43
government discretion and, 43
"hardness" of, 44
pension and deposit insurance, 43
unemployment insurance, 43
Extreme weather events
European floods, 206
fiscal implications, 21, 24–25, 130,
206
global costs of (figure), 24

Fabling, Richard
deadweight losses, 134
estimate of New Zealand's financial asset holdings, 183
fiscal impact of aging industrial
country populations, 18
public debt and asset management, 214
stochastic forecasting, 77
tax smoothing, 144n
Financial sustainability assessments
broadening the scope of the assessment, 155–158

Financial sustainability assessments
  (continued)
  current policy targets and, 125
  external vulnerabilities, 158–160
  fiscal gap indicators, 157–158, 161,
    166–167
  political economy dimension, 125
  questions policymakers should
    pose, 126–127
Fiscal gap indicators
  budget process and, 166–167
  financial sustainability assessments
    and, 157–158
  stochastic forecasting and, 161
Fiscal policy framework
  building the long term into the
    budget process, 163–177
  fiscal rules and, 152
  geopolitical tensions and, 220
  policy coordination role, 216–220
  population aging and, 217–219
  public debt and asset management,
    214–216
  restructuring a government's policy
    commitments, 202–214
  spillover effects on other countries,
    29, 153, 174, 228
  strengthening the analysis of long-
    term fiscal sustainability,
    153–163
  sufficiency of the aggregate
    approach, 177–202
Fiscal policy planning. *See* Analytical
    approaches to fiscal policy plan-
    ning
Fiscal rules
  biases against pro-growth invest-
    ments, 197–199
  biases arising from the absence of
    accrual accounting, 196–197
  concept and application of, 101–104
  countercyclical fiscal policy and,
    181–182, 200
  fiscal rule-based approaches to the
    budget process, 177
  government's freedom in respond-
    ing to adverse shocks and, 183

higher tax rates and, 201
  institutional mechanisms to sup-
    port, 104–108
  limitations, 152
  maintaining short- to medium-term
    fiscal policy and, 202
  practicalities of adhering to, 195–196
  public debt, 214
  stochastic forecasting and, 200–201
  tailoring to a country's situation,
    193–195
  uncertainty issues, 200–201
  variable, 103–104
  weaknesses in, 193–201
Fiscal sustainability, analysis of long-
    term
  arguments for bringing longer-term
    developments into the picture,
    154–155
  ensuring a long-term focus, 153–155
  extending the scope of analytical
    approaches, 160–163
  medium-term approach, 153–154
  strengthening sustainability assess-
    ments, 155–160
  time frame and, 153–154
Fitch Ratings IBCA, assessment of the
    impact of aging trends on the
    global capital market, 115
Foot-and-mouth disease, globalization
    and, 207
Fottinger, Wolfgang, intergenerational
    concerns about public debt, 102
France, medium-term fiscal frame-
    work within the formal budget
    process, 84; tax ratio, 189
Frederiksen, Niels Kleis
  estimates of the adjustment in the
    primary balances needed in 19
    OECD countries to achieve
    sustainability, 70
  fiscal impact of aging industrial
    country populations, 17
  GDP-weighted surplus gap, 194
  long-term debt reduction arising
    from sustainable fiscal consoli-
    dation, 183

Freeman, Paul K., tailoring financial instruments to the shocks a country is likely to face, 215
Futures studies, description, 83

GA. *See* Generational accounting
GAO. *See* U.S. General Accounting Office
General-equilibrium models, market resistance and, 146; saving and investment rates and, 52–53. *See also* Overlapping-generation, multicountry general-equilibrium models.
Generational accounting
　calculation of generational imbalance, 75
　country-specific studies, 73–74
　description, 73
　misleading nature of, 75
　usefulness of, 75
Germany
　closed airspace costs associated with the September 11 terrorist attacks, 208
　insurance coverage for flood losses, 207n
　medium-term fiscal framework within the formal budget process, 84
Giddens, Anthony, manufactured risks and globalization, 211
Global capital markets. *See also* Market reactions to fiscal reform
　baby-boom generation and, 159
　credit rating agencies and, 115–116
　market interest rates, 115
　risk premiums embedded in long-term interest rates and, 117
Global climate change
　adapting to, 23–24, 219–220
　agriculture and, 20
　considerations, 19, 39
　economic impact, 20–21, 39
　effects of abrupt change, 211

extreme weather events and, 21, 24–25, 130, 206
fiscal implications, 20–26, 39, 155, 206
impact on mean temperature and/or precipitation in the world's poorest countries, 130
low-probability, high-consequence climatic events, 25–26, 54
mitigation efforts, 25, 227
population increase and, 20
projected amount of temperature warming, 19–20
projected climate change indicators (figures), 22
public sector subsidies and transfers and, 23–24
Rio Treaty's requirement that governments prepare national climate change assessment reports, 88
sea level changes, 21
uncertainty about the dimensions of, 1–2, 47, 209–210
uncertainty about the future rate of technological progress related to, 139
weaknesses in the knowledge base concerning dynamics and economic consequences of, 219
Global political tension and heightened insecurity
　demand for petroleum, 37
　demand for water, 36–37
　income inequalities, 35–36
Global Trends 2015; types of threats the United States will face, 37–38
Globalization
　capital mobility, 29, 217–218, 228–229
　Internet and, 26, 28
　manufactured risks and, 211
　migration from developing countries, 29, 159, 229
　pressure for public infrastructure investment, 28–29

Globalization *(continued)*
   pressure for standardization, 28
   risks from, 207
   spillovers from bad policies in one
     country, 29, 153, 174, 228
   tax issues, 26
Gokhale, Jagadeesh, long-term fiscal
   imbalance estimate for the
   United States, 68
Goldman Sachs, assessment of the
   impact of aging trends on the
   global capital market, 115
Gordon, Bryon S., public saving rates,
   165
Government role in fiscal policy planning. *See also* Restructuring a
   government's policy commitments
   accrual accounting system and, 88
   accumulating resources in finan-
     cial "lockboxes," 59, 104–108,
     144, 177
   adaptations to government
     accounting systems, 88–92
   addressing long-term concerns
     through aggregate fiscal pol-
     icy, 100–108
   analytical approaches, 59–83,
     223–224
   assessment of long-term sustain-
     ability of a fiscal position in a
     broad and probabilistic way,
     56–57
   benefit parameter reforms, 110–111
   certainty of some structural
     changes, 221, 222
   changes in the quality or quantity
     of benefits or in the extent of
     coverage, 111–112
   commitment reform, 112
   common features of developments
     in, 2–3
   concept and application of fiscal
     rules, 101–104
   debt-service obligation projection,
     155–156

   deferring action, 3–4, 113–114,
     154–155
   domestic budget processes, 84–94
   durability of the government's pol-
     icy framework, 157
   expenditure policy rationalization
     and tax reform, 113
   financing parameter reforms, 109
   how government policies take
     long-term issues into account,
     123, 222–223
   identifying key risks underlying
     budget projections, 170–172
   indicators for clarifying long-term
     fiscal issues, 164
   medical care, 32
   multilateral surveillance of govern-
     ment budgets, 94–100
   need for a multipronged approach
     to, 223
   perspectives of different schools of
     thought, 7–9
   political economy difficulties in
     sustaining a tight fiscal policy
     stance, 180–185
   preemptive action, 112–113
   public debt and risk management,
     117–119
   quantifying the cost of contingent
     liabilities, 89–92
   questions policymakers should
     pose about the sustainability
     of their commitments, 126–127
   reinsurance, 24–25
   relying on the market, 115–117
   response to adverse events, 42
   restructuring specifics, 6–7
   "risk maps" for financial vulnerabil-
     ity to potential catastrophe, 171
   sectoral fiscal rules, 102–103
   specific policy reforms, 108–113
   strengthening accounting concepts
     relating to government debt,
     167–169
   uncertainty and, 227–228
   variable fiscal rules, 103–104

Greece, asset accumulation as a percent of GDP, 183
Group of Ten, studies on the fiscal implications of aging populations, 13n
Guest, Ross S., increase in consumption per capita, 7n

Hassett, Kevin A.
  government deferral of reform until a crisis emerges, 213
  model of government decision making under uncertainty, 140
Health care
  demand for sophisticated medical care from politically influential middle- and upper-income groups, 40
  government provision of public medical insurance to retired workers, 90
  high expectations about the standard and quality of care, 50, 205
  industrial country commitments to, 14, 156, 205
  medical and long-term care for elderly persons, 49, 156, 205
  rate of medical care inflation, 50
  technological change impact, 32–34
Hewitt, Paul, fiscal impact of aging industrial country populations, 17
HIV/AIDS
  adverse implications for the human capital base, 130
  economic impact, 35, 130
  globalization and, 207
  lack of long-term forecasts for, 55
  lowered life expectancy and, 1
  prevention programs, 113
  vaccine for, 35
Holland, John H., technological change in medicine in the next half century, 33

Holzmann, Robert, pension debt levels relative to GDP, 40; pension-related debt, 62
Howe, Neil, "Aging Vulnerability Index," 18
Hungary, government loan guarantees, 89

Immigration, political regime shifts and, 54
Implicit fiscal commitments
  "contingent liabilities" or "state guarantees," 44
  debt arising from, 155–156
  definitions, 44
  flexibility that governments have in interpreting their implicit commitments, 45
India, population increase projection, 13; young component of the population, 13
Indus River, tensions surrounding the demand for water, 37
Industrial countries. *See also specific regions and countries*
  "baby bust" following the baby boom, 60
  capital flow impact, 217–219, 228–229
  credit rating agencies' assessment of the impact of aging trends on the global capital market, 116
  economic impact of climate change, 20–21
  expectations of the government's role in health care, 156
  extent to which there is more or less risk to individuals and the choice between the public and private sector, 139n
  geopolitical tensions and, 220
  immigration and, 29, 54, 159, 229
  impact of aging populations, 1, 16–18, 154

Industrial countries *(continued)*
  importance of long-term fiscal
    issues, 39–41
  income inequalities and, 36
  labor market developments and
    "brain drain" from developing
    countries, 159
  long-term quantitative projections
    of revenue, expenditure, and
    the overall fiscal balance, 65–68
  policy commitment effect on future
    generations, 221
  response to natural disasters,
    156–157
  social insurance commitments,
    14–15, 156
  study of unfunded pension liabili-
    ties in, 70
Infectious diseases, economic impact,
    35; population pressures for
    migration from developing coun-
    tries link to infectious disease
    outbreaks, 29. *See also* HIV/AIDS.
Insurance
  adequate pricing of, 171–172
  development of new insurance
    products to cover emerging
    risks, 207
  DNA tests and genetic risk of major
    diseases, 32
  extreme weather events and, 24
  global capital markets and, 117
  government provision of public
    medical insurance to retired
    workers, 90
  government role in reinsurance,
    24–25
  terrorism risk insurance legislation
    in the United States, 38, 208
  unemployment insurance as an
    explicit fiscal commitment, 43
Inter-American Development Bank,
    tailoring financial instruments to
    the shocks a country is likely to
    face, 215–216

Intergenerational fairness
  country's present income per
    capita and, 9, 129–130
  developing countries' social time
    preference rate and, 129, 132
  identifying which generations
    need to be considered, 128
  lack of a single definition of "fair-
    ness," 130–131
  political nature of, 131
  public debt burdens and, 132
  questions governments should
    seek to answer, 132–133
  rights of unborn generations, 128n,
    129, 222
  scaling back commitments and,
    133
  tax burden of future generations as
    compared with current gener-
    ations, 131, 132
Intergovernmental Panel on Climate
    Change
  climate change assessment reports,
    88
  frequency and intensity of extreme
    weather events, 24
  incidence and impact of climate
    change, 20
International Federation of Accoun-
    tants, Public Sector Committee's
    agreement on an approach for
    treating public sector social ben-
    efit obligations in the public
    accounts, 91; social benefits defi-
    nition, 91n
International Federation of Red Cross
    and Red Crescent Societies,
    decentralization and risk reduc-
    tion efforts, 210n
International Monetary Fund
  assessment of the impact of aging
    trends on the global capital
    market, 115
  assessments of contingent liabili-
    ties, 97–98

International Monetary Fund *(continued)*
  Code of Good Practices on Fiscal Transparency and fiscal transparency manual, 88, 99–100, 167, 173
  medium- to long-run projections for fiscal policy planning, 65, 66
  member countries' obligation to submit to annual surveillance assessments of their economies, 94
  sensitivity stress tests, 98–99
  studies on the fiscal implications of aging populations, 13n
  surveillance efforts under Article IV and Articles of Agreement, 97, 174
  views on good practices for realistic fiscal sustainability assessments, 98
Internet
  "comparison shopping" of social insurance benefits and public services offered in different countries, 28
  growth of, 26
  measures of global interconnectivity (figure), 27
  value of business conducted by eCommerce by world region (figure), 27
IPCC. *See* Intergovernmental Panel on Climate Change
Iran, elderly population increase, 13
Iraq, elderly population increase, 13
Ireland, asset accumulation as a percent of GDP, 183; tax burden limit, 189
Italy
  adverse legacy of national debt, 148
  pension reform, 110, 227
  social commitment reforms, 205
  tax ratio, 189

Jackson, Harriet, relative merits of alternative measures of the debt-to-GDP ratio, 104n
Jackson, Howell E., estimates of the accumulated debt for the U.S. Social Security system, 168
Jackson, Richard, "Aging Vulnerability Index," 18
Jaeger, Albert, unfunded pension liabilities in industrial countries, 70
Janssen, John, analysis of New Zealand's long-term fiscal situation, 114; estimate of New Zealand's fiscal gap adjustment, 70, 72
Japan
  infrastructure investment, 199
  medium-term fiscal framework within the formal budget process, 84
  sources of long-term fiscal pressure (table), 268–272
  tax burden limit, 189
Jensen, Svend E.H., deadweight losses, 134
Jordan River, tensions surrounding the demand for water, 37

Kapner, Suzanne, insurance coverage for flood losses, 207n
Keen, Michael, tailoring financial instruments to the shocks a country is likely to face, 215
Kilpatrick, Andrew, spending windfalls, 182; stochastic forecasting, 200–201
Kopits, George, fiscal rules, 101; study of Ecuador's short-term vulnerability to financial crises, 119, 214, 216
Korea, medium-term fiscal framework within the formal budget process, 84; sources of long-term fiscal pressure (table), 268–272

Kotlikoff, Laurence J., country-specific studies of generational accounting, 73–74
Kraemer, Moritz
analysis of the dynamics of age-related burdens, 149
fiscal consolidation of "pioneer" and "laggard" EU countries, 148
fiscal impact of aging industrial country populations, 16–17
Kyoto Treaty, implementation questions, 219; preemptive action example, 112–113

Latin America. *See also specific countries*
demographic transition, 40
income inequalities and, 35–36
increase in the number of the absolute poor, 2
sources of long-term fiscal pressure (table), 238–241
Lee, Ronald
divergent treatment by the U.S. Social Security Administration and the U.S. Census Bureau in their construction of demographic scenarios, 68n
public's views on risk and political decision making, 139
stochastic forecasting, 76–80, 200
Legacy of past policy commitments, adverse legacy of national debt, 148; "legacy factor" meaning, 147
Leong, Donna, government debt management practices, 118, 214, 215, 216
Libya, elderly population increase, 13
Life expectancy, 1, 11, 39, 49, 52
Lockboxes for earmarked funds, 59, 104–108, 144, 177
Long-term care for elderly persons, 49, 156, 205
Long-term issues that can be anticipated
common effects, 40–41

concurrent nature of, 10–11
demographic changes, 11–19
environmental impact of the scale of global economic activity, 46
explicit fiscal commitments, 43–44
forecasting uncertainty in the 21st century, 47–55
global climate change, 19–26, 39
global political tension and heightened insecurity, 35–37
globalization, 26–29
HIV/AIDS and other infectious diseases, 35
identifying the country- or region-specific risk factors, the sources of fiscal pressures, and the key uncertainties, 40
implicit and explicit challenges, 41
implicit fiscal commitments, 44–45, 155–156
rapid technological change, 2, 31–35
shrinking agricultural land, 30
society's understanding of the world, 45–46
terrorist attacks and other catastrophic events, 37–39
transformative issues in the 21st century, 11–39
transparency of policymakers' environment, 46
uncertainty about the future and, 42, 45–46
urbanization pressures, 30
Low-probability, high-consequence climatic events
economic impact, 54
estimate differences, 54
infrastructure and, 25–26

Maastricht Treaty, budgetary guidelines, 148; specification for gross public debt limit, 102
Mad cow disease, globalization and, 207

Mani, Muthukumara, tailoring financial instruments to the shocks a country is likely to face, 215
Market reactions to fiscal reform. *See also* Global capital markets
difficulty of determining the range of forces, 147
effect of cutbacks in future expenditure, 145, 225
general-equilibrium effects, 146
negative supply response, 146
Ricardian equivalence effects, 145, 147, 179–180
side effects of policy actions, 147
types of market forces, 146–147
vicious circles in market responses, 146
McDonald, Ian M., increase in consumption per capita, 7n
McFadden, Daniel, Social Security and Medicare redesign, 78
McKibbin, Warwick, extension of general-equilibrium models to include climate change considerations, 83
Medical care. *See* Health care
Medium- to long-run projections for fiscal policy planning
elements, 65–66
false precision and, 68
forecasts of country outlays on age-related social expenditure programs, 66
IMF construction of, 65, 66
medium-term horizon of three to five years, 64–65
projections that estimate the NPV of fiscal balances over time, 67
projections with an infinite time horizon, 67–68
sensitivity to underlying assumptions, 67
unit-elasticity assumptions, 66
Merrill Lynch, assessment of the impact of aging on global capital markets, 115

Middle East. *See also specific regions and countries*
income inequalities and, 36
limited natural resources as a potential source of economic and political pressure, 39
population increase, 13, 36
sources of long-term fiscal pressure (table), 251–254
Miller, Timothy, stochastic forecasting, 77
Mills, Philippe, SGP's lack of rewards for virtuous behavior in good years, 182
Missale, Alessandro, public debt and asset management, 214, 215; public debt risk management practices, 117–118
Mody, Ashoka
Fiscal Hedge Matrix, 119
independent agency for budget oversight, 173
public debt and asset management, 214
Momigliano, Sandro, Italy's expenditure consolidation, 148
Monacelli, Daniela, Italy's expenditure consolidation, 148
Morocco, elderly population increase, 13
Moss, David A., risk management in the United States, 32
Multilateral surveillance of government budgets
assessments of contingent liabilities and, 97–98
IMF, OECD, and European Union countries' obligation to submit to annual surveillance assessments of their economies, 94
IMF's Code of Good Practices on Fiscal Transparency and fiscal transparency manual, 88, 99–100, 167, 173

Multilateral surveillance of govern-
    ment budgets *(continued)*
    IMF's views on good practices for
        realistic fiscal sustainability
        assessments, 98
    peer-group pressure to consider
        long-term budget issues, 94,
        97, 225
    primary focus, 97
    stress tests and, 97, 98–99
Munich Re Group, insurance industry
    and September 11 terrorist
    attacks, 207n; insurance indus-
    try's reliance on retrospective
    underwriting approaches, 25n
Musgrave, Richard, six broad objec-
    tives of long-term issues faced by
    governments, 124

Netherlands
    asset accumulation as a percent of
        GDP, 183
    budgetary fiscal rule, 103
    Economic Structure Enhancing
        Fund, 103n
    government loan guarantees, 89
    medium-term fiscal framework
        within the formal budget
        process, 84
New Zealand
    balance sheet approach to fiscal
        policy planning, 61
    fiscal gap adjustment estimate, 70,
        72
    Fiscal Responsibility Act, 85, 102,
        105
    fiscal rule approach, 104
    long-term budget planning, 84, 85,
        165
    Long-Term Fiscal Model projec-
        tions, 18
    medium-term fiscal framework
        within the formal budget
        process, 84
    "precautionary" tax, 135n

quantifiable and nonquantifiable
    contingent liabilities appendix
    to budget, 89
New Zealand Superannuation Fund
    flexibility of design, 85–86
    investment questions, 106
    lockbox for, 105–106, 177
    net asset accumulation separate
        from the overall budget, 183
    saving rate and, 108
Newell, Richard, uncertainty about the
    discount rate, 50, 51, 163; weight-
    ing of discount factors, 121
Nielsen, Søren B., deadweight losses,
    134
Niger, population increase projection,
    13
Nigeria, population increase projec-
    tion, 13
Nile River, tensions surrounding the
    demand for water, 37
Nonlinearities in fiscal sustainability
    dynamics of age-related burdens,
        149, 155
    intensification of the impact of some
        structural developments, 149
    medium-term fiscal sustainability
        and, 149
Nordhaus, William D., costs of climate
    change mitigation, 114
North Africa, population increase, 12;
    sources of long-term fiscal pres-
    sure (table), 251–254
Norway
    fiscal constraint relaxation, 183, 184
    fiscal rule approach, 104
    Government Petroleum Fund,
        102–103, 105, 106–107
NZSF. *See* New Zealand Superannua-
    tion Fund

OECD. *See* Organization for Economic
    Cooperation and Development
OLG-GE models. *See* Overlapping-
    generation, multicountry
    general-equilibrium models

Organization for Economic Cooperation and Development
analysis of the dynamics of age-
  related burdens, 149
assessment of the impact of aging
  trends on the global capital
  market, 115
Best Practices Code on Fiscal Transparency, 165
budget transparency code, 100, 167
composition of general government
  expenditure (table), 191
estimates of the adjustment in the
  primary balances needed in 19
  OECD countries to achieve
  sustainability, 70
expenditure profile rationalization,
  190, 192
fiscal impact of aging industrial
  country populations, 16
forecasts of country outlays on
  age-related social expenditure
  programs, 66
general government net financial
  liabilities in OECD countries
  (table), 184
member countries' obligation to
  submit to annual surveillance
  assessments of their
  economies, 94
overlapping-generation, multicountry general-equilibrium
  models and, 81
studies on the fiscal implications of
  aging populations, 13n
survey of debt management practices, 118
tax ratios, 186, 187
Overlapping-generation, multicountry
  general-equilibrium models
description, 73
feedback effects on critical fiscal
  variables, 82–83
interest rate sensitivity and, 81,
  82–83

policy reforms and moderation of
  the projected diminution in
  the growth of incomes per
  capita, 82
population aging and, 80–83
saving and investment and, 81–82
simplified grouping of the world
  economy and, 80–81

Pacific region, sources of long-term
  fiscal pressure (table), 268–272.
  See also specific countries.
Pakistan, population increase projection, 13; young component of
  the population, 13
Palacios, Robert, pension debt levels
  relative to GDP, 40; pension-
  related debt, 62
Pasek, Joanna
costs of global climate change to
  future generations, 7n
low-income countries' investment
  in technologies to control carbon emissions, 129
rights of unborn generations, 121n,
  128n
Penner, Rudolph G., information
  value of long-term forecasts,
  160; perspectives on long-term
  forecasting, 93, 95–97
Pensions. *See also* New Zealand
  Superannuation Fund
benefit parameter reforms,
  110–111, 227
benefit transfers and, 169
clawback provisions, 110
commitment reform, 112
developing countries and, 40
expected replacement rate of a
  state-provided pension estimate, 169
as explicit fiscal commitments, 43
governments' liabilities to those
  already receiving pensions,
  167–168

Pensions *(continued)*
  industrial country commitments
    to, 14
  PAYGO systems, 60, 61–62, 103,
    112, 133–134, 156
  pension-related debt, 62
  population aging and, 61–62
  prefunding long-term obligations
    and, 182–183
  projected government pension and
    health spending, selected
    OECD countries (figure), 14
  scaling up of minimum pension
    benefits in the United King-
    dom, 44
  social welfare function and, 122
  tax issues, 15
Petroleum, tensions surrounding the
    demand for, 37
Pinfield, Chris, consequences of
    "expenditure creep," 144n; tax
    smoothing, 181n
Pizer, William, uncertainty about the
    discount rate, 50, 51, 163; weight-
    ing of discount factors, 121
Political obstacles to fiscal reform
  budget crises and, 143
  complexity of the political econ-
    omy, 143
  decision making entities, 141–142
  differing motives of multiple
    agents, 142
  difficulty of sustaining policy deci-
    sions with a long-term focus,
    144
  discipline in fiscal decision making
    and, 144–145
  electorate's realization of its role in
    determining its own and its
    children's future, 143
  generalizations about the political
    economy of any country,
    142–145
  impact of actions on the personal
    interests of different groups
    within the electorate, 142–143

  mechanisms for addressing, 144
  pressure on governments to
    address long-term fiscal
    issues, 142
Population aging. *See also* Elderly pop-
    ulation
  age-related trends in public expen-
    diture, 69–70
  aggregate fiscal policy and, 100–108
  conclusions of recent studies on the
    fiscal impact of aging industrial
    country populations, 16–18
  credit rating agencies and, 115
  dependency burden, 203
  economic effects beyond the gov-
    ernment budget, 15, 18
  encouragement of increased fertil-
    ity and, 211–212
  fiscal implications, 13–15, 154
  fiscal policy challenges, 18–19
  generational accounting
    approaches to fiscal planning,
    73, 74–76
  immigration pressures and, 212,
    217, 229
  increase in the number of elderly
    persons, 1, 11, 13
  motivating factor for policies to
    limit government's net debt,
    84
  overlapping-generation, multicoun-
    try general-equilibrium mod-
    els, 80–83
  potential variability of fertility rates
    and, 79
  rapid economic growth and, 18
  saving and investment rates and,
    52–53, 81–82
  uncertainties related to, 217
  unemployment and, 18
Posner, Paul L., public saving rates,
    165
Public debt
  aggregate approach to, 185
  asset management and, 214–216
  bond market and, 216

Public debt *(continued)*
    catastrophe bonds and, 215–216
    fiscal rules and, 214
    government debt management
        practices, 118, 119, 214, 215,
        216
    intergenerational fairness and, 132
    rising risk premiums on, 224
    risk management and, 117–119, 137
    strengthening accounting concepts
        relating to government debt,
        167–169
    tailoring financial instruments to
        the shocks a country is likely
        to face, 215–216
    uncertainties about, 214–215
Public welfare systems
    industrial country commitment to,
        14
    overlapping-generation, multicoun-
        try general-equilibrium mod-
        els and, 82
    pensions and, 64

Quinet, Alain, SGP's lack of rewards
        for virtuous behavior in good
        years, 182

Raffelhuschen, Bernd, country-specific
        studies of generational account-
        ing, 73–74
RAND Corporation
    "globalization" definition, 29n
    Internet risks and vulnerability, 34
    technological breakthroughs possi-
        ble through 2015, 31–32
Rees, Martin, vulnerability to terror-
        ism, 38–39
Republic of Korea
    demand for sophisticated medical
        care from politically influential
        middle- and upper-income
        groups, 40
    government emergency assistance
        after the typhoons of 2002, 24n

Restructuring a government's policy
        commitments
    broadening policy approaches,
        211–212
    creation of new policy structures to
        reduce and manage risk,
        202–203
    deferring reform until a crisis
        emerges, 213–214
    as a means to ensure that the state
        remains relevant, 202
    reducing and managing risk,
        206–211
    scaling back, 203–206, 213
    specifics of, 6–7
    welfare objective implications,
        212–213
Retirement, age for, 14, 49, 196, 212.
        See also Pensions.
Ricardian equivalence effects, 145, 147,
        179–180
Rio Treaty, obligation of governments
        to prepare national climate
        change assessment reports, 88
Risk management. *See also* Insurance
    consequences of a government's
        approach to, 138
    current and future electorates and,
        140
    extent to which there is more or
        less risk to individuals and,
        139n
    future spending on public goods
        and redistributive transfers,
        138
    governments' need to deal with
        genuine uncertainty, 141
    how governments communicate
        with and involve the public
        and, 208–209
    independent pressures that may
        weigh on a government's
        approach to, 140
    infrastructure investment and, 209,
        210–211
    interdependence of countries and,
        228

Risk management *(continued)*
  moral hazard considerations, 208
  political economy considerations,
    140
  public debt policies and, 137
  public's views on risk and, 138–139
  restructuring a government's pol-
    icy commitments and, 206–211
  risk of inconsistency in a country's
    policies over time, 140–141
  types of risks governments may
    encounter, 137–138, 223
Russia, HIV/AIDS and, 35

SARS. *See* Severe acute respiratory
  syndrome
Saving and investment rates, cutbacks
  in future expenditures and, 145;
  population aging and, 52–53,
  81–82
Scarth, William, relative merits of
  alternative measures of the debt-
  to-GDP ratio, 104n
Schelling, Thomas C., costs of global
  climate change to future generations, 7n; low-income countries'
  investment in technologies to
  control carbon emissions, 129
Schick, Allen
  budget battles of the future,
    142–143
  extending the time frame of a bud-
    get, 155, 157, 165
  flexibility in the countercyclical use
    of fiscal policy, 193
  government debt management
    practices, 119
  perspectives on long-term forecast-
    ing, 93, 95–97
  survey of government accounting
    practices, 89
Schieben, Sylvester, fiscal impact of
  aging industrial country populations, 17
Scobie, Grant H., stochastic forecasting, 77

Sea level changes, 21
September 11 terrorist attacks
  demand effects on economies, 29
  effects on specific industries, 29
  fiscal implications, 38, 206
  Germany and closed airspace costs
    associated with, 208
  government compensation to vic-
    tims, 45
  governments' response to, 42, 117
  insurance industry and, 207n
  National Intelligence Council study
    of the risk of a terrorist attack,
    54
  U.S. General Accounting Office
    review of studies of, 209n
Severe acute respiratory syndrome
  economic impact, 35
SGP. *See* Stability and Growth Pact
Shoven, John, capital accounting for
  the U.S. Social Security trust
  fund, 168
Singapore, demand for sophisticated
  medical care from politically
  influential middle- and upper-
  income groups, 40
Skilling, David, "precautionary" tax in
  New Zealand, 135n
Slovak Republic, insurance coverage
  for flood losses, 207n
Smetters, Kent, long-term fiscal imbalance estimate for the United
  States, 68
Smith, Zoe, analytical differences with
  the generational accounting
  approach to fiscal planning,
  75–76
Social insurance
  aging population and government
    spending on pensions and
    health, 14–19
  "comparison shopping" via the
    Internet, 28
  debt arising from a government's
    commitments to, 156
  defined-benefit systems, 91
  developing countries and, 40

Social insurance *(continued)*
    disclosure of accrued liabilities and,
        168
    economies in transition and, 39
    legislated policy commitments to, 41
    medium- to long-run projections for
        fiscal policy planning and,
        65–66
    projected government pension and
        health spending, selected
        OECD countries (figure), 14
    quantifying the annual accrual of
        social benefit obligations by a
        government, 89–92
    scaling back on commitments to,
        203–206
Social welfare function
    capacity for implementation and,
        124
    description, 121
    discount rate and, 121
    distribution across generations,
        123–124
    government's approach to risk and
        uncertainty and, 124
    government's role, 122–123
    individual's utility as a function of
        consumption, 122
    interests of future generations and,
        121–123
    key factors on how government
        policies take account of long-
        term issues, 123
    rights of unborn generations, 121n
    risk and, 122
    "state of the world" probability
        function, 122n
    sustainability and, 124
South Africa, elderly population
    increase, 13
South Asia. *See also specific countries*
    HIV/AIDS and, 35
    income inequalities and, 36
    increase in the number of the
        absolute poor, 2

limited natural resources as a
    potential source of economic
    and political pressure, 39
population increase, 12, 36
sources of long-term fiscal pressure
    (table), 259–262
Southeast Asia, sources of long-term
    fiscal pressure (table), 263–267.
    See also specific countries.
Soviet Union, former, sources of long-
    term fiscal pressure (table),
    247–250. *See also specific countries.*
Spain, asset accumulation as a percent
    of GDP, 183
Stability and Growth Pact
    accrual accounting and, 197
    capital expenditure treatment,
        198–199
    fiscal implications of aging and, 174
    fiscal policy constraints and, 28,
        181–182
    fiscal policy safety margin require-
        ment, 128
    fiscal rules and, 101–102, 104,
        181–182
    flexibility of, 193–194
    long-run challenges facing countries
        with aging populations, 70
    sufficiency of, 195–196
Stabilization objectives, credit rating
    agencies and, 127–128; fiscal pol-
    icy safety margins and, 128
Standard & Poor's, analysis of the
    dynamics of age-related burdens,
    149; assessment of the impact of
    aging trends on the global capital
    market, 115, 116
Stochastic forecasting
    aggregative fiscal rules and,
        200–201
    description, 73
    development of, 76
    fiscal gap indicators and, 161
    historical analyses and, 161–162

Stochastic forecasting *(continued)*
  interest rates and, 79
  key sources of uncertainty and, 79
  methodology, 76–77
  multiplicity of fiscal risks and, 161
  objective of, 76
  relative probability of adverse out-
      comes and, 79–80
  strength and importance of, 78
Stress tests, 67, 97, 98–99
Sub-Saharan Africa
  HIV/AIDS and, 35
  income inequalities and, 35
  increase in the number of the
      absolute poor, 2
  population increase, 12
  sources of long-term fiscal pressure
      (table), 255–258
Sudan, elderly population increase, 13
Sustainability. *See* Fiscal sustainabil-
      ity, analysis of long-term;
      Financial sustainability assess-
      ment; Synthetic indicators of
      sustainability
Sweden
  medium-term fiscal framework
      within the formal budget
      process, 84
  Multi-Year Budget Framework, 87
  pension reform, 110, 111, 227
  social commitment reforms, 205
SWF. *See* Social welfare function
Switzerland, tax burden limit, 189
Symansky, Steven, fiscal rules, 101
Synthetic indicators of sustainability
  age-related trends in public expen-
      diture and, 69–70
  aggregative nature of, 72
  biased perspective of, 73
  deficiencies and weaknesses of gap
      indicators, 72–73
  equilibrating the present value of
      the long-term budget con-
      straint faced by a government,
      69

fiscal sustainability in OECD coun-
      tries: primary fiscal balance
      approach (table), 71
  intergenerational tradeoffs, 70, 72
  value of, 70, 72

Tax issues
  distortions of higher tax rates, 136
  equilibrium payroll tax rate and
      Social Security, 78
  expenditure policy rationalization
      and tax reform, 113
  generational accounting and, 75–76
  globalization and, 26, 55
  intergenerational fairness and, 131,
      132
  investment of surpluses to avoid
      tax hikes, 133–134
  limits on increasing the tax burden,
      186
  marginal tax rates, 8–9
  maximum acceptable tax rates, 135n
  pensions, 15
  political regime shifts and, 53–54
  public debt risk management prac-
      tices and, 117–118
  questions policymakers should
      pose about the sustainability of
      their commitments, 126–127
  scope for higher tax burdens,
      188–190
  social welfare function, 123
  tax competition, 26, 145
  tax rates as a debt-equilibrating fac-
      tor, 67
  tax ratios in OECD countries, 186,
      187
  tax smoothing, 117–118, 133–136,
      139, 178, 186
  technological change and health
      treatments, 32n
Technological change
  areas to be affected by, 31

Technological change *(continued)*
  computer viruses and, 34, 207
  DNA tests and genetic risk of major
    diseases, 32
  health care, 32–34
  potential for acts of destruction
    and, 34–35
  productivity growth and, 34
  risk of software or hardware break-
    downs and, 34
  speculating on technological
    change in medicine in the next
    half century, 33–34
  technological breakthroughs possi-
    ble through 2015, 31–32
Terrorist attacks and other catastrophic
    events. *See also* September 11 ter-
    rorist attacks
  catastrophe bonds, 215–216
  fiscal ramifications, 38
  probability of, 38
  "risk maps" for financial vulnerabil-
    ity to potential catastrophe, 171
  vulnerability to, 38–39
  weapons of mass destruction and,
    37–38
Tigris-Euphrates Rivers, tensions sur-
    rounding the demand for water,
    37
Tuljapurkar, Shripad, divergent treat-
    ment by the U.S. Social Security
    Administration and the U.S. Cen-
    sus Bureau in their construction
    of demographic scenarios, 68n
Tunisia, elderly population increase, 13
Turner, Dave, non-OECD regions'
    demand for capital, 218;
    overlapping-generation, multi-
    country general-equilibrium
    models, 80–83

UBS Warburg, assessment of the
    impact of aging trends on the
    global capital market, 115
Ukraine, HIV/AIDS and, 35

UN. *See* United Nations
Unborn generations' rights, 121n,
    128n, 129, 142
Uncertainties in the 21st century
  within existing economic and
    demographic models, 48–50
  expected changes in underlying
    models, 50, 52
  general-equilibrium effects, 52–53
  interactions between policy vari-
    ables and economic and demo-
    graphic variables, 53
  "lamppost" approach, 55
  political regime shifts, 53–54
  probability distribution, 54–55
  unforeseeable events, 55
United Arab Emirates, elderly popula-
    tion increase, 13
United Kingdom
  adjustments to the indexation for-
    mula and, 110–111
  Code for Fiscal Stability, 85
  debt management, 215
  Financial Services Authority's
    warning about the risks to
    insurance companies associ-
    ated with long-term annuity
    products, 92
  fiscal rule approach, 104
  "Golden Rule" for a balanced cur-
    rent budget, 85, 102, 196, 198,
    199
  long-term budget planning, 84, 85,
    165
  medium-term fiscal framework
    within the formal budget
    process, 84
  National Health Service strengthen-
    ing, 112
  pension benefits, 44, 63–64, 136,
    157, 204–205
  requirement that the social insur-
    ance payroll contribution rate
    be adjusted to ensure the sys-
    tem's financing on a PAYGO
    basis, 103

United Kingdom *(continued)*
   Sustainable Investment Rule, 102,
      198
   tax burden limit, 189
United Nations
   fertility rate projections, 13
   migration and the working-age
      population in the European
      Union, 212
   population increase projections, 13
United Nations Development Programme, scope for expanded
   provision of global public goods,
   220
United States
   accrued costs not reflected in the
      U.S. budget, 168–169
   actuarial calculations of the NPV of
      net benefits of alternative
      social transfer schemes, 163
   climate change and, 39
   compensation for farmers in the
      Midwest for weather-related
      losses, 23–24
   difficulties in sustaining a tight fis-
      cal policy stance, 181
   expiration of the Budget Enforce-
      ment Act, 87
   fiscal rule approach under the Clin-
      ton and Bush administrations,
      104
   long-term budget planning, 84,
      86–87
   long-term fiscal imbalance esti-
      mate, 68
   Medicare cost as a fraction of GDP,
      78
   medium-term fiscal framework
      within the formal budget
      process, 84
   population increase projection, 13
   private financing of health care, 188
   sources of long-term fiscal pressure
      (table), 232–237
   stochastic forecasting for demo-
      graphic and economic vari-
      ables, 77–78

subsidy cost of a government guarantee for direct loans, 89
tax burden limit, 189
terrorism risk insurance legislation,
   38, 208
types of threats the United States
   will face in the future, 37–38
Urbanization, developing countries
   and, 30, 39–40; projected population of world's largest megacities
   (figure), 30
U.S. Census Bureau, divergent treatment by the U.S. Social Security
   Administration and the U.S.
   Census Bureau in their construction of demographic scenarios,
   68n
U.S. Central Intelligence Agency
   futures studies, 83
   identification of possible situations
      that are sources of economic
      and political concern, 55
   National Intelligence Council study
      of the risk of a terrorist attack,
      54
U.S. Congressional Budget Office
   assessment of the long-term
      finances of the U.S. Social
      Security system, 77
   baseline analyses for a 75-year fis-
      cal projection period, 87
   independent budget scorekeeper
      role, 173
   stochastic forecasting models,
      77–78
U.S. Environmental Protection
   Agency, adapting to climate
   change, 20; U.S. Climate Action
   Report, 10n, 19n
U.S. General Accounting Office
   accrued costs not reflected in the
      U.S. budget, 168–169
   establishment of triggers signaling
      when the costs of existing
      budget exposures exceed a
      predetermined amount,
      175–176

U.S. General Accounting Office *(contin-ued)*
  "implicit exposures" definition, 44
  need for the government to pro-
    vide a list and description of
    fiscal exposures, 170
  review of studies of the impact of
    the September 11 terrorist
    attacks, 209n
U.S. Health Care Financing Administration, stochastic forecasting
  models, 77–78
U.S. National Intelligence Council,
  Global Trends 2015, 37–38
U.S. Social Security Administration
  divergent treatment by the U.S.
    Social Security Administration
    and the U.S. Census Bureau in
    their construction of demo-
    graphic scenarios, 68n
  long-term projection mandate, 66
  stochastic forecasting models, 77–78
U.S. Social Security system
  capital accounting for the trust
    fund, 168
  Congressional Budget Office's
    assessment of the long-term
    finances of the Social Security
    system, 77
  equilibrium payroll tax rate, 78
  estimates of the accumulated debt
    for the U.S. Social Security sys-
    tem, 168
  financing parameter reform exam-
    ple, 109
  fiscal sustainability issue, 107–108
  forecasting when the trust fund will
    be exhausted, 160
  lockbox for, 177
  payroll contribution rate and bene-
    fit amounts set to yield actuar-
    ial balance over a 75-year
    period, 103, 104
  stochastic approach for appraising,
    200
  trust fund as an autonomous bud-
    get entity, 107–108

van den Noord, Paul, functional classification of expenditure, 192
Violante, Giovanni L., capital flow
  impact, 217–218; overlapping-
  generation, multicountry general-
  equilibrium models, 81, 82

Weapons of mass destruction, types of
  threats the United States will face
  in the future, 37–38
Weather. *See* Extreme weather events;
  Global climate change
Weitzman, Martin L., uncertainty
  about the discount rate, 50, 51,
  163; weighting of discount factors, 121
Welfare systems. *See* Public welfare
  systems
WMD. *See* Weapons of mass destruction

Yemen, population increase projection,
  13
Young persons. *See also* Elderly population
  in developing countries, 1, 13, 36
  pressure on developing country
    governments to absorb unem-
    ployed youth into the military,
    37
  projected increase in, 13

Zviniene, A., pension debt levels relative to GDP, 40; pension-related
  debt, 62

About the Author

Peter S. Heller received his BA from Trinity College (USA) in 1967 and his doctorate in economics from Harvard University in 1971. After teaching for six years at the University of Michigan, he joined the International Monetary Fund, where he is now the Deputy Director of its Fiscal Affairs Department. He has written and lectured extensively on policy issues relating to economic development, fiscal policy, pensions, government expenditures, taxation, health care for developing countries, privatization, climate change, and aging populations. He was also an active participant in the 2002 World Health Organization-sponsored Commission on Macroeconomics and Health. He has written many papers relating to the Far East, Southeast Asia, and Africa. At the IMF, he has led or participated in missions to virtually every part of the world.